Composing for the Cinema

The Theory and Praxis of Music in Film

Ennio Morricone and Sergio Miceli

Translated by Gillian B. Anderson

Lessons transcribed by Rita Pagani and edited by Laura Gallenga

D1571492

THE SCARECROW PRESS, INC.

Lanham • Boulder • New York • Toronto • Plymouth, UK

2013

Published by Scarecrow Press, Inc.
A wholly owned subsidary of Rowman & Littlefield
4501 Forbes Boulevard, Suite 200, Lanham, Maryland 20706
www.rowman.com

10 Thornbury Road, Plymouth PL6 7PP, United Kingdom

British Library Cataloguing in Publication Information Available

Library of Congress Cataloging-in-Publication Data

Morricone, Ennio.
[Comporre per il cinema. English]
Composing for the cinema : the theory and praxis of music in film / Ennio Morricone and Sergio
Miceli ; translated by Gillian B. Anderson.
pages ; cm
Translation of: Morricone, Ennio. Comporre per il cinema, 2001.
Includes bibliographical references and index.
ISBN 978-0-8108-9240-8 (cloth : alk. paper) -- ISBN 978-0-8108-9241-5 (pbk. : alk. paper) -- ISBN
978-0-8108-9242-2 (electronic)
1. Motion picture music--Instruction and study. 2. Composition (Music) I. Miceli, Sergio, 1944- II.
Anderson, Gillian B., 1943- III. Title.
MT64.M65M6713 2013
781.5'4213--dc23
2013024914

♾™ The paper used in this publication meets the minimum requirements of American
National Standard for Information Sciences Permanence of Paper for Printed Library
Materials, ANSI/NISO Z39.48-1992.

Printed in the United States of America

To the students of the courses at Siena, Basel, and Fiesole

Contents

Translator's Note

Gillian B. Anderson

With almost four hundred scores to his credit, Ennio Morricone is one of the most prolific and influential film composers working today. In movie after movie his listeners come away with the conviction that he has achieved something special, and this is a conviction shared by composers, scholars, and fans alike. For all those who have wondered how he does it, these composition lessons will explain a lot. They are designed for composers, but Morricone's expositions are easy to understand and fascinating even to those without any musical training. To those with a musical background, they are of course even more profound. He discusses his relationship with directors like Leone, Pontecorvo, Pasolini, Petri, Scott, Beatty,Tornatore, the Taviani brothers, Zeffirelli, Joanou, and Joffé, analyzes some of his own scores, and reveals motivations that have not been taken into account in cinema studies, for the spaghetti western, for example. He describes recording session techniques and technology and many other specifics of his profession as a film composer.

Some things are especially noteworthy. Although Morricone's tunes are famous, he is not interested in melody per se. While giving the average spectator something to follow, he tries to write music that reveals the personality of the players and the character of the drama. He tries to compose music that is not just descriptive of what is already communicated by the image and that maintains its own internal logic. While doing what the director wants, he tries to add something that only the music can. He is passionate about musical expression, entering and exiting carefully to maximize the music's effect, creating dynamic changes by the addition and subtraction of instruments, relying on implicit sync points as often as possible, doing all the orchestrations himself so that the orchestral colors and emphasis that he wants will be realized. He always sets himself some purely musical challenge so that he will not feel like a mere artisan/servant of the director but an artist in his own right. Moreover, as Sergio Miceli points out, frequently Morricone uses the music as a force for redemption. These and many other particulars combine to explain why his music always seems to be doing something special, but in the end he insists that there is no one "right" or "correct" solution for a film's score.

His colleague, musicologist Sergio Miceli, is a pioneer in the field of film music. Although most professional film composers analyze movies intuitively, beginners, nonmusicians, and professionals alike will benefit from his well-defined, rigorous formal analyses. Miceli describes many of the signs or signals that a director, cameraperson, scenery designer, costumer, actor, sound designer, and script writer leave in a film. A composer must take these into account when deciding how to set the film to music. Miceli shows how different kinds of preexisting music cause one to read the same scene differently. He analyzes a number of films according to his system of levels, thereby describing a variety of musical solutions to many different kinds of film, and he even shows how sound design can be analyzed. As they have worked together for many years and do not always agree, Morricone and Miceli are shown to interact during their lessons to our mutual benefit.

This text is a transcription of lessons delivered live. Although we cannot run the films or play the recordings that were used, where possible I have added information about DVDs, videotapes, and excerpts on YouTube so that the reader can run the actual examples and listen to and watch the films being discussed. In this way one can partially reconstitute the original live lessons.

I would like to thank the Film Music Foundation for its support at an early stage of the work of translation and the University of Illinois Press, which published excerpts from chapter 4 in *Music and the Moving Image*, volume 4, number 2 (Summer 2011), pages 1–29. Finally, I would like to thank Lidia Bagnoli for her help and also Mario Militello of the Centro Sperimentale di Cinematografia.

Editor's Note

Laura Gallenga

This handbook was Ennio Morricone's idea. The text was transcribed and assembled from diverse recordings made during the film music seminars conducted by Morricone and Sergio Miceli between 1991 and 2000.[1] To the transcription of the recorded material Miceli added musical sketches, graphics, and various notes and remarks he had accumulated over the years from both teachers.[2] Miceli and the editor have performed the complex work of confronting and choosing between the different versions of the same theme from different editions of the seminar and in fact have created an ideal reconstruction that is a synthesis of lessons actually delivered over many years.

As for the structure of the seminar and therefore the book, it is important to emphasize that the parts treated predominantly by Morricone contain concepts expressed by Miceli, and vice versa. In the parts closer to his competence, Miceli refers often to the themes touched on by Morricone. Therefore, a selective and fragmented lecture would have restored neither the sense of the original lessons nor the thoughts of each teacher, as the work was based on alternation, exchange, integration, and the superimposition of the contributions.

Inevitably we have had to omit the analytical exercises performed by the seminar participants and the discussions pertaining to the students' compositional attempts. Their voices, however, are present in chapter 7, "Questions and Answers," a radical selection of the numerous questions asked of the professors during the different editions of the seminar. Further, by Miceli's express wish, his historical compendium of music for film, focused above all on the silent film period and intended as a generator of persistent dramaturgical models, has been omitted in this transcription.

After reflection and in consideration of the bond of friendship and of artistic and professional collaboration that has bound the two authors for almost twenty years, it has been a priority for the editor writing this introduction to conserve in the text some interventions and exchanges between Morricone and Miceli that are not always strictly pertinent to the argument being treated, but that faithfully re-create the climate in which the lessons were carried out. In this way, not only an authentic testimonial but also a sort of double human and professional portrait emerges. The perspective of the composer and of the musicologist, the extraordinary multiplicity of experiences of the one beside the didactic-speculative approach of the other, carry us to a series of agreements and disagreements, to a dialectical vivacity that represents perhaps one of the most significant aspects of interest in this work. To the reader it offers the possibility of approaching film-music themes from diverse angles with well-differentiated instruments of interpretation and appraisal. I have tried, in other words, to find a compromise between the simplicity required of a text in the framework of a handbook and the inevitable heterogeneous vivacity of a text with oral origins.

NOTES

1. At the Fondazione Accademia Musicale Chigiana in Siena (1991–1995), the Akademie der Musik in Basel (1992, with the participation of Hansjoerg Pauli), and the Centro di Ricerca e di Sperimentazione per la Didattica Musicale in Fiesole (1999) . . . and in 2000, with the participation of Franco Piersanti.

2. As a consequence, some of the references to precise times and circumstances that emerge in the course of the arguments offered during the lectures have been maintained in the final adaptation in order not to change the reasoning and references that follow. (Where possible, a clarification has been made in the notes.) However, we suggest that the reader consider these references in a very relative way.

Acknowledgments

The authors thank Salvatore Sica (seminar member at Siena), Nicolo Bellucci (organizer at Basel), and Simone Taffuri (course member at Fiesole) for having made available their recordings of the seminars. They also thank Rita Pagani for her patient and punctual transcription of large parts of the copious magnetic materials.

Abbreviations

ppp   *più che pianissimo*

pp   *pianissimo*

p   *piano*

mp   *mezzo piano*

mf   *mezzo forte*

f   *forte*

ff   *fortissimo*

fff   *più che fortissimo*

sfz   *sforzando*

AIFF   Audio Interchange File Format

CD   Compact Disc

DAT   Digital Audio Tape

dB   Decibel

DVD   Digital Versatile Disk

GB   Gigabytes

HD   Hard Disk

kHz   Kilohertz

LP   Long-Playing

MB   Megabytes

MP3   MPEG 1 Audio Layer III

RAM   Random Access Memory

SCSI   Small Computer Standard Interface

The notes are by the editor, Laura Gallenga, except when they are signed with the abbreviation SM (Sergio Miceli) or GBA (Gillian Anderson). DVDs and information about persons mentioned have been supplied by GBA. Ellipses (. . .) have been used to indicate omissions.

Chapter One

Introduction

The Composer in the Cinema

Ennio Morricone [EM]: I always say the same thing at the beginning of our brief course.[1] Do not delude yourself into thinking that this might be the time for you to learn how to compose music. . . . Responding to a suggestion from the artistic director of the Chigiana,[2] Miceli and I have consented to allowing your participation without requiring particular prerequisites,[3] but above all we believe that the course is designed to be most useful to those who have finished the seventh year of composition.

Those who do not know the art and techniques of composition might be curious about certain incidents associated with my profession. They will be able to learn about . . . film music's compositional praxis, what the composer does, his relationship with the director, with the production company, with the public, and in the end with the composer himself, but they certainly will not learn how to compose. Probably the course will end up illustrating the ideas that animate a composer who does not want to be passive with respect to the cinema and to motion-picture music. For this reason I will describe some of my experiences, but only those I can relate to you. However, I reiterate, I do not believe it is possible on this occasion to learn how to write music.

Sergio Miceli [SM]: For my part, I have to start with a discussion that has some analogy with what Maestro Morricone has just said. My area of competence also requires a certain step-by-step approach and a certain background of already-acquired prerequisites. . . . We have had to take for granted a preexisting knowledge of the syntax of motion pictures and of music, with particular reference to the epoch that goes from the nineteenth century

1

through to the so-called neo-avant-garde. Composing for the cinema . . . implies that one has knowledge of all the musical languages . . . to which I just referred and of categories and forms in the cultivated musical tradition.

It is my intention to tackle film music as a . . . twentieth-century phenomenon. It is not one of the marginal phenomena, either, if for no other reason than because of its enormous horizontal and vertical[4] diffusion. By "the twentieth century" I mean an extraordinary jumble of events, of experiences, of proposals originating from diverse sectors (literature, theatre, figurative art, but also science and technology—inevitably called upon for the cause of cinema and for certain aspects of contemporary music). Under many circumstances these have resulted in singular fusions.

In fact, if I had not put the phenomenon of film music into this context, I would have been merely . . . perpetuating the ghettoization that . . . I have always tried to combat. . . . It is my increasingly deeply rooted conviction that we ought to give special treatment to the study and practice of film music because it is a part of . . . the cinema, an expressive form that has the capacity more than any other to speak to human beings about the twentieth century. Its syncretism and efficiency is without equal. I say this frequently, and perhaps . . . I will have occasion to repeat it even during this course. . . . Made from so many languages, the language of the cinema sometimes is art but also has demonstrated its documentary value in a political and social sense, in the sense of customs and so on. Music has always been present in different ways within this language, sometimes assuming a decisive role.

ORGANIZATION OF THE COURSE

EM: The course has been organized along four . . . tracks. In accordance with the expertise of Professor Miceli, the first track is theoretical and analytical. Put in this way, it might seem erudite and a little abstract. Really, however, it presents a very effective method that the composer, the director, or the scholar can use to understand the relationships that exist between music and the cinema.

In the second track, I will be occupied with everything that has to do with compositional praxis: the writing, the business of the craft and invention, the way in which the composer can attempt to be himself . . . under the typical conditions for practitioners of film music. We have reduced all this to a series of themes that we illustrate in more detail later. However, we will alternate the theoretical and practical aspects because they are opposite sides of the same coin, and we predict that the connection between the two points of view will become more evident as the course develops.

The third track consists of an attempt at composition for an unedited short film,[5] while the fourth concerns the screening of four or five whole films[6] for which we will ask the members of the course to make an audiovisual analysis.[7] Finally, in the concluding part of the course, an encounter with a director will take place,[8] involving the projection of one of his films and the reconstruction of the phases of the work that resulted in the definitive version of the music.

Let's begin by talking about the composer's relationship to the motion picture business. It begins for me (but in general it happens exactly in this way) when I am called by the director. On the basis of a direct or indirect report that implies that he knows my . . . work . . . on other films, the director intuits, or believes he intuits, that I have certain affinities with his own work. He thinks he will be able to trust me.

Many directors, however, also make some unusual distinctions: "That composer will serve me for a dramatic film, but for a comic film he will not be good." In general, I do not share this type of superficial, even if understandable, judgment. In reality, a composer who dedicates himself to the cinema ought to be able to write the music for a comic film, for a dramatic film, for a war film . . . in other words, for a film of any genre. In short, the director has every right to think what he wants, but this "labelling" derives from a not-very-profound knowledge of the quality of his potential collaborator.

RELATIONSHIP BETWEEN THE COMPOSER, PRODUCER, AND MUSIC EDITOR

Sometimes the producer of a film or the music editor interferes with the director over the choice of the composer. This interference is a sign of a serious deterioration in a professional relationship. Being the one artistically responsible for the film, the director should be the only one with the right to choose his collaborators. Therefore, the intervention of the producer or of the music editor—who in Italy is the one who finances the soundtrack—presupposes a weakness in the director's contract or the absence of an accurate opinion of the value of the musical aspects of the film.

At this point it is reasonable to ask, "Why would the producer recommend or actually choose a certain composer?" It is definitely not for his or her musical value; rather, it is for the promotion of the film: the selected composer has a name that could be useful in the opening titles. I will give you some examples. Antonello Venditti[9] (with due respect to Venditti), Lucio Dalla[10] (with due respect to Dalla), and other pop songwriters are cemented to the cinema. However, composing for movies is so much not their real profession that . . . they are constrained to resort to the help of other composers. Therefore, above all one is dealing with a question of image. This is the producer's perspective.

To a certain extent what I have said about producers also applies to editors. However, editors have other criteria. In general, they often . . . turn to dilettantes or to little-known (even if competent) young composers. Because . . . they lack confidence when dealing with clients and in order to develop the assignment with the fewest difficulties, these unknowns or dilettantes tend to accede to pressure from the editor to reduce the size of the ensemble. In this way they betray the director's feelings and the exigencies of the film, a film for which of course a symphonic orchestra would have been necessary. For an editor who invests money in the soundtrack and who awaits a return on his investment, all this reduction translates into great savings and at the same time into a much more marketable discographic product.

For these reasons the editors fear the better and more recognized composers. Thanks to the force of their ideas, sustained by a stronger contractual authority, they do not consent easily to a similar reduction in the size of the ensemble. . . . An editor tends to want to save and to suggest a reduction in the performing forces even to the composer. Doing this he can spend 40 to 50 million lire. (This, however, includes everything: the studio, the technical material, the copying, and the performers.) With me, on the other hand, he will not spend less than 150 million lire. But even I can understand his dilemma because he has invested his money. If the film earns 40 billion [lire], the editor is due 0.5 percent; but not all films earn 40 billion [lire]. Therefore, he might not recoup even the amount invested, with the consequent risk that the artistic director will be fired. This is so true that I often suggest that the editors leave the honor of the music to the production company, with the possibility of eventually buying preexistent music.

Cecchi Gori[11] is an example of a producer-editor. In a budget of 10 billion [lire], 200 million [lire] for the music is almost irrelevant.

I, too, at the beginning of my career, was the prisoner of a producer who offered me a western film if I would agree to write the music for other genres of film. Thus, I found myself working for a director with whom I had nothing in common, just as he had nothing in common with me—it was a terrible relationship. In conclusion, in my experience, all the proposals that come from producers or from editors are unsound. . . . A director's request made directly to a composer is the only one that is professionally legitimate because it reinforces the offer to the composer that he use his own creativity.

THE COMPOSER'S FIRST MEETING WITH THE DIRECTOR

When the choice is clear, the relationship begins with a description of the film that the director has in his mind to do; or with the reading of the script; or, if the film is already shot, with a screening of the filmed material; or, finally, with the screening of the film if it has already been edited. One arrives in this way at the discussion about possible musical choices.

In general, I try not to have the director talk because first I want to express my own opinion. If he accepts it, it leaves me free to propose my own solutions. Sometimes the director is able even to anticipate the composer and to state his opinion. I repeat: I try to avoid this because I would like the encounter to be between equals. . . . The composer—in this case, I—can propose solutions in contraposition to those that the director might have in mind. (I admit that he has them.) I have even encountered directors—few, in truth—who have told me, "Do what you want; I don't know what to tell you." And in this case there is a greater responsibility, even a very heavy one. However, it does not mean that the composer should not come to a consensus with the director about the ideas he has espoused. In fact, because the director does not know exactly what to do, the composer has an even greater obligation to obtain the maximum consensus beforehand in order to give direction to a consistent, productive, and therefore economical process in the recording studio. (I refer, obviously, to the money invested by the music editor.) In conclusion, as much as possible the director should be conscious of what the composer is going to record, even if, with words alone, it will be very difficult—even impossible—to make him or her aware of it.

THE IMPORTANCE OF THE THEME

SM: Here it would be very good to refer to the statement you made at the 1990 conference "Music and Cinema" at the Chigiana.[12] It stimulated a discussion about the means the composer can employ to communicate his exact ideas to a director. Observe that the director is constrained in general to talk almost exclusively in terms of melody or about a theme.

EM: It is really a grave limitation, and at the conference I expressed my judgment to Monicelli,[13] to the Taviani Brothers,[14] and also to Piovani.[15] Often, what one is constrained to communicate pertains only to the creation of the melody to the neglect of that which is within the melody, which, in my opinion, is much more important. Thus, when you go to the piano to have a director listen to something, it is impossible for him to hear the sonority of the cellos or the attack of the basses that follows and then the clarinet that makes a certain sound after that. Therefore, one is forced to make him listen to a theme, a theme that might prove pleasing at that moment, but that later on he might not like because of the orchestration, which is the most important thing.

I have always thought that in motion pictures the theme is a minor element. In any case, in contemporary art music, composers do not write themes anymore. None of us is interested in making them. In the cinema, we create a theme because the public needs to follow a thread. They need to listen to the distinct and characteristic succession of sounds that are behind it. But beyond this necessity rests the very limiting fact that the composer at the piano can make the director hear nothing more than the theme. If the composer is a good orchestrator but a terrible pianist, when finally in the recording studio the director listens to the music that has been realized, he might marvel at a result that he did not expect, at colors that the orchestra gives to the theme. If instead, on the contrary, the composer is . . . a very good pianist but not a good orchestrator, the director will be disappointed because the theme that he liked at the piano he no longer likes. It can happen. Therefore, my advice is to have the director listen to the theme being played very badly. If he accepts it that way, it will certainly be more attractive to him when you have orchestrated it. I play it badly for him, also, because I am not interested at all in playing it at the piano. If necessary, I sing it to him in my off-key voice.

There is a certain director who after years and years confessed to me that he had not understood anything in my communications with him (though I had not suspected it). I had sung the theme to him badly. I had played it for him badly. So he had arrived in the recording studio thinking, "Finally . . ." One does not have the slightest idea about what the musical level of certain directors is. One of them, a dear friend, provoked me by saying, "Try that little piece again, there where the orchestra is tuning up."[16] But the orchestra was not tuning up: it was executing slightly abstract sounds that I had written for his film.

SM: Let's go into more detail, hypothesizing a film already definitively edited. It is not the only type of approach, as Maestro Morricone already has explained (and without doubt it is not even the most stimulating). However, it is the most common, and, in this expository phase, it is also the easiest to confront. In fact, from the moment that an analytical creative process (that is autocritical) has tools in common with a critical analytical process, . . . we can discuss a method applicable as much to a hypothetical film that needs a musical accompaniment as to a film already completely finished.[17]

PRINCIPAL ELEMENTS TO BE CONSIDERED BEFORE COMPOSING OR ANALYZING

EM: I anticipate later lessons by giving you some brief directions. First of all, start to observe the genre, the nature, the argument of the film, in what style it was shot. . . . Ask yourselves whether the subject, the general cutting, its constituent images, the photography, the editing, the dialogue, or the recitation seem unusual to you or whether they are within the norm. Ask yourselves, for example, whether the director wanted to make a popular film on a complex argument or vice versa—a very complex film with very simple images. And then, having made this ID kit of the director and the film in the case of an assigned work, take note of the way in which the composer has approached the intentions of the director. Be able to do it by analyzing his language on the harmonic level. To which tools did he have recourse? What is the nature of the melody, of the theme (if there is a melody and a theme), the rhythm? That is also very important. Try, in sum, to discover the reasons at the root of the choices that the composer made.

Here is a list of the principal elements you need to take into account:

- The geographic setting and the historical environment of the film.
- The characteristics of the costumes and the scenery design.
- The type of light and the treatment of color. For example: Does it deal with a veiled color, or is it dense? Is it toned toward one prevalent tonality, or is it sharp, with a very distinct tonality?
- Is the scene empty or full? Is it outside or inside?
- The weather conditions.
- The psychological condition of the characters.
- The presence of buzzing and of noises (the noises of airplanes, trains, barking dogs, etc., are considered significant).
- The presence of dialogue.
- Realistic sources of sound: a radio, a record player, and other sources of the sort; of bells, police and ambulance sirens, and other sounds of a traumatic nature that break the unity of the music you are writing.
- The presence of musical instruments playing a part in the narration that could be utilized in playback or for particular allusions.

We will summon these and still other principal elements, which will later enter more profoundly into the arguments Professor Miceli and I discuss. At this point it is necessary to establish, first of all, a common method of interpretation, a common vocabulary. Therefore we will begin with the audiovisual analysis, and then afterwards we will be able to enter into the practical details.

NOTES

1. The course in Siena was of variable duration from year to year, oscillating between seven days for the first edition to twelve days for the last. The lessons took place in the Aula Casella every morning from 9:30 a.m. to 12:30 p.m., while the afternoons were dedicated to watching whole films, for which the course members had to finish audiovisual analyses to present to the teachers the next morning. The edition at Fiesole took place in the course of eighteen hours over three days. Lacking the historical summary, the written test, the analytical

exercises by the course members, and the encounter with a director, in the treatment of themes one could consider it substantially equivalent to that at the Chigiana.

2. When Morricone and Miceli ran the course in Siena (1991–1995), the artistic director of the Fondazione Accademia Musicale Chigiana was Luciano Alberti. The proposition was made only to Morricone by Alberti as a result of the composer's brief participation at the International Conference of Music and Cinema, run by Miceli and held in Siena on August 19–22, 1990. (The *Atti del Convegno Internazionale Musica & Cinema*, edited by Miceli, are found in *Chigiana*, vol. 42, n.s. 22 [Florence: Olschki, 1992].) Morricone accepted on the condition that he be flanked by Miceli as co-teacher.

3. The same criteria were applied at CRSDM of Fiesole, while for the course in Basel, because it had limited enrollment, a preselection was made by the organizing committee, the International Seminar for Filmgestaltung.

4. By "horizontal" diffusion he means as a phenomenon that has been of interest to and interests every location; "vertical" diffusion refers to its capacity to involve diverse social classes.

5. The exercises consisted of a projection (three times for every morning, on three consecutive days) of a three-minute film. The members of the course, after having taken the timings and annotated the useful indications during the course of the projection, had two days to write and deliver the composition; the time available reflected the real time of the work. The more interesting scores were rewarded with a certificate of merit, conferred at the Chigiana and signed by Morricone and Miceli. At Siena, in the latest edition of the course, the selected pieces were performed in a final concert, entrusted to the class of Giuseppe Garbarino.

6. Even though the titles varied from year to year, the course always featured films for which Morricone had composed the music. According to the teachers' assertions, some of the course attendees demonstrated an analytic capacity and interpretative quality above the norm.

7. Exercises not reported; however, it is possible to recover some of the arguments.

8. In 1993 and 1994 Giuseppe Tornatore was a guest of the class, the first time with the episode *Il cane blue* (*The Blue Dog*), taken from the longer film *La domenica specialmente* (*Especially Sunday*), for which a Moviola was used. [DVD, Cecchi Gori Home Video, 2008.] The lesson-encounter took place at the Institute of the History of Cinema in the Faculty of Letters of the University of Siena. The following year the class featured the film *Una pura formalità* (*A Pure Formality*). [DVD, Cecchi Gori Home Video, 2011.] Notwithstanding the fact that the director had expressed a desire to limit the event's attendance to members of the course, the encounter happened in the presence of numerous journalists and took the form of a press conference more than a lesson because of the attention excited by the presentation of the film in that period at Cannes. In 1995 Mauro Bolognini appeared and encountered the students in the Aula Casella of the Chigiana, listening to and discussing the analyses of the film *La storia vera della signora dalle camelie* (*The True Story of the Lady of the Camellias*). [DVD, Ripley's Home Video, 2005.]

9. Antonello Venditti (1949–), singer, songwriter.

10. Lucio Dalla (1943–2012), singer, songwriter.

11. Mario Cecchi Gori (1920–1993), film producer.

12. At the International Conference of Music and Cinema, run by Miceli in Siena, August 19–22, 1990. See Sergio Miceli (ed.), "Atti del Convegno Internazionale Musica di Cinema," in *Chigiana*, vol. 42, n.s. 22 (Florence: Oschki, 1992), 108ff.

13. Mario Monicelli (1915–), film director.

14. Paolo (1931–) and Vittorio (1929–) Taviani, film directors.

15. Nicola Piovani (1946–), film composer.

16. Presumably Sergio Leone.

17. As already specified in another note, the discussion of the composition exercises has been omitted, being narrowly tied to unedited filmic material and therefore unavailable to the reader. However, as soon as the arguments in those treatises intertwine further with the theme of the abovementioned lesson, it has been considered useful to make a "montage" between the two parts. The ring of conjunction between them—that here we are summarizing—regards the composition of the ensemble proposed for the composition exercises, consisting of a quartet of strings plus contrabass, pianoforte, flute, oboe, and clarinet in B-flat. Concerning this ensem-

ble, Morricone hoped for a reorganization of the presence of the pianoforte—to use it within the ensemble rather than as a solo instrument. This reorganization was intended as much to make the course members value more highly a capacity for handling a heterogeneous ensemble as to avoid the easy shortcuts and commonplaces of amateur derivation (arpeggios and so on). Morricone observed in the end that the piano as protagonist can be justified in particular cases and cited as an example both "the beautiful musical comment of Nyman" for *The Piano* (*Lezioni di piano*) by Jane Campion (French, Australian, New Zealand coproduction, 1993) [DVD, Ciby, 2000, Jan Chapman Productions; Optimum Home Entertainment, 2006; Lionsgate, 2012] and one of his own experience tied to the film *Disclosure* (*Rivelazioni*) by Barry Levinson (USA, 1995). [DVD, Warner Home Video, 1994.]

Chapter Two

Audiovisual Analysis—Part 1

SM: The moment has arrived for us to look more closely at how we might approach the interpretation of a film *ex novo* on the musical level. We will do it in two phases. The first I will call the preanalytical phase, for which I have made a brief film that I have edited from outtakes. It is endowed with dialogue and effects,[1] but the music has not yet been supplied. In the second phase[2] I will demonstrate a method for the analysis of the audiovisual components, obviously privileging the music. In both cases I will refer to numerous examples, excerpts from films that are all very different from one other. . . . In the future these methods of analysis will help you both as a spectator and as a composer or director.[3]

At the request of Ennio Morricone, Fernando Ghia[4] has kindly put at our disposal some videocassettes, one of which has many outtakes from the definitive final montage of *The Endless Game* by Bryan Forbes.[5] From these outtakes I edited together a reduced series of scenes. I kept in mind the . . . interpretations that a musician might make while trying to formulate hypothetical solutions for the musical accompaniment. In part, I tried to favor one possible intention, but in part I tried not to, so as not to create an "ideal" excerpt and therefore something far from the reality in which a composer might have to operate. In this way I "invented" a little film that we will call simply *Cut Sequences*.

I was not familiar with Forbes's finished film. Therefore, I think the key to the interpretation of my edited narrative is more legitimate even if it is inevitably subjective, because it is based exclusively on the multiple messages the director launched in the course of shooting, using the technical instruments and system of signs that he had at his disposal. We will . . . return to this point a little later, but now I want to add that I tried to use scenes or sequences with a minimum of dialogue. Its total absence would have facilitated the task of the hypothetical composer too much. On the other hand, in a film like this, which is "without a story," the minimal dialogue could not be the carrier of precise and binding interpretative meanings or narrative, and in fact it is not. In the analysis that follows, you will find a maximum number of signals (although through a précis), not a literal transcription, as would be required, by comparison, in a shooting script deduced from the actual final montage.[6]

DEFINITIONS

Now we need to clarify my terminology. A **sequence** is a set of scenes that share a spatial or temporal unity. In it the elements of the narration are in some way unified or connected among the scenes. A sequence could also consist of a single scene, but within it there can be cuts in the editing.

A **single scene** is a fragment of a sequence, or an autonomous episode that is formally all one piece. It is characterized by spatial-temporal unity. That is to say, it must be free of cuts that would carry the spectator into another spatial-temporal sphere, but it could be endowed eventually with **connection cuts**. The most frequent cuts occur where there is a transfer from one room to another in the same internal environment, or where, taken from the editing, a change of framing occurs (for example, shot and reverse shot; subjective), or where there is recourse to the use of an optical or mechanical dolly (zoom), so a progressive change of the movie camera's angulation occurs—for example, the panoramic—that is or is not connected to the camera's physical movement.

A **piano sequence** is generally a long take using complex movements of the motion picture camera. The movements are obtained without cuts and therefore without edits. Of all the types of shot it is perhaps the most exacting, because everything has to function to perfection; otherwise, one has to shoot it over again from the beginning. The intent is obvious. The absence of cuts creates a continuity, a visual flow that immerses the spectator completely in the scene. I would define it as a choice place for music, but let's not get ahead of ourselves. Numerous examples of piano sequences exist, but I want to describe one that I like best. I refer to a masterwork of the musical, in which there is full concordance between visual and musical flow[7] : "Dancing in the Dark" from *The Band Wagon*, with Fred Astaire and Cyd Charisse.[8] In this case the virtuosity is twofold, because the dancers danced uninterrupted, without the aid of camera tricks, for the entirety of the single long take. The episode has a total duration of $2'40''$, and of this the first $2'11''$ is a single long take. Then there is a cut. What a shame . . . but remember the ultimate measure of the film *Some Like It Hot*: "Nobody's perfect."[9]

Having dispensed with these definitions, we turn now to some preliminary considerations. Obviously, the fewer the scenes that make up a sequence, the more powerful will be the potential unity of the sequence itself. And the same will be true for the single scene if in it the director or editor resorts minimally to cuts and the techniques already listed. The narrative proposition, the use of dialogue, and the mixture of shooting and editing techniques compromise, if they do not upset, this principle that less is more.

By defining these few specifics, I do not delude myself into thinking that I have established a complete . . . lexicon, and in this sense the suggested bibliography that you received in part will be useful. The significance that I attribute to certain definitions will be more precise, I hope, in the course of the preanalysis. In the meantime, we leave the truly technical aspects behind. . . . Now I will try to clarify . . . the possible definitions of didactic function, a fundamental semantic . . . aspect of the music-image relationship and then afterwards of color tonality.

DIDACTIC FUNCTION

We certainly know of (and we will see repeatedly) cases in which music plays a determining role in a film. Unfortunately, however, in the majority of cases the music is added when everything is already done—that is to say, when the film is mounted and already contains dialogue and noises. Clearly, in such a situation the music has been asked to play neither a primary nor even an equal interpretative role. Rather, the music has been used to underline or emphasize something that has already been said by other means (and, of course, has been said weakly or badly). In this way, the music risks being redundant and long-winded, putting itself on a didactic level (even if the diversity of language with respect to all the other components should attenuate the effect). This adjective, "didactic,"[10] contains many problems for film and film music, for which I request a moment of reflection.

When I speak of "didactic allusions," or of "didactic potential," or of "didactic tone" (if not actually didactic style), I mean that with the spectator in mind, the director has underlined something other than a feature strictly necessary to understanding the essence of the narrative. . . . The director sometimes does it through the dialogue, the style of the recitation, or the photography and shooting techniques, more often with the editing, and with still greater frequency by asking the composer to make sync points of the worst type. They are those typical orchestral breaks that are like the glottal effects every one of us has produced instinctively with our voices in infantile games in order to emphasize something. They represent the lowest functional aspect of music's contribution. But the insertion of music as an added expressive element under these circumstances implies an instructional function that goes beyond this type of solution. . . . Obviously, it is up to the composer to dignify this function, but for the moment I do not intend to deal with the means for doing so—this is an argument that Maestro Morricone and I will discuss further along. Right now I want to deal with the film context in which the music occurs.

Without being able to give the theme of didactic or instructional intent the depth of treatment that it deserves, I at least will say . . . that in a potential state, didactic intent is present more or less in any expressive form. Poetry is the exception. Being the "quintessential" language par excellence, poetry does without didactic intent, while music goes from a minimum grade (or zero) in so-called absolute music to a maximum grade in the symphonic poem, program music, and music for the stage.

I would put the musical and prose theatre in a category apart, because in both cases, even though with diverse mechanisms, results, and scope, instructional intention is an integral part of the "game," identifying itself sometimes with the very essence of the work. Think of the ancient Greek tragedies, of Shakespeare and all those cases in which the author speaks by means of a chorus or of an *historicus*. But don't dismiss the didactic presence as being only a feature of the classics. Think of that singular musical/rock film that is *The Rocky Horror Picture Show*, in which the function of the chorus is assumed by a criminologist.[11]

In the theatre of the first and especially the second halves of the twentieth century, the new hermeneutic function of the mise-en-scène carries us inevitably to the "quotation."[12] I could therefore continue by recalling Pirandello, in whose works the metatheatrical component transfigured the didactic function, and persist until the limited case of Brecht, who . . . exploited and increased the didactic function in the same way he increased the didactic function of the music.

Probably this mass of associations would horrify an entertainment historian (in the same way I am horrified when an entertainment historian or someone similar uses analogous musical-historical associations), but I use this mass of associations a little inaccurately to suggest that there were some preexisting references with which to confront a cinematic phenomenon. It is a phenomenon over which we cannot now generalize more. . . . If it is true that there is cinema and *cinema*, one might conclude that the greater the popular or commercial intent of a film, the more important the didactic potential might then be, but it does not necessarily follow.

On the other hand, the experimental and avant-garde cinemas have a didactic potential close to zero. (To pause for a moment on an interesting relationship between music and cinema, think of *Entr'acte* and *Ballet mecanique*.)[13] But it is not necessary to be experimental to repress the didactic function. Ingmar Bergman, for example, has the great merit of making instructional intent seem a poetic necessity, a trait that belongs moreover to the symbolist theater (with which, I have the impression, Bergman had some points in common).

In a language and in a culture light years away from the cinema of the Swedish director, there is something analogous in the theatre of Eduardo De Filippo. When he underlines certain fixed ideas through characters who repeat even a commonplace phrase more than necessary, the technique has both instructional significance and metaphysical potential at the same time. In sum, in light of profoundly diverse aesthetic conceptions, I can confirm that didactic characteristics are absent when the director is not preoccupied with supplying suggestions to the spectators[14] and when he does not intend to confer an instructional function on his own work.

Let's take a case of seemingly aristocratic but in reality (at least in my opinion) vilely populist and . . . vulgar directorial license. In the way he uses the motion picture camera, Franco Zeffirelli renders something of symbolic-narrative significance shamelessly didactic: Desdemona's famous handkerchief, which by itself is already very obvious in Verdi's opera *Otello*.[15] Zefirelli's ostentatious instructional intent, besides treating the spectator like an ignoramus, results in a deterioration of style. Such cases are extremely frequent, sometimes even in great masters of the cinema like Visconti[16] and Fellini,[17] and represent a symptomatic gesture of distrust of their own means and an attack on their own integrity. It is equivalent to exaggerating an expressive event, contaminating the essence in an artificial way. Most of the time the result is banal.

Being neither a censor nor a moralist, I frankly do not know how to establish the line of demarcation between eroticism and pornography, but . . . I use this metaphor to clarify my reasoning further. If the erotic genre alludes more or less covertly to sexual manifestations, then you could say that by comparison, the pornographic genre shows and flaunts them. (Paradoxically, however, . . . so much erotic . . . cinema has a miserable aesthetic and conceptual level.[18] By comparison, I find the pornographic cinema much more honest because it offers exactly what it promises without the pseudointellectual façade. But this is another subject.) Therefore, pornography could be defined as a "pure" explanation of sex.

A more ambitious didactic intent can lead to an appeal to symbolism. It is a terrain fraught with danger for many directors, even if they are good craftsmen. One of Sergio Leone's less satisfactory solutions from *Per qualche dollaro in più* (*For a Few Dollars More*)[19] is a demonstration of such a case. At the point in the film when the principal characters present themselves and their credentials to the public, Leone wanted to allude to a fixed idea, to the vindictive project that Colonel Mortimer (Lee Van Cleef) had in mind for the Indian (Gian Maria Volonté). There is an almost subliminal, crescendoing, rapid montage that shows alternately the face of the colonel (the hunter) and that of the Indian on a "wanted" poster, with a sync point underlined by pistol shots. Even if one allows for the fact that hyperbole is a typical stylistic feature of Leone, in semiotic terms this example contains a classic intrusion of the meaning sphere into the expressive one. It is ostentatious. In terms of cinema aesthetics, it is the result of the slightly coarse abuse of filmic tools that are more appropriate to an animated film than one with flesh-and-blood actors.[20]

SYNESTHESIA—COLOR PALETTE

Before turning to *Cut Sequences*, we must say a few words about color tonality. It is not a marginal annotation. Synesthesia is the principle of expression and contemporaneous perception of diverse sensory stimuli that are in agreement with each other. For example, one sees a color when one hears a sound. It does not belong only to the culture of ancient Greece, where it was born. In times closer to our own, it came to Padre Castel in the eighteenth century, to Wagner, to Scriabin, to the Schoenberg of the period tied to expressionism, and so forth. Today, beyond aesthetic features, synesthesia is very diffuse in video clips and in publicity. By comparison with these other examples, in our little film the opposite happens. The images will assume color and timbral significance analogous "superficially" to that of the music.

In the presence of a film endowed with its own chromatic coherence, it is absolutely appropriate for a musician to want to offer an equivalent sound. He or she has the advantage of a certain freedom by comparison to the sometimes slightly dogmatic or mechanical rigidity of recalled theorization. The composer often forgets that the color of a photograph is an artifice not inferior to the artifice of sound; like music, it has its own system of symbols, its own rapport between antecedents and consequents.

Let's look at four short examples.

The first is an example . . . in which color components are used for an expressive purpose and is among the most successful of its kind. It is from Martin Scorsese's *Raging Bull* (1980),[21] a film shot in a beautiful retro black and white but with some inserts in color that simulate amateur snapshots. They function as flashbacks or flash forwards of episodes from the private life of the pugilist Jake La Motta. . . . This is a case where the "signal" offered to the spectator, the neat and coherent separation between black and white and color, does not appear to be forced. It is entirely identifiable with choices of style and content.

The second example is from Hans Juergen Syberberg's[22] *Parsifal* (1982), a nonconformist film opera that is not very popular, whether because of the subject matter or because of the treatment to which it is subjected. This is a case of discovered manipulation, full of references and of metamusical and metatheatrical allusions in which the teaching method is the message, to paraphrase McLuhan. But within the context, the operation seems to me to be entirely legitimate. In fact, it would have been inconceivable to interpret Wagner on the figurative level without trying to use a system of color symbols. On the other hand, this extraordinary film opera is the apotheosis of the fiction (the film) of a fiction (the opera). The first artifice (Wagner) enters the mise-en-scène for half of the second artifice (Syberberg) under diverse cast-off skins, from the marionette to the showy portion.[23]

In Zeffirelli's film opera *La Traviata*,[24] the system of chromatic symbols appears much more natural. There are extremely cold tones against very hot tones, perhaps because they are tied to more direct narrative elements and to unequivocal interpretations. The prelude is like the container for the epilogue of the opera (a presumed epilogue, created for the film but legitimate in relation to the libretto). Thus the opera itself becomes a giant flashback of the prelude. Violetta is dying (note the prevalence of blue-green) and sees again her sumptuous mistakes (note the prevalence of yellow-purple).

As a last example, a video clip of Michael Jackson's *Thriller* is among the best, to confirm that the system of symbols of the language of color passes unscathed through epochs, genres, and styles. As an aside, I remember that the director, John Landis, had a privileged relation with music. (It is enough to think of *The Blues Brothers*.)[25] It is paradoxical, but the color relations in the video clip are the same as those present in Zeffirelli.

PREANALYSIS PHASE 1: *CUT SEQUENCES*

But let's turn now to *Cut Sequences*. The total duration is 7′04″.[26] According to the criteria already established, three sequences can be extracted.

> Sequence 1—containing two scenes
> Sequence 2—containing one scene
> Sequence 3—containing two scenes

The preanalysis is subdivided into three phases. Every scene will be examined according to the following aspects:

1. **Objective description of the visual/sound events**—A sort of screenplay inferred from the montage, with a minimum of added explanations.
2. **Synthesis of formal features (figurative, motor, auditory)**—To make a distinction between figurative and motor (dynamic) characteristics can seem arduous, since a dynamic pertains to the events (for example, the movement of the actors) and to the way in which the events are presented (techniques of shooting and of editing). But if we take the case of a scene endowed with constant figurative elements (for example, two immobile men seated in one place who talk for a

long time), animated by a play between close-up and very close-up, the distinction is legitimate and necessary.

3. **Analysis of the narrative**—Finally, on the basis of all the characteristics pointed out in the three phases, I will make some hypotheses about potential musical solutions, using preexisting musical compositions.

Let's turn now to scene 1 of sequence 1 from *Cut Sequences*.

Sequence 1
Consisting of two scenes for a total of 3′12″

Scene 1—duration 0′50″
External—autumn or winter dawn—suburban street—rain
Chromatic tonality (color palette) mainly cold

a. Objective Description of the Visual/Sound Events

Long shot. A milk truck enters from the left side of the frame, with a partially mechanical tracking shot to follow. *Much noise evident, natural dissolve.*

Approximately when the tracking shot stabilizes, there appears from the opposite side an auto, with headlights on, that stops a little after the point where the truck was parked. *Squeal of the brakes.*

A male figure descends. From the previous dynamics . . . one passes now to a greater general motionlessness. Consequently, the attention of the spectator concentrates naturally on the figure of the man. The auto departs again, not before the man passes in front. *Sounds of a small airplane off camera, presumably at low altitude.*

The mechanical tracking shot now pursues a movement that is the opposite of the one before, to which is added a moderate optical tracking shot, but it all appears natural due to the concurrent direction of the human figure and of the automobile. *The airplane persists, auto silent, except for the swish of the tires on the wet pavement.*

The man arrives at the gate of a little villa (the auto stopped many yards away). He carefully opens and closes the gate. He arrives at the main door with steps that are a little slow. *Light squeaking of the brakes—still the airplane off camera.*

b. Synthesis of Formal Features (Figurative, Motor, Auditory)

Figurative features: Very homogeneous.

Motor features: Variable but plausible. Total unity of space for the entire duration.

Framing with fixed features of the "composition" in a figurative sense (the branches in foreground) between the eighth and twenty-fifth seconds. Duration 17″ to 50″ altogether, equal to a third of the scene.

Two slow, mechanical tracking shots in opposite directions, and to the extreme limits of the scene, with a consequent great significance of symmetry.

One optical tracking shot associated with the second mechanical tracking shot, slow and of moderate range.

Objects/people in motion: Constant presence, but always supported, associated among themselves or included in the optical treatment, therefore muffled in potential dynamic autonomy.

Auditory features: Not homogeneous but plausible.

Presence of noises almost continuous even though of medium to low acoustic level, variable in nature but linked, with few superimpositions and with characters of symmetry analogous to those noticed in the visual component.

1. Truck in acoustic dissolve conforms to the mechanical tracking shot. Noise decisively muffled between the tenth and fifteenth seconds.

2. Breaks of the auto at the eighteenth second.

3. Airplane off camera crescendos at the twenty-third second (at about the halfway point of the scene).

3-4. Airplane continues/wheels on asphalt at the thirtieth second.

3-5. Persistence of the airplane sound at the forty-fifth second. *Squeak of the gate.*[27]

c. Analysis of Narrative

During this type of analysis one might use formulas such as "Here the director intends to suggest . . ." and so on. Obviously, in this case one is dealing with my personal interpretation, but in a certain way the director's intention is a legitimate concern even for a process of montage put together from preexistent material. The montage may carry some characteristics and potential meanings that survived my editing.

There is no "before" or "after" in this little film to which we have given the name of *Cut Sequences*. What we see is the whole story—or nonstory. In any case, the absence of a preceding narrative, or even of a prior event, should not concern us. Think of certain publicity shorts. Thanks to the characterization, to the editing, and to rapid associations, one presupposes a sort of story from the first frame of film. It demonstrates a notable expressive freedom. You may have noticed that some advertisements exist in versions with different durations. Their use depends on the hour and on the broadcaster for whom they are destined, but the story always remains intact.

In any case, we do not need the narrative component, because the intended story is not as important as the logic and linked succession of events nor as important as the climate, the emotions, and, in the end, the question without answer that the various scenes transmit. We will see how to make use of this consideration, treating the "musicability" of—the ease with which we can put music to—the whole film. Also, the duration of our little film should not present a problem. In comparison to so much of the televised publicity we are given to watch, *Cut Sequences* is almost a colossus.

You may agree in part or not agree at all with much of what I will say. This is probable especially . . . on the level of infinite interpretative features in psychological, semiological, and anthropological terms, in other words, on the level of the global aesthetic interpretation of our film. Whether you agree or not, however, does not matter at all. The purpose of the preanalysis is to demonstrate a method of approach to a film when the director either is not present or does not have precise ideas. It happens frequently in publicity work where the person one is talking to is the art director or someone similar, or when the director puts an unconditional trust in the composer. In any case, I repeat, this exercise is designed for circumstances in which one must insert a musical contribution into things that have already been made. It is unfortunately the norm.[28]

Now let's see what an analysis of the narrative can tell us. Scene 1 is only an introduction, but it is not neutral. The figurative elements are reduced to a minimum, and the directorial intent seems that of a "painless" contact with a particular reality. . . . One needs to emphasize the few mechanical tracking shots and the only optical tracking shot. The director has made the mobile subjects work to his advantage, limiting them to the support of the dynamics of the scene. The potentially significant events are reduced to the arrival of a masculine figure who descends from a car to enter a house. But, more than through the events, the director seems to send his messages by means of some subtle secondary allusions. Let's begin with the setting.

It is a little before dawn (so the light and the milk truck tell us). The color intonation is cold, therefore not very inviting. The asphalt is wet. The windshield of the car informs us that a light rain is falling. The overcoat that the man is wearing suggests to us that the season is autumn or winter. They are all elements that, without guiding us to a precise meaning, predispose us to a certain state of mind that we will attempt to define better a little further on.

We are in a typical suburb, presumably English, perhaps in the periphery of a big city, on a semideserted street with a few cars parked at the end. One is dealing with a minimum of signals, but they can be sufficient to allude to a middle-class environment, closed and reserved, tied to a routine of respectability. In this sense, the milk truck not only emphasizes the hypothesis of daybreak instead of sunset but is placed there to indicate a tiny periodic rite with which one associates the ordered and immutable life of a village.

The noise of an airplane at a low level should not be underestimated. It might be a sign of a nearby airport, which would mean that we are in a not particularly exclusive residential zone. . . . Considering that the noise is the product of a small motor action, it might be a tourist airport, but it is improbable that such an airport would be open at this hour. It could be a reconnaissance flight from a military base, which would lower further the social status of the village.

The environment does not communicate anything aggressive, nothing mysterious or disturbing. In any case, a sense of flatness and anonymity prevails. Up to this point, the psychological tone obtained from the sum of the ambient elements (season, atmospheric conditions, time of day) and the contingent ones (those just described) is vague but of a low profile. In this context, the man is a plausible element but also the carrier of a tiny trait of imbalance, obviously necessary because the story is being formed.

I hope my double role is clear to you. I make a distinction between my identification with the game, or acceptance of its more or less conventional rules, and the consciousness of the means necessary to realize it. In other words, I am reading the film in part as a spectator, in part as its "author." . . . Some of the observations that I have made up to now might appear excessively thin and have been aggravated by the explicit mechanisms to which, of course, I have had recourse. I run the risk of attributing to the events a significance superior to the one intended. But you have to remember, I repeat yet again, that this is an analytic laboratory intended to suggest a method whose application will depend on other contingent factors. For now we are not taking them into consideration, even if we will do so later on. Let's return, therefore, to scene 1.

Normally, in a place of this kind, it might be considered unusual to reenter a house at such an hour. It could be a return from a trip, but where are the suitcases (or at least one small bag)? And what if the man were a doctor? But in that case, he would have had with him the characteristic doctor's bag in the front seat of his car. On the other hand, the taxi (we'll still call it that) . . . stopped many yards away from the house in which the man entered.

The spectator would realize this as the scene matured. Was it out of consideration for the person who lives there? We still do not know, but one is dealing with a choice that should not pass unobserved.

Let's continue. The man descends without excitement from the side of the street, and he walks with secure step. But to reach the sidewalk, he does not go around the car from behind, as prudence and courtesy would dictate; rather, he runs along the length of it and cuts across the street from the front part. The gesture could denote disinterest on the part of the one who is driving, suggesting a superior condition. One could say that it is typical of a man accustomed to command, perhaps a military man or a policeman.

Having arrived at the little gate, the man slows up a little. The circumspection with which he opens and then closes the gate is evident. This detail emphasizes a posteriori the fact that the auto stopped a goodly distance from the house. But the auto is not a taxi, but rather a police car. It is clear only at the end of the scene that the car is not a taxi. . . . We note also that the car's stop would have been a good occasion to demonstrate the inside of the car with a cut in the montage, thereby also demonstrating the identity of the driver or at least how the person looked. Instead, at 50″ the director has avoided letting us see his face, but by doing this, he has immediately made us throw away the hypothesis that the car is a taxi. This sense of mystery can be added to the denotative elements we have noted up to this point. They are trivial, but there are a number of them.

Before continuing, I assure you that, further along, I will not descend to details of this type, not because the little film does not deserve it, but because, once the method is established, we will dwell on only those cases that can lead to new analytical aspects.

HYPOTHESIS FOR POTENTIAL MUSICAL SOLUTIONS

On the practical, operational level, it would be unthinkable to make a musical choice after having looked only at this scene while ignoring all the rest. Therefore, the segmentation by scene is due entirely to my desire to simplify and clarify my exposition. The hypotheses that I will make will inevitably take into account the whole work. They will carry knowledge of the whole film that you still do not have. On the other hand, if you encounter a director, the situation is analogous because he already knows the whole film and you do not. Regardless of the other auditory constants, the scene presents the potential for an extensive musical treatment. This is determined by its:

1. **Introductory character**
2. **General climate**, taking everything together—place, atmospheric conditions, luminosity—that induces us to take into consideration spe-

cific musical choices (dark timbres, mixed and/or suffused, with some variables)

3. **Contrast**—light but present—between a certain overall neutral atmosphere and some slightly disturbing characteristics insinuated by the human presence. The figurative and motor characteristics (associated with the presence of certain sounds, like the airplane) are understood according to schemes of concordance and of symmetry. There is the vague documentary style of an event shot in real time, or, to put it another way, total coherence between event and diegetic time. One can speak, therefore, of a general concordance with some premonitions of light discord.

I present a hypothesis expressed as the diagram that follows. The length of the horizontal baseline expresses the duration of the scene. The segment is divided in two parts. The time is indicated exactly in seconds (T for time line), from 00 to 50. The lower part (N—noises) has to do with the noises and their dynamics (according to crescendo marks not broken down into detail but in general). The upper part (M for music) sketches schematically the potential musical interventions, where ME stands for micro events (the asterisks) and P stands for pedal. The sideways forks underneath signs for crescendo and decrescendo obviously indicate the relative musical dynamics.

A musical interpretation could play with two coexistent registers, one of which would be in the bass. It could be . . . a connective fascia, a pedal, a more eloquent depth in the sense of timbre rather than rhythm or even less than melody. One could use it to "express" the general context, mixed at a

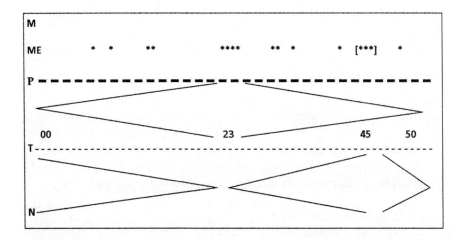

Figure 2.1.

medium-low volume, not louder than the peaks of the noises, which are important. Some microinterventions arising from the fascia (pseudopointillistic or pseudothematic, but soft) could insinuate a partial mobility and then could take over and thicken at approximately the moment the car reaches the sidewalk (23"). If it were necessary to confer on the musical composition a didactic or more tritely allusive role (hypothesize a specific request from the director), this could be realized (always with a light hand) with an implicit sync point[29] on the ultimate shot of the automobile, which is shown to be a police car. One ought to treat it only as a rhythmic rippling or contraction, a microthematic thickening (note the group of asterisks with square brackets in the diagram).

Elaborated differently or developed progressively according to jumbled clusters of rhythmic figures or semiphrases, this same material could be maintained in the sequence that follows. It seems opportune that we anticipate it, starting even at the end of this scene in order to give a sense of continuity to the differentiation and the development of events. For the stylistic connotation of the whole thing, one needs to avoid characterizations that are on the one hand too explicit or on the other hand dull, "generic" pieces. It goes without saying that the musical material used here, given the brevity of the whole scene, will remain in the spectator's memory. Therefore, the music needs to be chosen within the context of the solutions that will be adopted for successive scenes/sequences. For example, a solution filled with suspense . . . is to be avoided. (I use . . . preexistent music that, because of its limited diffusion, I predict will sound like an "original" composition.)[30]

A brief suspenseful composition could respond to our need for certain characteristics, like playability by the musicians or the intangibility of the argument. Although a certain sense of suspension and of expectation marries well with the scene, there is in our first musical example . . . something explicitly "positive"—empty stretches in a bucolic climate—that makes it oscillate between impropriety and lack of precision, without counting the scarce attractions implicit in the poverty of language. Again, one should avoid a horror solution.[31]

In effect, there is a basic beat over which one could put some interventions devoid of thematic characteristics—more or less those that we have hypothesized. The impact would be all too explicit and heavy. It might conduct the scene too easily into the context of a film of the horror genre. This is a case in which the music forces one's hand toward generalized (even if possibly legitimate) meanings but does so before the narration has developed sufficiently to justify them. I hope that it will be clear that I have chosen a "horror" example to go exaggeratedly in the opposite direction from the characteristics of the preceding example, establishing a sort of double border between the "little" and the "too much." It needs instead, as I have already said, an intervention psychologically incisive but not unidirectional, not immediately clear, and not too invasive on the dynamic level. Could it be a highly demanding contemporary piece?[32]

Here the musical language is too demanding, too obscure for the average spectator. It is unhooked from any sort of rhythmic continuity (which would be a constant and repetitive base), spaced freely between sounds in distant registers, and disposed against sharp chords of uncertain timbre and attribution. . . . These are musical clichés that are not totally inappropriate. . . . The composition was written so that it could be added as a soundtrack for any generic film and is entitled *Daybreak over the City*. However, . . . we do not intend to furnish the means for obtaining . . . good film music for a documentary without ambitions or for a film made for television. It is true that clichés exist in every musical genre, even the more noble (think of Bach, of Mozart), but one needs to surpass them, transcend them, reinvent them. . . . What would a jazz climate do?[33]

The qualities of the composition are not now in discussion. By making a similar choice, however, one falls into another cliché, although one of the film musical vices of the fifties and sixties. Even some extremely influential directors like Antonioni resorted to jazz for two motives. It stood for "neurosis and metropolitan alienation," and it was a reaction against the tear jerking that pervaded the Italian cinema of that period. Against this type one could contrapose a sort of impersonal and "objective" music, and by this time jazz was a topos.

Certainly, as happens inevitably with music composed for adding to a generalized soundtrack, there is no clear-cut personality in this composition. But then the general tone is not very far from that of our hypothesis, even if the sound "pressure" (acoustic and psychological) exercised on the spectator carries us . . . to the horror effect of example 2. The music forces the spectator toward generalized, possibly legitimate meanings, but before the narration has developed sufficiently to justify them. Jazzy example 4 employs an excess of means in relation to the weight of the narrative. It is a common defect of beginners (and of many professionals of modest talent).

If the director does not limit the complexity of the musical language, then one can obtain a still more valid audiovisual result that has a quality and musical intensity significantly different from that of example 4 but like that in the next case.[34]

The approach is bold. . . . It is a composition of great discipline. It is undoubtedly out of proportion to the quality of *Cut Sequences* (but this is exactly what frequently happens in the use that directors make of preexisting music . . .). I proposed it because I wanted to demonstrate another "territorial limit," in a way analogous to what I did with hypotheses 1 and 2. . . . This does not mean that a modest little film or one without endowment as a strong film automatically ought to have inferior music. It means, however, that the relative "caliber" of the film ought in some way or other to be relevant. If . . .

a composer had written this music for scene 1, he undoubtedly would have served the film to excess. It is a subject that we will develop later.

If one stays with the criteria of the journey developed up to now, among the infinite solutions available one could exercise a middle way. It would arise from a conscious use of contemporary musical language. Therefore, it would be endowed with a certain complexity but put at the service of functionality by means of recurrent figurations.[35]

To my mind, such a solution is very appropriate for the end of our discussion because it represents a balance, an ordinary interior that contributes to the connecting of single sound events (rhythmic, harmonic, in the end pseudomelodic) without concessions that are too obvious to the listener. I repeat, in this scene, perhaps the most difficult thing is to avoid having the music overclarify the figurative-auditory whole while maintaining its essential and well-designed simplicity. It needs to suggest more than to express, to insinuate more than to clarify. In sum, you should write little and then cut the better part of what you have written. You need above all to remember that the film continues, that you seed here for harvest later in the succeeding scene and perhaps in the sequences that follow.

ASYNCHRONISM

In this context the most inadmissible thing is to resort to asynchronism or incoherent juxtapositions (even if they are often very efficient). This is not so much because of the necessity to maintain . . . the already verified formal coherence, but, above all, in order to maintain the ambiguity of the whole. Moreover, because we are dealing with an introductory phase, we should not confuse . . . the spectator by such "poetic license." Because stylistic and/or psychological asynchronism is effective, the visual features and the narrative intent have to be explicit already if one is to use it.

The spectator has to possess a basic key to the interpretation of a work in order to appreciate the contrast between synchronism and asynchronism, so asynchronism almost never comes at the beginning of a film. Or if one is to make an exception, the relationship between the director and the music has to have so many precedents that it can authorize the deviation from a by now very established tradition. One thinks of the case of Rota-Fellini, where certain musical choices seem acceptable because "Fellinian," or the case of Morricone-Leone where, already from the first film, the grotesque, the ironic, the hyperbolic nature of the music had acquired an undeniable credibility. Then one thinks of the resort to classical music in science-fiction films, wanted and exalted by Kubrick in *2001: A Space Odyssey*[36] and others. In sum, even asynchronism in its various forms can be made into a model, but it has to be able to have a basis in an illustrious precedent, stratified culturally and already decoded by the spectator. Or it has to live on an inheritance, leaning on the prestige and the precedents of the authors.

Scene 2—duration 2'21"
Interior of a habitation
Neutral color tonality (but warm in relation to the preceding scene)

a. Objective Description of the Visual/Sound Events

Medium shot—interior 1—entrance to the house[37] —high angle shot—natural transition from scene 1.

Male[38] character enters, closes the door with care, and lingers at the bottom of the stairs looking (listening) up; then he starts to take off his overcoat/door half-closed.

From medium shot to medium full shot—interior 2—kitchen (linked cut of transition) (0'14")—The male character finishes taking off his overcoat and puts it over a chair, notes the cat. *Meows.* Salutes it with a nuanced cordiality.

Mechanical tracking shot from left to right. He approaches, caresses cat, and offers it something to eat, taking the plastic wrap off a plate. The cat refuses the offer and goes away. The man makes a ball of the plastic wrap and throws it away, *commenting tiredly*. Mechanical tracking shot from right to left.

The man goes toward the refrigerator, extracts a bottle of milk, and drinks it directly from the bottle, leaning against a piece of furniture. He goes to the exit carrying the bottle. *Noise of washing up—other meows.*

From medium shot to foreground—interior 3—stairs—landing (linked cut of transition)—1'00"—The man climbs slowly.

Arriving at a landing (mechanical tracking shot, then optical) and taking his time, he goes along the corridor until he reaches the door of a bedroom.

Reverse shot of the interior of the bedroom (medium full shot), which the man observes cautiously. The man extends his left hand toward the door.

Interior 4—bedroom (subjective)—1'25". Medium shot on a feminine figure who is sleeping in a double bed. The door is half-closed slowly.

Medium full shot—interior 4—new reverse shot. The man closes the door. Breathes.

He retraces his steps, but his eye falls on a print attached to the wall (the object is of an antique and noble manufacture). He stops to observe it thoughtfully. Mechanical tracking shot. He starts toward the bathroom. He enters it.

Interior 5—bathroom—1'40". From foreground to medium shot. The man enters, drinking again from the bottle of milk.

Medium shot contemporaneously with the image in a mirror. The man puts the bottle on the sink.

He extracts an object from the right pocket of the jacket, distances himself from the sink, exiting the frame but . . . remaining visible in the reflected image of the mirror.

Medium shot, reverse shot—The man sits on the bathtub. The object is a case that he is observing . . . and which he then opens. He extracts a decoration (detail of the hand—subjective).

Close-up of medal. He holds it in the palm of his hand. He caresses the figure in low relief with his thumb.

Very close close-up on his suffering and incredulous face.
The man raises his head and looks into space, lost.

Medium shot. The man moves his right arm and knocks over flasks that fall into the bathtub. *Sound of flasks.*

Presumed interior 4—2'20". In an empty frame, the face of a woman enters from the bottom in a very close close-up. Unexpectedly, she has awakened, calling, *"Alek?"*

b. Synthesis of the Formal Features (Figurative, Motor, Auditory)

Figurative features: Variable but consequential.

Motor features: Variable but pertinent. There are five different interiors in the same house. A pair recurs. There are two human beings and an animal.

The . . . woman has a foreboding quality because of the man's gestures and the noise of the falling flasks. Then, spied upon, she finally becomes the protagonist (a little more than 1″ from the end of the scene and the end of the sequence). The always moderate optics are worth noting. The point of view is natural, not in the least theatrical. Avoided (as is . . . typical in the interiors of many films) is the use of the forced grand angle shot in order to better encompass and describe the environment. Avoided also, therefore, is the distressing exaggeration of the scene that occurs in some cases when this length of focus is used. It is a type associated with the steady cam.

The intention, therefore, seems to be sympathetic and psychologically introspective, without artificial shifts. Only three stresses are created by the framing: the close close-up of the man who has observed the medallion, the detail of this medallion, and the close close-up of the woman as she awakens. Static moments alternate with dynamic moments for the entire duration of the scene. There are numerous indispensable, mechanical, and, in particular cases, optical tracking shots and a remarkable attention to linking the play of shots and reverse shots. (For example, note the closing of the door of the bedroom in which the woman sleeps, the result of three linked framing shots, of which the central is subjective). . . . In its apparent simplicity, the whole scene is well assembled.

Auditory features: Scarce and almost without influence, except for the flask noises at the end. After looking carefully at the scene, I believe that it is casual and disordered, whereas it has a rather precise latent scansion, as one can see from the simple graphic below. The scansion, if it can be defined that way, recurs every thirty seconds, with an initial dilation of double duration that corresponds to a false oasis of relaxation in the encounter with the cat. It is evident that these characteristics of symmetry facilitate the task of the composer, but of this we will speak later.

c. Analysis of the Narrative

Dealing with the second scene in the same sequence, which is linked naturally to the first scene, we are confronted with a case in which the acquired elements are permanent and therefore part of a psychological continuity. In other words, even though the scenario has changed, the spectator carries to the inside of the new context all the awareness he or she acquired in the previous one, with the addition of an increased level of curiosity and therefore of analytic attention. Every signal (visual, aural, musical) will be examined, even if unconsciously, with close attention to its allusive, explanatory potential.

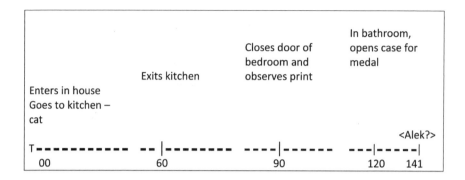

Figure 2.2.

Think about the fact that the two scenes involve a triple introductory significance. Scene 1 introduces the spectator to the film, but at the same time introduces a person in the scene, while scene 2 introduces that same person inside the place portrayed in scene 1. This naturally augments our expectation because nobody will imagine that now, on the inside of the house, as in a game of Chinese boxes, another process of introduction will happen. Instead, something has to happen, even if it is not definitive.

The man is middle aged. That could mean that what is done is done. He dresses in a dignified but anonymous way. He could be a functionary or, to advance a hypothesis already advanced, a military man or a policeman. The care with which he closes the glass door at the entrance and the look that he directs to the second floor (the latter barely didactic) could support the hypothesis that this is a much less usual return, perhaps a sign of a clandestine activity. The man's face denotes a state of prostration. The only nuance of cordiality appears in the encounter with the cat, from which he receives, however, a disappointment. The gesture, slightly irritated, with which he throws away the plastic wrap that protected the plate of food is fairly significant, but other gestures need to be noted. He left his overcoat in the kitchen. He carried the milk bottle with him, exiting with it. He continued to drink in the bathroom, where he abandoned the bottle on the sink.

It is evident that Alek goes about this house like its owner, but from this roaming around one obtains already a human profile with some specific, not exactly positive connotations. The man is visibly tired. He is disorderly by nature, or perhaps he is in a confused state, preoccupied with not waking up his presumed wife (remember the look with which he observed her, closing the door of the bedroom). Then one should note that for almost six seconds (so many, but with Sergio Leone it would have been six minutes!) Alek looks almost surprised by the print attached to the wall. It seems a sort of painful and embarrassing "memento" (another point that is a little didactic but at the same time enigmatic).

Finally we have the episode with the medallion. (Already in some preceding frames his hand went into his right pocket, as if he wanted to reassure himself that the object was there.) The expression on his face is of incredulity, of stupefaction, of embarrassment. It is as if that object had the capacity of making him exit from a painful state of amnesia. . . . Here the hypotheses are numerous. Ideals betrayed? Break from a completely different past? An injustice, a blackmail suffered? It is not possible to establish the reality, but in the end it is not important.[39] What counts is that already at this point the man exhibits a profound state of travail and of confusion, perhaps because he is a victim of his own self or of a not confessable and by now irreparable situation. . . . The unexpected, anxious awakening of his wife assumes the significance of a definitive break in a precarious and perhaps sanctioned equilibrium, at least on the symbolic level. It will be impossible to maintain a now unsustainable secret.

HYPOTHESIS FOR A POTENTIAL MUSICAL SOLUTION

The potential for musical treatment is very great, even if, were it to be in a feature film, we could accept it without music because the scene is so well assembled. What has already been observed about the naturalness of the photography (the use of medium focus and moderate grand angles) is very important for the musical component. It suggests that one could use expressive, logical means to support and increase the significance of all that is close to Alek's character and his private life. With respect to motor features, their variability has already been noted. The precision of the montage makes them natural. Therefore . . . it would be an error to put the music in competition (in the rhythmic sense, for example) with the visual articulation. I would avoid formal analogies and, of course, sync points.

Finally, what about the noises and the talking? Except for the wife's question, they are not important enough to create obstacles to the musical commentary. . . . The question "Alek?" is significant and ought to be maximized, if not . . . isolated. Thus it should be without music. . . . That moment of tension—I refer always to the awakening of the wife—might have been made using more time, for example, with the addition of an echo or a coda in the photography. This would have left the composer more interpretative room. (It might have been done also in consideration of the dry cut to the next sequence that carries us elsewhere in all senses.)

In order to obtain the extra room, I confess to having used the videotape recorders to obtain a still image of the wife's face (a result obtained without much trouble technically), but then I rejected it for two reasons. First, to create the required space, the still image would have had to last almost five seconds. There would have been a seemingly forced emphasis, a redundant enigma. And then a still image has precise semantic values. If you think of *8½*,[40] Fellini resorts to a still image to signal the interruption of Guido's[41] dream because of the ring of a telephone (off camera). It lasts not more than two minutes, chopping off the dreamlike female voice ("I want to put things in order . . . I want to do the cleaning . . . I want to put things in order . . . I want to do the clea—"), but it is unequivocal. If you remember the finale of the film *I pugni in tasca (Fists in Pocket)* by Marco Bellocchio,[42] the male character interpreted by Lou Castel dies at the end of an epileptic seizure while he is listening to *La Traviata*. The high note of the soprano is looped. Thus the sound becomes fixed, interminable. As has already been observed,[43] the passage from life to death occurs in that fixed position.

Second, as it is, scene 2 of *Cut Sequences* closes well, but it is throttled. After 1″ we are already in the next sequence. It is not a very good transition, but in the cinema it happens (if only because other material was not shot so that a fix would have been possible at the editing stage). The composer has to confront and try to resolve exactly this type of problem. Therefore . . . it is not bad that our little film has some imperfections . . . that make it other than ideal.

To summarize, the scene has a consequential character. It stretches to a point, a point of maximum tension, which is then resolved or overcome by a banal incident and by an "other" not contemplated in the film. We do not know, and will never know, what that man will say to that woman. We are not to understand whether Alek is hiding the medallion or whether he will be found in tears, nor whether the woman will greet him without asking anything, whether she will interrogate him mercilessly or scold him sharply. We know only that what we have gathered from the summit of a process of accumulation has for us a character that is partially liberating and semicathartic.

In light of these considerations, what should we put on the musical level? The scene presents a kind of latent crescendo that authorizes us to create something analogous in the musical sense, but by doing this, one would encounter two certain risks. The music might fall into the category of the "thrilling," and without covering the female voice, there would be the possible but fixed obligation to resolve the musical crescendo with a final marked difference in volume or quality of the music. The alternative . . . would be to support the scene according to the principles already seen in the preceding scene. It would be a sensitive, cautious, almost uncertain and therefore prudent sort of music (however eager it might be not to exist and, much less, to prevail). The music would let the images work. It would reduce the interpretive level and thus respect the need to render uniform the basic material used for the whole sequence.

Without repeating the hypotheses advanced for scene 1, let us look at some musical matches for both scenes 1 and 2, and therefore for the entire first sequence. It lasts 3'10", or 190". In our field, the numbers are not important as statistics to be used for their own sake. In fact, if we wanted to be symmetrical, we could conceive of a modular structure whose minimum element would have a range of 15". There could be a semiphrase "A" of 15" for which one would make a complement of a "B" of another 15". In any case, about . . . modular possibilities Maestro Morricone will be able to speak later in a much more concrete way. Returning instead to the hypothesized matches, remember that exact synchronicity and proportions have to be forgotten, because it is evident that I am using preexistent music. Therefore, let's think about language, form, and style.

> **First hypothesis**: Minimum interpretive level; a sort of continuum subjected to little variations, without events or any development.
>
> **Second hypothesis**: An interpretive level expanded slightly, therefore with greater musical eloquence and some indication of microthematic ideas.
>
> **Third hypothesis**: Interpretive will decisively expanded, with a decidedly diverse density of writing, whether with linear purpose or with the intention of using the differentiated participation by the instrumental ensemble.

In all three cases, though they use different nuances, the result might seem too important. In effect, whichever example one takes as the basic hypothesis, a melodic-harmonic characterization is lacking that might both concede something more to the spectator and possibly maintain the tension that . . . is already present.

Sequence 2
Comprising one scene, duration 1'26"

Exterior/interior—daytime—springtime
Neutral color tonality

I imagine that this subdivision might appear arbitrary. One is always dealing with an interpretation, for which I need to explain the motivation. I believe it will not be very difficult to accept the birth of a new sequence—the third—from the point at which Alek will distance himself from the monastery in order to go toward the sea. (The detachment from the place will not seem only physical, but to this we will return.) However, what has sustained one single scene in this second sequence might be a matter of opinion, though it contains an alternation of exterior-interior and of diverse moments perhaps not even pertaining to the same day. I ask that you accept it as valid. We will have occasion to return to these detailed analyses.

a. Objective Description of the Visual/Sound Events

Long shot—monastery encircled by a green lawn. Men that are working the land. *Voice off camera: Bible lesson—4".*

Medium shot—*monk reading*/linking shot—playback.

Optical and mechanical tracking shot to follow a second monk who enters carrying a little basket with some bread.

The object passes from hand to hand, revealing (aperture optical tracking shot) a long table at which sit a number of table companions of various ages, among whom is Alek, who is wearing a white shirt—30".

Medium shot of Alek in his room, where he is looking out the window. *Voice of the monk continues off camera.*

Long shot—subjective—men working on the lawn down below. *Voice of monk continues.*

Medium shot—reverse shot—face of Alek at window. *Voice of monk continues off camera—40".*

Long shot—exterior of monastery. Two brothers in conversation. Shot at their level. *Monk's voice continues off camera.*

Medium full shot of interior—Alek at the window. *Monk's voice continues off camera—47".*

Medium shot—Alek lying down on lawn near monastery. Over the same shirt he is wearing a dark sweater.

Medium full shot—passage of two monks (mechanical tracking shot to follow them).

Medium shot like the preceding—Alek is joined by a monk.[44] *Exchange of phrases suitable to the occasion.*

Medium shot—Alex in bedroom, in shirt, lying down on his bed. Looking fixedly at ceiling, then closes his eyes. Linking shot: *ultimate words of the monk off camera.*

Long shot—seen from above—stairway of the monastery. Alek descending in the company of a monk—1'26".

b. Synthesis of Formal Features (Figurative, Motor, Auditory)

Figurative features: Constantly very low. There is a notable alternation of long and of static-dynamic situations.

Motor features: Standard feature medium-high. If it is decisively high in the scene in the refectory, with an accurate optical and mechanical tracking shot that "describes" the place and the acts that happened there (it should be noted that the moment when the basket of bread arrives at the end of the table, the tracking shot is finished), one could not say as much for the succeeding scenes, which are made up of so many little motionless "upsets" of the montage and of continuous passages from long shot to medium full shot.

Auditory features: Standard feature very high. Having said this, I come to the problem of a number of scenes when auditory features are reduced to only one. The auditory component is very important in this sequence—I would say fundamental—and is the reason I chose it. . . . Make sure you notice that the voice of the monk who is reading a sacred text off camera begins with the sequence itself, outside. The voice proceeds with the scene, in the episode in the refectory, but the voice "punctures" that episode and develops in successive links that are more fragmented in appearance. Thus, that voice is a *continuum* of the monastery. It might even be an ostinato perceived by Alek (I do not know whether to define it as relaxing or obsessive). Or it might be the "comment" assumed by the director to be a comprehensive symbol of monastic life, and as such, audible before, during, and after the hour of the meal.

Because of this vocal presence, for semiotic and structural reasons I thought it indispensable to unify the entire sequence into a single scene. A doubt might arise at the sixtieth second, where there is live dialogue between Alek and the monk. (Note: The monk is the same one that read in the refectory. Therefore, I would opt for the interpretation that the ostinato is obsessive.) It would have been legitimate to consider this as a scene by itself, a buffered episode, the conclusion of sequence 2 and a connection between this and the following sequence 3. But also here the author plays in the same register, even if the ultimate words of the monk—relative to the conversation in the open air—are heard when Alek appears alone in his room. It thus reproduces the previous procedure, although in a way that is a little less satisfactory. This fragment could be the global conscience of the monastery, mediated through Alek's perception and memory, or it might be a sort of subjective acoustic. In conclusion, I would like to emphasize that in this sequence the director has used the noise-dialogue as a soundtrack with the same symbolic-expressive meanings that one usually could trust to the musical components. . . . In order to illustrate them, I have resorted to a terminology that will be the object of the second part of the audiovisual analysis.

One observation as an aside: the last fragment, the descent down the staircase in the company of a monk, should by rights pertain to the following sequence, in which Alek goes far away from the monastery to arrive at the beach. I say this because he is wearing a different shirt from the one he had on in sequence 2 and, as in sequence 3, it is outside his pants. But because of the long shot and the quality of the photography, it is not very easy to perceive it. Thinking therefore about the perceptive attention of the average spectator, we can assimilate the fragment of the descent of the stairs within the preceding moment simply because of its fragmentary nature and brevity. In sum, it is a case where to "make a mistake" makes life easier for the composer and an unequivocal decoding for the spectator. After an examination of sequence 3, you will understand better that, had I begun it with the fragment on the stairs, the sequence would have suffered a great deal.

c. Analysis of the Narrative

Let us begin with the season. On the basis of the clothing and the color of the vegetation, I have defined it as spring. If all this is not a flashback,[45] we are authorized to believe that time has passed since sequence 1. . . . On the other hand, the cinema has the specific characteristic of conducting us through time and physical or mental space on the basis of its own rules and conventions. The reasons can be clarified only at the film's conclusion. Paradoxically, the film composer has to intercept the more marginal-seeming signals and excavate the more recondite meanings in order then to "forget them." Through an interpretative more than descriptive process, he or she arrives at an absolute synthesis.

Turning to the sequence, . . . there is no doubt about the fact that it takes place at a monastery. It remains to be seen whether the guests are spending time there for a free spiritual retreat or whether the place is being used, for example, as a center of reeducation for ex-convicts. The latter is not that unreliable a hypothesis. From the first frame and in what follows, we see men at work. Alek's face in his bedroom does not convey happiness or serenity, nor do the faces of the other table companions express it. In this sequence nothing relevant happens, and this is its force and its intent. The director seems to want to transmit the sense of a slow passage of time, in the context of reduced and repetitive, monotonous activity. Alek seems to submit with a certain resignation but also with a deep bitterness. Beyond the figurative fragmentation about which we already have spoken, the scene captures a sense of immobility and lack of surprise. The conventional phrases that the monk repeats in the brief conversation with Alek confirm the same thing. The conclusions I will make after having analyzed sequence 3 induce me to formulate only one hypothesis for a musical solution.

Sequence 3
Consisting of two scenes for a total of 2′01″

Scene 1—duration 0′36″
Exterior—daytime—the monastery shot from a green slope near the sea
Late summer—color tonality warm

a. Objective Description of the Visual/Sound Events

Far shot of monastery. Alek advances on the lawn, which is thinner and of a brown color,[46] distancing himself from the monastery.

Medium shot—lawn—Alek proceeds. Mechanical tracking shot follows him. *Light pounding.*

Reverse shot—Alek enters from the right in far shot, descends toward the sea, and distances himself.

Scene 2—duration 1′25″
Exterior—daytime
From fence to lawn facing the beach—beach

a. Objective Description of the Visual/Sound Events

Far shot—fence. Alek climbs it and stops to observe the sea. *Noise of the sea.*

Far shot (telephoto lens)—young woman on the beach lying on a towel. She rises, then removes the beach robe, revealing a scanty bikini. She goes sinuously toward the sea (tracking shot following). *Noise of the sea.*

Medium full shot—Alek observes the scene. Climbs completely over the fence to exit from the frame lower left. *Noise of the sea.*

Far shot—From the profile of the green slope the young woman appears in the distance, going toward the shore. At the same time, Alek enters from the right. Alek observes her, then sits on the grass, always without taking his eyes off the young woman. *Sound of the sea louder.*

Far shot (telephoto lens)—portion of the sea—The young woman enters the water with long steps, and then she dives without hesitation. *Sound of the sea louder.*

Far shot as counterpart of preceding—Alek observes. *Sound of sea damped down.*

Medium full shot—Alek continues to observe. *Sound of the sea damped down.*

Far shot (telephoto lens as counterpart of preceding)—The young woman returns to the shore. *Sound of the sea louder.*

Medium shot of the beach, from lower to higher. Alek observes, partially covered by the grass. *Sound of the sea not damped down.*

Medium shot—optical tracking shot—The young woman exits the water, walks along the breakwater. *Sound of the sea—high.*

Medium shot of the beach, from lower to higher. Alek observes almost completely covered by the grass. Begins to lie down. *Sound of sea not damped down.*

Medium full shot—mechanical tracking shot to follow—Alek completes the gesture of lying down with hands behind his neck and observes the sky. *Sound of the sea attenuated.*

Far shot—The young woman walks through the surf, observing the sea. The beach robe is on, and she has with her the appropriate equipment. *Sound of the sea attenuated.*

Far shot—a scene between rocks and sand framed by branches. *Sound of the sea attenuated.* The End (without title card)

b. Synthesis of the Formal Features (Figurative, Motor, Auditory) Reported for Both Scenes

Figurative features: Variable but consequential.

Motor features: Variable but pertinent. Few but well differentiated are the environmental components that participate in the construction of the whole: monastery (suddenly abandoned), countryside, sea, Alek, and a beautiful young woman. The framings utilized for the same subject contemporaneously are very different. Just as various are the use of focal distance and the movements of the camera. The interventions of editing are continuous and decisive. Static moments are contraposed against others that are decisively dynamic. Scene 2 always associates the two opposing values with the people in the frame: the dynamism of the young woman and the static quality of Alek.

Auditory features: Not constant and not always coherent, but pertinent. The difference between the two scenes is the presence of the sea, above all on the acoustic level.

To underline: Though there are sources of discontinuity in the sound, the process used to mix the level of the sound of the sea should be noted. When the director wants to suggest the young woman's . . . point of view, the sound of the sea is very high, even if the framing shows Alek to be much closer than he would appear to her eyes. A moment afterwards, from Alek's point of view or at least from the point where he is, the noise is instead attenuated. We are therefore in the presence of the intersection between two subjective shots, even if obtained in a way that is a little free, made through some approximations of the choice of shot and angulation.

c. Analysis of the Narrative Relative to the Entire Sequence

Without exaggerating too much, I think that the director has given us a precise message that informs us that time has passed. I have isolated two still images from the monastery treated in diverse scenes[47] from which it is possible to note the difference of general color intonation: from the façade of the building; from the lawn, yellowed in patches and less dense; and from the bare tree in the foreground. This reinforces the choice of the subdivision between sequences 2 and 3 already discussed.

By comparison to sequence 2, sequence 3 contains a major narrative continuity and a not-indifferent psychological turning point. Let me explain better. If *Cut Sequences* had not shown the life of the monastery with such insistence, the appearance of the young woman would not have the impact on us that it does. The young woman[48] has a pleasing aspect, but . . . she becomes still more attractive in comparison with a dimension that is totally extraneous, the surroundings from which Alek comes. There is a unity of time, that of the walk. There is the tracking shot in front and then from the shoulders. There is the continuity of space, proposed for the connecting shots, but there is also this small spark given to the young woman.

I do not want to enter into a series of hypotheses about the symbolic potential of her presence (Alek, who distances himself from the monastery; the disrobing of the young woman; the pleasure of the dive and of the swimming; the vaguely voyeuristic aspect of the situation); rather, I want to emphasize . . . the contradictions in the man's behavior. At first he follows the young woman. He seems rather determined. You remember the gesture with which suddenly, after having seen her, he climbed the fence, choosing a place from which to observe her well, almost without taking his eyes off her. The successive play of subjective or pseudosubjective shots . . . coincides with the maximum degree of involvement and therefore of tension.

Then, however, when the young woman turns toward the shore, precisely at this point there is a shot that is extremely significant. There is the semicovered face of Alek, who almost seems to have hidden himself. Then, at the woman's approach, he lies down on the green of the lawn. One could say that the interest provoked in him by her presence has disappeared, or that demonstrations of sensuality have intimidated or embittered him.

Alek contemplates the sky now with a look and in a position similar to that assumed in the preceding sequence, when he was stretched out on the bed of his room at the monastery. He expresses inaction, resignation, and impotence. The shot of the young woman who is going away does nothing other than confirm the retreat and the extraneousness of the male character in comparison to that splash of vitality. With respect to the far shot that follows—the last frame—I confess to having mounted it only to allow the possibility of creating a not-too-meager coda, but it is clear that had the shot of the young woman passing to the shore been longer, it would have been better. The "finale" could have been earned. But, as I have said before, I tried to eliminate certain defects in the photography. Others, even though I would have been able to remedy them, I have left as they were in order not to create an ideal object for the composer.

HYPOTHESES OF POTENTIAL MUSICAL SOLUTIONS

There are three reasons why one would want to make the subject, and in consequence the musical material, uniform: (1) The whole film is brief . . . , (2) there is spatial continuity, and (3) the psychological intonation is uniform. One must take special care . . . with the point of maximum tension but without substantial deviation from the base, . . . because the final reaction of Alek refers back to the preceding mood. I was forced to put slight spatial and above all temporal deformities in relief, always within the scope of giving examples during the recitation of a method. In spite of this, I would opt for a unitary and comprehensive discourse that would be able to make the conflicting aspects of the episode end up as if within one network.

We could decide not to have the music interpret anything, creating only a musical background of a vague, even though participatory, tone. Then one of the examples we already have considered or others that are analogous . . . could be considered good. However, we will try to break up the discussion, revising the musical hypothesis of sequence 2. I grant that of the three sequences, this sequence could be at the limit of those without musical solution or with a solution that is mixed at a very low volume because . . . of the talking on and off screen.

Let's try Morricone's *Rifrazione*.[49] It is very intense, perhaps too decisively polarizing for the purposes to which we want to put it. For this reason, let's distinguish once again between musical quality . . . and the musical requirements of the episode. In other words, it is not always the best music that will guarantee the best result. Another demanding choice, although of a completely different nature, still applied to sequence 2, could be John Dowland's *Lachrimae Pavan*.[50] For sequence 3 we could adapt *Sumer Is Icumen In*.[51]

There is nothing extraordinary about creating similar matches (Kubrick has much to teach in this regard), even if, with a little affectation, these latter two cases have a geographical and thus cultural identity, because the film was shot in England and the music is English. . . . Even more, one could say that when using such bold juxtapositions, the "game" frequently functions beyond one's intentions or expectations. The linguistic and . . . anthropological contrast creates a spontaneous combustion that works to the advantage of both components film and music. In other words, a spectator, without any particular musical knowledge, can note better the nature of a Renaissance piece if he or she finds it associated with a contemporary visual situation, while these same stylistic characteristics can escape attention in a concert made entirely of Renaissance music.

Let us now turn to the two hypothetical compositions. The first has to be mixed very low and open some seconds after the beginning of the scene— let's say on the tracking shot in the refectory. Then it should be muffled decisively when the monk begins to speak. The second composition, instead, ought not to present particular mixing problems. It . . . presents some allusions that go beyond an ethnic society. . . . The round *Sumer Is Icumen In* . . . assumes, in fact, the significance of a sensual and disturbing flash and at the same time that of a spiral without progress, analogous to our discovery about Alek's condition. But effectiveness aside, how many spectators would grasp these allusions? Further, . . . it was not my intention to force you to write "in the style of" . . . (Maestro Morricone can tell you how ungratifying it is to receive a request of this kind.) I only want to invite you to reflect on the possibilities that are implicit if one chooses a pleasing, precisely intellectualized, and, as a consequence, slightly too exclusive, asynchronism. . . . *Lachrimae Pavan* instead has the effect of muffling . . . the stylistic connotations of the time in which Alek lives. (I'm always thinking of a not-very-educated ear.) As such, in its absolute nobility, it would be able to function like an intense, but at the same time discreet, subplot.

Let's continue with the hypotheses. Sequences 2 and 3 are very different from each other, but Alek remains in character. In fact, at the end of the last sequence his character is reconfirmed fully. Therefore, from the beginning of sequence 2 one needs to insinuate a character, a musical presence—Alek, his "theme"—that will return at the conclusion. And that same musical characterization has to be able to live alongside two other elements, the monastery in sequence 2 and the young woman—obviously not the personage, who does not exist, but the one that she represents—in sequence 3.

Again, this is a specification that causes me to take up and reexamine an observation I made earlier. The director has given us indications regarding the change of season that are interpolated between sequences 2 and 3. I do not expect a composer to make an abbreviated paraphrase of Vivaldi's *Quattro stagioni* [*Four Seasons*]. It does not have to be the latest news, certainly. But the musician does have to take into account and assimilate these facts— all those that will be discussed here—in his or her own mind . . . and then to synthesize and sublimate them in a tone that will be appropriate to the whole film.

Let us consider now how to arrive at a balance regarding the music for the whole of *Cut Sequences*. If sequence 1 presents an elevated opportunity for musical treatment, the following sequences instead create major problems. Clearly a uniform treatment could be made that is, however, . . . strewn with little, perhaps microthematic, discontinuities. I am thinking, in sum, of a Morriconian type of writing that has the capacity of making an atmosphere full of apprehensions and questions. Therefore, it would be "discontinuous." The spectator would have a minimum of horizontal development to hang onto. Think of the disassociation of stylistic-formal elements that are made to coexist in a schizophrenic way in an ambience that is suspended between grotesque and ironic. Think of a mixture of popular and cultivated inflections. Think of an example with a very complex tessitura, where the pseudo-theme (semi-ostinato) is of a modal nature, but is grafted to a latent tonal fabric.

Our little film is neither very affirmative nor unequivocal. It is marked by suspended and unclear behaviors. One has to take care of these characteristics in particular. This means that I am not positively disposed toward explicit, clear melodies, nor to those that are communicative and accessible. And then a melody requires resumption and repetition. Here there is not space to actualize it. The brevity of the episode—in general, but here above all—excludes the possibility, I don't say of development, but rather of recall. In a little film (or in a sequence) of a few minutes, it is therefore desirable to play over ostinatos that are opportunely varied to give a sense of expansion. If you think of minimalism, the pieces seem very much longer than they are in reality, exactly because of the reiterative process. And then the melody by itself, if well characterized, leads inevitably "from . . . to." It is always a little . . . biblical, in the sense that it has a beginning and an end. The melody frames, confirms, justifies, reassures, and creates a sense on the psychological level that is, if not unequivocal, at least sufficiently determined. This happens unless the composer wants and can utilize a micromelodic process made of small, ambiguous modal presences. In this way we come to certain compositional processes which are typically Morriconian. They are made from pseudomelodic procedures, fragmented, interrupted, picked up again, and never concluded, so much less reduced in a harmonic context than the clear and unequivocal connotation.

Departing from one among the infinite possible . . . characteristics of the little film and from how much the film, presumably, would have required of the music, I have made numerous hypotheses of potential solutions, none of which, however, notwithstanding the premises, has been revealed to be entirely suitable to the purpose. In other words, we have constructed and then destroyed, but I . . . hope that the demolition has appeared useful at least as much as the construction. In reality, I did not want to find a solution, but only to indicate an analytical method for arriving at one.

EM: This analysis is absolutely correct. It is exemplary for its rigor and for the method that it suggests. It has to be done. One could decide to stay outside, however, on a level higher than the fragmentation that comes through forcefully from the analysis. One could write music that covers the images entirely or that is born from the inside, but always globally, and that does not depend on fragmentation. For example, if you choose to put sync points on the text or on the movements of the actors, something that I always advise (except in rare, exceptional cases), the synchronicity would be in a musical form that would pertain internally to melodic or harmonic events. The synchronicity would involve a pause or the substitution of the timbre of one instrument that is entering or exiting for that of another. However, in a casual, not fractured, manner, the form of the music should be that of the film. To achieve this I believe that a detailed analysis is necessary in order to discover what the director wants, what he has done technically, and ideally which results he wants to follow on the expressive level.

At this point, one could ask what kind of music would be the more correct for a film in general or for this little film in particular. My response is that there is no such thing. If there are twenty-five of you who write a composition for *Cut Sequences*, you could propose twenty-five solutions, all extremely correct, exactly because a most correct solution does not exist. There is that which you feel, that which you succeed in writing with sincerity. The little film asks for abstractions that you then relax toward the end, when the young woman appears, or another solution that in this moment I do not know of. The solutions are many, but your technique, your fantasy, above all your coherence, are the elements that might be able to give to these images a significance superior to what they actually demonstrate.

SM: This clarification by Maestro Morricone permits me to add a basic rationale that I neglected previously. The nature of my contributions is based on two positions, on two distinct points of observation. The first is typical of my profession and, I believe, does not require other explanations except to say that I have a certain propensity for structuralism that, I think, up until now has been too obvious to need to be emphasized. The second arises from my frequent contact with composers who operate in the sectors of applied music. Many of them belong to the generations that succeeded that of Morricone, and they often keep me up to date with respect to their creative processes. In all these things I can affirm that, however good or bad they may be, their results have never started from a preanalysis of the type that I have just proposed, and of no other type either.

What does all this mean? First of all, by its very nature and established historical tradition, the praxis of the cinema has an improvised, aleatoric component that is unthinkable elsewhere (and let's leave out the fact that pedants draw negative conclusions). To this environment a musician has to adapt himself rapidly and with great flexibility if he is not to be branded as inadequate and as a consequence to become marginalized. From those of the grand masters to those that are merely routine, the cinema lives with extemporized solutions. As a consequence, the relationship between director and composer often can be characterized and conditioned by a strong component of irrationality. This is quite apart from the fact that many directors, above all the most sensitive to music, have a sort of Orphic relationship to music (but this is an argument that would merit being dealt with separately). They expose their own lack of defenses and lucidity, thereby leaving the field free to pure instinct. It is difficult if not impossible, therefore, except for certain exceptions, to think of a rigorous prearranged planning. But beyond the context and the circumstances, the absence of an analytic praxis by composers for whom I have great esteem means above all that a musician who is particularly well endowed and the depository of broad specific experience analyzes and elaborates a film automatically and "unconsciously."

Therefore, it ought to be completely obvious that the analytical methodology proposed here—or other equivalents—serves those who are inexperienced. It could be useful as a point of departure, as an alternative to chaos, as an antidote to mere impressionism, or as a psychological perception exercise. It would be in a way analogous to the educational function that the study of mathematics has for the mind, . . . thus finally as an exercise in aesthetic education. . . . For praise of a methodology, one could cite paradoxically Eisenstein, among the most radical formalists. However, he annotated his irritation when asked whether all the results of his film had been predicted in advance. "He who asks this kind of question," Eisenstein replied, "demonstrates his inability to understand anything about the way creative processes work."[52] Therefore, a balance has to be struck between theory and praxis without making absolute either one or the other. One acquires the ability to strike this balance with time.

I have noted that artists often are intolerant of theorization. It is a simplistic stance, presumptuous and often demagogical, above all irresponsible if carried into the didactic sphere. But one needs to pay attention also to the opposite reaction, to analysis for its own sake, which is useful to no one. I don't know how many of you know the film *C'eravamo tanto amati* (*We Loved Each Other So Much*) by Ettore Scola.[53] Those of you who have seen it will remember for certain the character of Nicola, interpreted by Stefano Satta Flores. I believe that Scola and the other screenwriters knew how to design the figure of the frustrated intellectual, the slave to a maniacal rigor that does not pay. They designed him with great authenticity, without indulgence but also without malice. There it is. It is not the type of approach that I intend to steer you toward, but neither do I intend to steer you toward carelessness.

EM: I, however, would like to return to the little film, because I still have a lot of things to say. Listening to the analysis of Professor Miceli, I agreed with him about everything except about the hypotheses of composition. I recognize, however, that my judgment anticipated his conclusions, where he demonstrated that it was only a hypothesis of departure that he himself then destroyed. However, while I listened, and so before knowing the outcome of the analysis, an idea came to me: how to make something negative become positive. Thus while he explained, I wrote a piece that now I will attempt to illustrate. In this little piece that was not written in accord with Professor Miceli, I realized exactly what he indicated in the first fifty seconds of the little film as the only road to follow. Before letting you see what I have written, I ought to clarify some things.

The sounds that we have listened to are the consequence of what is called a direct take.[54] Remember that the excerpts used were outtakes. They were not taken into the ultimate version of the film. Therefore, they did not have the benefit of the definitive treatment. In fact, in the elaboration, the editing, they remake it. Therefore, in a direct take they are casual. The airplane, for example, surely passed over by accident, and in a circumstance of this type I would ask the director to lower these noises.

In scene 1, I do not find any important synchronization. The first sync point I see is when the man enters the house. I would not give too much importance to the cat in the kitchen . . . it seems to me an incidental thing, while instead I find very important the moment when the man looks at his sleeping wife. However, here we find ourselves faced with a particular case. The film camera is on the man, who is looking; then there is a reverse shot, and one sees the woman who is asleep. Which of the two should have the sync point? One cannot do both. In my opinion, it is when he looks at her, because it anticipates the sensation that we will have immediately afterward.

I see another two important sync points when the man looks at the engraving and when he opens the box holding the medal. In the second case, the sync point is a little ambiguous. It could be on him while he opens the box or on the detail of the medallion. Also, here, what I said at the beginning is worthwhile: put the sync point on him, because his knowledge anticipates ours. Then there is the fall of the objects and the woman who calls out. There the music should interrupt them. Note that the voice breaks a silence that lasts almost four minutes. Were I to write the music, I would leave the silence in the monastery because it seems to me that music does not serve a useful purpose there. But it is also true that in the absence of requests from the director (who in our case does not exist, though Professor Miceli has in a certain sense assumed the role), in a little film like this, with not much dialogue and only a few noises, it would be legitimate to write a piece for its entire duration. However, standing by the hypothesis of not putting music to the scene inside the monastery, I would put the entrance of the music at the beginning of the exterior shot, but I would prepare it a little before, on the last interior shot. Then I would want a smooth sync point when the sea is first seen, while a decisive sync point ought to be on the woman in the bikini. Here, however, there might be a number of potential sync points, which might be unified by one idea: when Alek looks at her, when she throws herself into the water, when Alek looks at her again, and when she exits from the water (this seems very important to me), and then to the conclusion.

Let's remain with the piece that I wrote a little while ago for scene 1; let's look at it together (see Figure 2.3).

I did not want a dynamic crescendo but one that grows from the accumulation of the instrumental entrances. Contrabasses II begin; then contrabasses I enter. Violoncellos I and II are added, violas I and II, and then the violins. But the violins are divided in three, and the first play an F-sharp, the sound pole of the piece. It arrives at 24″ and at the end of measure 6, where the three sections of violins unite on a unison F-sharp. Immediately after the violas unite on C, the cellos on a D-flat, on an E-natural the contrabasses, giving place to a vertiginous close—vertiginous because unfortunately, I had little time at my disposal. Anticipating that I would continue with this music to the scene of the interior and not being able to write for the seven minutes of the film, at measure 9 I put a fermata. Note the indication to the strings, "All legato. All tremolo at the bridge and mutes and as soft as possible." This determines a sonority that is very dense but very soft. As I have already said, the crescendo indicated by the diagram of Professor Miceli is not realized by a crescendo symbol. It is interpreted by accumulation. This sound material very often dissolves when the violins reunite on F-sharp. Here the descending parabola indicated in the diagram begins. It continues on the unison of the violas, the cellos, and the basses and closes in a diminuendo, this time also dynamic, but above all in the average range of the chord.

I realize that the defect of the score is the same defect that the photography has, because the photography is too short. I would have wanted some of

Figure 2.3. Musical Example 1—Extemporaneous Fragments for Scene 1 of *Cut Sequences* (autograph of Ennio Morricone)

these sound events to expand. In the case of the entrances of the contra-basses, then of the violoncellos at the second measure, of the violas, and of violins II and III, if the scene had been longer, I absolutely would have had them divide over a longer period of time. The contrabasses would have entered imperceptibly. The violoncellos would have entered at the point at which Alek goes from the gate toward the house. At the first shot of the interior, I would have made the second violas enter, then later, in the kitchen, the first violas. On Alek's look at his wife, violin III, and on the engraving on the wall the second violins. I would have had the first section of the violins coincide with the frames of the medallion. That sync point would have had the maximum instrumental importance. I would have realized the idea of enlarging the significance of the figure and slowing down the entrance of the first part of the contrabasses to the third measure.

Instead, in the autograph score it all happens too quickly, even if the velocity of the piece is significantly reduced. "Quarter note equals 40" on the metronome means six seconds per measure. If the piece had had a unitary arch as I indicated, and here unfortunately so very much contracted, the entrances of the instruments that underline certain moments of the photography would not have fragmented the whole. They would have seemed like casual underlining.

Let's see now how I interpreted the asterisks, indicated by Professor Miceli as the entrances that ought always to be closer together in order to underline the crescendo and then conclude the piece. The contrabass solo enters with a free execution of the figures that are at the player's discretion. I have indicated only the pitch and the duration, but there it is the player that must interpret liberally. In fact, I wrote under the part "freely stretto." This would also have been able to be a sync point. If I had had more time, I would have fixed it in a precise moment of the photography, but instead I left it free to its own casualness. The same argument is valid for the very serious cluster in the pianoforte and again for the B-natural in the two muted horns that enter *pianissimo* and make a little crescendo, but apart from the crescendo of accumulation in the strings. Concerning the clarinets, I wrote that they play *pianissimo*. Making an acute dissonance, they could pronounce an "R." This is another possibility for synchronicity but inside, within the unity of the composition.

Note now the choices of sounds. The contrabass solo executes sounds without alterations, except a B-flat. All natural sounds, empty chords. This is because I wanted them to play again. The passage should not have a narrow dynamism but rather should make a vibration that remains in the air (and, in fact, for that reason there is the little indication of a ligature). I also wanted to emphasize that the sounds of the contrabass are different from those of the muted horns and of the clarinets.

But above all, and this is a manner of working that I would recommend to anyone. Inside of a very simple composition like this one it is important to find the motivations that lead one to want to write the piece, even if sometimes the piece is obvious. Here, in fact, departing from the contrabasses, there is a canon at the major third. This canon in two parts is taken up again by the cellos, then by the violas, and finally by the violins. The sounds that I have chosen constitute a minimal series and by progressive accumulation carry to the chromatic total by the fourth measure. Naturally this preparation, this rough dough of sounds that are so abstract and so confusing, clears up with the F-sharp proposed first by the first violins and becomes a polar situation of attraction. The accumulated tension, which is entirely chromatic as well as coming from the number of parts, melts progressively with the descent of the strings and with the appointment that the various sections take up in unison.

Note that at the contrabass solo I wrote "(in SP?)." SP stands for superimposition overdubbing of the instrument over a base recorded previously by all the rest of the orchestra. In the case of the contrabass solo a reason for overdubbing might be the wish of the composer to augment the dynamic level above that which would be perceptible normally. I wrote this part thinking of an acoustic contrabass (and for the player I would have turned to Franco Petracchi) because if I had thought of an electric contrabass (calling in this case Nanni Civitenga), its sound would have entered directly into the console of the mixer. Concerning the eventual superimposition of the clarinets, which in that high tessitura might not be able to succeed in playing *mp* or *pp*, the possibility of raising the level mitigates the difficulty for the player. (However, we will take up this argument of superimposition again when we deal with recording techniques.)

Finally, the piece concludes with a quotation from the beginning of the theme from the *Symphony of Psalms* by Stravinsky, here a tone higher. I did not have the space to make it proceed further. These four sounds, which are so important to the music of Stravinsky, can be our interior, moral pretext that gives us an opening of hope in the face of what we are doing, which we might consider even very futile. I say this to encourage you to search for something of yourselves inside and beyond the requests of the director. Sometimes very important requests are those that can help us, but in any case it is well to find a way to entertain ourselves while doing the work. And in this way, notwithstanding the various films so diverse from one another, it makes us carry forward a musical thought that with time could perhaps become something more consistent and felt.

NOTES

1. In cinematographic slang, "effects" means the entire repertory of visual and acoustic artifices used in film—night effect, wind effect, and so on.

2. Here, "second phase" refers to chapter 4: Audiovisual Analysis—Part II.

3. The first part that I will now show has a precedent in a seminar conducted by Ennio Morricone, Hansjoerg Pauli, and me in Basel some years ago, but I utilized the same material also at the Chigiana, as well as partially in other editions of the course. The seminar Filmmusik-Komposition und Analyse took place in Basel on January 8–12, 1992. Organized by the Internationale Seminaire fuer Filmgestaltung, it took place at the Akademie der Musik and was limited to a restricted number of students (twelve), who had received beforehand a very brief film to which to compose the accompaniment. The classes of musical computer information of the Akademie der Musik were then given the transcriptions of the scores, with successive recordings by sampling.

4. Whom all of you will remember as the producer of *The Mission*.

5. A TV serial broadcast in Great Britain in 1989 (TVS Film/Reteitalia), music composed by Ennio Morricone. [*The Endless Game*, VHS, 1990.] As a general clarification about the film utilized for this preanalytic laboratory, I need to say that I have never seen the TV film *The Endless Game* by Bryan Forbes, and I predict that you students can say the same. (If you have seen it before, you will have opted for other material.) [SM]

6. I remember that the shooting script is the textual base to which one turns—through the treatment, or storyboard—to shoot and then mount the film, but from the moment it is in the phase of elaboration, the director is able to move away from it. One can compile (typically for scholarly use) a script taken from a complete copy of the film, which assumes therefore the definition of a script deduced from the montage. [SM]

7. For a fuller discussion, see S. Miceli, "Dal 'naturale' al coreutica: Cinema e danza," in L. Quaresima, ed., *Il cinema e le altre arti* (Venice: La Biennale di Venezia/Marsilio, 1996), 71–79.

8. From *The Band Wagon* (variety show), directed by Vincent Minnelli (USA, 1953). [DVD Warner Bros., 2005.]

9. *Some Like It Hot*, directed by Billy Wilder (USA, 1959). [DVD, MGM/UA, 2007.]

10. "Intended for instruction." *Webster's Encyclopedic Unabridged Dictionary of the English Language*, s.v. "didactic."

11. Directed by Jim Sherman (GB, 1975). The criminologist is masterfully played by Charles Gray. [DVD, Twentieth Century Fox, 2002.]

12. See P. Puppa, *Teatro e spettacolo nel secondo Novecento* (Bari: Laterza, 1993).

13. *Entr'acte*, directed by René Clair, music by Erik Satie (France, 1924). *Ballet mécanique*, signed by Fernand Léger, music by George Antheil (France, 1924). For more information, see the relevant chapters in S. Miceli, *La musica nel film: Arte e artigianato* (Florence: Discanto, 1982), now in S. Miceli, *Musica e cinema nella cultura del Novecento* (Milan: Sansoni RCS, 2000), 139–67.

14. And we are not talking about the false, misleading didacticism of Ionesco or Flaiano.

15. Giuseppe Verdi, act 2, scene 4 (Otello, Desdemona, Emilia, Iago). The camera frames the handkerchief in an ostentatious way. The film opera is from 1985. [DVD MGM 2003.]

16. See S. Miceli, "Le musiche del film, Una breve analisi," in L. Miccichè, ed., *Il Gattopardo* (Naples: CSC/Electa, 1996), 28–39.

17. See the chapters dedicated to the association Rota-Fellini in Miceli, *Musica e cinema nella cultura*, 385–447.

18. Think of Italian actor Tinto Brass and even before that of director Giuseppe Patroni Griffi.

19. Italy, 1965. [DVD, MGM/UA 2007.]

20. But it is perhaps true that this type of cinematic production of the seventies was not aimed at the particularly exacting audience in the stalls. . . . However, since the enhancement of the linguistic aspects and a certain critical reevaluation of this line came much later, . . . it is precisely in the name of the exacting audience that one can and ought to advance a critique.

21. [Martin Scorsese Film Collection, MGM/UA, 2005.]

22. Richard Wagner, act I (Gurnemanz and squires). [DVD, Image Entertainment, 1999.]

23. For example, an ugly relief trampled on by singers reveals an enormous death mask of Wagner. For other notices, see "Opera e cinema: Seminario e tavola rotonda," in *Quaderni dell'IRTEM*, vol. 6 (Rome: IRTEM, 1988), 37–41.

24. Giuseppe Verdi, prelude act I, act I, scene I (Violetta, Valéry). The film is from 1983. [DVD, Image Entertainment, 1999.]

25. *Thriller*, USA, 1984 [DVD, *Michael Jackson: History*, vol. II, Sony Music Video, 1998]; *The Blues Brothers*, USA, came out in 1980. [DVD, *The Blues Brothers: 25th Anniversary Edition*, Universal Studios, 2005.]

26. Since the time code was applied to the video after the first phase of measurement of the timings, there could be some slight discrepancies that do not, however, compromise the estimation of the material. [SM]

27. The numbering indicates the succession of the entrances and takes into account the eventual recurrence and superimposition.

28. A very interesting way of proceeding would consist in creating a global laboratory, making a group of young directors realize a brief video fragment (for reasons of cost) after giving them a small subject and some trace of script and of treatment. One would have to proceed then to a drawing of the coupled director/composers, because to someone a music maniac director might come and to someone else a director who limits himself to saying, "Here put sad music" and "Here put happy music." (The reference is wanted. See "Colloquio con Ennio Morricone," in Miceli *Musica e cinema nella cultura*, 467–90.) [SM]

29. The concepts of implicit and explicit sync points will be dealt with later in the text.

30. At this point in the lesson, Miceli did not announce the title and author of the composition in order not to influence the judgment of the course members. The musical examples reported in the original text were recovered directly by listening. Therefore, they could differ in certain details from the original, above all in the instrumental attributions. In this case, one is dealing with *Suspense* by Robert Irancy for harp, treated in *Music for Radio and TV—Musical Illustrations Film Music Clubs*, LP MP 53, Ed. Montparnasse 2000, Paris, ca. 1970. See "Musical Example 1—Suspense," in *Comporre per il Cinema*, 30. [Ennio Morricone, Sergio Miceli, *Comporre per il Cinema. Teoria e prassi della musica nel film*. Ed. Laura Gallenga. Rome, Fondazione Scuola Nazionale di Cinema, 2001, Distributed by Marsilio Editori, Venice. Published as part of the series Biblioteca di Bianco & Nero - Documenti e strumenti, n. 3. B & N is on the spine and Biblioteca di B & N Blanco & Nero is on the front cover.]

31. *Epitaffio di Teo Usuelli*, part of the film *L'udienza* di Marco Ferreri, 1971, LP Cinebox MDF 33/45, 1972. Ed. Musicali Bixio SAM, Milan. See "Musical Example 2—Epitaph," in *Comporre per il Cinema*, 31.

32. *Alba cittadina* vers. II of Riccardo A. Luciani, belonging to the LP for adding the soundtracks to *Gli occhi sulla città* (*The Eyes on the City*), Publisei Ed. Musicali, PS/0109, 1977. See "Musical Example 3—Alba cittadina (Daybreak over the City)—Version II," in *Comporre per il Cinema*, 31.

33. *Alba in periferia* (*Dawn in the Suburbs*) of Riccardo A. Luciani, ibid. See "Musical Example 4—Dawn in the Suburbs," in *Comporre per il Cinema*, 32.

34. *Iter inverso per 16 strumenti* of Domino Guaccero. Composizione del 1963 full of extra musical purposes. Edipan, PAN LM 002. Disc connected to the monthly of contemporary music *1985 La musica*, Feb. 2, 1985. See "Musical Example 5—Iter Inverso," in *Comporre per il Cinema*, 33.

35. *Astrazioni* of Paolo Renosto, dated presumably around 1975–1976, belongs to a collection entitled *Musiche per un telefilm*, containing also compositions of R. A. Luciani, composed for *Rosa e il Mago*, prod. RAI, directed by Piero Nelli, recording Leo Records, Lr 11, "Promozione editoriale." See "Example 6," in *Comporre per il Cinema*, 34.

36. *2001: A Space Odyssey* (Kubrick, 1968). [DVD, Warner Home Video, 2012.]

37. The numbering of the interiors is not progressive but for identity purposes. It serves therefore to verify the eventual recurrences. [SM]

38. Played by Albert Finney.

39. British viewers, recognizing the queen, might have assumed that it was some sort of medal of honor.

40. The film is from 1963. [DVD, Criterion Films, 2001.]

41. Played by Marcello Mastroianni.

42. Music by E. Morricone, 1965. [DVD, 01 Distribution, 2006.]

43. Miceli cites here the article by Claudio Tempo, "Appunti di un discorso sulla musica per film," in *Teatro e cinema* 1, no. 1 (1976): 54, reported in Miceli, *Musica e cinema nella cultura*, 359.

44. The same of the Bible lesson. [SM]

45. For whose legitimization one would need in any case a much greater preceding development.

46. With respect to the analogous framing in the preceding sequence. [SM]

47. See the frames on *Comporre per il Cinema*, 41, and the first of the two frames, 48.

48. Played by the actress Monica Guerritore.

49. See "Musical Example 7—*Rifrazione* of Ennio Morricone," from LP RCA SP 10036, 1972. Dimensioni sonore 1. *Musiche per l'immagine e l'immaginazione. Comporre per il Cinema*, 54. Morricone was not present during the selection chosen by Miceli.

50. See "Musical Example 8—*Lachrimae Pavan* of John Dowland," lute tablature of 1605. *The Collected Lute Music of John Dowland*, transcribed and edited by Diana Poulton and Basil Lam (London: Faber & Faber, 1974), in *Comporre per il Cinema*, 54.

51. See "Musical Example 9—*Sumer Is Icumen In*," anonymous English round, dated around 1300. Transcription of M. Bukofser, *A Revision* (California University Press, 1944), reproduced in A. Della Corte, *Scelta di musiche per lo studio della storia* (Milan: Ricordi, 1949). See *Comporre per il Cinema*, 55.

52. The passage to which Miceli is referring is in S. M. Eisenstein, *Forma e tecnica del film e lezioni di regia* (Turin: Einaudi, 1964, 360) and is discussed together with numerous other technical writings of Eisenstein in Miceli, *Musica e cinema nella cultura*, 203ff and 229ff.

53. Written by Age (Agenare Incrocci), Furio Scarpelli, and Scola, the film is from 1974. [DVD, Brigham Young University, 2001.]

54. By "a direct take" he means the recording of noises and dialogue made on the set. It can be eliminated in a successive phase and reconstructed in the studio or conserved for the benefit of the recitation, avoiding thereby the artificiality of the dubbing. [SM]

Chapter Three

Production Procedures

EM: Reflecting on what we have said so far, I agree . . . that the composer should analyze how the director has structured a film. Then he has to invent appropriate musical structures that take into account the film's form and the director's style. For example, the repetition of a thematic idea can assume a significance of its own by virtue of its reiteration, even if it only involves timbre. . . . The form of the score cannot be predetermined. It has to assume its form from the way the movie has been assembled and the director has filmed it. It is a form that becomes *form* by virtue of the images. But let's return to the argument that I made during the exposition of Professor Miceli's method.[1] To cite an example, I would not be able to put to Fellini—to certain of Fellini's images—what Rota put to them, even though I know that it works well. That's why I ask myself once again, "Which is the *right* choice?"

In any case, the composer has to make a structural analysis. He has to analyze the editing and cutting of the montage, the motion picture camera, and the manner in which the film is shot and runs, but above all he has to analyze the psychological makeup of the protagonists. I think not only about their obvious character, but also about their thoughts, about their reflections, about their human or inhuman depth, according to the people with whom they associate. From there I arrive at compositional choices. While also respecting the requirements of the director, I research and find that subterranean way of bringing out the characters through the music. This is the film composer's great challenge.

Sometimes the director makes such crazy requests that the composer may want to gag. For this reason I say that the composer has to find his or her own way . . . by trying to apply the proper compositional rules coherently while harmonizing them with the exigencies of the director. Why the choice of a binary rhythm? Why a ternary rhythm? Why a melody in a certain mode? Why are there rhythmic accents? I make these choices by myself. I consider the director's requests, but he is certainly not able to foresee this type of thing. I do a job that respects me, that respects my professionalism while at the same time also respecting the film. This balance is what is difficult about our profession, and for this reason one wants tremendous patience, great love, a great desire for redemption, and naturally the technique to realize one's intentions concretely.

After so many years of work in the cinema I have developed a theory. To function well in a film, music has to have and to conserve its own formal characteristics—tonal relations, melodic relations if we want, rhythmic relations, instrumental relations—in sum, a correct internal dialectic. If this formal correctness and technique is present in the music and is applied to the images, the result will certainly be better. (Technique is still more important.) How have I arrived at this certainty? It came at different times when I heard and saw the music of Bach or Mozart or other composers applied to film. They were applications made as an experiment or from a desire for a definitive matchup. We all have seen this type of operation in Pasolini's *Accattone* (1961)[2] and in so many other films. Because these musical compositions were not invented for those scenes and because they have in themselves all the characteristics, the correct internal dialectic that I mentioned just now, they function on the emotional as well as the formal level itself.

COMPOSER AND DIRECTOR (WARREN BEATTY, *LOVE AFFAIR*, 1994)

SM: Since . . . the relationship with the director comes up again and again, resulting in the true *punctum dolens* of the situation, it would be helpful if you would say more about it, perhaps referring to some recent experience.

EM: I just finished recording for a Warren Beatty film, a story of excruciating love.[3] The film's own nature was revealed near the conclusion. It was, in a certain sense, a happy ending. Thus, almost at the conclusion, after a suspension that was adequately articulated melodically on the dominant, the theme attacked on the tonic (as you see, I speak of simple things: V-I). When I started with the tonic, I did not want to stop, all the more so because from that moment on, there was no more than a minute of music needed to arrive at the end of the film.

Warren Beatty . . . (I am concerned to be precise about it) is a very honest director who is full of doubts. In fact, one could say that he is certain of only his doubts (and here we understand each other well). Calling from Los Angeles, he kept me and my interpreter from New York on the telephone for three quarters of an hour in order to tell me that on the embrace of the protagonists—that is, after the attack of the theme on the tonic—he wanted the theme to come down in volume after a few seconds, because there would be dialogue.

The dialogue, in truth, is nonexistent. The actress, Annette Bening, says, "Mike . . . Mike, Mike," and Warren Beatty responds, "Why didn't you tell me?" and little else. In my opinion, the "deflating" that Warren is asking me for will harm the film, because it is too close to the conclusion. . . . I considered the film finished when the theme entered on the tonic. And . . . in response to my observation, even though he is an exquisite person, Warren was slightly offended. According to him, the film at that point is not yet finished, because the two protagonists embrace and kiss each other. He wants a synchronization point on the dialogue and another sync point, a crescendo, on the embrace and on the kiss—exactly what I tried to avoid. . . . (I hate sync points and crescendos on embraces and kisses. I find them unbearable.) And he, on the other hand, wants precisely that, a triumph, a thing that could not be more blatant and exterior. After this embrace and kiss, the two protagonists exit from the frame, and the motion picture camera is placed outside, showing a long panoramic shot of New York, maybe at forty degrees, to which I, instead of maintaining the theme, have put only a reiterated conclusion with the concluding sound from the theme itself, because I think that this scene leads to a surrender, to an ecstasy between the two lovers.

I said to Warren, "Leave your tension to the orchestra. It comes from the entrance on the tonic. Then you lower the level when she says, 'Mike,' and she repeats it to you another time and then perhaps a third time with tears in her eyes, maintaining still the same level when you respond to her, 'Why didn't you tell me that first . . . ?' Then, when there is the embrace, you turn the level up, and doing it in this way, you do not touch the tension caused by the instrumentation."

But he would not hear of it, and thus I will be forced to add another recording session with the orchestra. It does not cost me anything, but had he been more decisive, I would have done it when I recorded all the rest. I will do it alone, without his control, and I will send the recording to Los Angeles.

The problem is that at that prophetic point, Warren wants two solo instruments. I don't like it, but I have patience: in this case the director asked me for something precise, and I have to please him. And then it cannot be said that the scene will not function just as well, but I myself am not convinced that his idea will be the right one.

These are the kinds of little incidents that can happen, not always, but sometimes. The more I proceed in my profession, the more I am preoccupied about such things when I go into the recording studio.

When Warren Beatty came to Rome to let me see the film and to establish what kind of music to compose and where to put it, he did not succeed in making the decisions. At a certain point I had a discussion with him. I had to say to him that in order to write the score, I needed security. I could not write his uncertainty. I could not make the notes nebulous because I was uncertain.

Then, when he returned to Rome, he was visibly content with everything that I had done, but once again he carried all the doubts that he had had before back to America. So he telephoned me. I was very worried, so much so that having finished the work in four orchestral recording sessions, I scheduled the orchestra for six, seven sessions. Then there would be no loss of time, even considering two of his very intelligent corrections. . . . I recognized that I had been mistaken. Little things, but he was right.

But the uncertainty remained. In fact, I received a fax in which he said that the extra recording sessions to which I just referred should be cancelled; perhaps they were postponed for a month, or perhaps they were never done because another solution was found.[4]

Warren's uncertainty is a grave illness, but it is also a merit. I do not criticize uncertainty; all of us have so much. . . . Thus we had this dispute that then was resolved in a very human way.

I return now to a fundamental point that I touched upon at the beginning. In agreement with the director, the composer needs to decide what will happen before going into the recording studio, even if, I repeat, it is not possible for everything to be clear. When the director goes into the recording studio, he has to concede and yield to a margin of surprise. He cannot believe that everything that was said or all that he imagined will be found in an exact, letter-perfect copy. He has to have a little humility—and, I would say, abandon. Then, naturally, one can discuss and research the best solutions. Sometimes one needs to pay attention to the director, and the results frequently are not ugly, even if the contraproof, the solution proposed by the composer, cannot be heard by anyone. Therefore, nobody can tell whether it would have been preferable.

MUSIC COMPOSED IN ADVANCE: *C'ERA UNA VOLTA IN AMERICA* (*ONCE UPON A TIME IN AMERICA*) (LEONE, 1984)

In consideration of all this, the director's telling of a film's story can be very important, if not actually decisive. In some cases—those in which I have achieved the best results—the composer will record the principal pieces before the film is shot or before it is assembled. This is very useful, because in this way the composer makes the director understand the sense of the music in an unequivocal way. It eliminates at least 50 percent of the uncertainty and surprise that the director might have during a recording session.

I always find it very useful when the director falls in love with a theme or a musical situation. The fact that he listens to it many times over and understands it and makes it his own, and also sings it while he sleeps, means that in a way, even during the elaboration of the film, during the editing, during the mixing, he takes into account the way the music breathes, its tiny pauses. At the editing stage he actually may find strange synchronization points that the composer absolutely never would have thought of. Imagine: the actor in close-up simply raises his eyes, and the director finds a point of synchronization on that almost imperceptible movement (a type of synchronization that Professor Miceli defines as "implicit" . . .).

In *C'era una volta in America* (*Once upon a Time in America*) (1984),[5] Leone found an expressive concentration in De Niro when he raised his eyes while observing a photograph. He had my theme depart from that gesture. I never thought of it. All this came about thanks also to the fact that I wrote the music and recorded it as it was. It had an exclusively musical coherence. Then its application to the photographic realm permitted Leone to find such strange, light, not very obvious synchronizations—implicit, exactly—that no one, perhaps not even you, would have noticed them the first time you viewed the scene. But if one finds these coincidences, they become things of great intellectual stature.

To have this type of result, one needs the collaboration and availability of a director who does not consider the music just a servant, either to him or to the images.[6] In fact, under these circumstances it would be more accurate to say that the director has become the servant of the composer. Obviously, this is to the director's own advantage. Certain sequences in *C'era una volta in America* are examples of a very high quality of both direction and music. When the composer agrees with the director about certain ways of proceeding, it seems to me that the level of the music is raised and with it also that of the images.

Let's consider once again what I said before concerning my theory about the validity of preexistent music applied to a film. In a certain sense, and without making strange comparisons to the great composers that I mentioned previously, the process of writing the composition before making the film brings an analogous result. The music has and conserves its own formal characteristics. It guarantees to the composer the possibility of conceiving a piece in his own independent manner. Written in this way, the music has certain intrinsic, unmistakeable characteristics that I feel are the result exclusively of a composer's point of view. They are independent of any ideal identification with the film's features.

The use of preexisting music does not always work out smoothly. Do any of you remember the film *Cassandra Crossing*,[7] by director George Pan Cosmatos[8] (he smoked ninety cigarettes a day, as a result of which he trembled like a leaf . . .)? I had already made *Rappresaglia* (*Massacre in Rome*) with him, a good film about Rome during the war.[9] [For *Cassandra Crossing*] he asked me to give him some music that I might already have on hand.

To help him during the filming, it had to be something that would imitate the running of a train. A little while before, I had composed music for Aldo Lado's *L'ultimo treno della notte* (*Night Train Murders*),[10] into which I actually had inserted the sound of a train. I had written the music to that rhythm. It was already something, right? So I sent that piece to Cosmatos. But the film came out with the music of another composer, Jerry Goldsmith (very beautiful music, moreover).

I encountered Cosmatos five or six years later, and I asked him, "Excuse me, I sent you that cassette, why didn't you make the film with it?"

"But I didn't like it," he responded angrily.

He said it to me just like that: "But I didn't like it!" He didn't like it?! . . . But certainly I had not written it on purpose for his film! He had asked me for something provisional! Therefore, if the music is written in anticipation of a film (or if, as in this case, the director asks for a suggestion before the shooting), you need to be very careful. It can be a dangerous source of misunderstanding or disappointment. But it's the sort of thing that can happen.

This is the real significance of music written in advance: the director has to fall in love with it, making it very present in his film. It has to captivate the director to the point of conditioning the editing of the film and then of being very involved in the final mix. But let's not have any illusions: one needs some time. In this kind of thing, the falling in love does not happen immediately. Sometimes, in order to understand the music, the director needs to enter into it little by little.

SM: Although you are not doing so on purpose, I fear that to the ears of an aspiring cinema composer your . . . testimony about the problems encountered with Warren Beatty could sound like a potent means of dissuasion. . . . It gives us a perspective on trust. But, as far as I know, the creative-productive process put into action with Leone remains an exception in the panorama of the compositional praxis for film.

ESTABLISHING SYNC POINTS, THE ENTRANCE OF THE MUSIC

EM: That's true. So let us put our feet back on the ground. At the Moviola one needs to analyze the film and establish with the director the points at which the musical sequences enter and exit. Normally, when the director proposes to begin a sequence at a certain point (except in the case of a fundamental difference of opinion), always try to prepare the attack. . . . The entrance of the music is a very delicate moment. Therefore, begin a little before the point indicated by the director, advising him of this anticipation.

Then, if it is necessary, you need to establish the synchronization, or the meeting points between music and image within the sequence. . . . I do not love this process, but sometimes it can be extremely important. One needs, therefore, to put the letters A, B, C, D—sometimes up to the letter Z—in the schedule of timings, with a reminder that describes the event. For example, where an exterior begins . . . is very important, and the opposite, the passage from an exterior to a closed space, is just as important. Also, I think the music for a more intimate shot of a house should be different from the music for a street, . . . a panorama, or the sky.

Then you ought to establish the eventual presence of dialogue, making note of the point where it begins and ends. Equally, one ought to note certain important noises. In sum, one needs to take note of everything—all that the composer thinks could influence his creativity in composing the music. This does not mean, as perhaps I have indicated before, that the music has to be "fractured" because of all the synchronization points that the composer has established in agreement with the director. In cases where the synchronization is conditioning the writing, the best music that the composer can make is music that proceeds *over* the cuts, that is soft *over* the cuts, that does not break up the editing, that is therefore "round."

The composition always has to remain unified, but without fracturing it. You can add emphasis in a number of ways: by insinuating a timbre according to what you feel (or you can ask the director); by using the attack of a mandolin, the entrance of the bass, the shout of an instrument, or an orchestral unison; by having the whole orchestra unite in a unison *pianissimo*; or by having a harmony enter that until that moment was not present. The exception is that sometimes a cut in the image can be so peremptory and significant that it is necessary also to cut the music. It is a fist in the spectator's stomach, but this eventuality, when it manifests itself, is unequivocal.

Outside of these normal cases, the composer can give the director sound signals that call attention to occasions for potential synchronization. I'll give you an example. Some of you will remember the scene in *C'era una volta il West* [*Once upon a Time in the West*] (1968)[11] in which Claudia Cardinale climbs down from the train and arrives in a small town. When Leone told me about the film, he said absolutely nothing about the fact that there would be a close-up of a clock on the station building.

For that scene I composed a piece that used vibraphone and celeste.[12] By his placement of the visuals with the music, Leone made that casual choice become like the sound of a clock. This was very far from my original intentions. The actress passes from the tracks to the little piazza in front of the station, going through the building, and contemporaneously the film camera rises—a classic dolly shot—enlarging the field of vision until it includes the mountains on the horizon. For that point I had written a musical bridge, with a crescendo that I carried over to the reappearance of the theme. I did not know that Leone would transform that musical bridge into a cinematographic bridge. The woman enters the station, disappears, and next is seen reframed at the exit, at the opposite side. This is the work of the director. I only wrote the music, but the revision of this episode verified how much more effective the music could become with this type of treatment by the director. There are very few directors who react this way, but when one succeeds in establishing this kind of collaboration, the results are excellent, and usually one says that both the music and the film work.

TIMEKEEPING

We come now to the question of the stopwatch, or timekeeping. It is a very simple thing. . . . Having established, as stated already, the points at which there will be music and the eventual sync points, the editor furnishes the footage (or, as I request, the time in seconds). Otherwise, you have to have recourse to the so-called click track, a ten-minute film that is notched every twenty-four frames. Twenty-four frames equals one second. Therefore, it remains only to count the clicks and make the sum to arrive at the number of seconds. In general, the editor supplies the number of meters for each cue. I can offer you a system that streamlines the calculation of the number of seconds from the meters. I did not invent it; a person who occupies himself with copying the parts did.[13] To arrive at the number of seconds, you multiply the number of meters by a fixed number, twenty-two. Naturally this works only for 35mm movie film that runs at twenty-four frames per second, as opposed to the running speed of twenty-five frames per second for television.

ORGANIZATION OF THE SCORE

So now we arrive at the organization of the score. Pay attention, because at this point, due to inexperience, you can make many errors. One of my children, the only one who has studied composition and has begun to write music for film,[14] forgot some obvious things. This happened even though he had had some experience: he had assisted at some recording sessions for the cinema and also directed some of my nonfilm music in concerts. For this reason, confronted by his involuntary lack of order, I now feel the need to begin with the organization of the score. In previous courses I never explained many of these things, even though Professor Miceli invited me to do so. Every year, while we prepared the seminars, we had this friendly discussion, but I continued to think that the organization of the score was a superfluous thing. Now, having seen all that my own son forgot, I understand that

Sergio was right. So let's begin with the preparation of the personnel of the orchestra.

One cannot make an orchestration using a classical model. In the cinema, the instrumentation can be more diverse: five bassoons, a trumpet, a recorder, a violin, an out-of-tune piano, maybe a synthesizer. . . . It can be all of these things or anything; therefore there is no preestablished score paper as there is for the music of our great orchestral tradition. One needs to create the personnel roster, and it has to reflect the composer's fantasy, what the composer wants to achieve, the features that he intends to give to his melody, which then will not be only one melody any more.

Walter Branchi now cultivates roses and teaches electronic music. I remember one day a long time ago, he said to me, "You make all these songs, but then in the end they do not seem like songs." (He meant songs in the sense of melodies.) It made me realize . . . that orchestration was an extremely important phase of composition for the movies.

Orchestration is not only color; it also includes the connotations within and counter to the melodic part. Look, I am going to state a rule in which I firmly believe: counterpoint always pays. Counterpoint is such a fundamental thing that you want it in any kind of orchestration you write. For duets between any two instruments (two flutes? . . . a duet; two oboes? . . . a duet), you can create a very beautiful orchestration, even a traditional one, by making the pauses last longer and accelerating them, or by making responses. . . . In sum, a two-part counterpoint already gives something very important to the orchestration. And I am talking only about the horizontal parts and not the harmonic ones that are de facto coloristic. I am not talking about timbre, with which one can really work a lot. All this is valid for nonfilm music, but for film music it is fundamental—at least it is for me.

In this case, the orchestration belongs to the musical composition. It is not orchestration as one normally uses the word. And I don't like even to call it orchestration, because that would mean taking a piece written for piano, for a polyphonic instrument, and then transcribing it for orchestra. Instead, here one is dealing with composition. Therefore, up to now I have made a mistake by using the word "orchestration." The decision about the events that will occur in a score has to be made within the overall context of what precisely the piece will be. This is a thing of absolute importance.

So begin by writing down the performing forces: for example, a flute, seven clarinets, a trombone, a synthesizer, one percussion instrument, fourteen cellos (I have described an odd ensemble). I have a photocopy machine. Thus I can have all the score pages prepared with all the staves already labeled for the composing. As you see, I am confiding my ways of doing things to you, even the simplest and the most obvious, because when I have to write, I try to avoid distractions of any kind.

For example, I always write the page number, because otherwise the copyist can confuse the pages and not respect the order. The conductor would not be able to figure it out, and terrible tragedies could happen. Such an error happened to me in the early days of my career, when I made arrangements. It is an extremely grave type of error because the cost of the orchestra when it is time to record is very high.

After the page number, you have to write the title of the cue because in a film there are many cues. If we write only the number of the page, the copyist can pass from one cue to another without realizing it. You will think that I am saying things that are not useful. However, my son was going into a recording session with this kind of pastiche. I had to tell him what to do; for this reason I decided to tell . . . you as well.

What is the title of a cue? In film it is called "Music 1," therefore M1, M2, M3, and so forth (I once made a film for which I wrote 105 music cues). The film is divided into reels; at first they made ten-minute reels, and now they make twenty-minute reels. Therefore, each of the reels of film is also numbered successively—first, second, third, fourth—according to the duration of the film. I just said that the music is indicated with the letter M in order to distinguish it from other components of the sound: buzzing is called "B1," "B2," et cetera; noises, the special effects are labeled "ES"; the playback is labeled "PB."

But in the American system one does not write only M1. Before the M one puts another number that indicates the reel. 1M1 is the first musical cue in the film. 1M2 is the second cue of the first reel of film. 4M20 is the twentieth cue that is on the fourth reel of the film (because the music "M" has a unique number). It can happen that by shortening the film one reduces the number of reels (because if from a reel of twenty feet, for example, they retain three feet, that is not enough to make a reel by itself). In consequence, reel number 4 could become number 2 or number 3, but this doesn't affect the music, whose progressive numbering remains unvaried. This has the function in every case of distinguishing and identifying a cue: "Take 1M1 and put it at reel 5, in place of M23." One does it that way.

It is necessary for the score to display the number of seconds over every measure—in big, clearly visible characters—corresponding to the speed of the cue. If it is a fast tempo, we put a second and a half per measure. You want to write over the first measure 1 1/2″. At the end of the second measure write 3″, after the third measure 4 1/2″, after the fourth write 6″, and so on. Obviously these indications are independent of the film editor's measurement, which expresses in seconds the duration of the film. If at the center of a certain measure you have a sync point of 2 1/2″, or of 2″, or whatever, you have to divide the measure further. If the tempo is in 2/4 and the measure has a velocity of 2 1/2″, the sync will begin at 1/4″ and coincide with the second quarter of the measure. . . . And in this way you compose your score or your scribbling block.[15] I write directly in the score. I prefer it because by doing it that way, I already have the whole picture and control everything, and because I don't like to make successive transcriptions.

When you go to conduct your composition, you ought to direct it using a stopwatch. Those rehearsal numbers that you made at home on the score, therefore, you should be able to find while conducting. The eye will be on the score and on the stopwatch, nothing photographic, because at that point everything from the film already will have been taken into consideration. Also, a certain "license," a certain liberty that may have been inspired by the visuals, ought to have been programmed ahead of time.

To give an example, I frequently write the ritards into the score. Let us suppose that in a tempo of 4/4 I need a *rallentando*. That measure I change into a 5/4 or 6/4, and I calculate exactly the *rallentando*. If in that measure I have to make an *accelerando* instead, I write in 3/4 or 2/4 or in 5/8. . . . But in 5/8 or in 7/8 I do not use a *rallentando* or *accelerando* (or I try to use them rarely) because changes of tempo can become a problem for the orchestra. For this reason I adopt a very simple writing style based on the principle that the composer should resolve all the problems at home while he is writing. That is why the *rallentandi* and *accelerandi* should be converted into measures. But it is clear that one cannot apply this system in every case. Frequently, if the music is very regular, almost mechanical, I work with the click track, saving the orchestra and me from fatigue.

THE CLICK TRACK

SM: As you have recognized the necessity of explaining even the obvious things, do you want to add something else about the click track?

EM: The click is a metronome. The composer decides upon the speed that he needs for a cue he has written and indicates progressively the tempo, the relative duration, on the score. Let's make an example with a composition in 4/4 in which every measure lasts four seconds. If we want to put a sync point at the twenty-first second, we can make four measures of 4/4 and the fifth of 5/4 so that we are able to put the accent on the first quarter note and not on the second quarter note. This is essentially for a musical reason: one changes the meter in a way that puts the synchronization point on a strong beat. But there is this to say: many times the synchronization points are not exactly at the fourteenth or sixteenth second. Sometimes they are at 14.25″ or at 16.125″. . . . If one conducts without a metronome, it would be very difficult to find this fraction. If, for example, I have a sync point at 8.125″, then I divide the quarter note into four parts, and, at the moment that every quarter note is divided into eighth notes, that sync point at 8.125″ will correspond to the second eighth note of the measure. However, for fractions of this type I do not need to change the tempo, as I have explained before. I do not need to add that in certain cases I am able to anticipate the departure of the piece exactly to the fraction of time that permits me to find easily the desired sync point. This is obviously good if there are not preceding sync points that need to be taken into account. Is that clear?

SM: It is clear that the method exists but that the solutions are flexible.

EM: In fact, the composer chooses the line of conduct to follow on a case-by-case basis. There are situations for which one needs a calculator to make the subdivisions of the measure into various microfragments. (For this reason, music for animated films is composed first and the scene is edited to the music, because otherwise it would not be possible to find all the synchronization points.) Or, in cases of nonanimated film—which do, however, have complex sync points—where it is impossible to divide the second into tenths of a second, one will ask the director to add two, three, four, or five frames to the scene. If the director wants many sync points, the composer can ask that they be marked on the videotape copy with a mobile transverse band.

If in the course of a piece of a certain length there are changes of speed, the editor ought to prepare a click track before the recording session—sixty clicks for the velocity of four seconds per measure; or thirty clicks for the velocity of three seconds per measure; or eighty-two clicks for the velocity of two seconds per measure. Naturally, the composer is able to decide whether the clicks are to be audible on every quarter note or even on every eighth note if the rhythmic articulation of the piece requires it. The first four, or five, or eight clicks of the piece should correspond to the silent preparation of the orchestra because—I have not said this until now, having taken it for granted—every instrumentalist follows the clicks on headphones. I have prepared a list of the principal and simpler clicks for you.

Tempo	4/4	4/4	4/4	4/4	4/4	4/4	4/4	4/4	4/4	4/4	4/4	4/4	4/4	4/4	4/4
Duration of Measure	2"	2"¼	2"½	2"¾	3"	3"¼	3"½	3"¾	4"	4"¼	4"½	4"¾	5"	5"½	6"
Beats per Minute	120	106.6	96	87.2	80	74	68.4	64	60	56.4	53.3	50.4	48	43.6	40
Clicks	120	135	150	165	180	195	210	225	240	255	270	285	300	330	360

Figure 3.1.

In the last film that I recorded,[16] I did not want to use a click track, period. It was a romantic film, with music that was full of *rallentandos* and contractions. But it was impossible to have recourse even to tempo changes. Abstract music would have come out. It would have been absurd, because music written in 4/4 (or whichever other meter) has a tempo with specific characteristics. I could not insert a 5/4 measure in order to make a *rallentando*. For this reason, I resorted to a very detailed digital metronome. I did not indicate the *rallentandos* in a traditional way. I wrote the relevant metronome numbers, and this in some cases was even more effective, because it permitted me to decide what line of conduct to follow. I could begin a *rallentando* a half measure before I was supposed to if I was early, or if I was late, I could initiate it a little while after it was written.

In *C'era una volta il West*[17] I used neither a click track nor a digital metronome. In one phrase that was written all in 12/8 and that required a *rallentando*, I made a measure in 15/8 that was absurd. "Why not make first a 9/8 and then 6/8?" I was asked. Because in that moment those meters would not have worked for me. It seemed right to lengthen a measure of 12/8 rather than change the meter of two measures.[18] As you see, the themes that concern the preparation of the score overlap with those that concern the recording studio, and a rigid division of the discussion is impossible.

Naturally, after having found a point of encounter with the director . . . , the composer goes home to write his score. Here I recall the discussion that I had before about decisions regarding the performing forces, but this time from another point of view.

CHOICE OF INSTRUMENTALISTS AND SOLOISTS: EDDA DELL'ORSO

The composer ought to choose the performing forces he considers the most suitable to the music he has written or has in his mind to write. For this reason, the "discounts" that the editor might ask for in order to save money ought to be ignored. The composer is always and only at the service of the film. As it seems to me I have already said, commercial music applied to film is of no value to the film; it is valuable only for the eventual diffusion of the recording. Therefore, the composer should not betray his own specialty, beginning with his choice of performing forces.

The list of performing forces is submitted to the person who has to supply the orchestra. This person, the contractor, is the one who has to call the instrumentalists who make up the orchestra to ask whether they are available. . . . There are orchestral musicians whom I have always considered indispensable to my work, so much so that sometimes I have even postponed the recording sessions if these musicians have not been available. It has happened frequently, to give an example, with Edda Dell'Orso, a voice that for years I have wanted in my realizations. I assure you that it is very important to write for the instrumentalists, for the soloists, that we have in mind, because only they are able to respect our intentions.

I think about two colleagues who wrote for a trumpeter who was so ideal that in all of Italy they could not find a trumpeter capable of playing and recording their piece. This tells us that it is absolutely necessary to limit the musical and technical requirements to those that the available professional musicians . . . can meet. You cannot write for violin and put in passages that are so extremely difficult that a violinist may not know how to play those passages or may not be able to play them. One has to know one's collaborators in advance and have a realistic assessment of their capabilities.

SM: I make myself the interpreter of a question that perhaps someone would have wanted to ask. Can every composer expect to know in advance who the players—above all the soloists—will be, or is it subject to the influence and the prestige of the composer?

EM: It is valid for everyone. . . . The composer has been chosen by the editor, the producer, and above all, the director. He ought to enjoy their trust and ought to be able to work as he wants. Otherwise, the editor or producer will cause damage to the very product that he has financed. And then only the composer can know what his requirements are. In my experience, as I have already mentioned, I have always needed certain elements that give me something special. For example, I have always asked for the most talented musicians, even if they had to play something ordinary. Then there were times when they were required to give something more, something precise, something that was irreplaceable. In that case I absolutely could not permit myself to do without the most talented. In the most recent film of Warren Beatty, I asked that Edda Dell'Orso be hired. (Despite her slightly advanced age, she still sings well.)[19] Warren understood the necessity of using her too, so much so that we had her sing in two pieces not predicted at the outset. I think then of the late Dino Asciolla[20] . . . that great artist who made such incredible contributions.

There are then still more particular cases. For example, I called a particular percussionist because he was the only one who played a certain instrument that would serve my purposes; . . . searching for the instrument, I discovered that he was the only one to possess it. I had seen it in America . . . many years ago in a big factory of percussion instruments. It is a strange instrument: it contains water and has thin layers of sunburst decoration.[21] The player plays it with a bow: with the left hand he moves the instrument and with the right he passes the bow slowly from one sunburst to the other, by which it produces an uncertainty of frequency, of double and even triple sounds, if the horsehairs of the bow are soft. It produces a strange timbre, with which I remained fascinated. How could I settle for less? I utilized it with two directors,[22] and both were astonished. But one does not need to take advantage of a sound of this sort as a matter of course; otherwise, it would become too easy. . . . One needs to insert it in the appropriate context; otherwise, it becomes a species of almost useless whistling.

When I wanted to steal the sounds of certain types of animals for western films, I had to call on voices or instruments that imitated them. Therefore, everything depends on your thoughts, on what you . . . want your music to give to the cinematographic work, always with the consensus of the director.

MUSIC COPYIST

After you have written all the music, you give the score to a copyist. If the copyist makes many errors, it causes the orchestra to lose concentration. This translates into a waste of time and money, one of the most serious things. Therefore, one needs to pay a lot of attention to the work of the copyist and not . . . undervalue him. Instead, he needs to be considered one of the most important persons who collaborate with a composer. For some years now, I have made a photocopy of the score, and I have given the original to my copyist. The one who collaborates with me is extremely good and notices some of my own careless mistakes. When he is uncertain, he telephones and asks me, "Is it a sharp or a flat?" We both correct and thereby arrive at the recording studio with the errors reduced almost to nothing. And speaking of errors, you should not give the music to the copyist the night before the recording, as do some of my colleagues. (I won't criticize them. They have their reasons.) If you do it that way, it is not fair to blame the copyist for all the errors he makes. There have even been some who because of this repeated nocturnal sacrifice have become gravely ill and have died. Therefore, I pass the entire score to the copyist at least fifteen days before the recording session.

Another very delicate and important relationship is the one with the recording engineer. Sometimes the sound engineer does not help the director hear what the composer has written because he pulls up the level on the strings but does not let him hear the trombone, or vice versa. Therefore, the score is judged not so much by what there is, but by what there is at that moment in the headphones.

There is another calculation that one needs to make and that unfortunately forces the composer to become a species of minute counter. Let's say we have a film with an hour of music. How many sessions does one need with the orchestra to record sixty minutes of music? In practice, in one session of three hours (including a twenty-minute break, which then becomes almost half an hour), one records five minutes of usable music according to the pessimistic estimate, ten minutes according to the optimistic estimate. [23] Therefore, for an hour of music, between six and twelve sessions will be necessary. This difference of results in the same space of time depends on the orchestra. (One needs the orchestra to understand immediately the observations of the composer, who generally is conducting.) The difference also depends on the sound engineer and on the quality of the copying—aspects that I have already touched on separately. Given all these factors, it rarely happens that one can record ten minutes instead of five minutes; at most, one can do seven instead of six. In general, the spread ranges between five and ten minutes. It has also happened to me, in one session, that I have gotten only two minutes of usable recorded music.

I remember that on the fourth (or fifth) movie I did, a Luciano Salce film, [24] there was a huge amount of music. The opening titles were divided into six parts. . . . At the end of the first session (which back then lasted four hours; before that, when I was playing in the orchestra, it was five hours), I had finished only the first part, which is a few seconds long. I was still not very experienced in film work, . . . and I had written a score of a pathetic complexity. Probably the orchestra was mediocre (whereas the conductor, Pier Luigi Urbini, had a lot of experience; he was really good). We did not succeed in going ahead. The editor, one of those speculators with whom I no longer want to work—nor he with me—passed rapidly in front of the orchestra, making a show of his irritation. I remember it extremely well. . . . In conclusion, and perhaps I already have said this, one must simplify the writing. I do not say that one has to paralyze it; one must find solutions that are not banal but that at the same time can be realizable without too much difficulty on the part of the orchestra and the conductor.

PRERECORDED PLAYBACK: *LA LEGGENDA DEL PIANISTA SULL'OCEANO (THE LEGEND OF THE PIANIST ON THE OCEAN)* (TORNATORE, 1998)

Let's pass now to the problem of playback. Many times in the cinema it is necessary to write music even before the film has been shot. One typical case is that in which the director has predicted a scene with a dance in which the dancers obviously have to move in time to music. Occasionally, especially for dance pieces, I have attempted to avoid the assignment. For example, I advised the Taviani brothers in the filming phase of one of their films to utilize a piece of whatever kind would have an equivalent tempo and velocity. Then I would write a definitive piece with those same characteristics. However, a proposition of this kind is not always accepted. It is annoying, because not having seen the film, one is not informed about certain elements that might suggest certain solutions. (Then it means one must do twice as much work for the same film: at the beginning, before it commences, and then at the end). This naturally does not have anything to do with writing musical commentary beforehand, as I did for Leone's film. For prerecorded playback, one writes music for a scene that has not yet been shot, in which for their mimetic dumb show, for their dynamics, the protagonists are required to move to music. Above all, the serious thing is this: afterwards, it can't be changed. Therefore, it is a very heavy responsibility taken . . . blindly. But when one has to do it, one does it; one makes the sacrifice.

Sometimes the prerecorded playback does not have to accompany situations as banal as dances. Instead, it can actually be a piece fundamental to the life of the film. Anyone who has seen *La leggenda del pianista sull'oceano* (*The Legend of the Pianist on the Ocean*)[25] can understand that the pianist is playing music recorded months before and above all studied months before the filming began. The actor[26] studied piano for five months with a teacher who was a specialist in this type of operation. The director would not have been able to film if he had not had the music written and recorded ahead of time. In this case, the prerecorded playback had a fundamental function.

SM: In connection with this I would like to note something that has nothing to do with the composer but that damages the music and the whole film. As we know, playing an instrument requires a physical effort. It involves muscular and respiratory coordination. Gesture plays a part in the music. It is the music itself. It is not a gratuitous mise-en-scène, but a necessity intimately tied to the nature and quality of the sound. A strong and intense sound is not credible if the one who is shown to produce it appears immobile, relaxed, and uncoordinated. What comes forth is a psychological/physical disassociation and therefore a psychological perception that is very annoying as well as fake. It ought to be obvious, but frequently in the cinema it is not at all. If, in order to film a scene of a saber duel, one calls in a master of arms, why not do the equivalent for music? Italian art cinema is typical in this regard: grand ambitions, noble contents, problematic complexes, and then carelessness and amateurishness. . . . The cellist in *Il Casanova di Frederico Fellini*[27] does everything but pull the bow in a way that is minimally elegant or plausible. The head, the lips, and the cheeks of the flutist in the Taviani brothers' *Il prato* (*The Lawn*)[28] is inert . . . and let's forget about the fingers. Even to breathe into a blowgun requires a minimum of expressivity, of physical participation. Imagine what is required to play a transverse flute.

Certain Italian directors ought to look attentively at films like *Un cuore in inverno* (*A Heart in Winter*)[29] or *Tutte le mattine del mondo* (*Tous les matins du monde, All the Mornings of the World*)[30] and reflect. It is not so difficult to call in a master specialist to instruct the actors about a specific expressivity of gesture. I do not believe that this . . . renders a film exorbitantly expensive.

I inserted myself into the discussion on playback because the occasion seemed appropriate to annotate some of the bad habits of the cinema. Now let's see a positive example.

EM: We can examine again Tornatore's film *La leggenda del pianista sull'oceano* (*The Legend of the Pianist on the Ocean*), specifically the challenge between Jelly Roll Morton and Novecento, the protagonist of the film. Morton represents the pianist who has signaled the passage of ragtime to jazz, while Novecento, who lives and always plays on a cruise ship, appears to be a nascent star. He is destined to become the greatest pianist in the world. Morton comes to challenge him. He gives himself the airs of a braggart, enters into the hall and . . . in sum, it is not a pistol duel but a duel at the piano.

The first piece that Jelly Roll Morton plays and with which he proposes his challenge is one of his own pieces.[31] It was realized using the historic execution that remained from old recordings. How this old trick is realized I cannot say. . . . I'm sorry, but I can't tell you. . . . However, the pieces of Jelly are all realized by computer, starting from recordings of the period in a way that remains faithful to the original interpretations. To this performance our hero responds, but wanting to tease his antagonist, he plays, I think, *Stille nacht* (*Silent Night*). Jelly Roll Morton gets angry. The fans of Novecento get angry. Everybody gets angry. The challenger vents his anger by playing a piece that is still more demanding,[32] to which Novecento responds with the same piece, *Silent Night*, but does it a little faster. Then Jelly plays an overwhelming piece.[33] I have to say, it is extraordinary how he wrote and then executed it, because what one hears in the film is an exact copy of how he played it back then. He was really a great jazz player. . . . At that point, Novecento plays a piece that is the only original one composed by me in this sequence, *Moto perpetuo*.[34]

When I explained to Tornatore what I wanted to write for this extremely important point in the film, he was very skeptical. To talk about music to a director when you cannot play the piece in question obviously reduces the director's capacity to understand. (It was going to be a piece that neither I nor a number of pianists could play.) However, he accepted, and I went ahead with his confidence in me and my own confidence in the idea. But I told Tornatore, "Be careful, because here the editing will have to be insane, incredible, overwhelming. The piece that I want to write involves these things . . ." So saying, I "inflamed" him. However, he was convinced by everything afterward, when he listened to it. In this sequence, all the playbacks are prerecorded. The actors had studied them for a long time with a mute keyboard under the guidance of a master. It is clear that they do not play all the notes, but they are very convincing. I ought to say that I myself was very surprised at the result.

NOTES

1. [that there is no single "right" choice for the music.]
2. [DVD, *Pasolini Collection: Vol. 2*, Waterbearer, 2003.]
3. He is discussing *Love Affair* (*Un grand amore*), shot and produced by Beatty but signed by Glenn Gordon Caron, USA, 1994. [DVD, Warner Bros., 2002.] Warren Beatty was the principal star, while Annette Bening was the female protagonist.
4. This argument was originally dealt with partially and taken up again in a succeeding moment in the same course; it appears drawn with respect to the real dynamics of the facts.
5. [DVD, *Once upon a Time in America*: Two-Disc Special Edition, Warner Bros., 2011.]
6. In this case it absolutely was not.
7. A mediocre film of the catastrophe genre, shot predominantly on a train, produced in Great Britain in 1977 with an international cast including, among others, Sophia Loren, Burt Lancaster, Richard Harris, Ava Gardner, Ingrid Thulin, Alida Valli, Martin Sheen, Lee Strasberg, Lou Castel, and Lionel Stander. [DVD, Artisan, 2002.]
8. (1941–2005) [GBA].
9. Produced in Italy in 1973 with Marcello Mastroianni and Richard Burton. It dealt with the Italian partisan attack on the Germans in via Rasella and the German retaliatory massacre of Italian civilians of the Fosse Ardeatine in Rome. [DVD, No Shame Films, 2006.]
10. Produced in Italy in 1975, with Flavio Bucci, Enrico Maria Salerno, and Macha Méril. [DVD, Blue Underground, 2004.]
11. [DVD, Paramount Pictures, 2010.]
12. "Jill's Theme"—*C'era una volta il West*.
13. Donato Salone.
14. Andrea Morricone.
15. In musical slang, "scribbling block" refers to the rhythmic-melodic sketch without instrumentation (and sometimes without harmonization) made at the piano. . . . Generally, the composer of light music supplies such a draft to the arranger, but it is used also in the cinema when the author is working with collaborators.
16. [Perhaps *Bulworth* (*Il senatore*), directed by Warren Beatty, USA, 1998. [DVD, Twentieth Century Fox, 2003.]
17. *Once upon a Time in the West*. [DVD, Paramount Pictures, 2010.]
18. See "Musical Example 11—*C'era una volta il West*," in *Comporre per il Cinema*, 72. See in A how the rallentando is realized. B shows how the music would be if there were not a rallentando.
19. The reference is to *Bulworth*, confirmed by the presence of Edda Dell'Orso on the CD (RCA 09026 63253-2).
20. Dino Asciolla (Rome, 1920–Siena, 1994), violist. Among the major soloists of our time, for a short time he substituted for Piero Farulli in the celebrated Quartetto Italiano. For the cinema he recorded, among others, the music for *Marco Polo* and *Buone notizie* (*Good News*). Morricone dedicated two compositions of his chamber works to him, *Suoni per Dino per viola e due magnetofoni* (1969) and *Ombra di lontana presenza per viola, orchestra d'archi e nastro magnetico* (1997).
21. He refers to a waterphone, which is a metal bowl filled with water. Long rods of varying lengths are attached to the sides of the bowl (giving it the described "sunburst" effect) that can be either struck or bowed. The vibrations of the metal when modified by the movement of the water in the bowl create many eerie and odd sounds. It's not an uncommon instrument. You can find the website of its inventor, Richard Waters, at http://www.waterphone.com/. I am grateful to Bruce Broughton for this citation. [GBA]
22. It was not possible to recall their names.
23. These figures may be true for continental European musicians. In England and the United States, a three-hour session yields fifteen minutes of usable recording, and the twenty-minute breaks last only twenty minutes. [GBA]
24. The fourth film on which Morricone collaborated officially is *La cuccagna* (Salce, 1962) [DVD, Raro Video, 2012]; the fifth is *La voglia matta* (Salce, 1962) [DVD, Medusa Video, 2008]. Both were for the director Luciano Salce, and both were created in 1962.

25. Directed by Giuseppe Tornatore, 1998. [DVD, Medusa Video, 2007.]

26. Tim Roth.

27. Enrichetta, played by Tina Aumont; the film is from 1976. [DVD, Unilibro, 2010.]

28. Eugenia, played by Isabella Rossellini; the film is from 1979.

29. *Un coeur en hiver*, directed by Claude Sautet, France, 1992. The violinist is interpreted by Emmanuelle Béart. [DVD, Lorber Film, 2006.]

30. *Tous les matins du monde*, directed by Alain Corneau, France, 1991. Model, also here, of the gestural understanding of Gerard Depardieu (Marin Marais), Jean-Pierre Marielle (Sieur de Sainte-Colombe), Anne Brochet (Madeleine, daughter of Sainte-Colombe), and others. [DVD, E4 Entertainment, 2006.]

31. *The Crave*, track 20 of the CD (Sony SK 60790), the piece executed by Amedeo Tommasi.

32. *Jungle Blues*, not present on the CD.

33. *The Fingerbreaker*, not present on the CD.

34. On the CD cited it is track 8, with the title *Enduring Movement*. It is interpreted by Gilda Buttà.

Chapter Four

Audiovisual Analysis — Part 2

Elements for the Definition of a Film-Musical Dramaturgy[1]

EM: Many years ago, when I read Professor Miceli's theory of levels for the first time, I thought it was a great idea. It brought to light and rationalized something that unconsciously I had already felt in the compositions I had written for the cinema. For that reason, whether you are a composer or a director, I invite you to follow his exposition very attentively, because it could provide you with extremely useful tools. In fact, if directors were to take it into account, the work for musicians might be much easier, which would be all to the advantage of . . . films.

ORIGIN AND HISTORY OF THE METHOD OF LEVELS OR POINTS OF VIEW

SM: My method uses levels or points of view to analyze the function of music in a film. . . . I created it because I needed adequate and coherent tools for the study of a specific case, the association of Federico Fellini and Nino Rota. . . . I published the results at the beginning of the seventies, and later, . . . after revision, I published it in various versions and in different places.[2]

THE DISTINCTION BETWEEN ACCOMPANIMENT AND
COMMENTARY SCORES

Before I talk about the method, let me establish a common vocabulary. . . . In the analyses that follow I distinguish between an accompaniment-type score [*una musica di accompagnamento*] and a commentary-type score [*una musica di commento*] (terms generally used synonymously). The first type of score accentuates and supports the film using mere formal equivalence in the form of techniques ranging from onomatopoeia to rhythmic parallelism. Therefore, it depends on elementary musical codes or conventions. The second type of score is charged with interpreting, in all senses of the word, the narrative context and the symbolic needs of the film.

If I use an orchestra to evoke or imitate the sounds of a train under way, even if I superimpose sound effects, I am simply accompanying a scene onto which I am conferring an essentially superficial, though effective, reinforcement. If, however, onto that rhythmic base I fit a melody that is related to other key situations in the film, . . . I have superimposed a commentary onto the accompaniment. . . . I have elevated the character of the rhythmic base, . . . and the interpretative aspect of the melody now encapsulates it.

For example, Arthur Honegger's *Pacific 231* began as descriptive music in Abel Gànce's *La Roue* (1923)[3] but very quickly acquired a formal architecture with extremely noble antecedents (Bach). In this raising of its level . . . , it assumed an epic, extradescriptive stature and . . . a strong lyric evocation.[4]

On the other hand, far from mere formal equivalence, a commentary-type score has a quality and an intrinsic formal reasoning that are not necessarily faithful to the formal characteristics of a film's scenes. (It can extend even to extreme cases of decontextualization, or even of asynchronism, which can be of various types.) In the latter extreme cases, however, one can make such a score part of the world of signs (which is its traditional role in film), and it can refer to itself at the same time. . . .

"MICKEYMOUSING" AND THE MUSICAL

Now I would like to clarify further the characteristics of an accompaniment-type score. It is made up . . . of a monstrous series of sync points . . . because the synchronization, the temporal coincidence between the visual contents and the soundtrack, is a repeated and constant element. "Mickeymousing" in animated film is an extreme case of the accompaniment-type score's very "servile" way of proceeding. It involves the violent and redundant correspondence between music and movement that is not without notable humorous or even metaphysical resources. . . . I am not thinking . . . about the feature-length Disney productions that are in many respects closer to nonanimated films but about the classical MGM *Tom and Jerry* cartoons, where the relation between music and event is almost always played *ad absurdum.*[5]

The musical is another example of the servile accompaniment-type score. Think of Cosmo Brown's[6] tremendous number among the sets that are being prepared, or of his duet with Don Lockwood,[7] "Moses Supposes," in *Singin' in the Rain.*[8] That facial mime and those puppetlike gestures that challenge the force of gravity come from cartoons in which the music is totally synchronized. Think, for example, of Tom and Jerry in *The Cat Concerto.*[9] In this case, we are in the presence of adapted, preexisting music to which the cartoon has been cut, but the accompaniment-type score's very servile way of proceeding is still the same.

ACCOMPANIMENT/COMMENTARY FUNCTIONS IN THE SAME FILM: OLIVIER'S *HENRY V*

Naturally, it is possible to alternate the characteristics of commentary- and accompaniment-type scores within the same piece. William Walton has given us an example in the music for Olivier's *Henry V* (1944). In the battle sequence, when the archers shoot their arrows, the commentary takes a backseat to the underlining or accentuating function and therefore to the characteristics of the accompaniment-type score.[10] A fragment of this kind of accompaniment can lower the general tone of the commentary, or it can contribute to its elevation. (The latter is more difficult.) The choice between a lowered or an elevated tone depends on the solution the composer has devised and has to be evaluated on a case-by-case basis. In this sequence (here, as in the whole film), Walton's music does not seem to me to be particularly forceful. Therefore, the eventual damage that might have been caused by the exposed accentuating seems limited.

THE ACCOMPANIMENT-TYPE SCORE: PLAYBACK, MUSICALS

Playback . . . is one extreme type of the accompaniment type of score. It only superficially accompanies the images and does not try to interpret the film in depth. . . . The synchronism is absolute and legitimate . . . because it arises from a likely reality. A character plays an instrument, and the music has to be what he produces. Of course, one must add that there exist very interesting cases in which there is deviation or partial or total transfiguration of this playback situation. . . . The character dances, but he is following the music that is in his head. It is still in the technical-realization sense playback, but of what type?

Still staying with the accompaniment-type score, at the opposite extreme are the endless number of overstuffed musicals. They resort to the cinema of routine or to generic musical compositions (which are often defined exactly that way in the scores, especially French ones). I am reminded that ragtime was often the music of choice in the silent cinema.[11] It was a use probably permitted by . . . the mechanical nature and expressive neutrality of ragtime music. Today, ragtime music has been replaced by a vast oeuvre of easy listening and . . . pop music with many connections to . . . dance.

EXPLICIT AND IMPLICIT SYNCHRONIZATION (SYNC) POINTS

At this point, having already touched on the subject several times, I have to mention sync points, points of synchronization. As Maestro Morricone has mentioned already, I distinguish between explicit sync points and implicit sync points. The explicit sync point is a precise meeting place between music and image that the music accentuates in a very obvious way. It can do so by making a sudden crescendo, by holding a chord, by repeating a series of chords, by suspending a previous rhythmic flow, or by using a dissonant *sforzando* in a consonant context. . . . The solutions are endless.

In certain cases, this increased synchronization becomes mickeymousing. In a scene from *Dr. No*,[12] James Bond leaps from the bed and with a slipper squashes an enormous poisonous spider that has been put between the sheets. Five orchestral attacks are calculated to match the blows of the slipper inflicted on the insect (though the first with a slight delay), two long, three short. They are sync points without delicacy. One could not be much more explicit than this. . . . We are on the threshold of involuntary humor, even if the tone of the entire 007 series certainly does not lead one to take it very seriously.

In conclusion, sync points of this type are very diffuse in the comic genre, for example, where they reveal their kinship with pantomime. They play on . . . blatant artifice and very rarely demonstrate appreciable musical qualities.

Implicit sync points, on the other hand, can be defined as those that perhaps maintain an autonomous musical course. Together with a filmic event, they only slightly modify the structural musical characteristics of a composition. Also, they are slightly and, above all, subtly allusive. In other words, the implicit sync point underlines sentiments more than events, thoughts more than actions. The modification can be rhythmic in nature (a momentary suspension of or rippling in the music's flow), harmonic (a cadential pattern, actually suspended, irresolute, a dissonance on the inside of a complex mixture, a harmonic thickening and clarification due to a series of instrumental doubles), or timbral (the entry of an instrument or of a section, a unison, a jump in register). Every case remains coherently within the interior logic of the musical composition.

Maestro Morricone and I have demonstrated some concrete examples already, I in one way in the preanalysis for *Cut Sequences*, and Maestro Morricone in another way when he talked about *C'era una volta in America*.[13] Therefore, I will not say any more at this point, because later we will return to related topics.

METHOD OF LEVELS [OR POINTS OF VIEW]: INTERNAL, EXTERNAL, MEDIATED

Having established a common terminology, I can now describe my method of levels or points of view. Linguistic and semiological methodologies are the starting point for any analytical method that is to be applied to an audiovisual object like a movie or television program. They focus on an analysis of the narrative of a literary text and, within this, on the level of the statement, the so-called narrative point of view. The material is as compelling as it is limitless, but even if I had the time, I am not enough of a specialist to talk about it.[14]

For our purposes, it will be sufficient to remember the Platonic distinction between diegesis (the pure story, or the point of view of the omniscient narrator) and mimesis (the story taken from the point of view of the characters). These perspectives have been decisively elaborated on by contemporary scholars. From this platform the music theorists have proceeded in a more or less declared, more or less conscious way to make some propositions about the relations between music and film. . . . With diverse terminology and different degrees of systematic method, they refer us . . . to two categories of intervention by the musical component, the diegetic and the extradiegetic (with various subcategories). In the first case, one speaks of a "real" musical presence, located on the inside of the filmic narration. In the second case, we are referred with diverse nuances to what we define usually as the "musical commentary."

My proposal is different from all the others, not only because of the terminology that I have adopted but also because of the basic distinction that leads us to three categories instead of two (and without systematic recourse to subcategories). From now on, I will talk not of a diegetic level but of an internal level, not of an extradiegetic level but of an external level, to which I will add a mediated level. Because if I were to try to deal with only the internal level, I would have to refer to the others, I will anticipate now the global definitions in a reduced and schematic form.

Internal level	Musical source belonging to the scene
	Visible or presumable identification of the music-making source
	In certain cases coincides with playback
	Absence of the author
External level	Ubiquitous, indeterminate musical source
	Typical commentary-/accompaniment-type score
	Has a leitmotif function
	At the limit of expressive neutrality is a generic background sound
	Epiphany (sudden intuitive perception of reality) of the author
Mediated level	Interiorized musical source, identifiable with a character
	A sort of mimesis that is subjective sound
	It can also have a leitmotif function
	Absence of the author

INTERNAL LEVEL

Die Wunderbare Luege der Nina Petrovna (*The Wonderful Lies of Nina Petrovna*) (Hanns Schwartz, 1929)

The most obvious example of an internal level or point of view is in a scene that has a visible musical source, a radio apparatus, a hi-fi system, a musician that plays, and so forth. I can also cite an example of an internal level or point of view . . . in which the musical source is not in the frame, but the scene itself is left to support an entirely plausible assumption of live music making. If a couple enters a ballroom, anybody would think that the music heard from that moment on, because congruous, is coming from the location's orchestra. To reiterate, this example is the most obvious. It is calculated to represent reality accurately or with a rigorous documentary approach. The examples that follow show how and why the internal level, even though the author is absent . . . expresses many additional characteristics and nuances.

Our first example comes from one of the most interesting European late silent films, *Die Wunderbare Luege der Nina Petrovna*.[15] . . . I need to say something about the film, because you cannot see it at the cinema nor acquire it on videocassette.[16] . . .

The film was a German production, directed by Hanns Schwartz. . . . For its distribution in France it was thought opportune to entrust the music to a composer closer to the taste of the French public. The choice fell to Maurice Jaubert, without doubt one of the more important composers in the history of music for film.

The scene I want to analyze begins with a detail shot of an aquarium and then reveals the surroundings of a café concert. A little while afterward, in the background, . . . without emphasis or exposed didactic emphasis, a little instrumental group appears. . . . The waltz being played behaves with a certain ambiguity because the spectator can interpret it at first in a traditional way as underscoring. It seems to be music outside of the diegesis and thus of the commentary and external-level type. Since the successive shots inform us to the contrary (because only then do we see the instrumental group in the background), in an unconscious way the determination of its dramaturgical category remains uncertain. First it seemed to be of the external, then of the internal level. What will it be the next time we hear it?

I have chosen this example among many, because it is . . . very rich. Proceeding with the seeing and hearing, one could demonstrate the subtly ambiguous game it lends to the categorization of the music. Further on, in fact, it will not be possible to speak of the internal level with the same security, but at the moment these considerations are premature.

I do not believe that the internal level . . . is used by the director as a moment of mere and banal "realism." On the contrary, within the film, because of the ambiguity of its category, the music at an internal level . . . permits the "smuggling" of an expressive, emotive, and even symbolic presence into the diegesis in a totally natural and painless way. It is a sort of Trojan horse that has the great merit of downplaying the implicit artifice of every musical entrance. Obviously, the artifice or the memory of the artifice remains.

In general, the screenplay calls for this type of ambiguous entrance or intervention, . . . because it causes the characters to react in ways that are necessary to the narration. However, if one starts from the external level, the average spectator is not as aware of the significance of these interventions as he might be of other, more explicit interventions by the director. For exactly these reasons the internal level is particularly dear to those directors who have a radical, "pure" documentary conception of the cinema, or who see the cinema first of all as an ideological vehicle. Therefore, they have a "little or nothing at all" aestheticism and hide in the expedients of a consolatory display of spectacle as an end in itself. (Neorealism was also this way, and it is a real shame that the composers for neorealist films did not understand the essence of this characteristic.)[17]

Hidden on the Internal Level: The Marginalized Use of Music in the Films of Nanni Moretti and Gianni Amelio

As . . . an example of this "little or nothing at all" aestheticism, think of the Italian director Nanni Moretti. If you are going to the cinema to see one of his films, search above all for the thrill of the long single shot, the dizziness of the dolly, the frenzy of a montage full of cuts. Then remain disappointed. To see a movie about movie making, at least in Italy, one needs to turn to Giuseppe Tornatore or Bernardo Bertolucci.

I anticipate a probable objection: even Moretti has made some movies about filmmaking. This is true, but in the potentially "literary" and "chamber" sense. His metalanguage suffers from a rigorous egocentrism that is realized in hysterical scenes based exclusively on his monologues as both the protagonist and director.

A director that remains instead well hidden behind the camera is Gianni Amelio, but in the end . . . the result is almost the same. . . . In both cases, their films . . . show a "timid" if not marginalized use of music.

Il ladro di bambini (The Stolen Children) (Gianni Amelio, 1992)

For the cited authors, Franco Piersanti has generally been the composer. His duty has been arduous. He needs to interpret the film using many measures, without being able to be a protagonist, without prevarications, moving in the tiny space that is conceded to him, even in the temporal sense. This leaves the director the certainty (or the illusion) that the film is all under his expressive control and that the music does not add anything more than what he intended.

Think of *Il ladro di bambini* (released in the USA as *The Stolen Children*).[18] The musical commentary is reduced, justifiably, to a minimum, . . . while the music at an internal level, the ugly music that we are given to listen to, has an obvious denotative function. In contrast to so much that happens in Fellini (and, in part, in the films of the Taviani brothers), here the commentary-type music neither addresses nor helps, much less saves, the characters. Neither does it frame in a demiurgic embrace. (Think of Bolognini, Pasolini . . . but the list would be extremely long.) It is truly difficult for a composer to work under such conditions.

EM: It is not easy. I say so, because I have had directors like that.

SM: I have no difficulty believing it, even if I cannot imagine a compositional temperament like yours facing . . . a director who is ashamed of the presence of music. Nor can I imagine him dealing with you.

EM: In my opinion, it is a question of jealousy, a jealousy (I want to be clear) that I respect. It was like that in Zeffirelli's *Amleto (Hamlet)*,[19] where the protagonist's most beautiful monologue was realized without music.

SM: But in that case, even where you were allowed to compose, one could not hear much. When *Hamlet* arrived in the theaters, . . . I had a film music seminar at the University of Macerata. I went to see it with the students, and we all left feeling very disappointed. The mix penalized the music in a way that was like few other times I have heard. And this was certainly not one of those cases in which the director was ashamed of the music or in which he did not pay attention to the spectacle, even in the more glaring and "popular" sense of the term. But with Zeffirelli, we are a long way from the theme of the internal level. We mentioned him to call to your attention a type of cinema that, when it uses music, prefers music at the internal level. (But normally it uses very little music.)

Leaving aside now the examples of Moretti, of Amelio, and of a cinema that is little inclined toward the monopolizing presence of music, we need to remember that in a decisive way the internal level can contribute to the illustration of the social context or to the delineation of the psychological traits of a character, charging them with a didactic function that is otherwise cumbersome and that could damage the spontaneity of the narrative flow.

Io la conoscevo bene (I Knew Her Well) (Pietrangeli, 1965)

In order to illustrate this aspect of the internal level, I would like you to recall the concluding episode of a film that is among the most interesting in the Italian cinema of the sixties, *Io la conoscevo bene (I Knew Her Well)*.[20] As usual, I cannot offer a synopsis, but for those who have not seen it, suffice it to say that it deals with the story of a young girl who is ingenuous and a dreamer who "loses herself" while attempting to "make it" in the movie industry. She abandons herself to thoughtlessness and indifference until she realizes her own endlessly empty condition and commits suicide.

The film is the pitiless portrait of a specific environment, with the brief but memorable appearance of a magnificent Ugo Tognazzi.[21] It does not have a real musical commentary, because most of the music is taken from the cheapest consumer products of the epoch. (The film is also a good example of the utilization of preexistent music.) Fashionable dances and pop songs are the music that Adriana (Stefania Sandrelli) listens to continually, almost as if they were her narcotic. Accompanied by one of these songs, she throws herself from the terrace of her own apartment.

In this, my extremely biased description of the film, the fundamental experience of sound accumulation that the spectator takes into account in the course of watching a whole screening is lacking. (I can never insist enough on the importance of the antecedent-precedent relationship, whether it is in composing or in the evaluation of a work.) . . . The reiteration of the musical motif[22] leads to an effect of estrangement and semiotic reversal, or a kind of asynchronism. What might have sounded redeemed and festive reveals itself to be pitiless and obsessive, but above all extraneous. The internal level is unequivocal. The record player . . . accompanies Adriana's entire day and is extremely visible, but this film shows the degree of transfiguration that the internal level can attain.

Three More Examples of the Internal Level

The Man Who Knew Too Much

I have chosen three titles from among an infinite number of cases that demonstrate the expressive values of music at the internal level. The first is a fragment from Alfred Hitchcock's *The Man Who Knew Too Much*,[23] with music by Bernard Herrmann. . . . I am going to say what would be an obvious thing to motion picture specialists, but the mention of which is justified now by the fact that I am addressing mostly musicians. To relegate Hitchcock only to the circle of one genre, the mystery, would be a grave mistake. We are instead in the presence of one of the masters of the cinema *tout court*, whose linguistic and formal solutions should be put into an anthology of classics.

His is really a metacinema, from which derives, for example, the totally Hitchcockian habit of making a momentary appearance, sometimes in a very obvious way. (A city bus departs from the bus stop and closes the door in the face of a guy who is trying to get in, but that "guy" is Hitchcock.) In other cases, going to blow up a frame, we see in the background of a frame in the open air that there is a bridge with people facing each other, and one of them, perhaps. . . . But I don't know if it is correct to define it as a habit. Enigmatic self-citation and the marginal insertion of the author into his own work is a game of appearances ("to be or not to be, that is the question . . .") that can be referred back to the Flemish masters and to those of the Florentine Renaissance. All in all, without Hitchcock the cinema would be unthinkable, even for those who have never directed a mystery. Ask Paolo Taviani,[24] for example.

The movie fragment that I propose now has to do with an attempted assassination . . . in the Royal Albert Hall during a concert of Arthur Benjamin's *Storm Cloud Cantata*. (Here the game of auto-insertion has been extended to composer/conductor Herrmann.) The dramatic nature of the cantata assumes a double significance. Within the principal narrative context, its meaning changes and, consequently, its dramatic potential is amplified.

Ben (James Stewart) is searching for the box in which bounty killer Drayton (Bernard Miles) is waiting to ambush a visiting celebrity while Jo (Doris Day), Ben's wife, assists, impotent and upset. But the scene contains more than just a mechanism of emotive amplification. If the sound of the music accentuates the tension, the visibility of the musical notation and performers emphasizes instead their extraneousness to the events. The assassin watches for a crash of the cymbals as a signal to shoot, and the director "forces" the spectator to assume the same point of view by cross-fading several times to the percussionist, who with an absolutely tranquil expression is preparing for his entrance. With the musical crescendo there is a crescendo of events. In the contrast between pathos and impassivity, note the game of the movie camera. There is . . . a detailed close-up of the musical notation that rolls by (a lesson that Kieslowski took into account)[25] and a subjective shot of the percussionist, who with outstretched arms displays the cymbals in front of him in preparation for the upcoming crash. It's a shame that we cannot linger any longer on this film, because I would be able to demonstrate how from beginning to end the music assumes a determinant role on the dramaturgical level itself.

La dolce vita (The Sweet Life)

The second example is taken from *La dolce vita*.[26] . . . The film probably does not need any introduction. However, I will be examining a seven-minute episode that needs some explanation. Marcello (Marcello Mastroianni) accompanies his father (Annibale Ninchi) to a Roman nightclub. The father is visiting from out of town and is easygoing and slightly pathetic. He is the provincial Romagnolo figure incarnate. In an old-fashioned way, he begins to court his son's friend, a dancer (Magali Noël), who is ready to play the game with lots of spirit. She is typically Felliniesque (one finds her as Gradisca in *Amarcord*, interpreted by the same actress), a sexually generous woman who yields with cordiality and a bit of sentimentality.

The father pushes his advances until . . . he accompanies the dancer to her apartment. However, a little after their arrival, the woman, alarmed, is constrained to call Marcello, because . . . his father feels sick. The encounter between father and son follows. . . . It is one of the most humanly touching and above all measured episodes in all of Fellini's cinema. The psychological nuances of the characters overlap. They associate and disassociate. There is the embarrassment but also the tenderness of Marcello, the embarrassment but also a confused sense of blame from the dancer, the embarrassment but above all the bitterness of the father, who will take the earliest train that night to return home.

This ruinous parable that goes from euphoria to frustration, from illusory transgression to impetuous inadequacy, has a . . . musical anticipation in the central part of the scene in the nightclub. Among the nightclub acts there is a celebrated clown with a trumpet, Polidor. He plays an agonizing melody, typically Rota-esque, which returns again in the form of a waltz. Exactly at this point, watch carefully. The father will invite the young woman to dance.[27]

Polidor's number has an abysmal sadness. Only the circus as seen by Fellini has the ability to transmit it. With the sound of his trumpet, the clown, who is almost a new kind of Pied Piper, attracts a host of balloons and raises one of them. It explodes at the highest note, which is too "operatic," insistent, and clumsy. Finally the clown goes away, as disconsolate as he was when he arrived, followed by that flock of light and ephemeral entities. Only Marcello, in an oblique exchange of looks with Polidor (a very beautiful signal from the director! And without any didactic heaviness), seems to understand the profound uneasiness, if not the premonition, that the number transmits. And it is with premonition that one is dealing, or perhaps, to say it better, with an anticipation in a symbolic form of how much will come true in a little while. Or, in the end, it is something similar to the way one defines anticipation in narratological analysis.[28] Pay attention to the degree of dramaturgical responsibility that can arrive with a "simple" internal level. . . . This said, let's return to the last example that pertains to the internal level.

Non c'è pace tra gli ulivi (There Is No Peace among the Olive Trees) (Giuseppe De Santis, 1950)

The film is *Non c'è pace tra gli ulivi* (*There Is No Peace Among the Olive Trees*) of Giuseppe De Santis. The music is by Goffredo Petrassi.[29] It is an ambitious film, . . . atypical in the panorama of the Italian cinema of the fifties and . . . an example of a missed opportunity, above all, and perhaps almost exclusively, from the point of view of the music. . . .

To put the fragment that I have chosen into . . . context, I ought to say that the choices of the director resulted from research of an epic caliber, suspended between Greek tragedy (especially in the cuts of the montage with dialogue) and Brechtian estrangement. It occurs in the context of a pastoral community in which strong, archaic traditions do battle with a process of civilizing that demonstrates the typical contradictions in postwar Italy. There is the race to profit by illicit means and the taking advantage of those who are weaker, for whom the law does not seem able to create much of a defense.

Composer Petrassi's rapport with the cinema . . . was . . . extremely poor. . . . He had a basic misunderstanding that he shared with entire generations of cultivated Italian composers of the classical tradition.[30] Perhaps he was too preoccupied with the possibility of falling into a "vernacular" language or into an easy sketch. For *Non c'è pace tra gli ulivi* he offered a dense, complex music frequently related directly to the contemporary *Con-*

certi per orchestra. By so doing, he caused a fracture and an extraneousness that was not only stylistic but also psychological.

Said in another way, very little of what we hear pertains to the words, to the times, to the landscapes, or to the events of the film. It occurs to me that I might here anticipate themes that pertain to the treatment of the external level, but after the basic definitions have been clarified, I will say that Petrassi's commentary belongs to a level external to the frame because it can be described as so artificial and insensitive to the context.

Naturally, we need to clarify immediately an extremely serious potential ambiguity. No one believes that the musical commentary for a film like *Non c'è pace tra gli ulivi* should use only bagpipe, ocarina, and shepherd's pipes. Insofar as it is interpretative, art is transfiguring. It is allowed . . . any and every means. However, in an effort to turn a "base," primitive material into something epic, it should not ignore the context. This is especially true if the context is shown through an apparently realistic, expressive medium like the cinema.[31] However, in this case, the "miracle" of a film-musical dramaturgy does not happen. Rather, what happens is the manifestation of two dramatically distinct concepts, autonomous and uncommunicative. Petrassi's music does not succeed in making the story epic. It only makes epic the music itself.

I have said only a small part of what could be said about this situation. Obviously, the Petrassi "case" could contribute to the revelation of some basic problems regarding the music-cinema relationship. However, I ought to return to our theme, and I can do so now that I have put the episode into its context.

The most effective moment, in which the music is irreplaceable, is when the *carabinieri* (Italian police) are hunting the shepherd Francesco Dominici (Raf Vallone), who is evading an unjust incarceration. A young woman who is fond of him, Lucia (Lucia Bosè), tries to meet up with him in the mountains, but the *carabinieri* obstruct the passage to everyone. Lucia spurs on an accordion player and improvises . . . a saltarello in which the old and young who are collecting the olives become involved.

The saltarello, a traditional country dance, emerges with Lucia, the Beautiful One, at the center; the others, the Chorus, in a circle; and a shepherd who plays the grotesque figure of the satyr, the Beast. After having thus attracted the attention of the *carabinieri*, Lucia suddenly flees toward her hidden lover. Note the ambiguity in her look. (This requires little interpretative effort, because ambiguity is the most disquieting characteristic of Lucia Bosè.) While she is dancing, she feigns being carefree, while she is controlling the reactions of the *carabinieri*. The dramatic rendering results from the obvious and nevertheless charming contrast between the merriment of the musical episode and the true purpose of its manifestation. I find it an excellent use of the internal level.

Asynchronism

I can use this episode to talk once again about asynchronism, but I have to be careful. The concept of asynchronism was born . . . in a manifesto, or, better said, from a declaration about sound film signed by Eisenstein, Pudovkin, and Aleksandrov in 1928.[32] . . . It ought to refer above all to the commentary-type score, that is, to music of the external level. In the Petrassi case, the contrast or "counterpoint" (as one used to define it . . .) between music and image is unmistakable, because it is the result of the manifest expressive will of the composer. It is an expressive will in this case, however, that the music of the internal level muffles. It does so by virtue of the fact that the music assumes a significance because it belongs to the film.

Therefore, we can and . . . ought to distinguish between a contrast desired and a contrast suffered. However, these are distinctions that we could better investigate later. . . . Every time I speak of expressive will, I mean it from the point of view of the author or the spectator. In the eyes of the spectator, the internal level reduces the exposition of artifice, while the external level magnifies it. However, . . . from the point of view of artifice, there are two expressive wills equally knowledgeable and decisive.

Some will see in this distinction a kinship with Jean Molino's fundamental contribution, which was taken up by Jean-Jacques Nattiez in the context of the semiology of music. There he speaks of a *poiesis* process and of an *aesthesis* process. In the first case, one is occupied with the strategy of the creative act, while in the second, one takes into consideration the mechanisms of enjoyment.[33] Always simplifying, I could say that my method of levels privileges the *aesthesis* process, even if it observes it from the *poiesis* point of view.

EXTERNAL LEVEL

Bananas (Woody Allen)

It seems to me that Maestro Morricone and I have already had occasion to emphasize the extraneous and artificial nature of cinema music . . . but when we made this judgment, we were not referring to music at the internal level. On the other hand, "extraneous" and "artificial" apply very well to film music on the external level, and the most widespread way to insert music in a film is through the external level. . . . I want to analyze a brief clip from a film of the 1970s, *Bananas*[34] by Woody Allen, in order to demonstrate the characteristics of music at the external level. I will not give any explanation beforehand, because I would betray the director's intent and the reason itself for which I chose this example.[35]

While watching it, we all, justifiably, laugh.[36] I laugh a little less, however—and not . . . because I have looked at this scene on the occasion of every seminar. Nonfiction and the didactic are not able to compete with expressive synthesis, especially if they come from a genial director like Woody Allen. In this sketch, he has concentrated all of a long discourse on . . . the external level. . . . The implicit message . . . is as absurd as it is exhilarating, because . . . the external level represents a convention universally accepted and as such not discussable. However, we are here . . . to discuss or at least to reason about it.

I begin by noting that the external level, artifice *par excellence*, . . . shamelessly reveals the poetic meaning and substance of a work of art as a whole and the intentions of the director (and, as a consequence, of the composer). Borrowing this time from the semiotics of narrativity from the point of view of the external level, one can speak of the author's epiphany or sudden intuitive perception or insight into the essential meaning of something. This contrasts with the absence of the author at the internal level.

A particular musical choice, including the use of preexistent music, . . . appears as an aesthetic and sometimes, as Pasolini teaches, ethical proposal. It is expressed by skillful or artful contrivances or expedients that are applied to the characters and the work itself. This musical choice is part of the moral fable (apologue) that organizes a film; it can also assume the principal task of the apologue, even though it then will bear an inevitable didactic burdening.

In the case of preexistent music, the didactic burdening is directly proportional to the degree to which the music used is recognizable. But in such a case, another mechanism comes into play that in general does not seem to worry directors. A universally known piece of music, endowed . . . with a solid identity, has an enormous referential power that is closely tied to its natural location and to its traditional use, high or low as it may be. By carrying it abruptly into the cinema, one can cause a . . . serious aesthetic imbalance, a disproportion . . . between music and image. Only asynchronism, forced decontextualization, or the semantic short circuit put into action by a master like Kubrick permit one to avoid the occurrence of these negative phenomena.

The External Level and Pasolini

Pasolini, for example, . . . was neither preoccupied with the balance between recognizability and a potential teaching function nor with aesthetic disproportion. He assigned a direct demiurgic role, a precise moral judgment, to some of the most well-known music in the cultivated tradition.

In 1993[37] . . . I received from Gillo Pontecorvo the assignment to conceive and conduct a cycle of encounters on the theme of "Image and Music" at the Fiftieth International Exhibit of Cinematic Art in Venice.[38] . . . It all went well . . . with the exception of a . . . challenge that came from a movie critic whose name I do not remember (and it is not because I want to be diplomatic). He did not like my observations about the use of preexisting music in the cinema of Pasolini, declaring his criticism in a very animated way.

I recount this incident in order to make a basic observation that is useful to our work. Respect and admiration for a great artist ought not to exclude the possibility of legitimate critical analysis of his work. Obviously, I cherish the poet Pasolini, to whom I add my profound gratitude for a lesson that was fundamental for me, pertaining to the reading and rereading of the *Lettere luterane.*[39]

However, from a critical analysis of Pasolini's film work I extracted some unresolved aspects, contradictions, and inadequacies in the quality of his artful contrivances or expedients. . . . By so doing, I . . . surely did not influence the global esteem in which Pasolini was commonly held . . . , but my exposition was intended to be useful to students in a seat of learning.

The great Pasolinian lucidity, which he exercised on nonfiction, the narrative, and cinema, did not have a counterpart in his use of preexisting music. This was . . . not only because of certain brutal cuts to which he subjected the music. . . . Even an only slightly trained ear could hear these as serious amputations to a musical discourse in progress. (Think of the treatment reserved for Bach in *Accattone.*)[40]

At least in the first phase, from *Accattone* to *Il Vangelo secondo Matteo* [*The Passion according to Matthew*],[41] the music in the cinema of Pasolini has the characteristics of . . . a use that . . . I cannot define as other than *naïf.* It reflects an all-too-common comforting assimilation. . . . Gillo Dorfles says of it, . . . "Why shouldn't we allow a genius, even a very great genius from one artistic field, the possibility of enjoying *Kitsch* in another?"[42] I believe a lot in this possibility, but I would want to emphasize that one is dealing with enjoyment.

The use of preexisting music at the external level is the Achilles' heel of many directors, Pasolini included. It consists . . . precisely in the fact that they want to carry into their cinematic works music with which they have entertained . . . a deep, private, and intimate rapport. However, this use is in a context in which the expressive means should be entirely controlled and transfigured. . . . Theirs is a rapport of mere enjoyment that is dominated by empathy. It therefore is not lucid.

On the other hand, returning to the amputations of Bach, if . . . I recite a celebrated poem to a literary scholar, but I cut the most beautiful, even by as little as one half of an enjambment[43] —

> This hill was always dear to me,
> and this hedge that such a big part,[44]

—justifiably I will irritate him or her. Similarly, I am irritated by the brutal interruption of a musical discourse. The fact is that there are many (too many) who use music as if it were manna from heaven that has fallen by divine will and from which it is possible to feed oneself tidbits according to the necessity of the moment. For this exigency there is light music. It is made in small, digestible doses exactly for this purpose.

Pasolini on Music and Film

At this point, having dealt with the use of preexisting music . . . I would like to read a short essay by Pasolini about music and cinema. . . . In it the diverse insights of the poet, the essayist, and the director admirably intersect. It is here . . . to give the umpteenth demonstration of how the dazzling intuition of a great author is able to exceed theorization, sometimes with the flap of a wing. . . . Even though it represents a digression from our discussion of the external level, I . . . cite it to "compensate" for the criticism that I just expressed . . . and so as not to leave you with only a negative interpretation of the rapport between music and the cinema of Pasolini.

> The music of a film might . . . be thought of before the movie is shot (just as they think of the faces of the characters, the framing, certain attacks of editing, etc.): but it is only at the moment it comes materially to be applied to the film that it is born as movie music. Why? Because the encounter and eventual amalgamation of music and image have essentially poetic traits, or rather empirical ones.
>
> I have said that music is "applied" to film: it is true, in the moviola the operation that one executes is this. But the "application" can be made in various ways, according to various functions.
>
> The principal function is generally that of rendering explicit, clear, physically present the theme or the driving thread of the film. This theme or driving thread can be of a conceptual or a sentimental kind. But for the music the [kind] is indifferent: and a musical motif has the same moving force whether it is applied to a conceptual theme or to a sentimental theme. In fact, its true function is perhaps that of conceptualizing the emotions (synthesizing them in a motif) and of sentimentalizing the concepts. Music has therefore an ambiguous function (that only in the concrete act reveals itself, and becomes decisive): such ambiguity in the function of music is owing to the fact that it is didactic and emotive, contemporaneously.
>
> What music adds to the images, or better, the transformation that it works on the images, remains a mysterious fact, and definable with difficulty.
>
> I am able to say empirically that there are two ways of "applying" music to a visual sequence, and therefore to give it "other" values.
>
> There is a "horizontal application" and a "vertical application." The "horizontal application" happens on the surface, along the moving images: it is therefore a linearity and a successiveness that one applies to another linearity and successiveness. In this case the "values" added are rhythmic values and

give a new clarity—incalculable, strangely expressive—to the rhythmic silent values of the edited images.

The vertical application (that technically occurs in the same way) even though it follows the images in the same way, according to linearity and successiveness, in reality has its source elsewhere than in the principle [that drives the horizontal application]; it has its source in depth. Therefore more than through the rhythm, the vertical application comes to operate through meaning itself.

The values that it adds to the rhythmic values of the montage are in reality indefinable, because these transcend the cinema and bring the cinema back to reality where the source of the sounds has verified a real depth, not illusory as on the screen. In other words, the cinematic images, picked up from reality and therefore equal to the reality, at the moment in which they come to be impressed on film and projected on a screen, lose their real depth and assume a deceptive one analogous to that which in painting one calls perspective, but infinitely more perfect.

The cinema is flat, and the depth in which one loses, for example, a street in the direction of the horizon is illusory. The more poetic the film, the more this illusion is perfect. Its poetry consists in giving to the spectator the impression of being within things, in a real profundity and not flat (namely illustrative). The musical source—which is not recognizable on the screen and starts from a physical "somewhere else" that is "deep" by its nature—breaks through the flat, or deceptively profound, images of the screen, opening them to the confused and borderless depth of life.[45]

As you see, one is able to be a convinced dissenter and an agreeable admirer of the same person. There is no contradiction. Dogmatic deployments and conformity are rather sooner to be feared. . . . Pasolini himself left us a great lesson in this sense, very uncomfortable and very up to date. . . . In particular I am touched when Pasolini writes of a conceptualization of sentiments and of a sentimentalization of concepts. It is comforting, because without knowing his essay, I wrote something analogous many years ago—more than twenty now—about the processes of formalization of semantic values and of the making semantic of formal values in music for film. Then, if you will, one can find counterparts to the concept of horizontal and vertical application in some things that we have said up to now, but it is not a good idea to spell out things that are based on an intuition so deep and synthetic. Therefore, I leave it to you to find the eventual points of contact. Do you want to add something, Ennio?

EM: Let me give an explanation about the origin of this essay. It came out for RCA, in conjunction with a series of recordings (five of mine and five by Bruno Nicolai) entitled *Musiche per l'immagine e l'immaginazione* (*Music for Image and Imagination*). It was supposed to be music composed to be applied to images, but the images were not there.[46] I asked five directors to write what they thought about music in the cinema. I received contributions of diverse length and commitment. Petri was really lively, Leone also, in another way. Then there were the responses of Montaldo and Pontecorvo; they were all interesting, but Pasolini's was and remains a thing apart, because it is also poetry. But one thing that Pasolini did not write, that is implicit but that perhaps he needed to confirm, . . . is the reason why music and cinema are in such agreement. It is temporality that the two arts have in common. Look, he intends to say this, especially at the beginning, but he does not say it explicitly.[47] However, it is a great contribution that surprises me every time I hear it.

SM: The use of preexisting music has not been exhausted in these discussions, but once again we have to take up the thread of the discourse on the external level. Given that this is a seminar on composing for the cinema, we necessarily have to sacrifice certain aspects. However, I am convinced that it could be useful . . . to a composer in his or her work if he or she understood why preexisting music gives a certain particular character to a film scene. It is not an accident, therefore, that the next three examples I have prepared to illustrate the external level use music that was not written for the movie to be analyzed but that functions as if it had been.

Preexistent Music and the External Level: Samuel Barber's *Adagio for Strings* in *The Elephant Man* (1980), *Platoon* (1986), and *Lorenzo's Oil* (1992)

I will consider the finale and end titles of *The Elephant Man* by David Lynch,[48] the opening titles of Oliver Stone's *Platoon*,[49] and a sequence from the first part of *Lorenzo's Oil* (1992) by George Miller.[50] . . . These three movies have very different subjects and styles of direction, but there is one element that they share: the presence of the same music . . . at key points, the *Adagio for Strings* by American composer Samuel Barber.[51]

Recapitulating the discussion that I presented a little while ago about the intrusiveness and imbalance caused by the use of well-known preexistent music, I note that in this case things are very different. I believe that this *Adagio* is not too well known, at least in Italy (in spite of Arturo Toscanini, who "adopted" it, rendering it a great service). Or if it is well known, it is known almost exclusively in musical circles. However, to us the reactions of the average moviegoer and, still more important, those of the director are of more interest. Evidently it was well known to Lynch, Stone, and Miller, who did not hesitate to use it in their movies. (Who knows whether Stone knew of Lynch and whether Miller knew of Lynch and of Stone . . . ?) It has the enormous advantage of a quite reduced referential power, at least for European moviegoers, but maybe also for the American public, because Barber is neither Gershwin nor Bernstein. It remains to be seen why the choice was made, about which we can advance only some hypotheses.

Let's begin with Lynch's *The Elephant Man*. Remember all the characters in the film, the black and white, the optical filter effect,[52] and the voice-over. . . . The story is pathetic. The means for narrating it aim at a total immersion that repeats every stereotype about "monsters." Instead, however, the basic discussion goes against the grain, since it puts us on the side of the "monster." The scene is the finale in which John Merrick (John Hurt) dies, after having encountered the doctor (Anthony Hopkins), who has done a lot for him, and after we have observed the most meaningful objects and the portraits of cherished people found in his room. It is a leave-taking without traumas, knowledgeable and liberating.

Stone's *Platoon* has the peculiarity of resorting only to music of the internal level, the exception being the opening and closing titles, where one finds the *Adagio* (elaborated by Delerue). Subjected to the scene of the landing of the new recruits in Vietnam, the music fights with the effects—noises of the helicopter, shouts, cries, voice-overs. Sometimes it loses the contest, in fact, succumbs. I think it is the desired choice of the mix, because *Platoon* has the ambition of making epic a historical reality (with an openly autobiographical component). A documentary approach prevails over invention. The absence of other music at the external level in the course of the movie is confirmation of this situation. I have already spoken about the rigor of the documentary approach as an illustration of the internal level. It is here applied radically. The only declared artifice is in the frame around the film, in the opening and end titles, therefore a little outside and a little inside the story, at which point the author manifests himself and issues into the open.

Finally, Miller's *Lorenzo's Oil* deals with an event that really happened. The parents of a baby diagnosed with a rare sickness that attacks the central nervous system do not resign themselves to the baby's plight. Even though they are not doctors, they fight back by studying and gathering evidence to discover a chemical compound capable of arresting the mortal course of the disease. The film makes ample use of the most diverse preexistent music, but the fact remains that exactly in the scene where the parents of Lorenzo learn of the terrible diagnosis, transcribed for chorus, the *Adagio* of Barber enters. That the film is very moving goes without saying, although it is less effective than it might be because the tone, suspended between objective reports and the involving narration, is uneven.

The element that all three films have in common is compassion. . . . In the finale of *Platoon*, the repetition of the same *Adagio* that was used for the opening titles confirms a posteriori the character of compassion that was anticipated in the opening titles. Its use is more conventional in the other two films, because it coincides with the moments of maximum sentimentalism, right in the heart of the narration (though this coincides in *The Elephant Man* with the end of the film).

Personally, I find Stone's solution more elegant, but this is not the point. In similar cases, many directors would have resorted to Bach without worrying about the fact that it is widely recognizable or that it carries a heavy referential power or spiritual connotations (in the sense of being inevitably religious, liturgical, or paraliturgical). With Barber, none of this happens. His *Adagio* is a carrier of a sort of lay spirituality and actually of a more stylized characterization, even though it is attentive to the values of the nineteenth-century tradition. The phrasing is cautious, with its progression/regression by connected degrees of the scale. It does not affirm a theme shamelessly, while it also has the value of thematic construction.[53] There is a theme, but it does not assert itself. It expands in long chord bands over which it progresses, but it is not in a hurry to arrive at the climax, and at the end, when all is said and done, it is a music that refers to itself. Paradoxically, it is ideal music for moving pictures.

Visconti and Music

As you can well imagine after all that I have said, the musical choices of Luchino Visconti embarrass me. (I think, for example, of the *Adagietto* of Mahler in *Morte a Venezia* [*Death in Venice*], in spite of the fact that Visconti has justified the choice because he has identified Gustav von Aschenbach with Gustav Mahler.)[54] His choice works, even too well, but it tranquilly ignores all precedents and presupposes a virgin spectator, without historical memory or aesthetic conscience. (This is what disturbs me the most.) I do not know whether being a movie director necessarily implies a potent egocentrism, but to judge from the processes and from the results, one ought to say it does. They consider that everything is at their disposal. Music, painting, theater, and literature are all objects without historical identity that the directors can make use of, considering only what is most suitable for their needs. They are objects available as in an immense supermarket that holds a clearance sale at the end of the season. For every Kubrick who regulates the impact, there are many, too many, who are presumptuous (or ingenuous).

EM: In response to this point I will have to give an example from my experience. I was very, very young. I had graduated from the conservatory just a little while before, and, like so many other composer colleagues, I was looking for work. I went to do a tryout at the Accademia di Danza [Academy of Dance], run then by Mrs. Ruskaya. (I am not a great pianist, but what one had to play to accompany young girls who were dancing was a silly thing.) However, even before the test, there was a conversation. Mrs. Ruskaya told me that for one concert she had made two completely different choreographies, with different costumes and different scenery. For the first choreography, the music was the *Chaconne* by Bach; for the second, the music . . . was the *Chaconne* by Bach. And she said to me, "The audience did not realize that the music was the same." It was incredible, so much indifference and so much cynicism. . . . I did not bother to try out.

SM: Let's return to the external level. Even in their diversity, the examples with which we were just occupied demonstrate quite a . . . concordance between the climate of the narration and the characteristics of the music. We already mentioned briefly that the use (and abuse . . .) of asynchronism plays on dualisms: analogous/contrast, concordance/discordance, contextualization/decontextualization. In these dualisms, the epiphany of the author is at its maximum because it implies an exposed hermeneutic attitude. It induces the spectator to assume an analogous position, reflexive or at least interrogative. All this descends from Brecht, from well-recognized concepts of the epic theater and of alienation from which one can extract some analogies with the theoretical writings of Eisenstein.[55] It is clear that asynchronism is not an occasional find that a motion picture director adopts on a whim. Instead, it is the symptom of a precise conception. . . . All this has served to let me say that asynchronism is not a neutral technique but implies basic choices about which the composer also has to be knowledgeable.

Henry V (Kenneth Branagh, 1989)

In the infinite range of solutions pertaining to the external level I have chosen a singular . . . final example, an episode taken from *Henry V* of Kenneth Branagh, who is both the main protagonist and the director.[56] But before dealing with the film, I would like to examine an audio fragment,[57] because it will allow you to concentrate on exclusively musical characteristics. The composer, for those who do not know, is Patrick Doyle, and the orchestration, always important, but here in a particular way, is by Lawrence Ashmore, while the orchestra[58] has an exceptional director, Simon Rattle.

Here is music that I will define as having a low melodic, or . . . . thematic, profile. ("Melodic" and "thematic" are not synonyms. . . . In this case one ought to say "melodic," and in a little while you will understand why.) Notwithstanding the parsimonious means and in spite of its low melodic profile, the music communicates great intensity. The composition promises a development that then does not materialize, and yet it continues.

Unfortunately, I do not have the original score. Therefore, I have had to hazard a guess about certain instrumental attributions. . . . By listening, I have created a piano reduction, but it might not reflect exactly the original.[59] Diagramming, we obtain five parts:

1. Percussive figuration—pulsations
2. Harmonic progressions (in the form of a chorale)
3. Melodic parenthesis repeated and varied
4. Bridge (or response)
5. Repeat of 1 (varied instrumentally)—and so on

The piece does not conclude here, but what I have said will suffice for our purposes.

Having considered roughly the musical characteristics, we come to the film. The sequence to which this music is matched is long. Therefore, we might ask why Doyle didn't write a beautiful closed form with a nice melodic characterization or a strophic form of the A-B-A-B-C-B type, or even a theme with a lot of quick development. The answer is simple. In this film, the protagonist is (and ought to be) the Shakespearean text, and such musical procedures would carry the accompaniment too prominently into the foreground (I am not talking about the mix, but rather about the eloquence and the colloquial complexity of the music).

Motifs Instead of Themes

A little while ago I pointed to a problem of definition. I talked about a low thematic or melodic profile, opting for the second. Now I ought to clarify . . . the reason why it is advisable to make this distinction. In the cinematic sphere . . . extreme concern with the theme entails, in my opinion, a very risky discussion simply because there is not time usually to develop a theme. . . . To say it better, concern with the theme implies a utopian or idealistic situation. . . . If I say "theme," I ought to be thinking of a . . . formal musical development that follows. If it is not of the sonata type, it is at least of the variation type.

By convention we say "Lara's theme," "the jealousy theme," or "the desert theme" when we ought to say "Lara's motif," "the jealousy motif," or "the desert motif." Perhaps by labeling it thus, one risks aping the Wagnerian *leitmotiv*, but considering the analogy with certain formal musical functions, we would not be that far from the truth. On the other hand, even the nonmusical theme that they gave us in elementary school implied an unwinding (alias development). . . . Theme: What do I want to do when I am grown up? Unwinding . . . and here each one tries according to his or her capacity.

In music for the movies, however, this is what happens:

Theme: What do I want to do when I grow up?

Unwinding:
What do I want to do when I grow up?

> What do I want to do when I grow up?
> What do I want to do when I grow up?

et cetera, et cetera, according to the duration of the scene. In the best of the cases, the "unwinding" becomes:

> What do I want to do when I grow up?
> When I grow up, what do I want to do?
> Do I want to do something when I grow up?

The most able and courageous arrive at something like:

> . . . I want . . . to do . . . grown up
> (What . . . what . . . what)
> Grown up . . . to do . . . I want . . .

In situations that were very particular and almost unrepeatable, . . . Prokofiev and a few others finally told us what they wanted to do when they were grown up, but while their works are indispensable to know and study, they have not much to teach a composer who is working in the cinema *today*. This is precisely because, paradoxically, they have not written what is intended as the norm for film music in the context of a normal production. The lesson they have left us is clearly a very great lesson. It has a lot to teach us on the level of audiovisual interaction and dramaturgical mechanisms, but less about the composition process itself.

Today, in fact, one works for synthesis, and this leads us to another very interesting concept, economy of material. . . . When using an economy of material, one departs not so much from a theme as from a fragment, from a cell that can be elaborated and transformed enough so that it can be represented under another guise in a different context. In this sense, the Schoenbergian concept of *Grundgestalt* might come in handy.[60]

Henry V of Branagh

Turning again to Doyle, in this case we are dealing with King Henry's monologue from act 4, scene 3 that contains a prophecy. The music is not thematic and has a low melodic profile. Therefore, we are not able to talk about a "motif of something or other," since the music continually has to take stock of events and dialogue (and it does it extremely well). In the ultimate analysis, the melodic characteristics of the piece prevent the music from being singable and cannot sustain the representation of a defined object. It progresses, and not a little. It avoids any situation in which the process of growth would lead to a formal complication that might be to blame for taking the spectator's attention away from the text. (. . . In most cases, the Shake-spearean cinema is a sort of filmed theater.)

In its own way the monologue of King Henry behaves like a "crescendo" of exaltation. The music sustains it and inserts itself with light motivic and dynamic peaks "under" the text and in the pauses. It may seem rhetorical to you, but it is like a breeze that is at first discrete, whose always more intense gusts "swell" the spirit of King Henry and of his men. Note well the parsimo-ny of the compositional means and their scansion in relationship to the text—I was going to say they are "contrapuntal" (that is why there is not much counterpoint in the score). The skillfully made mix determines a unity of rare effectiveness, so much so that I feel like defining the episode as an excellent example of *melologo*, but you could categorize it more simply as an optimum example of the external level and of the use of implicit and explicit sync points.

I made a musical transcription from the soundtrack[61] that begins with the dialogue and follows. The beginning of King Henry's monologue coincides with measure 14. Other coincidences are indicated in the course of the mono-logue. Keep in mind that with the growing . . . musical dynamic there is an accompanying figurative dynamic that is represented by a mechanical track-ing shot. It follows, from left to right, and accompanies King Henry and his men, with some halts and cuts of montage that progressively bring us closer to his figure.

> Gloucester: Where is the King?
> Bedford: He went to observe their formation.
> Westmoreland: Of fighting men they have full three score thousand.
> Exeter: That's five to one. Besides, they are all fresh.
> Salisbury: 'Tis a fearful odds.
> Westmoreland: Oh, that we now had here but one
> 10,000 of those men in England that do no work today.
>
> [measure 14]
> King Henry: What's he that wishes so?
> My cousin Westmoreland? . . .
> No, my fair cousin. If we are marked to die, we are
> enough to do our country loss. And if to
> live, the fewer men the greater share of honor.
> God's will, I pray thee, wish not one man more.
>
> Rather proclaim it, Westmoreland, through my host,
> That he which hath no stomach to this fight,
> Let him depart; his passport shall be made,
> And crowns for convoy put into his purse:
> We would not die in that man's company,
> That fears his fellowship to die with us.

[measure 26]
This day is call'd—the feast of Crispian:
He that outlives this day, and comes safe home,
Will stand a tip-toe when this day is nam'd,
And rouse him at the name of Crispian.
He that shall see this day, and live old age,
Will yearly on the vigil feast his neighbors,

And say, "To-morrow is Saint Crispin's;"
Then will he strip his sleeve, and show his scars,
And say, "These wounds I had on Crispin's day."

[measures 36–37]
Old men forget; yet all shall be forgot,
But he'll remember, with advantages,
What feats he did that day. Then shall our names,
Familiar in their mouths as household words,—

Harry the King, Bedford, and Exeter,
Warwick and Talbot, Salisbury and Gloucester,
Be in their flowing cups freshly remember'd.
This story shall the good man teach his son;

And Crispin Crispian shall ne'er go by
From this day to the ending of the world,
But we in it shall be remember'd,—

[measures 45–46]
We few, we happy few, we band of brothers.
For he to-day that sheds his blood with me,
Shall be my brother; be he ne'er so vile,
This day shall gentle his condition:
And gentlemen in England, now a-bed,
Shall think themselves accurs'd, they were not here,
And hold their manhoods cheap, whiles any speaks,
That fought with us

[measures 53–54]
upon Saint Crispin's day.

By comparison, I remember so many of your student scores, which were sometimes well written but more often too charged, too present, too affirmative. With Doyle's music as an example . . . think about the possibility of working by subtraction more than by accumulation. His setting has the lightness that comes from the "said but not said." He starts a musical discourse that has the air of having been initiated previously. It is a procedure that guarantees great stamina and can exercise an eminent fascination. And if it is not clear what I am alluding to, look carefully at something by Mozart or

Brahms. . . . Of the former it should be enough to remember *The Magic Flute*, act 1, scene 12. An arioso of the officiating priest addressing Tamino jumps out splendidly from the recitative. Then it is repeated by the orchestra and chorus.[62] Of the second composer, . . . the attack of the first movement of the *Fourth Symphony* should be enough for you.

Music for Shakespearean Films—Music at the External Level but a Digression

At this point I would like to propose a comparison. Exactly a year ago I held a cycle of seminars at Irtem[63] on the music for films based on Shakespearean dramas. I discussed works by Olivier and Walton,[64] Welles and Lavagnino,[65] Kozintsev and Shostakovich,[66] Branagh and Doyle.[67] I even included a silent film, *The Life and Death of Richard III*, from 1912,[68] restored by the AFI and for the occasion assigned a new musical commentary by Morricone.[69] (For diverse motives that I will not explain now, I excluded the new reading by Zeffirelli with Rota and Morricone.)[70]

Let's examine the same king's prophecy episode from act 4, scene 3, but this time from *Henry V* by Laurence Olivier, with music by William Walton. . . . With respect to the predominance of the text, this is the most radical interpretation in the context of filmed theater. There is no musical commentary. I cannot talk at length about the characters of the film nor about the vision of the director, Olivier. Each film belongs properly to its own epoch and, in these two cases, to a certain conception of the cinema strongly conditioned by theatrical influences. I underline only the date, 1944. This *Henry V* assumed for the English a significance analogous to that in 1938 attributed by the Soviets to *Alexander Nevsky*.[71] It symbolized the defense of the homeland from the threat of Nazi invasion. Add to this, then, the prestigious presence of Olivier, one of the greatest actors of his time, and you will find perhaps an explanation for his style of recitation, so elegant and at times so "artificial" as to border on abstraction. It is in a deliberately fake scenic space, with visibly painted backdrops and rocks of papier-mâché that seem to have issued from a Giotto fresco. The battle is the exception. It was shot conventionally, like a mammoth production.

EM: Why wasn't music put in?

SM: I think the answer may be suggested by the fact that the length is still very theatrical. It is all another school. . . . Perhaps the director Olivier did not want music in order to concentrate the spectator's attention on the musicality of the actor Olivier's recitation. In any case . . . I alert you to the lack of a proper musical component. I do not know whether the metaphor of the music that swells the sail of the event and of the text of the Branagh version seemed fitting to you. I find it an extraordinary solution.

EM: It is very beautiful, but I would add one thing. We theorize, and it is right to do so, but then, in the cinema, strange things happen. Making *Amleto* (*Hamlet*) with Zeffirelli,[72] I was at the Moviola to analyze the film with the director, and the principal actor, Mel Gibson, was also there. At a certain point, we had arrived at the celebrated monologue, "To be or not to be . . ." I said, "I ought to write music, not necessarily melodic—perhaps consisting of chords." Gibson said to Zeffirelli, "But you think that my recitation needs musical support? You find it so insufficient?" As a result, the music written for that scene does not exist in the American version, while it is conserved in the Italian version. De Niro had a similar reaction in *C'era una volta in America*,[73] but in that case Leone did not pay attention to the actor's opinion. Now we are dealing with Olivier's *Henry V*.[74] . . . Who can say that the same thing didn't happen?

SM: It is a little different, because the director and principal interpreter were the same person. It is difficult to think of a divergence of opinion between the two of them. In any case, the music isn't there, but I maintain that the motive resides in the hypothesis that I just made. The director Olivier privileged the actor Olivier. As I pointed out a little while ago, in the economy of the whole film, the only moment in which the musician does his own work to the end is in the battle of Agincourt episode, because the model with which to compare it is the already-mentioned *Alexander Nevsky*,[75] the model to beat, and not only from the point of view of the film and musical realization.

Consult the first systematic study . . . on music in the cinema, issued in England in the fifties, translated also into Italian many years ago in the editions of *Bianco e Nero*.[76] The authors present an analysis of *Henry V* that recalls the audiovisual score for *Alexander Nevsky* deduced by Eisenstein[77] himself from the montage. Certainly the battle of Olivier–Walton does not have the force of the battle of Eisenstein–Prokofiev, notwithstanding the dynamic crescendo of the French cavalry, step, trot, gallop, charge . . . with so many dolly shots. Nor can the analysis of Manvell and Huntley confer more force to that scene, but it would be interesting to look at it again together.

It presents a series of sync points of the onomatopoeic type, to which I already referred, at the point where the English archers launch a swarm of arrows. It seems to me to be an example of an even slightly banal passage. In sum, it is a serious, commemorative, all very traditional external level. It represents an enslavement of the music to the image and has to do with the category of accompaniment more than that of commentary. However, above all in those years, there were concessions to the public in the stalls from which the cinema never refrained voluntarily.

On the contrary, the same episode in Branagh's version was realized with a very clever technique of photography and editing that lets us intuit a vast theater of battle, even though there are no scenes with masses of people in the true sense of the word. The certainty remains that Olivier did not want music where I believe anybody else would have put it.

EM: Naturally, we cannot question the authors in order to know their real intentions.

SM: No, this is certain, but it does not seem to me to be indispensable to do so. A historical-critical operation is based on deductive processes and inductive references. It is not based just on a single phenomenon but rather on context and relevant documentation. If one were to set a standard according to which a historical reconstruction could be made only with direct testimony, what could a medievalist do? If there are documents, they are welcome, but in any case they are evaluated prudently, because more than a few authors have "adjusted" reality to their pleasure, more or less in good faith. The important thing is a rigorous methodology, in which the final critical judgment springs from a historical investigation that is beyond reproach. . . .

Returning to our case and applying the reasoning made so far, my analysis of the Olivier-Walton association takes into account a general model drawn from all their collaborations and then compares it with the Shakespearean films of other authors. If one could deduce it and make a classification based on importance and on the presence of the components, one would expect the text of William Shakespeare to be in first place. The second place (but it could be a first *ex aequo*) would be for the actor Laurence Olivier. The third would be for the director Laurence Olivier. Only then would one choose the music of William Walton, which by its nature does not do much to impose itself, regardless of the exigency of the director. Having said that, I think of *Amleto*, in which the music, the little that there is, is never incisive.[78] I maintain that in Walton's case, he was using as a model the "entr'acte" or incidental music, and therefore the theater, more than film-musical commentary.

By comparison, the *Hamlet* of Kozintsev,[79] with music by Shostakovich, gives the measure of how much a Shakespearean film can be both cinema and powerful music while also paying the appropriate rightful tribute to its theatrical antecedents. Besides, Shostakovich had already written the stage music for *Hamlet*, and even this would be a very interesting comparison,[80] but we cannot make it here.

MEDIATED LEVEL

To explain the concept of the internal level and that of the external level, I resorted to the basic definitions of diegesis and extradiegesis. Therefore . . . , appealing to a terminology used in the analysis of literary texts, for the mediated level I now summon the so-called metadiegetic level.[81] . . . However-er, . . . I continue to utilize a term that refers . . . very clearly to a process of mediation that we will verify shortly through some examples. . . . It is precisely the mediated level that is without an equivalent term in any of the other audiovisual analytical theories that preceded mine.

By "mediated level," I mean a situation in which the character in a film expresses himself or herself not only and not so much through verbal lan-guage but rather through the music. In such a case, the music is not thought of or imposed from outside through the type of artifice that is universally accepted as coming from the musical commentary; rather, it belongs to the character, for some more or less explicit narrative reason. Thus, in the mani-festation of an episode with music ascribable to the mediated level, the spectator has the privilege of listening to the inner thoughts or perceptions of the character. It is a procedure like that of the voice-over, with the difference that instead of listening to words, one listens to music. Naturally, they cannot be thoughts in the form of verbal organization but must be emotions in a pure state, and obviously there is nothing better, more capable, than music to express them.

To say it another way, the mediated level is to the soundtrack as the subjective shot is to shooting technique. . . . The subjective shot forces the spectator to identify with the point of view of the character. It can be an easy solution and predictable, as in many thrillers, but it can also be dizzying, like the steadycam in *The Shining*[82] —the very low, wide angle shot at the height of the scene in which the baby rides on a tricycle along the long corridors of the great, deserted, but in a certain sense "inhabited," hotel.

If a character in a film exits from a bar in a state of intoxication and, walking in an alley, staggers, and if at that moment the motion picture came-ra frames that alley from a plausible prospective and sways, no one will doubt that he is dealing with a subjective perspective. But that same character can have a piece of music in his head that has already been heard in the film in another context. If it were to be presented again now in an unhinged form, rhythmically unstable, not perfectly in tune, it would be another example of the mediated level, this time more banal, tied to a process of physiological more than psychological mediation.

I emphasize the process of mediation in order to exhaust any eventual doubts about my choice of terminology. In every case it is music that existed previously in the film in another guise[83] and that in its definable manifesta-tion as mediated level is passed through the memory, the emotions, and the fantasy of the character. This is fundamental for the recognition of its function.

Already at this point three things ought to be clear. The first is the effectiveness[84] of the mediated level, where the presence of the music assumes a legitimization, a "spontaneity," that the external level does not ever have, even if we are used to the ruse. . . . In short, if all the music in the cinema were to intervene at the mediated and internal levels, Woody Allen's little scene with the harpist in the closet (with which I introduced the external level) would not make any sense, because when he first hears the music, it seems to be background music and thus is at the external level. Then it seems to represent his thoughts (mediated level), and then it turns out to be a real part of the scene and thus is at the internal level.

The second thing that should be clear has to do with the mediated level's design. Already during the screenplay phase of a production, the presence of music of this type needs to be called for in order to have the musical intervention at the mediated level assume the exact significance that is there. Or at least the diverse types of music in the film need to be planned and organized in such a way that the relations between the musical interventions are clear and unequivocal. This is more difficult, given the way most directors work, but if one is to make the relationships between the interventions clear and unequivocal, it must be done skillfully, and soon I will give a few examples.

The third thing that should be clear is perhaps the most important, because music at the mediated level has the power to interact with the dramaturgical structure. It assumes a primary role because it becomes a protagonist.[85]

Examples of Music at the Mediated Level

Die Wunderbare Luege der Nina Petrovna (The Wonderful Lies of Nina Petrovna)

The first example of music at a mediated level comes from the silent film to which I have already made reference. It confirms the fact that in the silent cinema a syntax was already established. Silent films arrived at the beginning of the sound film era with fundamental models already formed.

In *Die Wunderbare Luege der Nina Petrovna* . . . Nina Petrovna is played by Brigitte Helm. (Some of you, at least, will remember her in *Metropolis*.)[86] The waltz has a very obvious leitmotif function. . . . In an intertitle, Nina herself defines it as "my waltz." It is even presented at the internal level in a sort of playback *ante litteram*. (No one will be surprised to hear that in the silent cinema there were numerous cases of musical sync points, a source of joy and torment to orchestral conductors.)

The sequence to which I want now to draw your attention[87] belongs to the same episode that I already examined when talking about the internal level. It develops, therefore, at the same café concert. . . . Nina is accompanied by a lover, a colonel in the Cossacks.[88] Her attention will be attracted to . . . a young cadet, Mikhail.[89] In a preceding scene, he paraded his horse under her balcony, and she threw him a flower.

From the beginning of the sequence, the music consists of two rhythmically differentiated themes that alternate. Attributed to the café orchestra, opportunely framed in the background, it consists mainly of a waltz of multiple articulations and a *Tempo di Polacca*, which adapts itself with a light hand to the evolving of the events.[90]

Here we are confronted by the music of the internal level that seemed at first music of the external level type. . . . It plays with the ambiguity of the commentary. Therefore, it is related by marriage to the external level. The colonel realizes the relationship between Mikhail and Nina from their exchange of looks and is jealous without wanting to show it. He investigates. Nina lies, "He is my friend from infancy. We often played together as babies. We constructed sand castles." To this last intertitle, while Nina starts to mime emphatically infantile gestures, the theme in the *Tempo di Polacca* stops suddenly. It gives the precedence to a *Poco più vivo* section that has all the characteristic elements of a "Ring Around the Rosie" or of a nursery rhyme of the sort: "Oh che bel castello marcondiro-ndiro-ndèllo" ("O what a beautiful castle marcondiro-ndiro-ndèllo").[91]

The music is identified with Nina's lie and her expressivity. Therefore, the music does not comment on the episode but *interacts* with the scenic action, taking the responsibility then to fuse with the preceding theme and to disappear with the end of the fake infantile evocation. In reality, the solution is even more refined, because the comment of the colonel ("A fascinating falsehood") induces Nina to show an ostentatiously pouting expression that emphasizes the continuity between the evocation of infancy and actual infantilism, so much so that at this point the *Poco più vivo* music returns for the last time.

Colonel: "Is he an acquaintance?"

Nina: "Who? The young candidate down there?"

Nina: "He is a childhood friend. We played often together as babies."

Nina: "We constructed sand castles."

Colonel: "A fascinating falsehood."

Let's pass on now to a film that is much more contemporary. . . . You will see that every author interprets the possibilities offered by the mediated level in a different way. And when I say "author," I allude above all to the director, not to diminish the role of the composer, but to confirm beyond the shadow of a doubt that the author of a film is the director and that an intervention of this type presupposes above all a precise directorial will.

And it is obvious . . . that he who has realized this type of solution has not thought, "Now we have made a good mediated level for the music." Apart from the fact that for easy-to-guess motives a director is inclined to read many narratives and few essays, I would say that he has acted more or less from instinct, more or less consciously. Creative processes vary from individual to individual, and the most cultivated are not always the ones that have the most success. What is important is that the result is consistent with the other solutions adopted and is therefore unequivocal. In order to pull out general elements of technical and aesthetic appraisal, we need to research these constants, if possible without forcing, rationalizing, and contorting them into an artificial system.

Caro diario (Dear Diary) (Nanni Moretti, 1994)

The next example comes from Nanni Moretti's *Caro diario* (*Dear Diary*).[92] It may seem strange to refer to him again because we already have spoken about him in an uncomplimentary way. He is certainly not an author that concedes much to music, above all at the external level. Obviously, empathetic mechanisms are not included among his concessions. . . . But in *Caro diario* music has a greater space than in his preceding films. This is particularly true in one episode that is atypical because of the poetic intensity that it expresses . . . without rhetoric, . . . with a lot of moderation, almost modesty.

Moretti entrusts this scene to a fragment of the celebrated *Cologne Concert* by Keith Jarrett.[93] Moretti, on a Vespa, reaches the beach at Ostia and the place where Pasolini was murdered. Beyond the private, intimate meanings that the director attributes to it,[94] I find this solution very thought provoking because I believe Moretti succeeds in universalizing the personal. On this terrain, he overtakes a great director like Fellini, who many times "imposed" . . . something well known (and often cheap) that one could not get out of one's head but that one could not always unhook from its virtual universe.

Certainly Jarrett helps, because force and neutrality coexist in his language. Perhaps it would be better to say that it has an intensity and expressive polyvalence . . . that enables the listener to interpret it however he or she believes best. But this does not suffice to explain the cine-musical force of this extremely beautiful episode.

I am not yet talking about the mediated level. . . . In the eyes of the spectator, the relationships between the *Cologne Concert* and the protagonist-director live and die in the Vespa-on-the-beach episode.[95] . . . To consider it a mediated level or point of view, it would be necessary for there to be a preceding episode that would demonstrate Moretti as intent on listening to the same musical composition at an internal level. However, we are confronted by an open identification between mise-en-scène and reality (Moretti the protagonist and Moretti the director). One could say that all the preexisting music that does not appear at an internal level could be considered, in a certain sense, as being at a mediated level. It belongs to the musical-affective baggage of the director, who is not able to prevent it from belonging to the musical memory of the protagonist. It is a fascinating hypothesis, but at the moment I do not want to go there.

While using the same line of reasoning with which I have just emphasized the identification between the two faces of the film (direction and interpretation), I now arrive at the episode within the Vespa-on-the-beach scene that contains an example of music in the category of an unequivocal mediated level. It is where there is a dance floor in the open. However, . . . first I would like to make note of the references to dance that do not seem casual.

Beyond the sequence with which we are occupied, many of you will remember another point in this film. Moretti, being nosy about an apartment, uses the excuse of needing an inspection. He declares that he wants to shoot a film about a Trotskyite pastry maker of the fifties. Immediately afterward he says that it will be a musical. The proposal (apparently strange and improvised to draw out the embarrassment) takes shape . . . and demonstrates an "ill-concealed" attraction for a cinematic genre, the musical, which is almost completely extraneous to the Italian tradition. Here, just for a moment, I suspend the discussion about the mediated level, making a digression that finally ought not to appear to you to be one, because it will hook back up to the discussion of levels.

I confess to you that it took me years to understand that the musical is "an absolute type of cinema." I am not talking only out of a rational conviction but out of both rational and emotive involvement at the same time. It is an aspect that we have just touched on slightly in the first part of the audiovisual analysis, without being able to stop for so many masterworks of the genre, from *Top Hat*, to *West Side Story*, to *On the Town*, to *Hello, Dolly!*[96] (including even *Carosello napoletano* [*Neapolitan Carousel*]),[97] and that unfortunately we don't have time to go into more deeply.[98]

I brought up the musical in order to tie the allusions in the film by Moretti to a simple reflection. The musical is coexistence and hence the annulment of the levels. It enjoys a nearly absolute form of liberty with respect to the common audiovisual syntax. (This is true even if from one musical to another certain hierarchies are created, certain relations of reference from which they could be derived.) This liberty can be found even in films that have nothing to do with the musical.

Il bidone of Fellini[99] is a good example of it. . . . The music has a conventional job at the external level, but at a certain point one of the garbage-can men[100] whistles the same motif that until that moment was used at the external level, a music of which the character could not be conscious.[101] This is a procedure from the musical, and something analogous happens in *Caro diario*.

During the excursion on the Vespa, a typical South American dance is audible with a very high mix. It would seem a case of the external level, were it not for the fact that Moretti the director adds a dance in the opening to the scene. The same music continues without a cut and appears to be performed live, in sync (well, that is, in playback). It is an example of a common internal level that, however, has the ability to make us read the preceding part in a different way. Did Moretti the protagonist know already what he would have listened to from then on? Not he, but Moretti the director, yes, and from that moment the two are the same person. . . . This is why we returned to the previous point, . . . not only . . . because the bizarre participation of the director-actor in the execution of the piece should not escape attention,[102] but also because although it is not a musical, very little is lacking to make it one.

Moretti distances himself from the dance, but that mambo continues to be heard for a while, until he arrives at the Spinaceto neighborhood. We are therefore in the presence of a composition at the internal level that has had an anticipation and a coda at the mediated level. Finally, during the continuation of the trip on the Vespa, immediately after Spinaceto, a new musical presence enters the soundtrack, this time one with an oriental intonation. The protagonist follows it by very visibly oscillating on the scooter and snapping his fingers. Here the mediated level is still more evident because of the sync points, but the substance does not change. However, Moretti could come here and (as in a film by Woody Allen in which Marshall McLuhan materializes and a little angrily corrects the inaccuracies that have been attributed to him) tell us that in *his* film he had wanted simply to listen to and have the music listened to that he liked.

Allonsanfàn

In the course of the section "Images and Music at the 50th Biennial Exhibit of Cinema at Venice . . .," I encountered the Taviani brothers. I showed the final sequence and the end titles of *Allonsanfàn*[103] to them and to the public. The music was by Morricone.

This final sequence and the end titles had one of the many obvious and successful examples of music at the mediated level. I must add that it was precisely on the occasion of the biennial that the Taviani brothers declared their love,[104] an "impossible" love, for the musical. Attention—I am not suggesting a direct relation between this cinematic genre and the mediated level. I observe simply that some authors who are fascinated by the musical tend to break the conventions and the commonplaces of the music-image relationship.

To analyze this sequence of *Allonsanfàn*, initially I referred to the screenplay that was deduced from the montage.[105] However, the indications regarding the sound, and the music in particular, were too approximate, and I had to correct and integrate them.[106] Without being able to recapitulate the events that precede the sequence, I limit myself to recalling that we are in 1816. The nobleman Fulvio Imbriani (Marcello Mastroianni), already a Napoleonic official and ex-Jacobite, finds himself involved against his will with a group of men in a secret society, the Carbonari. The society is animated by revolutionary ideals in an expedition to the south of the peninsula. Between cowardice and skepticism, Fulvio betrays his companions, warning the parish priest of their intentions. Peasants confront the Sublimi brothers, who are members of the secret society, and massacre them. Only one is saved, Allonsanfàn, who, wounded in the head and in a state of shock, encounters Fulvio.

One needs to follow carefully both the dialogue and the musical entrances, because they are closely related to what the two men say to each other. Allonsanfàn raves and tells Fulvio of a fraternal encounter with the peasants that culminated in a collective dance, the same that the group had rehearsed during the preparations for the expedition. . . . With (A) I indicate the rhythmic scansion, with (B) the melodic motif.[107]

After the first agitated exchange in which Fulvio, incredulous, tries to bring his companion back to reason, Allonsanfàn asks him to be patient and adds, "I will tell you everything from the beginning." At this point, with the mix at a low level, one hears a series of rhythmic chords that introduce the tarantella (A) by Morricone. The music stops and then begins again, entering with the first melodic segment (B), repeated without progression, in coincidence with Allonsanfàn's account. At this point there is a rapid musical crescendo that covers Allonsanfàn's words.

Maybe it would be better to say that the music substitutes for the words. This is why one can talk of the formalization of this substitution of the music for the words, the thoughts, and in this case the raving of the character. The next signal is even more unequivocal. From the foreground shot and reverse shot used up to this point, one passes to a long shot in which Fulvio repels Allonsanfàn's embrace.

Immediately afterward, one returns to a foreground shot in which Allonsanfàn has an instant of confusion and silence and lowers his gaze. The music suspends the phrase and goes silent in sync, but immediately afterward the man shakes himself and with renewed energy begins to narrate again. However, we do not hear the words. In sync with the motion of his lips the tarantella picks up from the first melodic segment. This subjective sound is at the mediated level. The subjective visual follows and completes the materialization of the utopia/imagined scene. The Sublimi brothers and the peasants, mixed up, dance together.

Finally, Fulvio throws a pail of water in Allonsanfàn's face, shouting at him that it is not true, and, in sync, the music stops. One can realize such an extraordinary example of the mediated level, in which the montage and the mixing concur in such a decisive way, only when the presence of the music is predicted in the screenplay or at least the treatment. It presupposes a sensibility and also a certain musical preparation on the part of the director that can create a few problems for the composer.

EM: Yes. The Taviani brothers want to know everything beforehand. They want to establish what the composer ought to do and what one ought to avoid. I have stopped working with them for this reason, because I do not have the fun and the satisfaction of finding the solution for the scene myself. But they are people of great value.

SM: A shame. It is another paradox. First we have lamented the indifference and the ignorance of directors vis-à-vis music. Then, when we find two that are neither indifferent nor ignorant . . . I understand that your personality and your habit of working with a lot of autonomy should not suffer, but I understand them, too. I admire a specific audiovisual project in which the music assumes a primary dramaturgical role, but I realize that such a result excludes the possibility of the composer's having much interpretative liberty.

Use of the Mediated Level in the Taviani Brothers' Films

San Michele aveva un gallo (Saint Michael Had a Rooster)

This type of solution, that is, music at the mediated level, represents a constant in the cinema of the Taviani brothers. I think of *Il prato* [*The Lawn*][108] and even before of *San Michele aveva un gallo* [*Saint Michael Had a Rooster*].[109] In the latter, the protagonist (an intense Giulio Brogi) is an anarchist who has been captured following a failed act of insurrection. An instant before his execution, his death sentence is commuted to life imprisonment. At this point, the interior or manifest "monologue" assumes a fundamental role. To avoid madness in his solitary confinement, the anarchist imagines encounters and dialogue with companions. Therefore, the spectator has a way of entering into his thoughts and into his fantasies almost constantly. But all this is anticipated with great effectiveness in the first part of the film, in the scene in which Giulio is conducted to the scaffold. Here is a fragment of the screenplay realized from the montage, to which I have made some additions.[110]

Scene 16—village—exterior—morning

The two-wheeled cart drags Giulio toward the scaffold.

Ring of a bell.

Other bell rings and immediately afterwards:

GIULIO: "Eh, no bells for my funeral. No death knells."

Immediately funeral chorale enters (duration 11″) and following:

GIULIO: "Of music, yes, but not this. I know which . . ."

2″ of silence, then:

A fragment of the Capriccio italiano (5″ duration) enters, interrupted brusquely:

GIULIO: (sadly) "We are close, right? I know the way. Tell my companions that I want festive music and that it should enter only when the cart enters the piazza."

Strokes of the bell.

Full shot from above. The cart enters the piazza of the execution.

Immediately the *same fragment of the Capriccio italiano of Tchaikovsky enters*.

Now, as it pertains to the mediated level, the concept of the author's absence ought to be clearer, since in this case the choice of music literally depends on the character in the film. The musical rhetoric is its own autocelebratory rhetoric.

Il Prato (The Lawn)[111]

Il prato also contains an episode of the audiovisual subjective and therefore of the mediated level. In this case, however, unlike what we saw in *Allonsanfàn*, where the dramaturgical carrier is the music, we are confronted by a "closed" episode, almost a pretext to cross the border into one absolute, choral musical dimension (a . . . euphemistic way of saying once more, "the musical").

Following a fall, the feminine protagonist, Antonia, is in a feverish state. To avoid a hemorrhage, she is supposed to stay awake. Her lovers[112] try to prevent her from going to sleep. One of the two tells the fable of the magic flute, and at this point in her nightmare Antonia assumes the magic flute player role. She makes the king, the courtiers, and her countrymen, who have offended her, dance at breakneck speed . . .

Tre colori—Film blu (Three Colors—Blue) (Krzysztof Kieslowski, 1993)

Now I would like to move to *Three Colors—Blue* of Krzysztof Kieslowski, my final example of the mediated level.[113] When I first saw it in Venice in 1993, . . . *Film blu* shook me up. It was really remarkably important, something that the critics . . . recognized, and it appeared fundamentally grounded in terms of the dramaturgy, narratological structure, and implicit use of symbols. Its cine-musical processes were what I had defined almost twenty years before as the mediated level. Even more, Zbigniew Preisner's music throughout the whole film could be defined as being at a sort of global mediated level and therefore was without question the film's protagonist.

It would require a separate seminar to show you an analysis of all the relations, the allusions, the anticipations, and the recurrences entrusted to the music's presence, but such a complete presentation is not possible now. . . . However, one cannot confirm the primary dramaturgical function of the music without knowing the events of the film. Therefore, I will resort to an expedient, reading to you the partial synopsis of *Three Colors—Blue* from the catalogue for the Biennale in Venice.[114] However, I invite you to read the original screenplay as well. There you will notice that, notwithstanding the modifications made in the course of the shooting and the editing, the musical function is predicted in an unusually precise way.[115]

A terrible auto accident has upset the existence of Julie (Juliette Binoche). She escaped with one or two scratches but lost her daughter and her husband, Patrice, one of the greatest contemporary composers. Julie would like to commit suicide, but changes her mind at the last minute. The death of Patrice resonates greatly in the cultural world. Responding to the journalist of a magazine for a niche market, Julie denies that traces exist of the last composition that her husband was working on, the *Concerto for the Unification of Europe*. In reality, she will be the one that destroys what she thinks is the only manuscript. At home, Julie prepares her isolation from the world. She throws into the trash the cassette from the telephone answering machine and her address book. She empties her daughter's room. At the reading of the will by the notary public, she renounces a great part of Patrice's inheritance in favor of her brother-in-law. She doesn't want to need anything from anybody. But the magazine journalist suspects that the author of the music that made Patrice

famous was really Julie. And Patrice's young assistant, Olivier (Benoît Ré-
gent), tries to convince her to finish the grand *Concerto per l'Europa* with
him.

Obviously . . . in order to leave the pleasure of discovering the rest to the
spectator, the synopsis from the Venetian catalogue finishes at this point.
And the rest is that Julie tries to remake her life by moving to a popular
quarter of Paris, by making new friends (like the beautiful Sandrine, the
neighbor who performs in a sex show),[116] and by trying to destroy thereby
whatever ties she had with the past. But the connection is not suppressible
and manifests itself always in a musical form. The more Julie dedicates
herself to other activities, the more the unfinished music assaults her, surprises her, shocks her. It is a vital energy that wants to survive and that, little
by little, will induce her to complete the unfinished composition. There is
more, obviously, but I have to cut it off here even if it doesn't deserve such
treatment.

The unfinished composition manifests itself initially in fragments that are
neither immediately recognizable nor associated with the source (in short,
there is no didactic forcing). Only in the finale will the music appear complete, recalling visually, as in an ideal embrace, the diverse presences that
have animated the story: every one of her existential conditions, inscribed
between the advent of a new life (the son of Patrice and of his lover, at the
fetal stage) and the end of another life (Julie's mother). And it is not an
accident that the text utilized in the *Concerto per l'Europa* belongs to passages from the first epistle of Paul to the Corinthians: "If I speak in the
tongues of men and of angels, but have not love, I am only a resounding gong
or a clanging cymbal."[117] I find this summary solution very sincere, particularly intense, and not at all rhetorical. It has a vague relationship to the
catwalk finale from Fellini's *8½* and the finale from Bergman's *The Seventh
Seal*,[118] even if the context, the linguistic intonation, and the spiritual intentions are profoundly different.

But we are coming to the fundamental point. In the film there is no music
until Julie observes the ceremony of exhumation of her husband and daughter on a little monitor in the hospital. That funeral music, played at the
internal level by a small group of wind instruments, anticipates the thematic
beginning of Patrice's not yet completed composition. The first musical manifestation of the mediated level arrives when Julie, still in the hospital, is
awakened from a state of drowsiness by the same measure of the funeral
music, but this time for full orchestra, while she is illuminated by a blue light
(obviously, this will be a recurring chromatic symbolism). Released from the
hospital and having returned home, she enters into the music room and
approaches the piano, upon which she finds a musical sketch. The same
incipit sounds in a piano version, without her having touched the keyboard.

Later Julie returns to the room to read that sketch, and we read it with her because a subjective shot frames the musical staves in macro detail . . . and runs sometimes along the few measures, alternating with a foreground shot of Julie. The musical sketch is short, but Julie repeats the phrase in her mind until, to liberate herself, she makes the lid of the piano fall all of a sudden, and this causes an interruption in the soundtrack.[119]

Life, its continuity and its renewal, besieges Julie in different ways and circumstances . . . but it is the music that prevails. It comes at night while she is seated on the stairs of the palace where she has gone to live (vocal instrumental fragment and blue light). It comes when she is in a café and encounters a young man who was a witness to the accident. (There is a fragment associated with a dissolve to black, as a subjective shot of her eyes, either closed or looking wide open into the abyss.) It comes when she exits from the water of the deserted swimming pool to which she goes habitually (someone's unexpected and powerful entrance paralyzes her movements). As if this were not sufficient, there is an enigmatic traveling recorder player who is stationed in front of the café she frequents habitually. He intones the development of her husband's composition. It corresponds to the vocal part (the text of the Apostle Paul), while in a later scene this musician will play the motif that we know from the beginning.

Obviously, this music does not want to die. Is it the spiritual patrimony of the entire human race? What more is there to say? . . . It does not embarrass me to speak of being moved to tears. In fact, if the emotion survives an analytical and therefore lucid approach, I am proud of it and am very grateful to the authors that provoked it in me.

Apropos the work of Preisner, over time I have collected critical evaluations that are couched in terms of a certain delusion that Preisner's music is not of the avant-garde type. I do not agree. Perhaps once in a lifetime a film music composer has an opportunity that is as charged with great responsibility and as exalted as this. I have the impression that his music was evaluated by his critics according to the usual parameters of the commentary-type score, while in this case we are at another level.

As regards the musical language, the aspect that has provoked the most perplexity, I find that Preisner's choice is faithful to the subject and to the context. The solemnity of the funeral transmitted over the television, the conservatory assignment (deducible from one of the first scenes, in which Patrice's assistant collects the dead man's papers in a sumptuous studio), the commission received for such a celebrated composition, and the interest of the press all locate the figure of Patrice in an academic more than an avant-garde context. Behind the façade of the French setting, there is a Polish director and a Polish composer, whose point of reference is presumably Szymanowski or Lutoslawski rather than Penderecki. This conclusion is reinforced by the totally cinematic prudence with which the contemporary music is employed.[120] In short, for all these reasons, it is unthinkable that Patrice would be conceived as being able to write like Boulez.

TRANSITIONS BETWEEN THE LEVELS

The Duelists (Ridley Scott)

Now that we have clarified the dramaturgical functions of each of the levels, we can demonstrate their development and their global or partial use in a single narrative context. We can take into account some factors like the mix, quality, and spatial disposition of the sound that can influence the result, sometimes even decisively.

Let's begin with Ridley Scott's *The Duelists*.[121] Still very far away from *Blade Runner*,[122] his masterwork, it is a very interesting first film which in the use of photography, of filters, of light, and of the extremely elegant and meticulous recreations of the environment demonstrates a debt to Kubrick's *Barry Lyndon*.[123] Many of the scenes contain references to actual paintings, and the faces are perhaps too superficially beautiful. The story involves an absurd challenge between two Napoleonic officials, interrupted and revived many times in the course of fifteen years. The music is by Howard Blake. As usual, the leitmotif of the film is anticipated in the opening titles, but it is an extremely brief appearance, about 40 seconds in length. A more extensive version returns in the end titles.

For my analysis, I extrapolate three fragments from the first part of the film, with consequent cuts of the intermediate scenes. The cuts do not compromise one's understanding of the image/sound relationships.

In the first fragment, we are confronted with a typical example of music at the internal level. A medical official, friend of Lieutenant Armand D'Hubert,[124] enjoys playing the transverse flute (a four-keyed wood instrument that I think fits perfectly with the year 1800, when the story begins), and he plays it as he is able—that is, pretty badly. This "realism" is important,[125] . . . but for the developments that the director wants to attribute to this musical appearance, it is not enough that the spectator can establish its source. It is important to notice the way in which the sound has been recorded, naked and crude, without reverb, as it really would resonate in a room. Therefore, notice that a choice of the type of execution and of acoustic are related to each other.

In the second fragment, at the end of a subsequent conversation between the two friends, the medical official begins to play the flute, but after a foreground shot of him (an extremely brief playback that lasts a little more than one second) there is a cut. The subsequent shot shows the exterior of a palace under floodlights and the window in the same apartment illuminated with an optical tracking shot that widens the field. Here it is very important to note two things. The entrance of the flute is presented with a much more stable and in-tune sonority than in the preceding fragment. From the cut onward, the sound gains in quality and sense of space contemporaneously with an acoustic dissolve that accompanies the optical tracking shot. This is the extremely well-taken-care-of transition from an internal level to another, more ambiguous one, which is prepared—and prepares us—for its definitive transformation into an external level.

In the third fragment, set in Hapsburg a year later, Armand encounters an old acquaintance, a prostitute[126] whom he treats with gallantry, almost affection. There is a cut to the bedroom of the official's apartment, where the couple is having intimate relations. After a brief conversation about the acquaintances they have in common, the two begin to make love, and the musical motif returns, this time in the strings, at a typical external level. That is all there is here, but it does not seem inconsequential to me. To give us this external level within the narration, therefore excluding the frame of the titles, Scott has used nineteen minutes with a careful preparatory progression, based fundamentally on the quality and mixing of the sound. This does not take into account that a recurrent motif, a main theme born from an internal level, assumes a credibility without equal.

Per qualche dollaro in piu' (*For a Few Dollars More*) (Sergio Leone, 1965)

The next example is from *Per qualche dollaro in più*, the second collaboration between Leone and Morricone.[127] The scene is that of the "triello," a duel between three people, according to a new word invented by the director. I believe that everyone has seen the film, at least on videocassette (even if this is not the same as seeing it in the theater); therefore, it will suffice to recall the narrative elements that are identified with the musical ones.

Two identical musical watches give rise to everything. One belongs to Colonel Mortimer, the other to his sister.[128] In a flashback, immediately after the murder of her husband, we see Mortimer's sister violated by a Mexican bandit, the Indian. During the rape the sister takes her own life, and that gesture disturbs the bandit. He morbidly reads her watch, listening to it either in order to pronounce clearly his pistol duels or in the moments when he is obliterated by drugs.

I summarize for brevity's sake. The music produced by the watch (obtained with a celeste) is recognizable at the internal level not only because of the gesture of the character, who opens the cover to activate the music-box mechanism, but also because of the sound, which is presented by itself, without any rhythmic or harmonic support. However, for the moments when the Indian is under the effect of drugs (a psychophysical, exalted state shown with photographic effects), this same sound is transformed. It is half-covered, wavering (harmonics in the strings, elaborated electroacoustically), and anyway more full bodied. Evidently we have a mediated level. Finally, after the motif is associated obsessively with the character of the bandit, it becomes his leitmotif. It is appropriated by a recurrence of the original gesture.

The alliance between Mortimer and the Monk (Clint Eastwood) is casual. The former wants to vindicate his sister's murder while the latter is a bounty hunter. Anyway, in the final showdown with the Indian, Mortimer comes unarmed and is subjected to the rite of the music-box watch: "When the music ends . . ." This phrase is not new. It is a good example of psychoperceptive "blackmail" of the spectator, who is constrained to identify with the hearing of the designated victim. Above all, one is constrained to assimilate the enlargement of the musical forces, which have exited from a certain degree of musical "realism" as if one were still dealing with an internal level.

The evolution is noteworthy. As the sound of the music box is about to stop, it gives way to another. In a full shot of the dusty open space, the theater for the duel, a detail shot of the bounty hunter's hand enters. It holds the other watch, which has been taken from Mortimer. (Even after many years, I still find this sudden unexpected change, this play of distance and closeness, extraordinary.) The Monk says, "You were not very attentive, old man." What follows . . . you know. To sum up, in the beginning the music is at the internal level, and the first growth that follows (light chordal support from the strings, percussion from the sound box of a guitar) could be understood legitimately as a leitmotif-type reworking of the original proposal for the Mexican, that is, music of a mediated level type.

I . . . recognize that its dramaturgical function is not as explicit, unequivocal, or, in other words, decisive as we have seen and felt in preceding examples. Here the process of identification between character and music is more quantitative than qualitative. This is without counting that it could be taken back to a necessary intermediate degree of orchestral growth, to a simple function of connection between the internal and external levels.

This brings me . . . to the moment in which the trumpet (or the organ, depending on the episode) articulates the Bach grace note (mordent). In every way, the aspect that I find the most successful is the bonding of the spectator to the musical event through the levels. . . . It is fundamental to remember the reabsorption of the musical ensemble, or rather the return to the thin sonority of the music box, that heralds the extraction of the pistols in the final part of the scene. Represented by the most impudent and artificial of external levels, the trespassing on the violent and autocelebratory rhetoric of the confrontation appears now as a momentous "license," inscribed between the initial "realism" and the final "realism" of the music box. One can only regret the overall range. If there had been a still greater expansion, the growth could have been more progressive.

EM: It would have required much more footage.

SM: Still another time that there was not enough film shot to allow for a remedy of the situation during the editing phase. . . . I have not been able to emphasize until now the joints, the metrical analysis, between the insertions of dialogue in the form of ritual sentence and musical semiphrases. Here is one example to demonstrate all of them: "Indian, you know the game," and immediately the trumpet enters.

EM: I would like to emphasize one thing above all the others that Professor Miceli has said. If the musical intervention is predicted in the shooting script and the director shoots knowing it ahead of time, then everything will turn out well. If instead the music results from an improvisation made afterwards, with decisions that are made when the director or composer is in front of the Moviola, or even by the composer alone, a good result is less likely. In my opinion, the music in *The Duelists* (Scott, 1977)[129] is wasted because it does not have the space to expand.

SM: One has it in what follows. Here I have wanted to demonstrate only the genesis, the transition from the internal to the external levels.

EM: Yes, yes. But the third fragment is really entirely too brief to allow one to clarify the musical idea well.

SM: I don't agree. At that point, the development of the musical idea is not important, and it will have a way to express itself better further on. Have you seen *The Duelists*? . . . There, I believe that your conviction depends on the fact that you haven't seen the whole thing. Certainly if you judge the scene in isolation, as a composer, naturally you will find that the music has been sacrificed. But you ought to take into account the fact that the scene is brief. The sex act is a foreseen epilogue, lacking in particular meanings, and the prostitute is not the woman of his life. To give major space to the music would have signified an importance that the scene did not require. The fact that a man and a woman are making love does not mean necessarily that the music ought to interpret it in a positive way or with more extensive means. For example, and I have even written it,[130] I have never understood why you and Leone reserved such a "positive" and even "romantic" treatment for the bitter intercourse and blackmail of Jill and Frank in *C'era una volta il West*.

EM: In the cinema there is an element of chance that is well accepted, whether by the composer or the director. I am thinking of certain unpredictable solutions that happen only after the music has been composed. We let these miraculous events go. Sometimes they come from a director's intuition, other times from the composer, at times even from the editor, who can come up with an idea to put the music at a certain point to surprise the composer and director. At that point one looks, one listens, and one decides whether to leave it alone, as, for example, in the finale to *Allonsanfàn*. Those two orchestral and choral interventions are heard very briefly, piercing.

SM: That is another solution which I think was unfortunate. I always wondered how it came about.

EM: I had not written for that scene, I wrote for a preceding situation. . . . The Taviani brothers put it there, and I thought, "Well, okay . . ." Perhaps they wanted to give a great blow to the stomach of the spectator. It could have been a novelty, because one does not hear in the cinema pieces that are so short, fast, and traumatic.

SM: But it really damages the essential nature of the film. It is an excessive and too invasive external level. It is more artificial and extraneous than one could possibly imagine. The shuffling of the mass of farmers that arrive menacingly and the whistling of the wind. The attack of the tarantella in the opening titles of *Allonsanfàn*[131] sufficed.

EM: As I said, often one has to improvise.

SM: Certainly, extemporaneity also plays a role in the creative act, and hyperdeterminism is not by itself a guarantee of success for the final result.[132] . . . We have already touched on this point, but perhaps we should reconfirm it. Read the theoretical writings of Eisenstein and then the reconstruction of Eisenstein and Prokofiev's developmental phases for *Alexander Nevsky*.[133] They, too, improvised, devised extemporaneous solutions. But subject the analysis to examination. These improvised solutions prove to a degree to be a consistent part of the general picture. The "secret" is all there, in the consistency.

Naturally, there is always someone who, occupying himself with these things, misunderstands. To write freely without verifying is an extremely simple thing. (One makes mistakes even when documenting oneself; imagine what can happen without such documentation.) Take the famous audiovisual diagram of *Alexander Nevsky*.[134] I don't even bother with the books that define it as an "audiovisual score for the realization." Nothing is more false. Eisenstein made that diagram a posteriori and constructed it as part of a very evident formalist conception that has nothing to do with the operation of the film, improvisation included.

One needs to distinguish. To improvise is a good concept, but if I apply it to Sergei Eisenstein, I cannot apply it in the same way to a minor Italian director like Sergio Corbucci. But I have a suspicion that I feel always and that I give to you as such. . . . I suspect that in the Italian cinema the improvisation of the Taviani brothers (or of Sergio Leone, or others) has some point of contact with the improvisation of Dario Argento[135] or Carlo Vanzina.[136] There is a common base of craftsmanship that includes genial intuition, great skill (referring to Leone and to the Taviani brothers), and a shoddier more-or-less-ism.

Henry V (Branagh)

Let's pass now to the final example of a transition between levels, for which we turn to a musician and a director who have already excited our admiration, Doyle and Branagh. We deal again with *Henry V*[137] and more precisely with the hymn of thanksgiving, *Non nobis, Domine*, after the battle.

We begin with the long single shot. I think all of you know what it is, and I remember that I already called it to your attention, even if only in passing.[138] It involves a way of shooting that does not resort to the solution of continuity. They shoot without a break. It requires a virtuosity that does not resort to editing. All is more fluid, more connected, and it assumes great importance for the music. In this episode, immediately after the spiritual proposition expressed by King Henry, the long single shot coincides with the soldier who begins to sing by himself (internal level)[139] and goes forward until the ultimate seconds, at which point there is a break and a foreground shot of King Henry. As we are looking at a scene involving masses of people, the only one in the whole film, you can intuit the difficulty that justifies my discourse about its virtuosity. But I am not talking about an exhibition of cleverness for its own sake.

Note the double movement. The mechanical tracking shot follows the king's walk from left to right. It loses him, finds him again, slows up almost to a stop, and starts again, while an opposite transverse cut intersects the space and all the supporting actors of the story from the bottom to the left. In short, and without scandalizing you by the comparison, here there is also some analogy with the recapitulation of *8½*[140] and with the conclusion of *Three Colors—Blue*.[141] It is an extremely beautiful undertaking, even just from the point of view of visual dynamics, perfectly connected with the primary role that the music assumes for you. The soldier intones with a loud voice, "Non nobis, Domine," and begins to walk. After the first strophe, other voices in unison join in, but, all things considered, the mix remains *live*.

Then, at the following strophe, a light harmonic support entrusted to the strings takes over (and meanwhile the sound is made cleaner, more refined), while at the next strophe the chorus presents a contrapuntal writing and intones in a way by now professional. For this reason, it cannot be considered an internal level anymore. Now even the orchestra is reinforced and alone develops an episode, always more agitated, that carries to the conclusive shot, where the chorus and orchestra assume a more celebratory tone. It arrives, all in all, at the most sumptuous external level almost without realizing it.

EM: Terrific. A perfect enterprise, realized in an extraordinary way. Here there is all the time that one would need. I think of all the times that someone has said to me, "Can you make twenty seconds of music?" . . . You can make nothing! It is the amount of time that counts. I did not know this film before, and I really admire it.

SM: Consider also that this work represents a double debut. It is the first film both for Branagh and for Doyle, who had been predominantly an actor.

EM: There is such knowledge evident that really they should not be called beginners. What I have noted, which I like, is that the soldier sings badly. He sings a theme that, apparently, in that moment even seems ugly, but that then little by little transfigures itself. This is a positive thing. I believe that he made it on purpose not to be sung well, to make the theme appear at the beginning a little less beautiful, just to hold back the gradualness of the development.

SM: In fact, a different version of the thanksgiving hymn returns in the end titles. The soloist intones from the beginning with a totally different confidence and vocal quality (here the "realism" from the direct drive does not serve a purpose anymore). Also, the tempo is different, a little quicker. All in all, care is reserved for even the smallest details.

Those of the Academy . . . who awarded to this film only the Oscar for costumes understand so little. On the other hand, think of the Oscar for music for *Il postino* and for *La vita e' bella*.[142] I hold Bacalov and Piovani in great esteem, but I think they themselves realized that they had been miraculously rescued by the commonplace stereotypes associated with "being Italian"and the "Mediterranean" that the American jurists harbored. They are musicians who are too intelligent and expert not to know it. Certainly, on the other hand, you do not go to the ceremony and give back the statuette with an offended air. Therefore, we say, better for them. The reality is very clear to those who work in the motion picture business, but not certainly to the great public or the journalists who are ready to sing the praises of their glorious homelands. The truth is that one is dealing with commercial music, a commonplace trade, in which Bacalov for his part and Piovani for another are only employed so much.

Too bad, because above all *La vita é bella* merited a more profound oration. Don't misunderstand me. I have said "profound," not "intense," because the dramaturgy of a film is not served only by musical protagonism, raising one's voice and throwing it to the melodramatic. I intend to say more, sensibly adhering to the singular coexistence between the tragic and comic elements that characterize the films of Benigni. However, it would not be fair to attribute the responsibility for the result only to the composers. The neo-realist cinema has demonstrated to us that a director who is not demanding with the music obtains what is merited, even if the film would have merited much more.

EM: In this *Henry V*, the music really achieves a good result. One feels the collaboration with the director and the projection of the screenplay. In the preceding lessons when I spoke about temporality, I wanted to arrive exactly at such an example. Here the result is extraordinary, not only for the bravura of the composer but also for the bravura of the director who has wanted it to be really like this.

SM: Here I conclude my exposition of the method of levels and the related dramaturgical functions. I exhort you to use it in a systematic way to analyze the work of others so that you can better understand your own work and to use it to be more exigent with your own and with your interlocutors. I say a thing that is halfway between an omen and a joke. If generations of compos-ers of applied music were formed with a solid theoretical base (this or an-other . . .), it would render a little more difficult the life of those directors who treat music as a last-minute remedy, who have not even a clue about music's potential and who do not respect even its minimum requirements. It would create conflicts, but the result would be to the advantage of the cine-ma.

NOTES

1. Excerpts from this chapter were published in *Music and the Moving Image* 4, no. 2 (Summer 2011), 1–29.

2. Sergio Miceli, "La musica nel film e nel teatro di prosa: L'avvento dello specialismo," in G. Sallvetti and B. M. Antolini, eds., *Italia Millenovecentocinquanta, SIdM—CIDIM—CIM/ UNESCO, Musica nel 900 italiano* (Milan: Guerini e Ass, 1999), 223–30. For more informa-tion, see Miceli, *Musica e cinema nella cultura del Novecento* (Milan: Sansoni RCS, 2000), ix–xiv, 372ff.

3. *Pacific 231* signaled the debut of Honegger in the cinema. For the same director he composed the music of *Napoléon* (France, Gance, 1927). In all, Honegger composed the music for about thirty films (some in collaboration).

4. The more important realization of films made to *Pacific 231* (France, Jean Mitry, 1949). [DVD, *Avant Garde: Experimental Cinema 2*, Kino, 2007]. For other attempts, see J. Mitry, *Storia del cinema sperimentale* (Milan: Mazzotta, 1971).

5. Miceli covers this theme in more detail in the introduction to G. Bendazzi, M. Cecconel-lo, and G. Michelone, *Coloriture: Voci, rumori, musiche nel cinema d'animazione* (Bologna: Pendragon, 1995), 13–18.

6. Played by Donald O'Connor.

7. Interpreted by Gene Kelly.

8. Directed by Stanley Donen and Gene Kelly, USA, 1952. [DVD, Warner Home Video, 2010.]

9. Directed by William Hanna and Joseph Barbera. Animation by Kenneth Muse, Ed Barge, and Irven Spence. Music by Scott Bradley. Academy Award, Best Cartoon of 1946. [DVD, Tom and Jerry Spotlight Collection, Warner Home Video, 2004.]

10. For a detailed analysis of this episode, see R. Manvell, J. Huntley (revised and enlarged by R. Arnell and P. Day), *The Technique of Film Music* (London: Focal Press, 1975), 94–107. [DVD, Criterion, 1999.]

11. See the chapter "Il Ragtime, Intrattenimento come riproducibilita," in Miceli, *Musica e cinema nella cultura del Novecento* (Milan: Sansoni RCS, 2000), 445–51.

12. *Dr. No* (Terence Young, 1962), produced in Great Britain with music by Monty Norman and the signature tune of John Barry. [DVD, *James Bond Ultimate Collector's Set*, MGM/UA, 2007.]

13. *C'era una volta in America* (*Once upon a Time in America*) (Leone, 1984). [DVD, *Once upon a Time in America*: Two-Disc Special Edition, Warner Bros., 2011.]

14. For specific terminology, see A. Marchese, *Dizionario di retorica e di stilistica* (Milan: Mondadori, 1978). For the basis from which it was born, indirectly, the student of the method of levels would have to return to such authors as Gérard Genette, Vladimir Jakovlevič Propp, and others, but a concise and systematic approach, more than sufficient for our purposes, is already possible to find by referring to A. Marchese, *L'icina del racconto* (Milan: Mondadori, 1983). Other critical and bibliographical references can be found in Miceli, *Musica e cinema nella cultura*, op. cit., 329ff. [SM] [See Jeff Smith, "Bridging the Gap: Reconsidering the Border between Diegetic and Nondiegetic Music," *Music and the Moving Image* 2, no. 1 (Spring 2009): 1–25, and David Neumeyer, "Diegetic/Nondiegetic: A Theoretical Model," *Music and the Moving Image* 2, no. 1 (Spring 2009): 26–39, about the sources for the terminology used in music. GBA]

15. Title in Italian. [YouTube: "Wunderbare Luege der Nine Petrowna (1929)," posted by Samotaaar; 33 videos.] For the reconstruction, the postrecording, and the first study of this music, see C. Piccardi, "Controlettura musicale di un film," in Sergio Miceli (ed.), *Atti del Convegno Internazionale Musica & Cinema*, "Chigiana," vol. 42, n.s. 22 (Florence: Olschki, 1992), 135–99. On the same film, see Miceli, "Analizzare la musica nel film," in Miceli, *Musica e cinema nella cultura*, op. cit. At the Conference Convegno Internazionale Musica e Cinema, Siena, 1990, the musical functions in *Nina Petrowna* were also the object of debate. See Gianni Rondolino and the reply by Carlo Piccardi in Miceli (ed.), *Atti del Convegno Internazionale Musica & Cinema*, op. cit., 225–34. If I had been able to develop a brief historical summary, I would have indicated the phenomenon of "localization," using two musical versions of *La Corazzata* of Eisenstein. He is referring to two fragments of the same film, *Bronenosec Potemkin* (*Battleship Potemkin*), USSR, 1926, with music by Nikolai Krjukov (Soviet distribution) and Edmund Meisel (German distribution). [DVD, Kino, 2007.]

16. I believe I was among the few to have become familiar with it, above all for the musical component, until Carlo Piccardi, who is an atypical musicologist—that is, of vast competence and without prejudice— presented it in a restored and newly recorded version in 1990 in Siena at the *Convegno Internationale Musica e Cinema* (*The International Conference Music and Cinema*) that I organized for the Accademia Chigiana.

17. But it is also symptomatic that though Rosselini, De Sica, and all the other directors were involved in a phenomenon as courageous and innovative as neorealism, we have accepted without question their ancient, conservative, non-innovative rhetoric and language for the musical component itself. [SM]

18. *Il ladro di bambini* (*The Stolen Children*) (Gianni Amelio, 1992), music by Franco Piersanti. [DVD, Arrow Films, FCD317; Medusa Film, 2007.]

19. *Hamlet* (Franco Zeffirelli, 1990), coproduction USA-Italy. [DVD, Warner Bros., 2004.]

20. *Io la conoscevo bene* (*I Knew Her Well*) (Antonio Pietrangeli, 1965), music by Piero Piccioni, with, among others, Stefania Sandrelli, UgoTognazzi, Enrico Maria Salerno, Mario

Adorf, Nino Manfredi, and Jean-Claude Brialy. [DVD, Medusa Home Entertainment, 2009. Scenes on YouTube.]

21. (1922–1990). Italian film comedian. [GBA]

22. "Letkiss," executed by the Orchestra of Yvar Sauna.

23. *The Man Who Knew Too Much* (USA, Hitchcock, 1956), starring James Stewart and Doris Day. [DVD, Universal, 2006.] Remake of the film of the same name shot by Hitchcock in 1934.

24. He is alluding to the film *Il prato*, in which the director enters rapidly in a car of the Milan subway.

25. See others in the discussion of the mediated level.

26. *La dolce vita* (Federico Fellini, 1960), music by Nino Rota. Of the many actors and actresses, we remember at least Marcello Mastroianni, Anouk Aimée, Alain Cuny, Annibale Ninchi, Nadia Gray, Magali Noël, and Anita Ekberg. [DVD, Medusa Film SPA, 2003; Butterfly Music SRL, 2010.] Many years ago Rota gave me a photocopy of the piano reduction for *La dolce vita*'s score.

27. See "Musical Example 12, 'Polidor from *La dolce vita*,'" in *Comporre per il Cinema*, 87.

28. The implicit reference is principally to the fundamental studies of the already-cited Gérard Genette.

29. *Non c'é pace tra gli ulivi* [*There Is No Peace among the Olive Trees*] (Giuseppe De Santis, 1950), with Raf Vallone, Lucia Basé (debut), Folco Lulli, and Dante Maggio. [DVD, Lux Film, Cecchi Gori, 2008.]

30. This argument has been treated by Miceli in diverse publications.

31. Put in this way, one touches lightly on a big, basic problem. We are well aware of the fact that realism in the cinema is only apparent, but we are not supposed to forget that the average spectator generally lives the filmic experience in a less critical way. [SM]

32. See V. Pudovkin, *La settima arte*, Italian translation of diverse writings (Rome: Editori Riuniti, 1974), 131–35. The version published in Eisenstein, *Forma e tecnica*, op. cit., 523–24, is to be avoided because it is badly translated and incomplete.

33. One is dealing in reality with a three-part partition, for which see J.-J. Nattiez, *Musicologia generale e semiologia*, edited by R. Dalmonte (Turin: EDT, 1989), 8ff. (original edition Paris, 1987). For a more concise alternative, see, by the same author, *Il discorso musicale: Per una semiologia della musica* (Turin: Einaudi, 1987), 3–12.

34. *Bananas* (Woody Allen, 1971), with music by Marvin Hamlisch. [DVD, *Woody Allen Collection, Set 1*, MGM, 2004]. Distributed in Italy with the title *Il dittatore della Stato libero di Bananas.*

35. I owe this recommendation to Sergio Bassetti. [SM]

36. After an amorous disappointment, Fielding Mellish (Woody Allen) goes to a country in South America and receives an invitation to a dinner given by the governor. The scene begins by showing the protagonist in his hotel room, at the moment he has received the invitation. Fielding is lying on the bed and repeats a number of times, in ecstasy, the formula of the invitation, "To dinner with the governor . . . ," while a harp arpeggiates in crescendo (external level). That crescendo distracts Fielding from his fantasies and induces him out of curiosity to look around inside, to find the source of the music (mediated level). The protagonist opens his closet and finds a harpist, who excuses himself, saying that he can never succeed in finding a place to rehearse (internal level). End of the scene.

37. Miceli alludes to the fact that Pontecorvo was thinking of giving an assignment to Miceli and had asked the advice of Morricone.

38. He gave "carte blanche" (without reference to Totò in the film *I due colonnelli* [*The Two Colonels*] . . .), and I treated myself to a very stimulating as well as demanding experience. In nine encounters I took into consideration the music in the "silent" cinema (with the collaboration of the pianist Bruno Moretti and of my dear friend and colleague Hansjoerg Pauli), synchronies and asynchronies (with Morricone and Pontecorvo), audiovisual thinking (with the brothers Taviani), the prose theater in film (with Franco Piersanti), the film opera (with Riccardo Muti), film musical metamorphosis (with Giuliano Montaldo), and the alternative culture (with Sergio Bassetti and Angelo Branduardi). It all went well, I believe I can say (except for a

certain "lack of discipline" by Muti, who, ignoring the list of anticipated examples, became impatient with the projectionist).

39. In the last year of his life, Pier Paolo Pasolini published this series of articles in the *Corriere della Siera* and in *Mondo* as part of a pedagogical project that was modified as it proceeded. The series remained unfinished and was published posthumously by Einaudi (Turin, 1976).

40. It signals the debut of Pasolini in the cinema. [DVD, *Accattone*, Medusa Video, 2006.] From Bach there are fragments of *Cantata*, BWV 106, of the *Passion according to Matthew*, BWV 244, and of the *Brandenburg Concerti no. 1*, BWV 1046, and *no. 2*, BWV 1047. For a more detailed analysis, see S. Bassetti, "Letteratura musicale tra passione e ideologia nel cinema di Pier Paolo Pasolini," in S. Miceli, ed., *Norme con ironie: Scritti per I settant'anni di Ennio Morricone* (Milan: Suvini Zerboni, 1998) and R. Calabretto, *Pasolini e la musica* (Pordenone: Cinemazero, 1999).

41. The film is from 1964. [DVD, Waterbearer, 2003; Legend Films, 2009.] There are compositions, among others, by J. S. Bach from the *Passion according to Matthew*, BWV 244, from the *Mass in B minor*, BWV 232, from the *Concerto in E major*, BWV 1042, and from the *Concerto in D minor*, BWV 1060; by Mozart from the *Maurerische Trauermusik*, K. 477; and by Prokofiev from the *Cantata* op. 78, extracted from the film *Alexander Nevsky*. For a complete, detailed list, see R. Calabretto, *Pasolini e la musica*.

42. See G. Dorfles, *Nuovi riti, nuovi miti* (Turin: Einaudi, 1965), 176f. Miceli had already had recourse to the same citation apropos Fellini in *La musica nel film*, cit. now in idem., *Musica e cinema nella cultura*, op. cit., 432–33.

43. [The running on of the thought from one line, couplet, or stanza to the next without a syntactical break.]

44. Naturally, he is dealing with Leopardi's *L'Infinito*, taken from a series of enjambments. It continues, "blocks the sight of the infinite horizon/But sitting and looking, endless/spaces beyond that, and superhuman/silences and very deep quiet."

45. The text of Pasolini has been reproduced in A. Bertini, "Teoria e tecnica del film," in *Pasolini* (Rome: Bulzoni, 1979) and more recently in Calabretto, *Pasolini e la musica*, op. cit.

46. *Dimensioni sonore 1—Musiche per l'imaggine e l'immaginazione*, RCA SP 10036. Here already cited for the use of a composition by Miceli, see chapter 2, "Audiovisual Analysis—Part 1."

47. The thought of Morricone is developed in appendix 1.

48. *The Elephant Man* (GB, Lynch, Paramount, 1980), with original music by John Morris, starring Anthony Hopkins, Anne Bancroft, and John Hurt. [DVD: Music Video Distribution, 2007].

49. *Platoon* (USA, Oliver Stone, 1968), with original music by Georges Delerue, starring Charlie Sheen, Willem Dafoe, and Tom Berenger. [DVD: MGM, 2008.]

50. *Lorenzo's Oil* (George Miller, 1992), starring Nick Nolte and Susan Sarandon. [DVD, Universal, 2004.] Miceli owes this communication to Sergio Bassetti.

51. Transcription from *Quartetto*, op. 11 of 1936.

52. Optical filter, or gelatin, that softens the borders and attenuates the contrasts.

53. See "Musical Example 13, 'Adagio for Strings,'" in *Comporre per il Cinema*, 97.

54. *Morte a Venezia [Death in Venice]* (Luchino Visconti, 1971). [DVD, Warner Bros., 2006.] Miceli is referring to the fourth movement of *Symphony no. 5*. For other notices about the musical choices of Visconti in this film, see L. Miccichè (ed.), *Morte a Venezia di Luchino Visconti* (Bologna: Cappelli, 1971), 74ff.

55. See the chapter "Asinchronismo e straniamento" in Miceli, *Musica e cinema nella cultura*, op. cit., 203–15.

56. *Henry V* (Branagh, 1989). [DVD, MGM, 2000.]

57. On CD EMI CDC 7499192, it corresponds to track 10, *St. Crispin's Day—The Battle of Agincourt*.

58. City of Birmingham Symphony Orchestra.

59. See "Musical Example 14, 'Prophesy of Henry V,'" in *Comporre per il Cinema*, 99–101.

60. Known also as "basic shape." For a clear explanation, see David Epstein, *Al di là di Orfeo, Studi sulla stuttura musicale* (*Beyond Orpheus: Studies in Musical Structure*), ed. M. De Natale (Milan: Ricordi, 1988; New York: Oxford University Press, 1987).
61. See "Musical Example 14, 'Prophecy of Henry V,'" in *Comporre per il Cinema*, 103–5. Here and there the prechosen photograms represent a synthesis of the framing (shot, reverse shot) that constitute the sequence. [SM]
62. Speaker, "Sobald dich fuehrt der Freundschaft Hand Ins Heiligtum zum ew'gen Band."
63. Institute for Research for the Musical Theater, Rome.
64. *Hamlet* (Olivier, 1948) and *Henry V* (Olivier, 1944). [DVD, *Olivier's Shakespeare*, Criterion Collection, 2006.]
65. *Othello* (Wells, 1952), whose restoration with new execution of the music one finds briefly examined in Miceli, *Musica e cinema nella cultura,* op. cit., 292ff.
66. *Gamlet* (*Hamlet*) (Kozintsev, 1964).
67. The same *Henry V* here discussed.
68. *The Life and Death of Richard III* (Calmettes, Keane, 1912).
69. The composition was analyzed by Miceli in *Musica/realtà* 18, no. 54 (1997): 185–99.
70. He is alluding to *Romeo e Giulietta* (1968), with music by Rota [DVD Paramount, 2007]; and to *Amleto* (1990), with music by Morricone [DVD, Cecchi Gori, 2007].
71. *Alexander Nevsky* [*Aleksandr Nevskij*] (USSR, Eisenstein, 1938).
72. *Hamlet* (Zeffirelli, 1990), coproduction USA-Italy. [DVD, Warner Bros., 2004; Cecchi Gori, 2007.]
73. *C'era una volta in America* (*Once upon a Time in America*) (Leone, 1984). [DVD, *Once upon a Time in America*: Two-Disc Special Edition, Warner Bros., 2011.]
74. *Henry V* (Olivier, 1944). [DVD: Criterion, 1999; *Olivier's Shakespeare*, Criterion Collection, 2006.]
75. *Alexander Nevsky* [*Aleksandr Nevskij*] (USSR, Eisenstein, 1938). [DVD: Criterion Colletion, 2001; Eureka, 2003.]
76. R. Manvell, J. Huntley, *The Technique of Film Music* [1957]. Revised and enlarged by R. Arnell and P. Day (London: Focal Press, 1975) (translated into Italian from the 1957 edition *Tecnica della musica nel film*, ed. Bianco e Nero, 1959).
77. See Eisenstein, *Forma e tecnica*, op. cit., 321–61.
78. *Amleto* (Zeffirelli,1990). [DVD, Warner Bros., 2004; Cecchi Gori, 2007.]
79. *Gamlet* (*Hamlet*0 (USSR, Kozintsev, 1964). [DVD: *Hamlet*, Mr. Bongo Films, 2011; *Gamlet*, Chicago, Facets Video, 2006; *Gamlet* Moscow, RUSCICO, 2003.]
80. He is referring to the *Suite*, op. 32a, from 1932.
81. See V. J. Propp, *Morfologia della fiaba* (Turin: Einaudi, 1966; original edition, Leningrad, 1928). For the references to the studies of Gérard Genette and for more information, see S. Miceli, "Analizzare la musica nel film," in *Cinema e musica nella cultura,* op. cit., which consists in a substantial amplification of the essay "Analizzare la musica per film" ("A Revised Proposal of the Theory of Levels"), *Rivista Italiana di Musicologia* 29, no. 2 (1994): 517–44.
82. *The Shining* (Stanley Kubrick, 1980). [DVD, Warner Bros, 2008, USA.]
83. Internal level, but there could also be cases of "interference" with the external level.
84. (But I would like to say "fascination.") [SM]
85. He intends the term as the realization of a syntactic function, according to the Greimasian theory. See A. J. Greimas, *Semantica strutturale* (Milan: Rizzoli, 1968; original edition Paris, 1966); idem., *Del Senso* (Milan: Bompiani, 1976; original edition, Paris, 1970). [SM]
86. *Metropolis* (Germany, Fritz Lang, 1926). [DVD, Masters of Cinema, 2010.] The film returned, to the upset and attention of later generations, [which was] caused by a rather unusual musical operation [a rock and roll score], made by Giorgio Moroder in 1984.
87. A more detailed analysis is found in Miceli, *Musica e cinema nella cultura,* op. cit., 363ff.
88. Played by Warwick Ward.
89. Played by Franz Lederer.
90. See the beginning of the *Tempo di Polacca*, "Musical Example 15, 'Tempo di Polacca' from *Die Wunderbare Luege der Nina Petrovna*," in *Comporre per il Cinema*, 111. A more

extended illustration of this fragment and of the succeeding example is found in Miceli, *Musica e cinema nella cultura,* op. cit.

91. See "Musical Example 16, 'Poco più vivo' from *Die Wunderbare Luege der Nina Petrovna,*" in *Comporre per il Cinema,* 111.

92. *Caro diario (Dear Diary)* (Nanni Moretti, 1994). [DVD, Warner Bros. Entertainment, Italia SPA, 2009.]

93. *The Cologne Concert,* CD ECM 1064/65.

94. As often happens to a director when he chooses preexisting music.

95. With a noninfluential return in the Isole episode, where he appears always at the external level. [SM]

96. *Top Hat* (Mark Sandrich, 1935), music by Irving Berlin, with Fred Astaire and Ginger Rogers [DVD, Universal, 2007]; *West Side Story* (Robert Wise and Jerome Robbins, 1961), music by Leonard Bernstein, with Natalie Wood, Richard Beymer, Russ Tamblyn, Rita Moreno, George Chakiris [DVD, MGM, 2003]; *On the Town* (Stanley Donen and Gene Kelly, 1949), music by Leonard Bernstein and Roger Edens, with Gene Kelly, Frank Sinatra, Jules Munshin, Betty Garrett, Ann Miller, Vera Ellen [DVD, Warner Bros., 2008]; *Hello, Dolly!* (Gene Kelly, 1969), music by Jerry Herman, with Barbra Streisand and Walter Matthau [DVD, *A Celebration of Song and Dance,* Twentieth Century Fox, 2007].

97. *Carosello napoletano [Neapolitan Carousel]* (Ettore Giannini, 1953), music by Raffaele Gervasio (with elaboration of traditional popular music and traditional repertory), choreography by Leonide Massine, with a vast cast and actors dubbed by celebrated singers. [DVD, *Sophia Loren,* Lionsgate, 2008.]

98. See Miceli, "Dal 'naturale' al coreutico, *Cinema e danza,*" in L. Quaresima, ed., *Il cinema e le altre arti, La Biennale di Venezia* (Venice: Marsilio, 1996).

99. *Il bidone* (Federico Fellini, 1955). [DVD, Medusa Film SPA, 2003.]

100. Roberto, played by Franco Fabrizi.

101. For an analysis of the Fellini-Rota association from *I vitelloni* to *8½,* see Miceli, *Musica e cinema nella cultura,* op. cit., 385–447.

102. Still, an observation regarding the linguistic liberty and the implicit winks. Moretti, it is said, stops at the edge of the dance floor and observes the couples dancing, then jumps on the stage of the complex, inserts himself, and sings the refrain together with the musicians. But, pay attention, it could be a "dreamlike" insertion because in the cut of the editing occurring immediately after the ultimate vocal strophe, before finding him again intent, as in the beginning, contemplating the dancers, the dolly frames the musicians, and one does not see a trace of him. In other words, if the time that is running is "objective" and uninterrupted during the song, Moretti could not be on the stage and, a fraction of a second later, be at the edge of the dance floor. [SM]

103. *Allonsanfàn* (Paolo and Vittorio Taviani, 1974). [DVD, Delta Video, 2009.]

104. But it wasn't the first time. See F. Accialini, L. Coluccelli, A. Ferrero, "Su *Allonsanfan* e altre cose: Conversazione con Paolo e Vittorio Taviani," *Cinema & Cinema* 1, no. 1 (1974).

105. S. Piscicelli (ed.), *San Michele aveva un gallo—Allonsanfàn di Paolo e Vittorio Taviani* (Bologna: Cappelli, 1974).

106. The analysis is in S. Miceli, *Morricone, la musica, il cinema,* published in the series *Le Sfere* (Milan: Ricordi-Mucchi, 1994) (Spanish translation: Valencia, 1997; German translation: Essen, 2000), 256–61.

107. See "Musical Example 17, 'Tarantella from *Allonsanfàn,*'" in *Comporre per il Cinema,* 117.

108. *Il prato (The Lawn)* (Taviani, 1979). [DVD: ArtHaus, B000PKHW3S, n.d.]

109. *San Michele aveva un gallo [Saint Michael Had a Rooster]* (Paolo and Vittorio Taviani, 1976), with music by Benedetto Ghiglia. [DVD, Fox Lorber, 2005; Butterfly Music SPA, 2010]. While it was released in 1976, it was actually produced in 1972.

110. The elaboration by Miceli was already published in 1982 in *La musica nel film,* op. cit., and successively in *Musica e cinema nella cultura,* op. cit., 361f.

111. *Il prato (The Lawn)* (Taviani, 1979). [DVD: ArtHaus, B000PKHW3S, n.d.]

112. Played by Michele Placido and Saverio Marconi.

113. *Trois couleurs—Bleu* (Krzysztof Kieslowski, 1993) was a French-Swiss-Polish coproduction and belonged to a trilogy that included *Trois couleurs—Blanc*, 1994, and *Trois couleurs—Rouge*, 1994. [DVD, Disney-Buena Vista, 2003.]

114. *50th International Exhibit of the Cinematic Art*, Edizioni Biennale (Venice: Fabbri Editori, 1993), 76.

115. K. Kieslowski, K. Piesiewicz, *Tre colori: Blu Bianco Rosso* (Milan: Bompiani RCS, 1997) (original edition 1992).

116. Played by Florence Pernel.

117. The same passages present in *The Mission* (Roland Joffé, 1986), but here in Greek.

118. *8½* (Fellini, 1963). [DVD: Criterion Films 2001]. The celebrated film, *Det sjunde inseglet* (Ingmar Bergman, 1956). [DVD, *The Seventh Seal*, Criterion, 2009.]

119. For the fragment, see "Musical Example 18, 'Thematic Cell from *Film Blue*,'" in *Comporre per il Cinema*, 121.

120. I have taken as a reference, very banally, the major figures of Polish music of the first and second halves of the twentieth century without the pretext of knowing the real models to which Preisner was looking eventually in his compositional activity. [SM]

121. *The Duelists* (GB, Ridley Scott, 1977), starring Keith Carradine and Harvey Keitel. [DVD, Paramount Home Video, 2002.] This film is based on a short novel by Joseph Conrad, *The Duel*.

122. *Blade Runner* (Scott, 1982). [DVD, The Final Cut, Warner Home Video, 2007; 30th Anniversary Ultimate Collector's Edition, Warner Home Video, 2012.]

123. *Barry Lyndon* (GB, Stanley Kubrick, 1975) [DVD, Warner Bros., 2001] had been released two years earlier. The actress Gay Hamilton appeared also in Scott's film.

124. Respectively, Tom Conti and Keith Carradine.

125. Something similar was realized in *The Mission* in the scene in which Padre Gabriel plays the oboe at the first contact with the Guarani.

126. Played by Diana Quick.

127. *Per qualche dollaro in più* [*For a Few Dollars More*] (Sergio Leone, 1965). [DVD, in the *Clint Eastwood Collection*, MGM, 2007.]

128. Played by Rosemarie Dexter.

129. *The Duelists* (GB, Ridley Scott, 1977). [DVD, Paramount Home Video, 2002.]

130. Miceli, *Morricone*, op. cit., 150.

131. *Allonsanfàn* (Paolo and Vittorio Taviani, 1974). [DVD, Delta Video, 2009.]

132. I heard it, for example, from so much "absolute" music written on a theoretical level in the sixties.

133. *Alexander Nevsky* [*Aleksandr Nevskij*] (USSR, Eisenstein, 1938). [DVD, Criterion Collection, 2001; Eureka, 2003.] They are reported and discussed in Miceli, *Musica e cinema nella cultura*, op. cit., 229–45.

134. Reproduced in various texts, it appears perhaps for the first time in Italy in Eisenstein, *Forma e tecnica*, op. cit.

135. (1940–), Italian film director.

136. (1951–), Italian film director.

137. *Henry V* (Branagh, 1989). [DVD, MGM, 2000.]

138. See *The Band Wagon* (variety show). [DVD, Warner Bros., 2009.]

139. It involves Doyle himself, who plays the character Court.

140. *8½* (Fellini, 1963). [DVD, Criterion Films, 2001.]

141. *Trois couleurs—Bleu* (Krzysztof Kieslowski, 1993), *Trois couleurs—Blanc* (1994), and *Trois couleurs—Rouge* (1994). *Tre colori: Blu Bianco Rosso* (Milan: Bompiani RCS, 1997) (original edition 1992). [DVD: Disney-Buena Vista, 2003.]

142. Respectively, *Il postino* (Michael Radford, 1994) [DVD, Disney-Buena Vista, 2004] and *La vita e' bella* (Roberto Benigni, 1997) [DVD, Cecchi Gori, 2005].

Chapter Five

Premix and Final Mix

The Recording and Sound Design

OVERDUBBING

EM: I can write a normal score for a normal recording session. The microphones will be located according to the audio engineer's specifications. Alternatively . . . during the process of writing, I can call for overdubbing, which requires a different microphone setup. I gave you an example already as a coda to Professor Miceli's analytic exposition in chapter 2.

Superimpositions can be dictated by practical or artistic considerations. For example, if a particular instrument needs to receive special treatment, it can be recorded separately and superimposed over the orchestra. I might decide to call for overdubbing if one group of instruments produces too much sound with respect to the others present in the hall, thereby making it impossible to control the volume levels separately. For example, the trumpets will have entered the microphone for the violins. If I ask for a higher level on the violins, inevitably the level of the trumpets will be raised. The mix—that is, the complex equilibrium between the sixteen or twenty-four tracks—will be compromised. Sometimes the mobile sound barriers that enclose and shield an instrument, most frequently the percussion, are not sufficient. Therefore, one has to make a separate recording and then . . . superimpose it over all the rest.

Creative Overdubbing

The other type of dubbing, which to me is the more important, is the creative one. In this case, all the music is written specifically to be overdubbed—all made up of superimposable sections. I compose a piece of music that is, let us say, aleatoric. It is free, open. The entrances of the individual instruments and those of the orchestral sections can be almost casual. (They are not casual with respect to their relation to the picture, however.) The material in the score is not written vertically but horizontally. Then all these occurrences are organized vertically during the mix. Writing in this fashion, I anticipate a staggered recording session and call . . . for an entire orchestra, but not in one plenary sitting.

In some cases I have needed an orchestra of sixty players, but I have first called ten players. I have made them record the beginning of the first part of the section to be superimposed. I have them record on one track or two separate tracks. (I make this decision together with the audio engineer.) Then I call another ten instruments, and then later another ten. Thus one completes the entire ensemble of sixty players in six recording sessions.

In such a way one can make an infinite number of combinations for the definitive mix. I can mix the single track of strings or a part of the strings. Then I can mix it together with that of the brass, which are as free as the strings because the sound of other instruments has not contaminated their tracks. Or I can mix those strings with little instruments or with certain percussion instruments and also with the keyboards. I can make trios. I can make quartets. With recordings thought of in this way, I can make quite a lot of types of instrumental combinations with the same number of players. This is not something that all composers do. It is a process I have adopted very frequently. It began with the need to economize, and then it became a creative affair. With respect to the cost savings, recording in this way, I record in one session with ten instruments twenty minutes of music. During the following session, with another ten instruments we have still another twenty minutes of music, but already with the possibility of multiplying the combinations. In sum, this procedure gives some very useful results.

Also, the creative potential . . . is obvious, but one has to write the score thinking of this approach ahead of time. One can't do it on the spur of the moment as it is happening. One can obtain music that is a little freer, a little chromatic, a little dissonant, but one can also get a tonal result, simply tonal. In certain scores organized in this way,[1] I anticipate on the same page a lot of diverse situations, even with three times as many strings. Therefore, it is a way to invent everything, and it is very stimulating, very entertaining. Then one goes to mix.

During the mix, the director watches the film but cannot understand anything. I will be recording and mixing a score with various sections that, in their "incompleteness," cannot give the listener the composite final idea right away. Naturally, I have to have explained this procedure ahead of time. The director will have been both scandalized and irritated, precisely because he will not be able to control anything nor even express an opinion. To do so, he would have to wait until the end of the recording and mixing process. However, at that point he would only be able to say that the result was not to his liking.

In sum, there are great risks involved in this type of procedure, and in the course of my career I have taken them a little at a time.

Boisett (*L'attentat*, 1972) [*The Attempted Assassination*]

One of the first directors for whom I applied this method was Yves Boisett (*L'attentat* [*The Attempted Assassination*], 1972).[2] He never called me again . . . or rather, he called me only after many years. When I proposed the technique of superimposition, he understood the mechanics, but he was not very convinced. We had already established the synchronization points where at opportune moments we would open or close certain tracks, though to us the track had only one main line. The piece became in this way a kaleidoscope of sounds, of unpredictable events, that gave a defined result that was in a certain sense aleatoric.

SM: It would be opportune at this point for you to add some words about the film, about its climate, for the benefit of those who have not seen it and also in order to justify the choice of instruments you made.

EM: *L'attentat* essentially takes place in France, but it deals with the political problems of a North African country. We did not have at our disposal the original, that is, indigenous instruments, so I took some of the percussion, those that I had. I added the mandola that had to be an imitation of the Greek bouzouki and perhaps seemed like the plectral instruments of North Africa, and in this way we proceeded.

I did not want a rigorous reconstruction of the folklore of the place. On the contrary, I wanted an illusion of that folklore, which was all the more necessary, as I would never have been able to hire North African instruments and instrumentalists. As an alternative, we might have remade the music of the place, but that was not possible either, because the editor had already invested the money for written music in another way. Therefore, he was not able to obtain the existing rights to music of North African provenance.

On the other hand, no one had asked me to write music with precise ethnic connotations. The film was not a documentary about North Africa. I was able to make music that I could regard as having an occidental interpretation. Precisely because of the technique of superimposition I could make a compromise between an illusion of the music of North Africa and the musical commentary that I wrote in a traditional way. One can distinguish the various sounds of the violin, the plucking of the strings, the reeds, and percussion. Upon reflection, this piece was influenced by one idea. It is the identification of a theme by its timbre (here, practically speaking, there is not just one theme; there are many). It is identified by its brevity, the brevity of a theme that comes from examples of primitive music passed on orally by virtue of memory. It is music made from brief melodic, rhythmic, and timbral engravings or parentheses. On the other hand, I have spoken of African music, which is repetitive to the maximum degree. Therefore, it is right that there is this sense of repetitiveness here, and therefore of . . . I don't want to call it boredom . . .

SM: Of persistence.

Modular Elements

EM: Of persistence, yes, because it is music made from little parenthetical digressions. The piece is pretty long. I called it *Sinfonia Dell'attentato*[3] . . . In this version I haven't even used all of the parentheses. The final written version of the superimposition involves a situation that has often entertained me. If there is someone in the ensemble that doesn't know how to play the way I like, I don't let him play. The score is so open that I can eliminate parts I have written. In that case, I say that I have changed my mind and that I no longer like what I wrote. I take all the blame, and only those whom I like play, and this also is a great advantage.

SM: In film work the composer has to struggle with a musical temporality that is not absolute but is tied to the scene and to the sequence. At the same time he has to guarantee that the piece succeeds in having its own logic. . . . Modular writing eliminates these problems.

I have defined "modular writing" as a system that pertains to the technical part of superimposition, but in limited cases it creates a relationship with the film that is no longer temporal in the conventional sense. In fact, in a contribution of a traditional nature (I mean to say the development of the theme assigned to the melodic arch), the temporal dimension is clearly recognizable. It has a beginning and an explicit end that coincides more than once with the filmed episode. It is not by chance that one speaks of such music as a "closed form." But here instead we find a musical continuity that influences the architecture of the film itself and consequently its temporal perception. (It is sufficient to think of the way it influences the assembly of the film.)

EM: The manner of recording the elements that form this music, precisely the so-called modular elements, requires a further clarification. At the time that I made *L'attentat,* I did not have a recording machine with twenty-four but rather one with sixteen tracks. Therefore, on this machine I recorded all the rhythmic elements that had to be in sync. Then, on a machine with eight tracks, I recorded those that were "suspended"; that made long, taut sounds; . . . that did not have to be in sync. Today one can record forty-eight tracks as a matter of course. Many groups do it, many ensembles. [4]

Instead, I am talking about recording on forty-eight tracks but also many fewer. The composer decides what to write and what to superimpose. It is a concept that arises from the absolute necessity of being creative and of imposing one's will on the multitrack machine, instead of being submissive to it, as some rock groups are. In order to make a CD they may remain in London for three or four months and spend millions and millions. I've never been able to dispose of a sum like that. The pleasing thing that I have discovered about my compositional system is that in a piece written in this way, everything seems to arise from a sort of spontaneous germination. Consequently, at the entrance of a new element, the preceding one seems to transform itself. Still, the thing repeats itself and multiplies with the entrance of each new component. One realizes a form proceeding from itself, in the sense that it is born every time from the components themselves that make up a part of the composition. No component attacks assertively in this mix. Even if an instrument has to attack immediately, without being gradual, one doesn't raise the potentiometer. One merely presses a preset button that directly sets the prearranged level. In this way the attack is imperative.

Now we want to move on to another type of piece that compares with this idea, although with different consequences. I imagined it for the episode of a UNICEF film. [5]

Bambini del mondo (*Children of the World*) from *Ten to Survive*

SM: An animated film.

EM: Yes, animated, for which five composers were hired; to each one of them two pieces were entrusted. Initially I had thought about making a piece using choirs of children from all over the world. Except . . . there was no money to be made and not even an editor. UNICEF was to finance the project.

Therefore, I thought I would get at least the satisfaction of drawing on original Japanese, Algerian, Arab, Italian, Hebrew, Greek, South American, Indian, Spanish, and Portuguese . . . sources. To obtain a piece a little like that of *L'attentat*, one could work from a kaleidoscope of children's songs with a variety of ring-shaped tracks (loops). ("Loop"—do you know what it means? One finds the right place to splice the beginning of a tape to its end. One makes the splice and lets the loop run *ad infinitum*, and one records it.) If a piece is thirty seconds long, you have doubled or tripled it. A single melody always repeats from the beginning without end. But the original idea was not realizable because it was impossible to find the songs with all those choruses of white voices.

In the end I had at my disposition a chorus of thirty children. So I wrote the songs thinking of the Japanese tradition (so to speak, because it was always my chorus—imagine what kind of Japanese I would have made!), of the Indian tradition, and so forth. In short, I had recourse to a variety of scales, a variety of melodies that were not authentic but invented. I thought from time to time of Spanish or Portuguese or Jewish music. Working with the technique of superimposition, I obtained sixteen children's choirs that sang sixteen different things. Each one was on a track, and I also inserted little compositions that had the function of glue, the connection between the various choirs. Then I had pedal points recorded, not so much for the intonation of the kids as to create a certain clarity for the listeners, a reference point, a polarity. The result was not what I had imagined if I had been able to use authentic choirs, but it is a result that I remember as a very positive experience, that even had certain beneficial results. . . . The movie business served to give me experiences of this type, experiences that probably have made an important contribution to the music I wrote outside of the cinema.

SM: Also, if we are moving on a predominantly technical level, it seems to me important to emphasize that *L'attentat* of Boisset for one kind of sound and *Ten to Survive* for another left you a freedom of choice that was truly unusual. As such, they are solutions that remain a little at the margins of routine procedures.

EM: It is exactly as I have said. In fact, Boisset was not so happy. It is true that the director is able to control all the elements of his film. He is the boss of the dialogue. He directs the actors. He decides the scenery design, the costumes, the dubbing, the noises, the air, and the birds. However, if over the music he has no control, at least initially, the contribution of the composer can surprise him negatively or positively. In the case of Boisset, as I told you, I had warned him, explaining all the details, but by this time I knew from experience that this explanation would not get through—or that very little of it would.

But one also can understand Boisset's unhappiness. Because I utilized superimpositions, he would have listened to the final results when the orchestra would no longer have been available. If at that point he had said, "I would like the oboe to do a certain thing . . . ," I would have had to respond that it was impossible. In short, the directors in these cases are really excluded. If I have been able to operate in this way, it is from a certain prestige that I have earned in the eyes of the director.

Returning to the piece for the UNICEF film, I can add that not all the modules are monophonic, even if the polyphonic ones are in the minority.

The counterpoint is apparently casual. I started with specific scales before composing the individual songs. Therefore, apart from the pedal points, I had absolute control over the scales and the consequences of all the sounds used. The relation of cause and effect arose afterward, from the mix to the modules. Still, it was always my choice. Let's be clear: the tracks are not synchronized at all, in the sense that in one particular track I knew that there was the Spanish song, in another the Portuguese song, in another the Chinese, in another the Mexican . . . but enough. . . . At the beginning I made all the modules enter together gradually, and just as gradually I made them diminish, but a successive control was possible (and this I exerted in certain cases). It consisted of timing and annotating the tempi of diverse modules.

SM: Because a point of reference seems appropriate, in my work on Morricone there is a substantially detailed analysis from which I can extract some other information. The generating cells are fifteen; some are tetrachords, others pentachords. I list the ethnic areas as the author has annotated them in the score:

1. Europe
2. Western Europe
3. China
4. Senegal
5. Jewish culture
6. Japan
7. Japan (Asian area)
8. South America
9. North American Indian
10. Africa
11. Europe
12. South America
13. Africa
14. Western Europe
15. Asia

But all the tetrachords and pentachords . . . come from a generating scale of ten notes. Extrapolating the sounds from diverse melodic modules and carrying them into the confines of an octave, I obtained this series of notes: F, G-flat, G, A, B, C, D-flat, D, E-flat, E.[6]

EM: It seems to me that there were eleven . . . . It isn't a chromatic total, there is not a dodecaphonic foundation, but we have a clearly perceptible modal majority. The pieces are all catchy.

SM: I would like to add something else. In the score one finds a point that I even reproduced in the book. Morricone distinguishes three categories of reference, or, if you prefer, of compositional characteristics. One has to do with the tessitura, one with behavior, and one with relations. For the tessitura he distinguishes between A (high-pitched), M (medium), and B (bass). For that regarding behavior there are other symbols: MEL is for melody, PED signifies pedal (although harmonic behavior, indicated between parentheses), and DIN is for dynamics. The final category, the relations, consists of two options: CO, that is to say, consonants without alteration; and DI, namely dissonances.

Let's turn now to the modules that are characteristic of the project. If we take, for example, no. 13, Africa, it is made of only two sounds. We find the symbols B–DIN–CO in the score. This signifies that that module has been constructed in a low tessitura, with dynamic behavior and with consonant relations, and so forth. This example can render the idea of the planning of the project, even if the project hides a polarity of a tonal nature that it does not behoove us to specify now. The text, enunciated in diverse languages, is always the same: "We are the children of the world."

EM: If I had abolished all the polarities, a much more incisive, much more aggressive piece would have issued forth, with voices of children that come from afar, arrive in front of the listener, and then turn back. . . . Yes, the piece would have been a completely different thing, but the aspect that pleased me about the overdubbing is exactly this: the same material transforms itself according to its disposition, giving place to completely different results.

Indeterminacy in *Giù la testa* [*Duck, You Sucker*]/*Invenzione per John* (*Invention for John*) (Leone, 1971)

The same experience was created with a much easier, catchy, and as Professor Miceli has said, efficient piece of music in a film where it was necessary that the public not have any difficulty understanding. The film is *Giù la testa* (1971) of Sergio Leone.[7] The composition is in the opening titles, and I called it *Invenzione per John* (*Invention for John*).

SM: In effect, I owe the discovery of modular technique to this composition, which you then verified in *Bambini del mondo* and in still other pieces. In the preparatory phase of my book I asked Maestro Morricone for some scores written for *Giù la testa*, and according to his customary modesty, he dictated them to me without comment or any particular directions. It did not take much to understand that *Invenzione per John* was not the usual score, to be read contemporaneously horizontally and vertically, but rather one that I subsequently defined as a mother score [aleatoric score], based on the principle of modularity. I admired then (and still do) and remember extremely well the pleasure it gave me to imagine combinations, superimpositions, that were different from those realized on the film's soundtrack or on the recorded disc. The person who reads music becomes a type of potential composer. Thus, in infinite ways, like a child who constructs the pieces of Meccano, an erector set (from my time) or of Lego (today), I forget that someone else created those pieces there.

I would not want to say now in a summary way what I wrote after long and serious thought. . . . However, I need to make sure you understand. Much more than in *L'attentat* or in *Bambini del mondo*, *Invenzione per John* wanders from a normal melodic, harmonic, and rhythmic conventionalism to an (apparent) indeterminacy that is not far from some contemporary music. There is the unfailing whistling that elsewhere, in other sections of the film, will be a microthematic element. There are the little falsetto voices that sing, "Sean-Sean-Sean," another characteristic element of this soundtrack. Therefore, it is a species of synthesis of all the music in the whole film. But recognizing these elements also makes them evaporate, floating on an extremely changeable base that is not the type of base one usually means. To illustrate this, it suffices to open the track of one of the two string sections, the one that is the most "free" from harmonic references, which associates it with sounds that are more vivid and isolated and tend toward dissonance. They are the direct progeny of a pointillist concept toward which Morricone has looked forever in order to transfigure the final result. But which final result? The one that I have in mind, not the one that is given for listening on the LP recording.[8]

I can have you look at the extrapolation of some modules from the mother score for *Invenzione per John*, each one of which can be characterized in very different ways. The first one, for example, refers to four masculine voices in falsetto. It is one of the longest modules in the whole system.[9] The next, on the other hand, is module 1 of the strings. It is a varied augmentation of the *Marcia degli accattoni* (*March of the Beggars*) and assumes both a coloristic-harmonic (vertical) and contrapuntal (horizontal-vertical) function.[10] It might be interesting to compare it with module 2 of the strings, which is arrhythmic and more fractioned with respect to the other modules.[11] To this "linearity," although fragmented and subsequently segmented by the aleatoric operations of entrance and exit, one adds pseudopointillist interventions, as in the module assigned to piano and electric bass.[12]

Basically, it is a return to the concept of a theme with variations, but closer to that of the preclassical period than that of the eighteenth and nineteenth centuries.[13] It remains to be said only that modular compositions perhaps have a weak point in that it is impossible to perform them live.

Live Performance of Modular Compositions

EM: It is a fair observation, but in theory it is possible. The conductor would have to give entrances according to preestablished times in a specially prepared score where it would be written, for example, "At twenty-three seconds the six children of chorus C enter."

SM: But it is all less controllable, without taking into account the absence of the dissolves, of the gradual entrances and exits.

EM: Certainly. However, I have done it. The occasion came in 1982 as the result of an invitation from a convent of nuns in Rome. They wanted me to write a piece to be played publicly to celebrate an anniversary of their mother superior. Having no intention of accepting this assignment, I said that to write such a piece I would need a chorus of three hundred children. They responded that it would not be a problem. Then I added that I would need a big circular hall in order to be able to divide the children into various choirs, and the nuns told me that there was a circular hall. I said finally that I would need a separate amplification system for each choir (of sixteen to eighteen) as well as another system for the propagation of a reference pitch for the intonation of the various choral groups. They were not fazed by this request either, so I was constrained to accept. The experiment went very well. I realized and directed it for free, because it was worth it just to have the experience.

Krǎsnaja palata (*La tenda rossa, The Red Tent*) and *Mosé* (*Moses*)

To conclude the discussion of overdubbing, we can refer to two other cases: a little composition from *Mosé* (*Moses*)[14] and another from *Krǎsnaja palata* (*La tenda rossa, The Red Tent*).[15] In *La tenda rossa* the choirs were created for another purpose; they were placed in a circle and immediately received an electroacoustic treatment via a modulator. The results would have been unthinkable without the overdubbing.

SM: *Krǎsnaja palata* was about the polar expedition of Umberto Nobile with the dirigible *Italia* and the race of solidarity that sprang up to support the explorers.

EM: In fact, after an introduction entrusted to synthesized sounds, there is an acoustic situation that begins with a signal, a request for help using the Morse code "S-O-S." It leads as a consequence to the opening of an orchestral piece constructed on nine pulsations—three short, three long, and three short[16] —

with the entrance of successive voices. Toward the finale, a prevalence of synthesized sounds returns. And this sound of the synthesizers is responsible also, or rather above all, for the composition drawn from *Mosé*. Inevitably, the arguments superimpose themselves. One would want to talk about synthesizers and samplers, but right now our attention is directed to the problem of multitrack technique.

SM: After so many demanding references, I think it would be appropriate for me to insert a basic observation. It is completely understandable that, taking a cue from the subject of overdubbing, Maestro Morricone would propose compositions like the *Sinfonia da L'attentato*, *Bambini del mondo*, and a section from *La tenda rossa*. He cites examples that emphasize the way in which a composer in the cinema can take his own craft seriously (if he has the talent).

But someone legitimately could ask, "What are their applications to film? Were there scenes, were there sequences, that were long enough to permit the insertion of the music?" I know for sure that it wasn't that way, Ennio, so for that reason it would be useful if you would refer to the real solutions adopted. Sure, we are talking about overdubbing, but I would not want those who are following . . . to make the mistake of thinking that a film music oasis exists where one can ignore so many of the requirements of cinematographic narration or the laws of the marketplace. Instead, what we have heard even confirms again what I have already observed. We are in the presence of exceptional cases in which the composer has earned the liberty of using a language that unfortunately does not prove anything. (I am not talking about overdubbing.) In other words, they are testimonials of great interest, but being the privilege of very few, they can be admired more than hoped to be put into practice. The cinema with which one perhaps might collaborate will ask something completely different of those who are following our discussion. And anyway, you yourself at the beginning of your career came to the attention of the great public and of the critics (open-minded or malevolent as they may have been) not with these radical experiments but with music of a completely different type.

The Recording versus the Soundtrack on the Film

EM : I agree. The music for *La tenda rossa* lasts twenty-three minutes, and in the film one doesn't ever hear it all. That for *L'attentat*[17] lasts seventeen minutes, and also in this case it is never complete but returns at different moments in the film. For this reason, I made a special mix for the LP, collecting the various fragments that I had prepared for the film. In this way, I developed a unique composition exclusively for the recording.

SM: It seems unmistakable that the cutting of a soundtrack disc documents the work of composition more than does the recording that operates in the film. In certain cases, however, there is an enormous difference between the recorded discographic version and that which one can hear of the soundtrack on the film. Pausing on the film *L'attentat* itself, after comparing the two versions, a certain delusion can result. There is a problem with the general technical quality of the film's sound. Then, at the point where the music intervenes in a big way, at the encounter between the demonstrators and the police, the music also has an unhappy coexistence with noises. Finally, in comparison to the seventeen minutes of the discographic version, the most consistent presence in the film does not last more than approximately three minutes. That's the reason why I believe it is important to clarify the difference between one operation of speculative research, which we find on the recording, and the reality of its application.

EM: There is still more to say about pieces thought of in this way, written in this way. They really need time to be affirmed. It is absolutely necessary that the spectator have the time to listen to the music. Therefore, if writing of this kind is to be utilized for ten seconds, it's better not to insert it, better not to even think about it. In *L'attentat* there was the possibility of listening to the music at length, but in the mix Boisset betrayed me a little (perhaps because of his delusion). There were moments in which it would have been possible to put in more music. We mixed it together. However, he then removed it unbeknown to me, privileging the effects. Many directors understand this type of writing only years later. This means that in the commercial cinema, if experiments are made, one pays for them afterward. I have paid for them. And luckily, no one ever protested against me. In fact, the work can be rejected and the assignment given to another composer, with the consequent doubling of expenses. It happens rarely, but it happens. Not to me, luckily.

To remain on this concrete aspect . . . cuts do not happen only to music that is difficult to comprehend. Sometimes the director and composer decide already at the Moviola stage that they ought to prepare some pieces in reserve, knowing at the outset that perhaps they will not go in the film. It is normal. It can happen finally that a piece serves to cover noises that did not come out very well. It can be frustrating for the composer, but it is a part of the work in the cinema.

THE PREMIX AND FINAL MIX

The Use of Noise

I mention now the premix and the final mix. The difference between the two phases should not require explanation. We have, however, spoken of the premix phase many times without identifying it by name. One might say that separately, superimpositions represent a particular case of premix. The premix is an operation done to give equilibrium to the diverse orchestral components for the final transfer into two stereo channels (or, in more sophisticated systems, if the film calls for it, Dolby Surround, and so on). On the other hand, the mix consists of the mixing of music with dialogue and effects. It involves a mixture that is not real, because the various tracks remain separate to allow the insertion of dubbing afterward. (The part that is not modified is, in fact, called the "international track.")

The music track endures a series of interventions in order to be adapted to the film. Here the director has the ultimate word. Under the best circumstances, he could treat the music well, allowing it to be heard; or he could treat the music badly, not allowing it to be heard enough. In general, in my opinion, one must take into consideration that the music that one hears badly seems ugly even if it is the most beautiful, and vice versa. Mediocre music makes its own contribution to a film. But frequently after having worked so much, the composer feels disillusioned by the way in which his music has been sacrificed. . . . The recordings save us. Through them, the document of what we have really done remains and can reach the spectator, but it is only a partial consolation if the presence of the film music has been compromised by the mix.

With respect to other sound elements, such as noise or dialogue, one . . . has the prospect of using noise itself as an integral part of a composition. These are very difficult experiments that you attempt only when you know that the film will not make any money for you. I have used noise in some films, in some isolated scenes, but I applied it in full only once, in Virginia Onorato's 1972 film *L'ultimo uomo di Sara* (*The Last Man of Sara*). I used exclusively casual sounds, recorded live, mounting them in the Moviola with various premixes, anticipating them even in the composition that I made for the film.

I remember another attempt that has some analogy with the preceding one. It was in Elio Petri's beautiful film *Un tranquillo posto di campagna* (*A Tranquil Place in the Country*),[18] above all in the dream episodes. I attempted to interpret the nocturnal nightmares of the protagonist, a painter played by Franco Nero. Chromatic, abstract images are seen, one a warped palette. Here the music does not replace the sounds of reality as in the preceding case. It is another thing. One is dealing with a process of identification with the images, but it is of great effectiveness. The film earned extremely little: this it is well to say.

Solutions like this one depend on the confidence the director has in the composer, on friendship, and on the confidence that passes between them. Directors are not always ready to receive certain messages, to attribute to music a significance and an expressive possibility that can seem totally over and above their own actions—above all, over their own roles.

The very first film I made with Faenza was an eccentric film, *Escalation* (1968),[19] which did very well. He told me that he did not have the foggiest idea what to do regarding the music. It left me totally free. I invented sounds made with the voice, sounds from the throat and the larynx, which were realized by Carlo Nicchio in various overdubs. I would not apply this type of solution to just any film; I would use it only for certain moments when, such as in this case, the bizarre character of the protagonist was elated.[20] A director might verbally accept certain ideas and then nullify the consensus during the mix. Faenza wanted to cut those sounds, but he did not do it. In no way does this very unusual type of intervention play a part in the negotiations between composer and director, at least in the initial phase. It is the sensibility of the composer that causes the decision to transfer to the score the sounds that come directly from the images, independent of dialogue, noise, and other things.

Critique of the Music for *Il sorriso del grande tentatore* (*The Smile of the Great Tempter*)

I will cite a concrete example. The film *Il sorriso del grande tentatore* (*The Smile of the Great Tempter*)[21] is set during our time, in a religious convent. The architect Umberto Turco had made extraordinary scenery designs that included various styles of ecclesiastical architecture. Thus I wrote music based on choirs that passed in review, and I mixed together, in a disorderly way, the texts of the five sequences of the church, with musical references to diverse epochs of liturgical music, and for this idea I was criticized very strenuously by Professor Miceli.

SM: Aside from . . . solutions of this type, if I explain them only in musical, technical, and historic terms, they are communicated badly to the director. He remains a little out in the cold, don't you think?

EM: Not really. The director accepts a plan like this ahead of time. He does not go in search of an adventure (which in any case he could refuse if he wanted to). The composer confides his own idea. He explains it to the best of his ability, at the piano first, before going into the recording studio. I told Damiani my intention to respect the scenery-design approach to the film, and he accepted it. In this case we were not confronted by a thematic idea, which is always easier to communicate. We were confronted by a thought, a stylistic plan that prevailed throughout, so much so that these musical moments of the Christian liturgy that I passed in review were completely mixed up. As with the rest of Turco's scenery, it had mixed, not distinct, Romanesque and baroque elements. Therefore, I served the film in the manner that I believed best, and the director shared this choice with me. Then, many years after, I listened to the critique of Professor Miceli.

SM: Don't get started on that argument, because my judgment is irrelevant to the mechanisms you are explaining. I can only say that with the years, studying your music, or rather other themes regarding other authors, I too have modified certain opinions. It gives me pleasure, because I believe that it is always better to put everything on the table for discussion and not take refuge in an untouchable position. But on this point, with the passage of time, I have become surer of my original judgment.

EM: Now you can talk about it.

SM: Anyway, the argument about the diverse architectural styles seems a pretext to me. I have seen the film again and again, unfortunately, but I have never noted all those stylistic architectural mixtures. The dominant tone, a little cold and a little kitsch, is that characterized by the typical modernism of certain churches and sanctuaries constructed from the end of the war to today. There is only one discordant element. It pertains to a brief scene shot in a chapel that looks as if it is from the seventh or eighth century (and that seems original to me, not reconstructed by the scenery designer). Therefore (if I can be sincere right to the end), this argument about the mixture of architectural styles reminds me of another discussion that took place years ago. I asked you about the motive behind your choice of the organ (and the citation of Bach) in the scene of the duel in *Per un pugno di dollari* (*A Fistful of Dollars*).[22] You responded by saying that the duel took place in a church, and therefore . . . I began to suspect that in the presence of certain very courageous musical choices (good or bad as they may be, and to this point I will return later), you need to cook up a justification, an extramusical alibi. Perhaps you don't remember well *Il sorriso del grande tentatore* [*The Smile of the Great Tempter*][23] (it is better that way). Everyone remembers the surroundings in which the duel took place in Leone's film. It is a little deconsecrated church, a tiny, dilapidated building, containing all manner of stuff and reduced to a stable. It is not the Basilica of Santa Croce in Florence nor Notre Dame in Paris (which makes you dizzy when you enter, and you think instantly, "Organ"). Therefore, I believe that you wanted to use the great sonority of a great organ and the grand citation of the pungent opening of the *Toccata and Fugue in D Minor* no matter what.

Pretexts aside, as far as my reservations about the use that you made of the five *Sequenze ufficiali* of the church, I have observed in your music an iconoclastic vein that is slightly gratuitous and in any case out of proportion to its purpose. This would open another chapter that concerns, in my opinion, a certain confusion between the display of means, the musical solutions that you have utilized, and the quality, the weight of certain films to which you have applied them. To put it briefly, Damiani is not Ken Russell (and Russell in his turn is not Kubrick). I believe I have intuited the motive that, on the other hand, you yourself have declared on many occasions. In a film you always give the maximum. (This is in your nature.) If it concerns a film without economic ambitions, you use the occasion to experiment. But there remains the fact of the imbalance between the two components.

Returning to *Il sorriso del grande tentatore*, you know how much I appreciate stylistic mixtures and daring juxtaposition (and you have made extraordinary ones). However, I am perplexed by this cheap accumulation that . . . involves . . . all five of the great hymn-sequential models of Christian song. Any one of them is the carrier of specific and linguistic musical values, and each is also very far from the others. Even more, it disturbs me to hear them entrusted to female tribunes full of sighs and erotic winks. It is worthy of a television jingle produced by an economics faculty or a university student festival. It has the exaggerated use of a drum set that seems to be stolen from a dance of the third order from the Italian Riviera in Emilia-Romagna.

Respect for religion does not matter to me (even if for others it might be a valid argument). For me it is above all a question of musical taste and moderation. I know well (and one feels it clearly) that this also is an experiment tied to the process of superimposition, as in *Bambini del mondo* and similar works. The hearing of it does not console me nor render the results pleasing for me.

Let's take up again the thread of strange solutions devoted to particular stimuli.

L'umanoide (The Humanoid)

EM: Then let's talk about *L'umanoide* (*The Humanoid*).[24] I have never liked the little marches in the stratosphere that John Williams has written for American science-fiction films by Spielberg and others, even though I think that Williams is a very fine composer. I am not making a qualitative judgment. Also, in those circumstances Williams is very able. I think his choice is dictated by the film and record industry. It seems to me that the sky, the infinite, deserves something better than a little march. For *L'umanoide*, which is an Italian science-fiction film, I wrote a fugue in six parts—"Incontro a sei" ("Encounter in Six")—with a double subject and a double counter-subject. It is a double fugue in the real sense of the word, because there is an orchestra that performs a fugue for three voices and a synthesizer with the voice of an organ that performs the other fugue *a 3*. These two parts were recorded separately and then put together. Naturally, I wrote a fugue for six parts. Here the vertical control is total and the overdubbing doesn't matter, because it is a fugue on an absolutely tonal foundation.[25] So . . . I thought that for the journey of a spaceship into the stratosphere, it would be more appropriate to make something of this sort than a little march.

SM: Certainly, yours is one interpretation that is more than legitimate, but it is also a confirmation of what I said before with respect to your tendency to give your all, no matter the stature of the film. . . . Lado is not Kubrick (just to repeat myself, but first I was thinking of *Clockwork Orange*;[26] now, evidently, I am thinking of *2001: A Space Odyssey*).[27] But the trouble is that Lado is neither Ridley Scott[28] nor Andrei Tarkovsky.[29] But I would not want to attack Lado, who, I would hope, had good reason to decide to make a science-fiction film in Italy. It seems to me that the discussion basically has to do with the traditions and possibilities of Italian cinema. It is a cinema that has been very important in comedy, serious drama, farce, . . . and the production sui generis of some master directors, but it is without a past and a future in the musical (notwithstanding certain potential inclinations of Moretti and the brothers Taviani, about whom I have already spoken) and science fiction. I believe that this is incontestable.

Now I return to the "little march" of John Williams (as Maestro Morricone called it), in order to say that it seems to me a legitimate choice and also totally credible considering the context. Certainly, in idealistic terms, the equation of an "infinite space" with "great forms" has an indisputable logic, but the saga of interstellar wars is the interpretation of a modern fable. It is a fable for youngsters and nostalgic adults by a baby American civilization that has a very short historical consciousness. America has existed for two centuries, little more, full of disguises "a posteriori"[30] and mythological roots. Therefore, if our Italian mythology is in the remote past, America's mythology, apart from the epic poem of the West, is in the future—a future, on the other hand, to whose construction they have given a decisive contribution. They needed a film-music dramaturgy that would have recourse to models of self-celebration and triumphalism, with a sincere and massive dose of self-irony.

I believe that Spielberg and Lucas entertained themselves first and foremost as monstrously able children to whom the use of an extraordinary toy had been conceded. (While saying this, we should not forget their great professionalism.) And to that winking and unruly toy it was not appropriate to put Bach and his dizzying abstractions, but rather a simplified synthesis of a universally comprehensible musical world. Therefore, it seems natural to me that the model ought to have been that of the late-nineteenth-century symphonic poem, with a touch of the triumphal bellicosity of the operetta. Above all, it is a model already aligned with the tradition of the school of Hollywood music, which was in good measure of middle-European origin (Herrmann, Rozsa, Korngold, Steiner, Waxman . . .). Choosing Bach or something that would remind you of it would have fallen into the serious and therefore the ridiculous.

EM: However, when I see scenes like those in *Star Wars*,[31] I continue to be disappointed. One is able to kid around, but in my opinion there is nothing entertaining about writing like that. Those are choices dictated by commercial motives. Instead, to write a fugue *a 6* was very fatiguing. This is my way of saying to you that the craft of the cinema composer should never be routine. One needs to stimulate oneself, to conduct experiments, always finding a way to entertain oneself.

Recently I wrote a canon in retrograde only because it is not a conventional canon. It did not suffice to put the subject of the canon and the retrograde in the melody, because the piece had always to be catchy, transparent, and correct in all the vertical appointments and harmonies. In this film, *Canone inverso* (*Inverse Canon*), of Ricky Tognazzi,[32] which takes place in Prague during the Second World War and also contains gypsy music that I wrote, the protagonists are a pianist and a violinist. The playback program called for a part of Mendelssohn's *Concerto for Violin, Piano, and Orchestra*,[33] a youthful work that we handled by using a preexistent recording. (The choice of Mendelssohn was required because something tied to Jewish culture was needed.) The screenwriters and the director had listened to this concerto for a long time. The piece with exasperated energy had to have a very great impact, as in the best of the romantic tradition. However, they found the Mendelssohn *Concerto* a little weak in relation to the function called for in the film. In fact, at the end of the film, . . . the concerto is interrupted by German soldiers breaking in.

In this craft one has to pass from rock to a romantic concerto. At a certain point, the director asked me, "Why don't you write it?" Now, if one listens to a fragment of this romantic-style concerto with its tonal foundation, it is even too romantic and too intense, but that's the way the director wanted it. He literally implored me on this point, which calls for an explanation. The principal protagonist is a violinist. He has a nervous temperament and has been in love with a pianist forever. . . . He has engaged a violin studio especially in order to . . . play with her, a thing they finally succeed in doing at the end of the film.

The canon in this piece is an anomaly. Concerti written in the romantic era would not have had one. Its presence was born of a cinematographic necessity that was not suggested by the director. I suggested it myself. Tognazzi wanted the piece to last two minutes, but I told him that in such a short time it would be impossible to do anything and that it would have to last at least between four and four and a half minutes. This condition he then accepted, and afterward he also gave me precise synchronization points for it in the film. There was a second theme that I had not predicted and that, while I was still writing, I had to insert at two minutes, twenty seconds, as a result of a telephone call from Prague. On the point of tears (it happens to all directors who are passionate about their work, and it is not a ridiculous thing), Tognazzi begged that the violinist be dramatic, "harrowing." I told this to Gabriele Pierannunzi, a top-notch violinist, and more than that it seems to me I could not have done.

SM: That canon is a slightly unusual solution, because from Viennese classicism forward it was a form that did not excite much interest, only to reappear timidly in the late romantic period, but in the chamber music genre more than in the concerto, and then above all in the twentieth century.

EM: Make note that I said I found that I had to modify the romantic form.

SM: You are not talking about a modification, because the representative forms of romanticism are immutable. They are consigned to history itself for having certain distinctive characteristics. If we modify them, we are no longer able to define them as romantic forms (and naturally, this is true for any other epoch). But one can talk about contamination and of stylistic medleys. Now let's listen, calling attention to the fact that the premix is not definitive.

EM: Yes, it is not definitive. Unfortunately, one hears that the contrabass is lighter than the trumpet. Then there are other imbalances where one does not hear the piano well enough. Unfortunately, we mixed the piano in half an hour because we had to send the recording to Prague, where they were filming. However, if in the assembly there were a *pianissimo* in the violin or in the piano, in the final mix we would have taken it into account, raising the level of the instrument to the detriment of all the rest. The orchestra was recorded live, while for the violin and piano we had recourse to dubbing exactly for this reason. The execution was entrusted to Gilda Buttà, who played also in *La leggenda del pianista sull'oceano* (*The Legend of the Pianist on the Ocean*).[34]

It does not finish in E major because there will be the aforementioned interruption at this point in the film. It seemed illogical to me to conclude the piece with the arrival of the German soldiers. Therefore I closed with an avoided cadence.

After so many films, I have to be ready for anything. To be able to make music for the cinema, one has to study and experience all fields of music. It is not easy to accept, but I realize that in the taste and culture of the director, as well as in the people, in the listeners, the difference between a very beautiful and a very ugly piece is minimal. Someone might say, "This piece is extraordinary," and another might say that the same piece is repugnant. My advice is that you learn to suffer.

SOUND DESIGN, MIXING, AND THE COEXISTENCE OF
MUSIC AND EFFECTS

SM: The examples tied to the experiences of Maestro Morricone are exhausted, at least at this point. Therefore, let us examine more closely the topic of mixing. The not-always-peaceful coexistence between music and effects is repeatedly skimmed over. I will save you from a very long list of films that have contributed to the history of cinema whose effects were defective in a very obvious way. One will do as an example for all. I invite you to reexamine and listen again to the sound chaos of *Le notti di Cabiria* (*The Nights of Cabiria*).[35]

But let's go beyond the attention paid to a single author. About mixing one has to say that stereo sound and the successive audio techniques applied in the cinema have made a contribution not only from the point of view of the spectacle. Dolby Digital, Dolby Surround, and more generally the multitrack system, with its relative separation of the channels in the projection hall, constrain one in a major way during the production phase, but they guarantee results that are far superior to those of the past. In other words, if in the premix one has to carry everything to a single monophonic track and in stereo to two, the multichannel system permits the conservation of a fractionalization of the sound sources that is more faithful to the original channels (sixteen tracks, twenty-four tracks, and other). It has the possibility of steering and mixing successive distinct instrumental sections with distinct extramusical sources.

Aside from quality and the dynamics of the sound, one can easily verify a major spatial definition not only at the cinema but also in common domestic sound systems (provided that the VHS player and the television are at least stereophonic) and above all in home theater systems. In these, the old magnetic supports, even though emerging in more recent cases from digital matrices, cede inevitably to the field of the laser disc and the DVD. There is a jump in quality without comparison not only on the acoustic level, where the sound has the quality of a CD, but also on that of the visual. Aside from the higher resolution of the image, one thinks of the passage from 4:3 to 16:9.[36] A film created recently is able to teach us many things. It is a demonstration that the technical side of things is, or ought to be, a means (not an end) to expand the expressive range of the creators.

Analysis of Music and Effects in *Dances with Wolves* (*Balla coi lupi*)

To demonstrate this, . . . I will examine part of a film in a little analytical laboratory that I have created. You have gone to spectacular films, typical of the Hollywood productions of recent years but of little interest in terms of content. However, while working, it is necessary to entertain ourselves . . . , so I have chosen a film, *Dances with Wolves* (*Balla coi lupi*),[37] that in my opinion is spectacular and has interesting content even though the soundtrack does not present the emphasis on technology and the special effects of other, later films. It is the debut of Kevin Costner as a director and from the first screening struck me, among other things, for certain characteristics of its sound design.

Personally, I don't put much value on the Oscars in the musical category because of the very debatable criteria for deciding to whom a score should be attributed. However, in this case, the film, made in the 1990s, obtained seven Oscars, among which was the Oscar for John Barry's musical score and, of more interest to us at this point, for sound design.[38]

I have analyzed the opening titles and the first episode. The opening titles . . . functioned as a prologue and introduced . . . the protagonist and therefore the story. I tried to characterize the entire sound treatment for these two cues. To do it, I used three different copies of the film (unfortunately all in VHS, while waiting for a DVD edition). I compared them with each other in a preliminary way. The first is the "short" version, dubbed in Italian;[39] the second is the "long" version, hi-fi stereo, Dolby Surround, still dubbed in Italian;[40] and the third is in the original language, English, a wide-screen extended version (three hours and forty-three minutes), obviously in Dolby Stereo.[41]

It is obvious that in order to evaluate the sound itself, the version in the original language has to be the one used for reference. The dubbed edition would have had to be altered to accommodate the changed equilibrium between the dialogue, effects, and music. The listening took place . . . under three different conditions: [1] with a good domestic sound system with amplification and external diffusion (thereby bypassing the television, which was utilized as a monitor in 16:9), then [2] by means of a sumptuous home-theater setup (to which I had access for the occasion), and then [3] with headphones, for a more selective verification of the preceding hearings. In the end, in order to confirm objectively certain auditory sensations, I converted a fragment of the sound track (about nine minutes and thirty seconds) into AIFF format,[42] subjecting them to a complementary software[43] spectrographic analysis. We can see a part of the spectrum, very contracted in the horizontal sense, relative to a little less than two thirds of the soundtrack examined [see Figure 5.1].[44]

I have summarized the results of the analysis in a diagram that requires some explanation, namely a legend. I have not subdivided the clip in the horizontal sense because on the narratological level, the passage between its various parts happens practically without . . . continuity. I remind you only (but you will find it in a subsequent graphic) that the opening titles are divided into two parts (the first with title cards on black, the second in

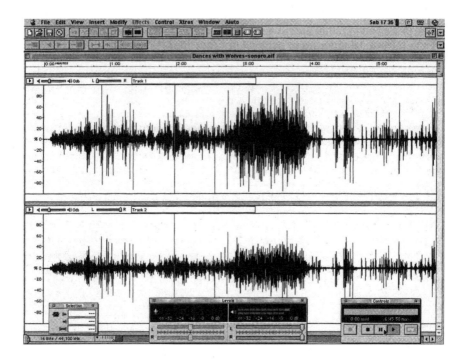

Figure 5.1. Spectrograph of Dances with Wolves

superposition). Interposed between the two is a brief episode that represents prior events and the entrance on the scene of the protagonist. I doubt that anyone here has not seen this film. However, I will recall it for you.

On a rudimentary operating table, in a camp hospital in the open air, lies a Northern soldier whose leg is being prepared for amputation. Profiting from the momentary absence of the surgeon, the man, wincing with pain, puts his boot back on and returns to his platoon. At the end of the second part of the opening titles, we are carried onto the field of battle and into the first episode of the film. It is the suicide ride of John Dunbar that causes the improvised attack of his men and the destruction of the Southerners.

Now returning to the diagram (Figures 5.2–5.4) and commencing with the column at the left, we find the time, a concise description of events (therefore a synthesis and not a script adopted from the montage), and the music. The other five columns indicate the spatial arrangement of the sounds (area at the left—area intermediate left—central area—intermediate right—far right). . . . To be clear, the reproduction is not multichannel. It is limited to track 1 (left channel) and track 2 (right channel). Just as a sound located as being in the center is a "virtual" reconstruction obtained from the perfect equilibrium between right and left channels, so equally, even if with less clarity, one can talk about the "intermediate left" or "intermediate right" location simply by unbalancing the same sound source between the two channels.

The more frequently encountered example of this "virtual" reconstruction is the moving sound that changes position rapidly from one extreme to the other of the channels. Above all in these cases, it is the brain that compensates for the missing parts, thereby creating a sense of continuity that does not actually exist. There are other expedients for expanding the sound image. They include phase inversion and forced reverb, thanks to which the sound loses brightness but assumes an unusual spatiality (also profundity) and a sort of apparent mobility. And here I will stop. . . . One could subject a musically neutral recording to first electronic and then digital elaboration on the timbral and spatial acoustic planes.[45] The possibilities are enormous.

Returning to the diagram, the letters indicate the nature of the sound taken into consideration.

M = Music
D = Dialogue
N = Noises

Taking as an example the noises, the scale of intensity, reduced to four values, is indicated this way (in descending value of the sound from more intense at left):

N—(N)—n—(n)

As you can see, they are approximate indications for the dynamics. For any particular sound event, you could have created a precise value in decibels, but it would have been a useless complication with respect to what I propose to demonstrate to you. In musical terms, N is able to be *forte*, (N) *mezzoforte*, n *piano*, and (n) *mezzopiano*, but because we are not dealing exclusively with musical dynamics, I preferred this neutral denomination.[46]

The vertical arrows ($\downarrow$) indicate a continuity of location of the sound in the course of a limited episode, those that are transversal (/ \), a repositioning (to which it will be important to return). The horizontal arrows ($\rightarrow$) are valid only for sounds that undergo a perceptible spatial change in relation to the images, presumed or visible, that produce them. The greater the number of arrows, the greater the velocity of the change of location. Within the limits possible, I have placed the description of events and the relevant sounds on the same horizontal line. Clearly one is dealing only with major references because, as happens frequently in the assembly of sound, the tail of a sound event pertains to a scene that continues, even if only for a little while, into the frames of the successive scene or vice versa. Into the last frames of a scene the sound for the next scene will already have entered. It is a sort of acoustic dissolve utilized to "read" and to soften the passage between diverse situations. Now let's look at the whole diagram in detail in figures 5.2, 5.3, and 5.4.[47]

The diagram reveals the existence of a mix that is the result of a precise and complex audiovisual design. Some episodes warrant comment. First, you will have noted that all of the music happens at . . . four key points: from 00:05 to 00:50 of the opening titles; from 01:27, at the entrance of the protagonist on screen; from 02:56, in the change of scene that introduces the theater of war; and from 06:22, as soon as John Dunbar rides against the enemy's front line. In the first three key points, the noises and dialogue are nonexistent or very marginal. Therefore, the music shares the principal role with the image. In the fourth, the attack is all musical, and many of the noises that follow arrive after having been treated in a very opportune way, as we will see better in a little while. . . . Through the fruition of stereophonic spatiality, the work of mixing allows the coexistence of components in a cinema sound that was unthinkable in the past.

Let's take the clip from the end of the first part of the opening titles, that is, from 00:51. Up to this point the spectator has listened to music reproduced in all its dynamic and spatial dimension.

Therefore, the passage to a diverse acoustic space . . . carries with it certain problems, above all, as in this case, if there is no interruption in the music. The lowering of the musical level to *mp* from *m* and the central location of the dialogue and noises, D/R, create a focus on the noises, with the consequent loss of an intermediate spatiality in the music. However, it is restored at 01:27. The passage of a carriage pulled by horses (02:04) proves to be an element of relative disturbance. The visual reference is absent. The corresponding acoustic transfer is presumed, and the brevity of the episode makes it assume an incidental character for "color." In other words, the music is covered, but the reason justifies the effect. This does not take into account the progression of ascendant chords in the strings and brass[48] that carry the second thematic idea to a solution. It is signaled by a recurring military drum figuration, the "martial bridge." It is barely finished when noise occurs over the final chord, held and beating again—in other words, without too much damage. Still faithful to a succession joined to musical segments, a crescendoing ostinato of staccato and repeated chords is born here (02:13), coinciding with the first attempt by John Dunbar to stick his injured leg into his boot. It concludes with the cry of pain that accompanies the second, this time successful, attempt.

TIME	EVENT	MUSIC	AREA LEFT	AREA LEFT INTERMEDIATE	AREA CENTER	AREA RIGHT INTERMEDIATE	AREA RIGHT
00:00	Beginning opening titles						
00:05	continues	*Main Title - Looks like a suicide* (birth of *John Dunbar theme*)	M ↓	M ↓	M ↓	M ↓	M ↓
00:50	End 1st part opening titles						
00:51	Camp hospital. Dialogue between doctors. Ambient noises. Big fly buzzing	"Martial" bridge onto which is grafted...	(M) N		(M) D N		(M) N
01:27	"Entrance" John Dunbar. Groan	...2nd thematic idea	M	M	M n	M	M
02:04	John observes a mutilated man. Carriage passes by (FC)		(n) ←	n ←	(N) ←	n ←	(n) ←
02:13	John tries to put the hurt leg in the boot. Groans, buzz	Ostinato of staccato Chords in *crescendo*	M ↓		M ↙ ↘ N		M ↓
02:35	John reclines head suddenly. Buzz of large fly in pause between chords.	*Crescendo* continues	M ↓ n ←←	(n) ←←	- ←←	(n) ←←	M ↓ n ←←
	John breaks a cane, puts it in his mouth, and puts leg in boot. Groan	Held chord (in synch)	M ↓				M ↓
02:56	Camp of the opposite side	Variation on the second thematic idea	M	M	M	M	M

Figure 5.2. *Dances with Wolves*—Spatial distribution of the sounds

Time	Scene	Music/Comment	1	2	3	4	5
	Beginning of 2nd part of opening titles	Abbreviated insertion of the *John Dunbar Theme*	↓	↓	↓	↓	↓
03:53	End 2nd part opening titles	continues	M		M D		M
03:55	Cavalry platoon arrives	continues	(n) ←	n ←	N ←	n ←	(n) ←
04:00	"St. David's Field – Tennessee 1863"	continues music ends	(M) m (m)		(M) m (m)		(M) m (m)
	Northern general observes the sides from on high	and other officials		D	D		
04:12	John at the Northern camp. Rifle shot aimed at him. Another shot and the whistle of the close bullets.		N (n) →→→	n →→→	D (N) →→→ D n (D) (N) →→→	n →→→	(N) →→→ (n) →→→
	Crazy laughs and shout in the distance. Interposed dialogue with fellow soldier		n		D r D ↓		
05:40	John observes horses, then distances himself while	Repetition of 2nd thematic idea (varied)	(M) ↓		(M) ↓ D ↓		(M) ↓
	Fellow soldier fires, continues to talk unawares	Bridge			N D ↓		n
06:22	John, in saddle, leaps over barrier (comment of Northern general)	Theme "in 3" of the ride	M ↓	M ↘ D	M ↓ (N)	M ↙	M ↓

Figure 5.3.   *Dances with Wolves*—Spatial distribution of the sounds (continued)

06:22	John, in saddle, leaps over barrier (comment of Northern general) and launches himself toward Southern lines. Reactions of opposite faction.	Theme "in 3" of the ride	M ↓	M D	M ↓ (N)	M	M ↓
	Many firearm shots, shouts, neighs.		N M ↓ N	(N) (N)	M ↓ N	(N) (N)	N M ↓ N
	Dialogue among John's fellow soldiers.	suspension	(M)		M D		(M)
07:14	John stops in the middle of the field. Northerners exult. Southerners challenged to try again.		n N N ↘	N	N	N D	n N N ↙
07:53	John continues his ride along the enemy line. He lets the bridle go, raises his arms. Explosions.	Resumption of theme "in 3" of the ride with added choir	M ↓ (M) N	M (N)	(M) ↓ M N D	M (N)	M ↓ (M) N
08:40	Assault of Northerners. Shots, horses' hooves, moans,	Blasts and *John Dunbar Theme* more animated and articulated.	M ↓ N ←	(N) ←	M ↓ N ←	(N) ←	M ↓ N ←

Figure 5.4. *Dances with Wolves*—Spatial distribution of the sounds (continued)

[notation of quarter rest, half note, quarter note, quarter rest, quarter, quarter, quarter]

This simple but effective figuration begins with the brass (two times) and passes then to the strings. After two analogous repetitions, the strings retake it in abbreviated form at the octave *sforzando*, with a held conclusive chord that functions in synchronization with the change of scene.

The typical stereophonic positioning of the sounds is the beneficiary of a particularly careful treatment. It is consistent with the emphasis on the extreme area for the [music] and on the central location of noises (in this case, the suffocated groans of the protagonist). In fact, the debut of the ostinato for half of the brass favors a prevalent centrality for the music. The same figure in the strings determines an enlargement on the musical front, with a consequent "appropriation" of the central space from the noises. It is made even more significant because it is synchronized with the second attempt of the protagonist to put on his boot, which is accompanied by sounds of various sorts. . . . Thanks to the fact that we direct our attention to frequencies in the high range, the passage of the strings from a high-pitched to super-high-pitched range emphasizes the spatial element carried to an extreme. But this is not enough. Exactly at the second repetition of the figure on the part of the strings a tiny sound arrives, a lightning sound event that we would consider a virtuosity of mixing. At 02:35, when John Dunbar throws his head back in pain at the conclusion of the first attempt to put on his boot, the buzzing of a big fly enters the right ear of the spectator, traverses the brain, and exits from the left ear.[49] The event, not new but here more obvious,[50] is located exactly in the pause of the ostinato, before its repetition. Afterward we will try to listen to it, the quality of the audio equipment permitting. In the meantime (because one does not say that I hear flies like others see the Madonna), observe this detail on the spectrogram:

The area examined is between the end (2:23.2) and the successive attack (2:36.6) of the violins on the ostinato. The central part, evidenced by a rectangular area of more secure tonality, frames the buzzing of the fly. I have a duration of 0.0571 of a second, as indicated in the little window at the bottom to the left, labelled "Selection." Observing track 1 in the top spectrogram, one notes that the maximum peak is at 2:35.7 and, in correspondence to its diminishing (2:35.8), it grows in track 2. The point of insertion—the subtle vertical line that intersects the spectrum and that runs during the hearing—one finds a little after 2:36, and it corresponds to the point of reduction in track 2. The dynamic difference between the two channels, to which we owe the effect of transfer, is very evident in the window located at the bottom in the center (labelled "Levels"), even though the images have been "frozen" immediately after the maximum peak of track 2, which skims along the under 8 decibels against the under 24 of track 1.

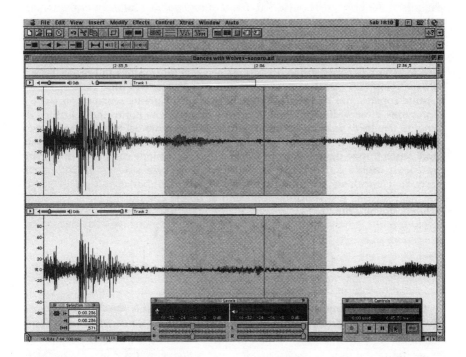

Figure 5.5. Detail of spectrogram

It would be safe to hypothesize that the music was written and recorded to the final edited version of the film. (I don't have information regarding this, although the Hollywood practice leaves little room for procedures that do not conform to the norm.) This means that the final mix must have been preceded by a reassembly of the sound effects (all or in part). Otherwise, the insertion of the fly into the musical pause would have been impossible. As you see, I have not considered the hypothesis that John Barry calculated a synchronization of this type in advance or that, like the airplane in chapter 2, the fly is a completely extraneous accident.

Many other points of the clip would be worthy of specific comment, but for brevity let's go to 06:22, namely to the beginning of the ride. As I have already anticipated, the musical front is initially compact, but some problems of coexistence are created immediately following the arrival of a repertory of sounds that are very nourished by effects. Coincident with the comment of the general who observes the scene from on high ("Looks like a suicide"), the theme begins with the trombones and passes to the trumpets, then to the violins, and finally to the horns, while the strings play in counterpoint with a simple figuration of accompaniment. In all these cases, including the violins, the sound has its origin predominantly in the center, while the explosions, pawing of the hooves, shouts, and many other sounds scatter over the whole acoustic stage. The justification (not indispensable) is that the frame presents diverse subjects, among which is that of John in the saddle. In other words, the spectator's hearing is in the center of the action. Thus, in the chaos, the thematic component maintains its cohesion and plasticity nearly intact. The . . . strings in a high-pitched register, at the extremes of the acoustic area, defend themselves by reason of their strategic position and their acoustic nature with the help of the percussion. Although it has already been noted, it is well to emphasize that the entry of the violins with the theme conserves the centrality of the other sections, with the cellos and basses assuming the figuration of the accompaniment. Very interesting, at least from my point of view, is the brief episode that follows (from 07:14 to 07:52). In the sudden absence of the music, the enthusiastic shouts of the fellow soldiers and those of scorn and of challenge from the enemies make a game of close/distant, of crescendo and of filling in waves of the space, that confer to this acoustic episode a profundity that is truly unique.

The second part of the ride presents a procedure that is a little different. My diagram cannot do it complete justice. The horns still assume the central role of major force and compactness, but the entrance of a very reverberant chorus vocalizing in crescendo together with the explosions results in a hard location. They sound as if in the distance. I remind you that John Dunbar drops the bridle, opens his arms, and closes his eyes. He leaves them as if waiting for the coup de grace. His is a state of abandonment that is almost heroic. These oscillating sounds, which are a little out of focus (as a result of reverberation), are the equivalent of his state. One could talk even of an acoustic subjectivity, of a sign of the function of the mediated level. A Southern soldier receives a bullet in the forehead (08:40). It is the signal for an attack by the Northerners. John Dunbar exits provisionally from the scene. All of a sudden, the music turns to its habitual plasticity. With an ambiguous *incipit*, blasts of the trumpet, it courts the internal level. But it is only an allusion, because to these blasts is grafted a more animated version of the John Dunbar theme. It is assigned to the trumpets (located in the center), the only ones perhaps that can emerge from the acoustic and spatial chaos of the battle.

There. I hope I have demonstrated the importance and the possibilities of the work of the mix. It would not be presumptuous to hypothesize that the premix was conducted with a view to this final phase or that it must have been possible to intervene until the very last moment, having recorded and conserved the music on multichannel matrixes. Although indirect, there is evidence for this hypothesis in the fact that on the CD this same musical episode (not perfectly synchronized with the soundtrack, from the ride on-ward) has a conventional spatial disposition.

EM: At this point once again I have to affirm what I have already said about the importance of Professor Miceli's analyses. His method and this kind of scientific rigor are models that you should apply in your profession as composers. But I have to add also—and here the analytic work does not enter at all—that the music of John Barry does not seem to me a particularly important model. Sure, there is great skill, but then there are others who orchestrate the pieces.

SM: In fact, the object of this work was not the music of John Barry (even if to me personally *Dances with Wolves*[51] seems one of his better results; "Two Socks," the theme of the wolf, for example, is very intense even if it is not developed enough). But I like the fact that you have touched on the argument about orchestrators. Naturally, it does not apply only to John Barry but also to all the American film composers, who by tradition assign the task of orchestration to collaborators. To tell the truth, one is dealing with a practice that one notes also in composers here at home, but there are exceptions— though few—and Maestro Morricone is one of them. This is itself the sign of a concession by the craft that one encounters when there is an industrialized other, the cabinetmaker against the industrial designer. On the contrary, precisely because I predicted that we would arrive at this theme, I prepared a step back to our first colloquium in September 1979, which was published in 1982 in an appendix to the book *La musica nel film* (*Music in Film*).[52]

COLLABORATORS[53]

SM: You were never served by collaborators?

EM: Never, and it is an absolute moral principle. Unfortunately, when I collaborated with Nicolai[54] —and it is one of the reasons that I had to stop— some people believed that he helped me in some way. He only helped me conduct. He would arrive in the studio at the last moment. He would not know the score. No, absolutely no collaborator.

I like to write. It is my craft, the only thing that I know how to do. I cannot give to others tasks that I feel are profoundly mine.

SM: And in the case of works that you knew in advance would not give you satisfaction?

EM: A secondary film, you say? Why haven't I given those to others to do? But what should I have done? The orchestration? The melody? If I could not do a film, I would refuse to do it (but I rarely turned one down), and instead I sacrificed. I worked hard.

Also, I began this profession as the orchestrator-arranger for musicians who were making money while I was making nothing. I did it for certain composers who are still working today. Therefore, I was exploited, and after this experience, for moral as well as artistic reasons, I was unable to exploit others. If you want to see, all my scores are autographs. With some force I could rewrite all of them.

SM: That you knew. Is it pretty diffuse, the habit of using anonymous collaborators?

EM: I have to say that the tendency has been diminishing for quite a while, but some illustrious composers for the cinema still have recourse to this type of collaboration. It is something that I have never understood, because even if you give someone a well-done short score, really clear, the orchestration is the music. The fact that you put "ponticello" for the violas, or "pizzicato," it is a part of the music; it influences the whole sound. Therefore, for me it is an unacceptable thing as a matter of not only moral but particularly musical principle. The boss of the music is the one who writes it from beginning to end, beautiful or ugly as it may be.

EM: I have to confirm fully what I said twenty years ago.

NOTES

1. The definition of "score," inevitably but generically, cannot do justice to the principle. If one can speak of an aleatoric score [mother score], in which the degree of simultaneous vertical legibility (from section to section) is only potential, one remakes a composite concept of modularity. For a more expansive treatment of this concept, see Miceli, *Morricone*, op. cit., 158ff.

2. [VHS Lange, B004AH2DY0.]

3. LP, General Music ZSLGE 55121.

4. They record any kind of thing on forty-eight tracks, even if they have to make a very simple piece. As they are not masters of experimentation, these men do not know what they ought to do. They don't know what should be excluded, they don't know anything: they have the tuning of C major with the good sound of the guitar and nothing else. Then one needs a month to find one line among those forty-eight tracks.

5. *Ten to Survive*, on LP *Antologia General Music*, GM 33/01-4, then in CD NST 01-1/2. For more information and for a detailed analysis, see Miceli, *Morricone*, op. cit., 229ff. The film is beyond repair, but a copy is deposited in the Archive of the RAI. Besides Morricone, Nino Rota, Egisto Macchi, Luis Bacalov, and Franco Evangelisti were involved. The film therefore was composed of ten animated shorts produced in as many countries. The chorus of white voices of the ARCUM was directed by Paolo Lucci.

6. *Comporre per il Cinema*, generating scale of *Bambini del mondo* (*Children of the World*), 134.

7. [DVD, *The Sergio Leone Anthology*, MGM/UA, 2007; *Sergio Leone—Cofanetto Grandi Classici*, Mondo Home, 2007.]

8. *Invenzione per John*, soundtrack on LP Cinebox MDF 50. The composition was never reissued on CD.

9. See "Musical Example 20, fragment of mother score for *Invenzione per John (Giù la testa)*," in *Comporre per il Cinema*, 135.

10. See "Musical Example 21, fragment of mother score for *Invenzione per John (Giù la testa)*," in *Comporre per il Cinema*, 136.

11. See "Musical Example 22, fragment of mother score for *Intervenzione per John (Giù la testa)*," in *Comporre per il Cinema*, 136.

12. See "Musical Example 23, fragment of mother score from *Invenzione per John (Giù la testa)*," in *Comporre per il Cinema*, 136.

13. For a more detailed analysis, see Miceli, *Morricone*, op. cit., 162.

14. "Nella voce di Dio" ("In the Voice of God"), from the TV film *Mosé*, directed by G. Del Bosio, 1975, CD NST 01-2.

15. "Altri dopo di noi" ("Others after Us"), from the film *Krăsnaja palata* (*La tenda rossa*), directed by M. Kalatozov, 1968, CD NST 01-2. [DVD, Cecchi Gori, 2007.]

16. In Morse code, whose use was recently officially abolished, the letter *S* corresponds to three dots and the letter *O* to three lines.

17. *L'attentat* [*The Attempted Assassination*] (Boisett, 1972). [VHS Lange, B004AH2DY0.]

18. *Un tranquillo posto di campagna* (*A Tranquil Place in the Country*) (Petri, 1968). [DVD, CD, 2007.]

19. Roberto Faenza (1943–), film director. *Escalation* (Faenza, 1968).

20. Luca, interpreted by Lino Capolicchio.

21. Directed by Damiano Damiani, 1974. Recording Beat CD CR 18, comprising "Veni Sancte Spiritus," "Victimae Paschali Laudes," "Lauda Sion," "Stabat Mater," "Dies Irae," and a composition entitled "Con serena gioia."

22. *Per un pugno di dollari* (*A Fistful of Dollars*) (Leone, 1964). [DVD, *Sergio Leone Anthology*, MGM/UA, 2007.]

23. *Il sorriso del grande tentatore* (*The Smile of the Great Tempter*) (Damiani, 1974).

24. Directed by Aldo Lado, 1979. [DVD, American International Pictures.] He then is referring to *Star Wars*.

25. Recording on CD New Sound Trails, NST-CD 01-2.

26. *Clockwork Orange* (GB, Kubrick, 1971). [DVD, Warner Home Video, 2007, 2012.]

27. *2001: A Space Odyssey* (Kubrick, 1968). [DVD, Warner Home Video, 2012.]

28. Miceli alludes here to two masterworks of the type: *Alien* (GB, 1979); and *Blade Runner* (USA, 1982).

29. He is referring to *Solaris* (USSR, 1972). [DVD, Criterion Collection, 2002.]

30. (Think only of the weight of rhetoric and of prudery in the Italian culture of the 1800s, surviving at least until the Second World War.)

31. *Star Wars* (Spielberg, 1999, 2002). [DVD: 20th Century Fox Home Entertainment, 2011].

32. The film is entitled *Canone inverso* (*Inverse Canon, Making Love*) and was produced in 1999. The soundtrack was published by Virgin/Cecchi Gori Music, CD 8489422. [DVD, Cecchi Gori, 2000.]

33. *Concerto in D minor for piano, violin, and string orchestra* (1823).

34. See "Musical Example 24, Finale of a *Concerto romantico interrotto* (per *Canone inverso*)," in *Comporre per il Cinema*, 144–45.

35. Directed by Federico Fellini, music by Nino Rota, 1957. [DVD, *Nights of Cabiria*, Criterion Collection, 1999.]

36. He is referring to the dimensional relations of televised images, where 16:9 (or widescreen) permits a view that is wider and without lateral cuts for films shot in Cinemascope. In reality, things are much more complicated than that which could be presented hurriedly in the text, because of the actual state of the systems of digital transfer; in the support of the DVD, they behave very arbitrarily and incoherently on the part of the production houses. There is the tendency to realize DVDs in 4:3 letterbox format (a format contained in the original cinematographic format—that is, 2.30:1), avoiding thereby the use of the anamorphic video (the system of vertical compression of the image, analogous to that obtained with optical means in the cinema) with its very heavy consequences for the resolution. To understand these notions in

greater depth and to keep up to date with the discussion, I suggest regularly consulting periodicals from the sector, such as *Videotecnica*. [SM]

37. *Dances with Wolves* (Costner, 1990). [DVD, *Dances with Wolves—20th Anniversary Edition*, MGM/UA, 2011.]

38. Attributed to Russell Williams II, Jeffrey Perkins, Bill W. Berton, and Greg Watkins.

39. Copy of a monophonic televised RAI transmission and therefore unreliable technically. [SM]

40. Fox Video – Life Int. – 3017SA, duration 240 minutes. [DVD, CVC, 2009; Warner Home Video, 2009.]

41. PolyGram & Guild Home Video— GLD51212, also the CD of the soundtrack, Epic 467591 2. [DVD, *Dances with Wolves—20th Anniversary Edition*, MGM/UA, 2011.]

42. AIFF (Audio Interchange File Format) is an audio format developed by Apple Computer, utilized generally to master a musical CD. In this case, the conversion from analogical source (the audio exit of the VHS player) to digital was accomplished with AudioCatalyst v. 2.0.1 with a 44.1 MHz, 16-bit stereo on a PowerBook G3 series "bronze" 400 MHz. [SM]

43. SoundEdit 16, v. 2.07. [SM]

44. See spectrograph in *Comporre per il Cinema*, 147.

45. For a deeper knowledge of this theme, see S. Miceli, "Analisi della prima trasmissione stereofonica italiana," in *Tempo e spazio: Problemi di un rapporto tra opera e televisione. Atti del Seminario internazionale, Quaderni dell'Irtem*, 11 (Rome, 1991), 57–88.

46. Otherwise I would have had to notate the intensity of music that rarely goes under (M), so better not to compromise the legibility. [SM]

47. See *"Dances with Wolves—Spatial Distribution of the Sounds,"* in *Comporre per il Cinema*, 149–52.

48. These and successive references to the orchestral makeup are made with the benefit of the inventory but without the verification of the score. [SM]

49. The spectrograph shows instead a proceeding from left to right caused by a banal inversion of channels at the audio analogical entrance of the PowerBook. [SM]

50. The buzzing of the insect has a pair of anticipations in minor relief, more easily perceptible with headphones because of their lesser intensity and their superimposition over the music. [SM]

51. *Dances with Wolves* (Costner, 1990). [DVD, Warner Home Video, 2009.]

52. Miceli, *La musica nel film*, op. cit., *Appendice. Il musicista nel cinema d'oggi*. Colloquio con Ennio Morricone, ora in idem., *Musica e cinema nella cultura*, op. cit., 467–90.

53. Ibid.

54. Bruno Nicolai (1926–1991), composer and orchestral director. [GBA]

Chapter Six

Compositional Elements

*Timbre, Use of Themes, Characteristic Stylistic Features,
and Combinations of Styles*

SM: At this point we . . . can test some analytical hypotheses and examine some of Maestro Morricone's compositions a little more closely.[1] To facilitate the task, Morricone himself will make a preliminary analysis before each . . . projection. . . . Precisely because we have talked about the music before and will do so again, this new arrangement will allow us to focus specifically on compositional elements. Let's begin with *Indagine su un cittadino al di sopra di ogni sospetto (Investigation of a Citizen above Suspicion).*

ANALYSIS OF *INDAGINE SU UN CITTADINO AL DI SOPRA DI OGNI SOSPETTO (INVESTIGATION OF A CITIZEN ABOVE SUSPICION)* (PETRI, 1970)

EM: We have decided to begin the analytical experience with *Indagine* because I was in complete agreement with the director and it presented me with very simple choices.

The score has two fundamental pieces. There is the piece that is presented immediately after the opening titles. It is in binary rhythm and has the function of characterizing the whole film. Then there is another piece of great sensuality that develops in tertiary rhythm. It is united with a particular, more unusual harmony. I recommend that you watch the whole film. The application of the two pieces, especially the first, occurs under such diverse circum-

163

stances that it assumes a different character in each case. While watching the film again some days ago, I thought that I would not change anything. . . . The ambiguity of the first piece adapts in the right way at all the appropriate moments in the film.

SM: Because this is the first analysis, do we want to formulate some other elements?

EM: Very well.

Theme I[2]

Tempo of a tango/march (chosen for its popular and grotesque characteristics). The rhythmic scheme gives a sense of instability and uncertainty.[3]

Instruments

Out-of-tune piano, mandolin, woodblock, English horns, bassoons, Sicilian mouth harp, Thomas organ (fart), small out-of-tune clarinet in E-flat, strings.

- Bad intonation of the instruments as a symbol of degradation
- Arpeggiated theme (triplets) as a sense of common popularity
- Harmonic, chromatic connections for adjacent notes of the scale (creepy, poisonous, serpent-like, falsity)

Theme II[4]

Represents the shocking (but also grotesque) sensuality of the protagonists.[5] The 3/4 time gives a smoother result than the 4/4 of Theme I. It is an abstract and sleepy theme, brief and incisive. It is formed from three elements. It takes its shape little by little by accumulation.[6]

ANALYSIS OF *L'ATTENTAT* (BOISSET, 1972)

SM: And now it's time to give the preliminary analysis for the music for *L'attentat*.

EM: We have spoken about this work on several occasions. Therefore, I won't repeat what has been said already. I can add only that all the music in the film (excluding the waltz at the embassy, which is of the diegetic or internal-level type) is written in a scale I created for reference purposes. From this I extrapolated certain elements, distributing them to diverse instruments or groups of instruments.

Instrumental Groups

A—Double reeds: oboes, bassoons, and contrabassoons
B—Percussion: various-size skins (drum heads)
C—Strings: they play microtones, fourths, and thirds of a tone (think of Oriental music)
D—Plectral instruments: mandolas, mandolins, mandolincellos

To these are added white voices, electric guitar, and synthesizer. In my chart you can find these elements and the pertinent tracks.[7]

ANALYSIS OF *IL PRATO (THE LAWN)* (TAVIANI, 1980)

SM: Now let's move on to the preanalysis of the music for *Il prato* (*The Lawn*).

EM:

Theme I[8]

The intonation is purposely popular and archaic . . . because of the place where the story develops and also the "fable" that is told in the film.[9] It presents a strange harmonic character, obtained with plagal cadences arrived at with the lowered sixth (VI) (chromaticism) in the internal harmony. This gives rise to an equivocal tonal continuo that leads me to define the piece as "modal."[10]

Theme II[11]

Conceived to be based on the name of Bach,[12] transposed until it covered twelve notes completely, and therefore a dodecaphonic procedure harmonized in a traditional way. For contrast, it opposes the harmonic and melodic elements of Theme I, which is essentially diatonic.[13]

ANALYSIS OF *IL DESERTO DEI TARTARI (THE DESERT OF THE TARTARS)* (ZURLINI, 1976)

SM: And now it is time for *Il deserto dei tartari* (*The Desert of the Tartars*).[14]

EM: Here there are also two principal themes.

Theme I[15]

Theme I, in B minor, is the theme of the family, of memories, of nostalgia.

Theme II[16]

Theme II, in D major, is the theme of the desert, of the sacred, and of its mystery.

I sought an analogy between the two themes in the way they enter (attack) and in their prosecution. The long-held sounds of both always represent the interval of a just fifth. It is the motor for them.[17]

ANALYSIS OF *THE MISSION* (JOFFÉ, 1986)

Nothing is left but to sketch out the notes on *The Mission*.[18] In this film one has to take into account the following:

1. The ethnic music (Indians of South America—Argentina—Colombia).
2. The musical traditions of the Catholic Church after the Council of Trent, carried to South America by the Jesuits.
3. The fact that one of the protagonists of the film plays the oboe; therefore, he is the carrier of a specific post-Renaissance instrumental experience tied to its own epoch.[19]

All this determined the following creative process, in chronological order:

A. Composition of the oboe's theme, initially constrained (intervals and contractions of melodic values) by the source music for the scene in which Padre Gabriel plays.[20]
B. Superimposition of the oboe theme, with implicit harmonizations, over a motet in Palestrina's style.
C. Superimposition of **A** and **B** over an ethnic theme (deceptively ethnic). The themes **A, B,** and **C** are executed in isolation or in the possible combinations of **A-B, A-C, B-C,** or **A-B-C**.[21]

From the ethnic theme, except for one added sound (mi), I extracted the expanded elements for the creation of another, more reflective theme, used often in a rhythmic, percussive manner but with wood flutes and in dissonant situations.[22]

SM: This concludes the section containing Morricone's analysis. Nevertheless, we will consider *The Mission* later from another perspective.[23] Let us move now to the subjects predicated in the chapter heading: timbre, use of themes, characteristic stylistic features, and combinations of styles.

TONE COLOR—*PER UN PUGNO DI DOLLARI* (*A FISTFUL OF DOLLARS*) (LEONE, 1964)

EM: I have always believed that the inventive use of tone color is one of a film composer's most important means of expression. Under the influence of this way of thinking, I began to experiment with music made expressly for the stage, but above all for the protagonist in *Per un pugno di dollari* (*A Fistful of Dollars*) (1964)[24] and all Leone's other films. The western helped me, because the genre, at least as Leone intended it, is picaresque, exaggerated, excessive, playful, dramatic, entertaining, and caustic.

The caricatured figure of the protagonist is delightfully forced by the director. . . . Many years after we made the film, Leone confided . . . that in order to have Clint Eastwood recite in the way he did, he invited him to associate very bad swear words with his antagonist. Those terrible words (which I cannot repeat) remained verbally unexpressed. Leone wanted them to burn inside the actor, transforming him into a grim countenance.

In the presence of this kind of direction, especially a director used to excellent results, it was necessary for me to use unusual sounds that would be able to equal these excesses. . . . Everything, including the soundtrack, had to appear to be much more than it really was. Thus, therefore, I called for bells, whip, whistling, anvil, clay whistle, voices, and . . . so many other things. The necessity of making the film seem epic caused me to augment the tone of the instrumentation and to resort to a chorus, to crescendos, to strings with their galloping rhythm (think of the strings of Monteverdi in *Il combattimento di Tancredi e Clorinda*), and to all the other artifices in existence in order to give the music the necessary quality. Finally, the character of Leone's movie took off, and the film became credible.[25]

PER QUALCHE DOLLARO IN PIÙ (*FOR A FEW DOLLARS MORE*) (LEONE, 1965); *IL BUONO, IL BRUTTO, IL CATTIVO* (*THE GOOD, THE BAD, AND THE UGLY*) (LEONE, 1966)

For the same reason I used the Jew's harp in the second film, *Per qualche dollaro in più* (*For a Few Dollars More*). On the other hand, in the third film, *Il buono, il brutto, il cattivo* (*The Good, the Bad, and the Ugly*),[26] a thematic idea is transformed into the verse of the coyote. . . . That's how it is with the war episode, the episode of the opening titles. Five or six trumpets . . . blare in the space of a few seconds, making an incredible uproar. After other similar choices, there were even those who accused me of not having the score under control. Those sonic interventions happened effectively "outside" the images. They were aimed directly at the spectator. I can understand the reason for the criticism, but it is absolutely not true that it was a sign of my inability to control the score.

In Rome recently I heard a composition by Ligeti that was a great comfort to me. It is called *Concerto per violino e orchestra* (1992), but some call it *Due ritratti* [*Two Portraits*] because the piece has diverse stylistic origins. There is a very difficult solo for violin (but the violins of the orchestra also have soloistic parts). All of a sudden, four ocarinas enter. It is such an unusual intrusion, incredible in that context. But I have to say that the discovery gave me such pleasure, thinking about what I had done for Leone, even if in a much simpler way. In sum, I found a correspondence that consoled me.

SM: This is a case in which we do not agree. I do not believe that the association is legitimate.

And I will not be more specific, nor will I make a hierarchy among composers. I simply will say that an "absolute" compositional process cannot be compared to a "concluded" compositional process. (Note well that I have spoken of compositional processes. If you had spoken of single, circumstantial compositions, my judgment would be even more radical.)

I think I understand very well the profound motives that cause you to experience this kind of comfort. I have touched on the subject many times in my book, but I find it a little simplistic and as a result a little offtrack, above all for those who are in a formative phase of their careers. I don't believe that a Viennese coachman at the end of the 1800s would have felt himself ennobled by the fact that Mahler used his post horn in the *Third Symphony*. No, it is not a direct parallel. It is as if one were to say that the significance arises from the context or from the decontextualization, operations at which you are a master.

The same instrument used in diverse contexts assumes profoundly different significance and values. You have used the marranzano (Jew's harp) in a western film, creating thereby a commonplace. You have disturbed the human voice by marrying it with the howl of a coyote, realizing a game, crossbred with anthropological and zoomorphic allusions that are fundamental to the thesis of the film (in addition to being extremely pleasing on a musical level). You have taken the names of two protagonists in another western[27] and transformed the phonetic characters into semantic values— "Sean," "Juan." You have created two incisive little leitmotif-like identities that are able to reassume within themselves the psychological qualities of the characters. Doing things in this fashion, you have given a turn to the way music for film is conceived. So of what importance are the ocarinas of Ligeti?

It was stated that at this point we would briefly treat a particular aspect of Maestro Morricone's music in the western cycle of Sergio Leone. . . . It is something that goes beyond the inventions that are possible using tone colors, even if it takes its idea from them.

MUSIC FOR THE FILMS OF SERGIO LEONE – THE MODEL – THREE AUDIENCES

In almost all the films of Leone,[28] the principal musical composition is based on a tripartite organization, on a stylistic, formal segmentation. It is a recurrent model. The beginning is always entrusted to a thematic segment that we might define as archaic or minimal. The instruments utilized in this segment are in fact simple, humble instruments, from a human being's whistle that has the supremacy of need to the marranzano (Jew's harp), from a rough argilophone to recorders and panpipes, from a mouth harmonica to the acoustic guitar. In this context, the acoustic guitar occupies the most elevated position. The same concept also applies to the accompaniment, which is generally percussive, made up of whip, anvil, castanets, bells, and so on. This first segment is complete and autonomous but acts as a bridge to the successive segments.

The second segment is characterized by a change in intonation. It is always entrusted to the electric guitar. The music is written in a rock 'n' roll style. In this case, the segment can also be intended as an autonomous episode or as a response to and "development" of the preceding segment. With the exception of the electric guitar in *C'era una volta il West*,[29] where the sound is very aggressive, distorted, and hard, it is a tame rock 'n' roll. It is powerful in its rapport with the antecedents, but by itself it is fairly inoffensive.

The third segment introduces new elements that are borrowed from the system of the "classical" music tradition: string orchestra and vocalizing chorus. Every so often there is a trumpet soloist (as, for example, in the piece accompanying the duel, in which its presence is obligatory), even an organ[30] and a reinforcement of the percussion. In this case also, the segment enjoys full autonomy. In any event, it presents itself as the recapitulation and comprehensive phase since, other than assuming a variant role, it appears superimposed (or underimposed) on the preceding segments. They are represented here in a complete or abbreviated form, or without some of the elements present in the original version.

Schematically, the basic structure is seen in figure 6.1.

Obviously, depending on the context and the circumstances, each of the three segments can appear isolated from the others in the film. (They thereby represent the primary form of the modular music concept we have discussed

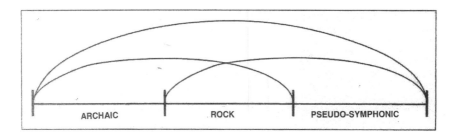

Figure 6.1.   Segmented Structure of Scores for Leone Films

already.) However, the more interesting aspect of the segmentation lies in the founding concept, which affects the progressions . . . and even the coexistence of the stylistic elements. The stylistic elements are very distant from the progressions, although they are all tied to a unique connective fabric. Composing in this way, you address three types of public that are profoundly different from one another, not only from the cultural but also from the generational point of view.

Without a doubt, the first segment is the most original and characteristic, especially from the point of view of the inventive use of tone colors. However, it is also original because of its ability to express an implicit essence every time it is used regardless of the context, and for expressing . . . anarchic individualism, simplicity and primitive force, eroticism without rhetoric, sentimental neutrality, authenticity, and nonconformity. As a result, the first segment is absolutely natural and timeless. The connotative function is identified with the denotative. It is without doubt the more refined and allusive of the three segments.

The second segment brings about a noteworthy leap, but not only from the stylistic point of view. The heroic character—but also the rhetorical character—transforms and actualizes itself. The unconventional component remains (Who remembers the motto "Sex, drugs, and rock 'n' roll"?), but, civilizing itself, it identifies with a group or a clan. Can electric amplification carry us to so much? In the metaphorical sense, I believe so. In any case, beyond the impact, the aggressiveness is diluted by the clean melodic strumming and the absence of friction and contrasts. Here, if you will, a door opens onto the more influential part of musical consensus (and consumption).

With the third segment we slide into social integration, into the "return of reason," in which a cloyingly rhetorical, triumphal, autocelebratory tone and an absolutely conventional timbral and harmonic system dominate. In sum, good feelings prevail, and in this way lower-middle-class taste recovers its proper reference points and security even if, as a result of the partial or total coexistence of the three segments, everyone has to search for his or her preferred part in the interior of the others and in doing so has to listen to them. In this way one can explain, at least partly, the reasons for an extremely rare kind of intergenerational and intracultural success that has lasted for some thirty years. At the same time, it denotes what I would define as a restorative process, a painless process, the fruit of great ability—which is, by the by, restorative. (If we had time, I would demonstrate it also within Maestro Morricone's concert production.)[31] This is the point to which timbral invention and stylistic characteristics, among others, can carry us.

EM: It is incredible. When Miceli analyzes, I discover what I wrote! I would not have thought it when I composed this music. I was thinking about something completely different.

SM: That's natural. There is a rational control during the writing, but fortunately everything is not determined or hyperdetermined. Otherwise, talent would make no difference, and we would not be able to distinguish the difference between Mozart and a software program designed to imitate him (which has been created). Also, in its own way, the critical process can be a creative process, or recreative, but it has a completely different nature. In sum, do you find yourself in some way in what I said?

AUTOCELEBRATION OF SONORITY

EM: Yes, only I did not do it on purpose. I did not deliberately . . . write for three different audiences. Celebration of sonority for its own sake is one of the principles that inform my composing, both for and outside the cinema. The theme is not as important. If from this moment today we were to destroy form, the traditional understanding of it, I believe that if a second formal element were born from the first, and the first continued in the second, and so it went, this would be a correct way to proceed. I believed this even before applying myself to the cinema, and in the cinema I have put this same procedure into action in a briefer form.

As you see, I have said things that confirm your analysis, but I have reported as I was thinking while I wrote. In a seminar during which this same discourse took place, someone asked me whether, in the segmentation, there is one part that has more importance. I responded, and I repeat it now, that I do not know. I thought about a progression of sonorities in order to arrive at the exaltation that in my opinion was required by Leone's film. Perhaps the first segment is more important, because it is the one that causes the seed to develop that gives birth to the other segments.

I know perfectly well that melody is an obligatory presence. It is the only element with which one can reach an understanding with the director, even though it is up to the composer to find the way to drown that melody in other solutions. But melody is not so important. . . . If you take away the melody from all my pieces of this or other types, the piece still will remain . . . on its own feet. But the theme helps the director and serves the public. Perhaps I am deceiving myself by thinking that while following the theme, people also assimilate and appreciate the instrumental solutions.

SM: I hope to interpret correctly what you have just said. As a composer, you tend to minimize the importance of the melodic material, ensuring that your structures can live independently from that material. As a composer for film, however, you recognize that melody has a function that cannot be discarded and therefore is important.

EM: Certainly the theme is extremely important, even if I personally have always considered it of little significance. For this reason, especially in the first films of Leone but also . . . on many other occasions afterward, I have attempted to distinguish it, to subtract it from its conventional function. In some cases I have augmented the result with timbre, in others with the pursuit of a theme made of intervals. I have had to concentrate on something that could redeem the low vulgarity of the theme, even if vulgarity is present to some degree in the third fragment about which you talked, the one in which, with the addition of the chorus, all the strings shriek.

THE "OLD-FASHIONED" CHORUS

SM: Considering the refined and inventive nature of the first segment, for the third, one could speak of "deliberate concessions in the pit to the bad taste of the audience." I have always wondered—and never asked you explicitly— whether that chorus, which is a little "old-fashioned," was supposed to be exactly like that, or whether the editor couldn't offer anything better.

EM: If you are referring to Leone's first film, it wasn't as though there was much money or much ambition. Perhaps it might be "old-fashioned," but it still ought to be the consequence of the first two segments. Naturally, what you say interests me a lot, since it is extraordinarily thorough and to the point. By contrast, I remain embarrassed when speaking about myself and what I write. I am always uncertain about whether to talk about all the things that concern me, because many are also intimate things. I could strip naked in front of you. I will do it, if therefore I succeed in doing it without hiding myself, but it is not easy.

TIMBRE AND THE FEMALE VOICE

SM: Let's return to timbral solutions, listening to an example from *C'era una volta il West* [*Once Upon a Time in the West*] with the vocal part entrusted to Edda Dell'Orso. It contains Jill's theme.[32] Beyond the explanation that you have already given about the necessity of resorting to trustworthy performer-collaborators, how do you explain the recourse so frequently to a feminine voice? Isn't it a little bit in contrast with your tendency to experiment constantly?

EM: It's true that I used it too much. I used it ten or fifteen times. Others abused it in a not-always-very-adequate manner (there were certain exceptions where it was used very, very well), and this circumstance actually provoked an inflation in the frequency of its use. At a certain point, one was not able to use it anymore. I took into account the fact that the public appreciated it tremendously, but above all I thought about . . . Edda Dell'Orso's great quality and her capacity to adapt herself to whatever the requirements were. . . . I made her do all sorts of things.

I remember the arrangement I made of a samba in F minor, the story of an insane woman who, the day after the end of carnival, is still dancing. In her head she remains overwhelmed by the carnival. I harmonized the piece in a way that was pretty normal, and the voice sang a series of very strange dodecaphonic intervals in counterpoint. It was extremely difficult to insert this line precisely in a tonal context, but she did it with great facility. Certainly, experiments bring some solutions, and the solutions at a certain point exhaust themselves. Therefore, one needs to transform and renovate them.

OBSTACLES TO RENOVATION

SM: In my previous observations I did not take into account a fundamental element, namely the director. He or she can be an obstacle . . . to renovation (and in this case we are talking about timbral components, but the arguments could be extended to other elements).

I pause to consider *C'era una volta in America* [*Once upon a Time in America*],[33] one of the more important cine-musical results not only of the Leone-Morricone association but of all the movies after the Second World War. It seems to me that exactly there the resistance to renovation is evident—or, if you prefer, the persistence of tested stylistic models of which the director is fond. I understand, even if without enthusiasm, the sensuality of the angelic vocalization in *C'era una volta il West* [*Once upon a Time in the West*], fortunately compensated for by the harsh and grating presence of the electric guitar.[34] I don't understand, however (it even disturbs me), that same sickening eroticism on varnished paper, ideal although nonexistent, in the last extraordinary film of Leone.[35] Where does sentiment end and sentimentality begin? For me, the sentimentality (or worse) begins precisely when the female voice enters.

EM: The director also was infatuated with this type of voice. Therefore, sometimes he even forced me to use it more than I myself would have wanted. I already have talked about the most recent example with Warren Beatty, so you can see that such an obsession is normal. When directors listen to something that fascinates them, they want still more of it. Tornatore, for example, liked the clarinet. In the past I never used it, except when an out-of-tune clarinet served me (all the available clarinettists played out of tune), and I took them only in that case.

But in *Nuovo cinema Paradiso* (1988)[36] I used an in-tune clarinettist. . . . He was one of the two first soloists[37] of the Santa Cecilia orchestra, and he played in an extraordinary manner. Tornatore therefore had good reason to ask me to make the clarinet more present. This is to say that on many occasions, recourse to a determined timbre happens not only when there is a beautiful feminine voice but also when certain instruments are played very, very well. For the composer, this repeated use can be translated into a label, which is yet another danger that arises in our profession. Instead, we always ought to take the best and then have the courage to put it to one side.

THE SOUNDTRACK ALBUM

SM: I would like to turn for a moment to the discussion about the major ambitions of a production, above all with respect to the international market and to the hypothetical repercussions that such ambitions can have on compositional choices. In contrast to the previously discussed films, these ambitions seem very obvious in *C'era una volta il West* [*Once upon a Time in the West*].[38]

Knowing the results, with obvious repercussions for the record market, a director for one reason and a composer for another may more or less consciously regard the possibility that some music can live with a greater autonomy than normal with respect to the media of film music. At the beginning of his or her career, I do not believe that a composer deals with problems of this type. However, when a certain notoriety is added and the composer enters into the mechanics of big productions, it is possible that he or she might be more readily inclined to construct one or two complete forms that would have two combining capacities (usually the theme attached to the principal character and the music for the opening titles). On the one hand, there is all the functionality necessary for use in the film; on the other, complete emancipation from the film. My hypothesis can be confirmed from the analysis I made of the music written for *C'era una volta il West* [*Once upon a Time in the West*]. Here, in fact, the fragmentation already seen in the preceding films where I spoke of a tripartite form, of stylistic segmentation, becomes a macrosegmentation. Therefore, the diverse segments are able to operate with still greater autonomy, with the malleability and the concision necessary for the film (though each one by itself is already a complete piece), or the segments are able to connect together, making the "big piece of pieces" that can be devoted to pure listening. It is a perfect mechanism, is extremely efficient from all points of view, and provokes such admiration as to over-shadow (at least to my ears) the "infamous" vocalization.

EM: Thank you, but in reality I have never thought about making a recording while writing for a film. To the person who has pressured me in this way, I have always replied that I would write music for the film. If the director could make the most of the mixing and was then pleased, then the recording too could be a success, but it was not obligatory. This has always been my response. Certain composers first prepare the recording and then apply it to the film. Perhaps it might be useful as an approach, but it does not concern me.

SM: Now let's approach some cases of maximum interaction between diverse components, with particular reference to tone color and, more general-ly, stylistic characterizations. They are meant to be like precise connotative identifying features in the interior of the film. This is without forgetting the thematic characterizations that are seen not as mere symbolic functions in the service of the film narrative (or the typical comment, the main theme) but indeed as equal and sometimes primary narrative elements.

THE FINALE OF *THE MISSION*[39]

EM: Let's occupy ourselves with the finale[40] of *The Mission*. In this film I had a problem that became evident only little by little and that was anticipat-ed by neither the director nor the producer. The film takes place in a Catholic mission in South America,[41] in the first half of the eighteenth century. The priests teach music to the natives, transmitting to them what was done in Europe in that epoch. What's more, the Jesuit who heads the mission[42] plays the oboe. There is a liturgical context that needs to be present, one that is tied to the western tradition, and in this case . . . specifically to the sacred-music tradition. (I told you already about the use I made of the "Palestrina-like" chorale). . . . Then, appropriate to the place, one had to consider the music of the Indians, an ethnic music.

I wanted to mix together these three ideas, and I did it throughout the whole film, mostly in pairs: oboe and music of the Indians, music of the Indians and liturgical chorus. Only in the finale did I mix together all three components with the idea of interpreting the communion of the priests with the Indians. (I had projected it from the beginning, so I did it without any strain). The technical commitment of the music is analogous to the commitment present in the communion between them. Achieving this result was a great source of satisfaction for me, because it was difficult to find a way for the autonomy of the three components to be maintained and yet for them to be able to be shuffled together.

SM: It is interesting to note that the potential dialectic that we saw already from *Per un pugno di dollari*[43] onward as well as the modular concept appears here at its maximum. In fact, although the technical procedure is different, it is not difficult to find here what you call the "shuffle," the inheritance of the process of superimposition and the segmented construction about which you have spoken.

I think we are all in agreement that with *The Mission* one is treated to one of the best film scores of all time, and not just with respect to Morricone's productions. But let's try to reconnect briefly to its principal characteristics, using the method of levels in order to verify the unconventional nature of the solutions adopted in it. [44] Initially, as source music at the internal level, there is a total identification between Padre Gabriel and the oboe that is suggested ever more frequently. Diverse recurrences of its presence occur in the film in which the oboe is audible without the Jesuit doing the playing. Therefore, the sound of the oboe represents Padre Gabriel, and in musical terms it has the capacity of formalizing and synthesizing his ethic, his faith. Thus one is dealing with a mediated level.

By fundamentally the same mechanism, whether in the "original" songs or those learned from the Jesuits, the Indians' music is, respectively, an emanation of Indian traditions and the manifestation of a nascent cultural assimilation. It is also the carrier of new spiritual values. It could be another mediated level and obviously seems so the more the act of actually singing in chorus is visually absent from the film. The third mediated level is represented by the a cappella choirs. . . . They express unequivocally the two faces of Catholic civilization. One is spiritual, and one is colonial. (The first is not extraneous to the second.) Therefore, this choral song not only represents a fascination with grandeur that is communicated by its refinement and by the force of its polyphonic architecture but also embodies the doubts and travail of the old prelate sent by the pope,[45] the arrogance of the Spanish viceroy,[46] and the shrewdness of the Portuguese.[47]

Already, while dealing with the methodology of levels, we saw that the external level, regardless of musical quality, is always destined to seem like an artificial act. However, it is accepted by convention and for its undoubted ritualistic and autocelebratory potential. But in this case—and saying it this way brings us back to the passage in question—in *The Mission* the mixing of the three themes at the mediated level and their preexistent classification in the film take the mixture to an external level, but one that has been deprived of its major defect. Their coexistence is the seal, but with, above all, the most powerful and the least didactic, as well as the least rhetorical, meaning that one could possibly imagine.

On careful examination, one finds a component "extraneous" to the musical appearances legitimized by the development within the film: the presence of strings.[48] But their insertion imitates the parts of the a cappella chorus and as a result presents melodic recognizability against tone color diversity. But this insertion of the timbre of the strings is enough to insinuate into the piece a stylistic swerve and a temporal slide. This is the music of artifice that reveals the falling of the curtain. At the point of transition between fiction and reality, it offers itself as such to the spectator. In this gesture I see even a secret autobiographical allusion, a declaration of belonging, of artistic and spiritual identification (a little like when Renaissance painters would make a self-portrait in an angle of an altarpiece), but on this point I cannot go further, being in the presence of the composer.

Instead, I can add one more thing. Considering the symbolic values that each musical line carries within itself, we have a continuous situation of agreement and of conflict, a dialectic rapport between the parts that has a precise significance in the film, verifiable also like the logic of the score. In contrast to Morricone, I favor a negative, pessimistic meaning for the fable, so where he speaks of communion, I think of the failure of a utopian community. When, a little while ago, he said (approximately) that "the technical commitment of the music is analogous to the commitment present in the attempt of the Jesuits to enter into communion with the Indians," it gave me a lot of pleasure. Without our ever having consulted about this matter, I find his explanation very close to what I wrote using only the score for *The Mission.*

In fact, a constant in Morricone's work (that you find in the first production for concert from *Musica per 11 violini* onward) consists precisely in making formal values semantic and semantic values formal. What is purely building-block material is organized in such a way that it assumes a character analogous to that which pertains to the narrative context. The musical elements "act" like "actors" on the stage, responding to a script, which is then a precise, incorporated study of symbols. This kind of treatment is very rare in the history of the relationship between music and cinema. One thinks of *Alexander Nevsky,*[49] but the match is improper, because the relationship between director and composer, their way of working, guaranteed already on paper an uncommon result. Often I tried to imagine what would have hap-

pened to *The Mission* had Joffé acted not like Eisenstein but at least like
Leone. The theme of the oboe, as I've already said, gives rise to everything
else, and even the harmonic plan remains the same.

EM: Yes, the harmonization is that one, except at one point where I changed
it because after being in D major so much, I could not go to B minor; I would
not have been able to make the modulation to VI—it would not have supported the whole foundation. Well, one feels this imperfection at that point.

I want to point out something else. The drumbeat is casual—not in time. I
wanted that grave sound to be exactly that way. It ought to bring to mind the
booming of the cannon heard in the film, but there is another reason. Every
time that I have heard Argentine and also Brazilian music, but above all
Argentine, there always has been a strange drum performed almost casually
(maybe it wasn't written casually, but I found it casual). Therefore, as a little
effort at authenticity, I wanted to insert that characteristic.

SM: This, as I said, is one of the highest results attained by music in the
cinema, in both the formal and conceptual senses. Unfortunately, it is a
missed occasion equilibrium-wise with respect to the reciprocal relations
between music and images. . . . Joffé must not have been conscious of the
extraordinary potential at his disposal or rather thought that it was too late to
intervene in favor of a more complex result.

EM: I have to add one thing to what you have said. Joffé is a great director,
but he is one of those who are afraid of music. Perhaps he fears that the
expressivity given to a scene by the music puts into relief one of his deficien-
cies. This I came to understand during many discussions about *The Mission*,
but above all in other films where we worked alone, whereas for *The Mission*
there was an Italian producer[50] who invited him to leave things as they were,
as I had planned them. For example, in the finale, during the massacre, Joffé
had wanted to mix the *Ave Maria* by Guarani and the theme of the oboe. I
would not have wanted it, but he didn't pay attention to me and made a mess.
In any event, I am certain that he is afraid of music, for it is true that during
the most expressive moments of a film he always keeps the music very soft.

SM: You can console yourself that you wrote music that will last, that by its
being thought of precisely for that film, for its multiple features, you demonstrated immediately that it could live an independent life. The appropriations
that have been made in diverse situations and the reactions of the public at
concerts demonstrate it.[51]

EXPLICIT AND IMPLICIT SYNCHRONY:
IL BUONO, IL BRUTTO, IL CATTIVO[52] [*THE GOOD, THE BAD, AND THE UGLY*], "L'ESTASI DELL'ORO" ("THE ECSTASY OF THE GOLD") (LEONE, 1966)

EM: Let's go to the next example. Someone will remember that in one of the preceding lessons I touched on the problem of synchronization, a subject already treated by Professor Miceli on the theoretical level. Now I would really like to return to the distinction between explicit and implicit synchrony.

Being inclined to value his own actions, the director often asks the composer to emphasize this or that point by making synchronizations, until he wants so many that they could ruin the score. The advice that I give, and that I want to repeat, is that you not alter the synchronization passively as the director asks. Rather, make it come into play musically. Think of the piece as if it were natural that it had these carefree rather than dry cuts. The score surrounding the images should run fluently (without "fracture–ization"). The best synchronies are those that one does not feel, those that arrive via a musical logic (or also casually), not by a logic that is only cinematographic. This is really fundamental.

There is an example to which I always willingly refer because it is a great piece of cinema and, it seems to me, a successful enough piece of music. I am referring to *Il buono, il brutto, il cattivo* [*The Good, the Bad and the Ugly*]. Here, within three feet, twenty seconds of film, Leone asked me for twenty-three or twenty-four sync points. (Now I do not remember the exact number. More than twenty-five years have passed.) The problem was to pay attention to them without paying attention to them, making them happen in such a way that the music would not be adversely influenced by such a heavy-handed request. Therefore, by lengthening the phrases that I wrote, I sometimes passed from an even meter to an odd one. Sometimes I accelerated or used the entrance of an instrumental section to match up with certain images. Precisely from this point of view, it seems a very successful example. Leone was enthusiastic about this recording. There is some synchrony that is not very precise, but he preferred this execution because it was better, more spontaneous, since it was made directly with eighty instrumentalists without overdubbing.

You see, in this case the movie sequence was projected during the recording session. Naturally, there were problems in the premix because, for example, the trumpets entered into the microphones of the violins. At a certain point we understood that we had to send everybody into direct play, because those who play listen to the others and are stimulated.

There would have been two ways of correcting the small imperfection in the synchrony: interfere in the film by proceeding . . . to a new mix in order to earn five, ten, fifteen, or twenty-four frames of film; or execute the piece again. The first alternative was not possible because no film remained available (and it would have been unthinkable to repeat the same frames to lengthen the projection). With the second way, a new execution would almost certainly have been less spontaneous, less effective, so Leone decided to sacrifice the visual synchrony a little to the advantage of the music.

SM: This is an obvious case of external level, even if it occurs in the mind of the person who has a fixation about gold (therefore it makes an allusion to the function of the mediated level). But one cannot talk about the real and precise mediated level, because the director did not send the spectator some explicit signal about it. If, of course, in the preceding scenes of the film we had heard in the background fragments of the melody coinciding with Tuco talking about the hidden treasure, the cue "L'estasi dell'oro" ("The Ecstasy of the Gold") would have been an evident case of mediated level, but it didn't happen that way. The piece appears here for the first time. [53]

One understands the fixation with gold because the musical phrase is reiterated, using a melodic ostinato with subtle variations (or, better to say, "license"). As Maestro Morricone has said, these variations are the consequence of a writing that is stretched out in search of sync points. As a result of their "lightness" they are implicit synchronies except for the final frames, which coincide with the dry conclusion of the piece in which Tuco finally finds the grave with the name for which he was searching. Noteworthy is the coincidence between the function required and typically Morriconian stylistic features (the dilating of the phrase on long-note values beyond the probable melodic arches).

In . . . "The Ecstasy of the Gold" one observes the presence of all the typical ingredients of the sonorous imaginary western: the voice of Edda Dell'Orso, the little mocking voices, the galloping rhythm, the chorus, the percussion (free and unleashed at the finale), the orchestral crescendo by quantitative accumulation rather than in a dynamic sense. If then one pays attention to the film's editing and the use of the motion picture camera, one can individuate many subjects, many types of ending, during which the spectator identifies with the point of view of Tuco, played by Eli Wallach. In sum, in this cue we have an example of the orchestration of every audio and visual element. The spectator is involved to a maximum as a result.

Let's remain with the theme of implicit synchronization and the important function of thematic material, introducing another example, not by accident related still to Sergio Leone.

SYNCHRONY IN *C'ERA UNA VOLTA IN AMERICA*[54]

EM: I had composed and recorded the piece before the film, actually before Leone started shooting. It was an exceptional case with respect to production practices. I am referring to *C'era una volta in America*. Editing the film to that "preexistent" music, Leone had stocked up on a series of imperceptible coincidences or sync points, realized or potential, but of course lacking a few, just a few. Thus he asked me to rewrite the piece to make these sync points more perfect. I had to take the synchronization down to a tenth of a second, and we had to utilize an entire recording session. The execution, torturous for me and the orchestra, ended up worse than the first recording because I proceeded casually, without the constraint of using a metronome. But Sergio was content and preferred the new recording, not really because it was more expressive but because of all the sync points that he had invented.

SM: He is referring to the episode in which Noodles returns to the place of his own adolescence. There he encounters Fat Moe[55] in his bar. The example may appear to have long stretches before the music enters. (In reality, there are two points at which the music enters. One is at the beginning of the sequence.[56] The other is when Noodles, left alone, observes the photographs hanging on the wall, and it lasts until the flashback and the sonorous connection of the theme[57] with Amapola.) This teaches us another thing, which perhaps I have already mentioned. A musical entry assumes its full significance and correct expressive weight if it is understood in relation to the events that precede it. In this sense, the mechanism of antecedent-consequence (well known to every composer) has to be applied to an audiovisual object, too.

We now can examine the music detached from the images, beginning with the theme "Poverty,"[58] which opens the sequence. Note the enunciation of the thematic material. It has been assigned to only a few instruments with harmonic support from the also much-reduced strings. This is a constant in Morricone's writing. After this beginning, a progressive enrichment in the central part follows. In this case, there is contrapuntal differentiation only in detail, in harmonic function (horns, violin II, and violas), and there is a progressive reabsorption that brings back the initial essentials. The harp articulates the coda and the connection to the piece that follows.[59]

The theme "Once upon a Time in America"[60] is less articulated than the preceding example because it is based on a reduced cell that is uniform rhythmically. It is subjected to little variations, almost transpositions. But this uniformity renders it particularly ductile, adaptable to the radical transformations that also happen in the movie. Think about the central part of the cue "Childhood Memories." Entrusted to the panpipe, the theme breaks off, and "Once upon a Time in America" is transformed into a jazz-band motif.

This is possible precisely by virtue of the character of the rhythmic-melodic cell. Therefore, if you write a highly articulated melody that is also tormented rhythmically, don't think you'll be able to adapt it easily to another context.

In the final example, "Deborah's Theme,"[61] as in "Poverty," we find more important evidence for the function of the pedal. It actuates the delicate passage between silence and music. We can observe the melodic dilation and the use of the pause that "breaks" the semiphrases with a sense of suspension, of expectation. It is an expectation that comes less frequently from measure 11 onward, when the articulation builds toward the climax. It is a constant character that I would say is typical of Morricone's melodic development. We also will verify this statement with other examples that occurred before this film.

Among the many things that one might say about this extremely beautiful film-musical episode, one needs to be privileged above the others because it touches on an argument that has general validity. I referred to it a little while ago: . . . that is the attack of the music, the way in which the music enters into the film. It is an extremely delicate moment that rarely receives the attention it deserves. I could make you see and listen to so many episodes from diverse films. They are all admirable works for one reason or another, including the quality of the music, but the attack of the music receives very little attention. Even directors like the Taviani brothers, who we have said already have a musical sensibility well above the median, on this point sometimes let me down.[62]

It is a delicate situation, because the question of artifice again enters into play. Certainly, if the music is from the internal level, there is no problem (or the problem is different, as we have seen). If a person is listening to the radio, if it has begun to play, or if the music arrives through the open window (on the condition that it is an unequivocal signal from the director in that sense), the legitimization is automatic. On the other hand, if the entrance is of an external-level type and is not prepared properly, it can shriek exactly because of its artificial connotations.

PEDAL POINTS—HOW THE MUSIC SHOULD ENTER AND EXIT

EM: I agree absolutely. In general, I use pedal points. Perhaps I use them too much, but they are useful. To begin with, they are the simplest things. One wants a pedal that is not irritating but that makes the listener feel like the music is entering or has entered. The theme that enters without preparation risks not being received the way it might merit, while a pedal predisposes, signals, creates an expectation. And then, apart from the exploitation of the theme, it is the passage itself from silence to sound that has to be prepared, but without coarseness, in a simple way. It is a way, I would say, that is almost "nonmusical." The same thing is true for the exit. It ought to be expressive but delicate. It needs to return to musical silence with discretion, without exception. These are fundamental rules that one runs into, but the tendency that directors have to stuff their films with music has the consequence that the musical presence is disqualified and does not offer . . . the contribution that it might have made.

SM: It ought to be an event, and it isn't anymore. It is a little like that current linguistic vice, so irritating, that leads to the abuse of the adverb "extremely." Instead of strengthening a statement, it flattens everything.

EM: It is exactly like that. Think about certain films of Hitchcock during which, in an hour and a half of film, there is an hour and a half of music, music also very well and attentively done on the part of the composer. But . . . it is thrown away because completely useless, a music that accompanies the personages, the events, the gossiping, the noises . . . with so many crazy sync points. Today, by comparison, one tends to put less music in a film, making one listen to it more.

SM: I spoke a little while ago about the Taviani brothers.[63] . . . In the film *Il prato*,[64] for example, a fundamental role is entrusted to the music in key episodes, but a more observant analysis demonstrates that those same compositions return a little wearily in other parts of the film in which they are not as decisive. These "fillers" thus finish by damaging even the better contributions.

EM: In the section dealing with *C'era una volta in America*,[65] we referred to three cues, and this permits us to talk about stylistic solutions, another aspect that we planned to deal with. The thematic idea, chromaticism, and orchestration, especially the folk chromaticism in the first cue, come from the epoch in which the film develops. I remember that when I was a young boy I listened to *Appassionatamente* by Rulli.[66] It was a little like this, nostalgic, antique, and modern. . . . Those waltzes were the typical musical artifacts of an epoch. From the associations that come from the scenery design and the costumes, one needs to work not so much to resolve the situation with a predominant theme but rather, if necessary, to try to give the music a background environment, a plausible sonorous climate, that also includes the thematic idea.

STATE OF GRACE (STATO DI GRAZIA)[67]:
THE THEMATIC IDEA AND CHROMATICISM

Another very different way to confront the same stylistic-formal problem can be found in the film *State of Grace (Stato di grazia)*.[68] (The execution of one of the three sections of the strings excluded the use of the other two. I reserved the right to choose one of the three options in the recording studio. Also, for the rest of the orchestra it was up to me to decide who played and which of the instruments called for would be among the personnel.)

Here the principal theme,[69] a thing reduced to a minimum, operates on two notes, three notes of adjacent degrees of the scale: it stops . . . picks up again . . . stops . . . picks up again. . . . What is happening inside this theme? There are some events, little events. For example, that of E-flat together with E-natural (we are in C major). That E-flat signifies the blues for me, what one makes in the "rotation" of the blues; it is not the same E-flat, but by inserting it here, it places me in an epoch, in a season, in an American environment that I have synthesized in this way.

Besides, inside this insignificant theme—which, however, can be extremely expressive—I have added a game based on the harmonics of C. I used them up to the fifteenth, that is, F-sharp, and a superimposition of B major arrives together with that F-sharp and E-flat, with the seventh major degree of the chord of C major. These so-called dissonances in an absolutely tonal theme are present in two ways. The first involves those fixed dissonances, like the E-flat and the F-sharp. The second is based on mobile dissonances that fluctuate throughout the entire score. There is this game of double significance for the dissonance in the allusion to the blues and in the intention to organize around the theme something that renders it more interesting. I would like to emphasize the fact that this insignificant theme repeats every so often. Before attacking the second parenthesis, there is a long pause, during which the dissonances that I mentioned are clearly inaugurated and developed. As far as the harmonization of the piece is concerned, there are four chords: the tonic, C major; the sixth degree of the scale, a minor; the subdominant, F major; and the dominant ("doctored," not particularly exact), G major. They are four chords that I have tried to "destroy," however, in the way I have just explained.

State of Grace (Stato di grazia) — Music as Redemptive Force

I would like to stay with *Stato di grazia* (*State of Grace*) and with its tone color and thematic and stylistic solutions. (In fact, it is impossible to distinguish one aspect from the others.) I would like to share with you an unpublished, private fact about the music that I wrote for the final scene in the pub. It is the one in which there is the shoot-out, the massacre. I have to say ahead of time that this is one of the most violent films for which I have ever composed a score, but the violence is, in my opinion, a little gratuitous. In an attempt to render this kind of violence more acceptable to the public, I felt that I absolutely had to redeem it with the music. I could not consider making violent music for a violent scene. In that scene, the director had not wanted to put music (as in fact he did not). I wanted to try to convince him, and I proposed something that he did not understand but that he accepted. So I wrote a piece for organ and orchestra.[70] . . . I wanted to suggest not so much the traumatic situation as, above all, the "sacral" rite of murder. It would have suggested a vendetta conducted by a heroic figure against a group of bandits.

I had wanted the music to include the noises and sounds and drums of the St. Patrick's Day procession.[71] The playing of the funeral march should have corresponded with the slow motion of the Irish gang. The pact was that the director would remount the sounds of the drums over the music. Without even consulting with me (because from Los Angeles to Rome it was a little difficult to do it), Joanou did not insert what I had written. Instead, he only thought to put the sounds of the drums. Perhaps he was right (but the counter-proof does not exist).

An idea of this kind would have arrived at the correct conclusion with Leone, while Joanou, this very talented young man, wrote me a letter (the only director to have done so) in which he said that that music was incredible. He had not expected so much. . . . But, in the end, he removed a piece of that kind! It is also true, however, that . . . the music for the end titles[72] begins in a much better way, and the framing of the young woman[73] who assists at the procession among the crowd becomes a sort of grand message of tranquillity attained, of peace arrived at, after so much violence.[74]

SM: I take a cue from this interesting direct testimony to express a basic disagreement. Beforehand, however, I need to make some preliminary remarks.

The category of film to which *State of Grace* belongs is certainly not that of *Pulp Fiction*. The model seems to me Sam Peckinpah more than Quentin Tarantino. And in any case, even if it were Tarantino, I don't believe that *State of Grace* expresses, as you said, "a gratuitous violence." If you intend to deal with individuals who live in Hell's Kitchen, violence is the base. It is itself the fuel of the story. To sweeten or censor it would be absurd. Anyway, I don't think that Joanou would consent at all. . . . On the contrary, the violence to which "good" and "bad" indifferently have recourse exhibits itself almost "objectively." It is as if violence were an unavoidable medium within that environment (but to this point I will return a little later). This is the preamble.

Coming to the point, I can understand how a composer of your stature is inclined to take responsibility for the more profound values of a film. You have marked with your imprint dozens and dozens of movies.[75] You have left an indelible mark on the cinema and always assumed your responsibility as few others do. However, while musical language has the power to express the inexpressible, I do not believe that one must always ask the music to accomplish the job of hyperbolic exaltation, of judgment *super partes*, of deliverance or of salvation. It might have been valid for Leone, who depended on artifice itself, on hyperbole, for Joffé (even if he did not know how to make use of all its great capacity), and for who knows how many of the others about whom I am thinking and whom I will not enumerate now. But it cannot be valid all the time, and I believe it is not valid for this film by Joanou.

Brecht said that "music is not an ark on board of which one can be saved from the flood." I think it is such an important thought that sooner or later I will find a way to use it as an inscription in an antiromantic and anti-idealistic context.[76] Up to now this has been a basic principle. (And having said this, in a certain sense we thus return even to the discussion of music in science-fiction films.) No matter how much of your music was or was not used, it seems too obvious to say that it was extremely potent, that we perceived your footprint. But when you say that you wrote in that way, thinking that you would redeem the violence of the scene in the eyes of the public, bestowing on it a sacred meaning, I feel that I have to take Joanou's part, and for many reasons.

First of all, recalling my preliminary remarks, a director does not shoot a film in that way to then deaden it exactly where the significance manifests itself completely. Terry does not confront the Irish bandits (whom he infiltrated, thanks to their mistakes) as a policeman. In fact, by unmasking himself, he consigns to Frankie, the head of the gang, his own policeman's badge in the form of a challenge. By confronting the bandits in the bar instead of having them arrested, Terry reduces himself to their state, and in this there is precious little of the heroic or the positive. By acting thus, he returns to his own worst origins and loses the woman he loves, the only one in the story able to dissociate herself from the environment, the only one to intuit, first sadly, then with a glacial detachment, that Terry is being sucked into the spiral of violence.

The moral fable therefore puts on a blacker pessimism, and the framing of the young woman mixed with the crowd, who assists at the procession with a hard and absent expression, is another explicit message on the part of the director. That setting is the result of a conscious choice of shot, bitter but determined, definitely dissociated from the condition of Terry, who in fact in the cross-editing one sees shown on the ground, wounded, empty, brutalized, surrounded by the cadavers of his adversaries. In sum, the director did not want to redeem anything or anybody at all. So how can you say that he was wrong if he did not want to follow your proposal?

Finally, the music that enters in the finale and then with the end titles is a version of the same piece that repeatedly returns in the film and that you explained before. When I heard it for the first time, I remember thinking that it was one of the most interesting propositions of all the music that you have written in the last ten years. But also here there is a singular difference of opinion between us. You said a little while ago that this insert was supposed to signify a message of tranquillity, the achievement of a condition of peace. Frankly I do not see how.

Let me explain better. I find the piece and its application to the film excellent, also in this finale. The thing that astonishes me is your a posteriori interpretation. I neither see nor feel messages of tranquillity or of peace. But it is not a subjective fact; it is based on precedents. The piece, I repeat, is a version of the cue "Hell's Kitchen"[77] . . . that has skillfully accompanied the entire film and its terrible climate (about which we have spoken). It is an extraordinarily appropriate piece for the endless anxiety that it communicates. Here, in the finale of the film, it does not present formal modifications with the consequent slipping of expressive, psychological significance. Therefore, I think that the interpretation you give it today is autoconsolatory. You are feeling again that temperament that makes you search for a role of redemption and salvation in music, the function that exactly here has been denied to you. This confrontation of opinions and interpretations has seemed very useful to me, because beyond the personal exchange it can demonstrate to those listening the multiplicity and disputability of the choices presented to the director and the composer. The choice of a theme—or, if you prefer, of a musical character—can have enormous positive or negative implications for a film, because it is always also the interpretation of an interpretation.

EM: I'm a peaceful type. When there is a duel, I always try to soften it. This was particularly violent. I was afraid that it would be interpreted as a barbarism and nothing else, but the director did not want to soften it. Perhaps he had wanted to take away exactly that sacredness that I wanted to give it, but that was a holiness of revenge, of redemptive vengeance.

SM: You say that with this music of yours the encounter would have been softened. I cannot imagine what you would have been able to write if you had decided to render it harder.

Let's summarize. The cue "The Shootout" was not included in the film, but it is possible to listen to it on the CD, a confirmation of how much the disc is a comprehensive testimony of the work actually carried out. It is not the first time that a piece thought of for a film has not ended up being utilized. It happens, of course, that it is used elsewhere—and you have some examples to propose—but it is better if you talk about them.

USE OF THEMES DISCARDED BY OTHER DIRECTORS

EM: Perhaps it has happened; now I do not remember. . . . But there was Leone, who developed a particular habit. He had a taste for the themes that had been rejected by other directors, and he took them. Almost all the themes of his films had this origin. There is a precedent that can be explained.

In *Per un pugno di dollari* (*A Fistful of Dollars*),[78] Leone wanted to insert the *Deguello*, a composition for trumpet, full of ornamentation, that he had heard in the film *Un dollaro d'onore.*[79] I threatened to leave the film because I could not accept that there would be music by someone else in an important scene. Leone conceded, asking me, however, to write a piece that resembled the *Deguello*. Constrained to make a type of imitation, out of a kind of revenge I took a theme[80] that I had written and used years before for *I drammi marini* of O'Neill,[81] adding the trumpet and melismas typical of Mexican music (as well as the soloist, Michele Lacerenzo). Later I confessed to Leone the truth, and from then on he always wanted my preexistent themes, but above all those rejected by others. It was a diverting habit; he would tell me, "What has that foolish Z— thrown away? This? It is very beautiful." And it was done.

SM: It is an anecdote that I know, but it is always exhilarating to hear it from your own lips. However, there remains a point to clarify that is a little more serious. How can you reconcile this casualness with all that we have said (and that we will yet have to say) about the relations, about the subtle interactions that exist between a film and its music? Let's say that the composer has a beautiful theme on a cassette, a theme really too important for a film in which, for a thousand reasons, it was not used. He who listens to it can ask, "On the basis of what processes is it able to be applied to any other situations?"

EM: Yes, I understand what you are asking. . . . There is no theme that cannot be corrected and then, by adapting the instrumentation, applied to a film. Certainly, if I make a theme all in whole notes that has a profoundly spiritual sense and then apply it to a film full of scoundrels like *State of Grace*,[82] it will be difficult for it to function (even if music has the possibility of adapting itself to everything).

For a while I threw away the rejected themes. Then I understood that I ought to keep them, not only because of Leone's habit but above all as the result of another observation. Often directors choose the worst of all the potential themes. Therefore, I conserve them in order to use them if, for example, I have to write diegetic music . . . for another film. However, in that case I always advise the director.

In general, I have the director listen to six or seven themes, among which is one of the previously rejected. Sometimes the choice has fallen exactly to that rejected one, to the injury of the themes written specially for the occasion. For Roland Joffé's film *The Scarlet Letter* (*La lettera scarlatta*),[83] I wrote six themes, and he chose the three ugliest. . . . I tried to give him some advice, but he did not want to listen to me.

SM: Aside from the problems of comprehension and unity of point of view with the director, and even though you have declared many times that the theme is not even that interesting for you, the fact remains that your themes are recognized, remembered, and well loved by the public. In sum, there is something about them that makes an indelible impression. . . . Personally, I do not believe that the more profound characteristics of a composer's nature can be explained, revealed at their deepest level, and therefore transmitted. Still, I am certain that those who are listening to us would like to know more, perhaps not about the technical level so much as about your predisposition fundamentally at the moment in which you set about confronting a problem. Take, for example, an ambiguous situation.

THE PROCESS FOR CONFRONTING A PROBLEM

EM: They are situations that are very difficult to realize. . . . Now, before the shooting begins, I ought to write the music for Tornatore's next film.[84] In it, the grotesque and the sensual will be present contemporaneously. It is a problem. I need to reflect on the way I will resolve it, . . . on how I want these two components. He asks me to resolve them in the simplest manner. However, I still do not know how. I wanted immediately to make it more complex. However, Tornatore wants the simplest, most tonal music, even naively tonal.

The film is shot in Sicily. The place can also determine certain types of sound. However, it is not easy to respond, to make oneself so naked. What thing can determine not only how to do the instrumentation but also how to compose the themes to characterize them? Sometimes pauses are sufficient. Unusual sounds are sufficient, a dissonance put in a tonal piece that suggests something very simple, perceptible to listeners, because in the cinema the listeners do not concentrate on the music. It also might not matter to them at all. The dialogue, the story are the more important things.

DIFFERENCE BETWEEN HEARING AND SIGHT

One has to think (I resort to this argument frequently) that the cinema monopolizes our two most important sense organs, those of hearing and sight, but with diverse results. From our first waking moments onward, sight is the organ that we exercise with a natural analytical capacity. However, we do not exercise our ears in the same analytical way. Therefore, film music is penalized by comparison to what is seen.

Besides, there is a further disadvantage due to the fact that the brain does not give the ears the possibility of listening in a way that can distinguish between two different types of signal. In the end we (experts, trained people) can follow a fugue in two voices; with a fugue of three voices we already have some difficulties. We feel the vertical harmonic foundation; for a little while we follow the three moving parts, but then we have difficulty. Returning to our discourse, this means that if the music for a film is not clear and incisive, it does not stimulate one's brain in an efficient way. With that kind of music, nothing is important. It might just as well not be there, because one just as well could have a film without music.

MUSIC THAT ONE DOES NOT HEAR

I frequently say that music is the only useless guest at a film, useless because it is not part of the film. The life of a film plays out away from the music. The music is something added by the director, by necessity or by habit (more rarely for real poetic reasons). One always puts it there; therefore, let's also put it there this time. Although it was contrary to my interests, on more than one occasion I have said to certain directors not to put music in a film because there was already a pastiche of sounds that would make the music completely useless. It seemed honest for me to say so.

Sergio Corbucci, for example, did not pay attention to me, and in fact in his films one does not hear the music. For that reason and not by its own fault the music can make a bad impression. If it is there and one does not hear it, it is as if it were ugly or as if it were not present. It happens, therefore, that music is isolated, but that is not the only thing. Since it is always an unexpected guest, we should never make it enter all at once.

If music is to mean something . . . to people, it has to be prepared. And in order to prepare it, we need some seconds. One has to prepare the listener to be interested in that which the music will signify better further on. If we begin immediately with the theme and they miss the beginning of it, the public will lose something important.

THE ENTRANCE AND EXIT OF THE MUSIC
FOR INTELLIGIBILITY

I know that I have already touched on this point, but I reassert it because it is very important and because it is connected to the discussion of the theme from which we departed. For the traits that it proposes, the attack of the theme, the debut of the first notes, is fundamental to its recognition.

Pontecorvo[85] maintains that the music in a film has to be that which they cannot express in the film's colors, movements, or dialogue. It has to be something else entirely. If we lose the attack of a musical cue that has this significance, we lose 50 percent of its potential. We risk making it useless.

In *C'era una volta in America*,[86] I began frequently with a pedal point. You have heard it. A study by Professor Miceli[87] began, "In principio era il pedale (In the Beginning There Was a Pedal Point)," like that, a little ironically, in a way "biblical."

There you are; I am saying that a pedal point is the simplest and least disturbing thing for the listener. This is valid not only for the beginning of a piece but also for its conclusion. The music tiptoes in, knocks, and asks permission, and the director opens with the correct message and allows the public to listen to it. When it goes away, it says goodbye very softly and closes the door very softly. The music ought to finish its participation in the scene with the same good manners and care with which it entered. For the same reason, it leaves space for the sounds that appeared at the beginning to disappear in their turn. This is valid for me and for some directors, but it is not valid for all of them. A lot of music is ruined by the lack of attention to this process.

FLORENTINE CONCERT—USE OF NOISE

Now I would like to talk to you about an episode that taught me a tremendous amount; thus I hope it will be useful to you as well. Many years ago I went to Florence, to the Conservatory Luigi Cherubini, to do a concert with the Gruppo di Improvvisazione Nuova Consonanza (New Consonance Improvisation Group).[88] We were supposed to do the second part of the concert, and thus we thought to assist with the first part. The concert was supposed to start at 9 p.m. The public waited with much courtesy, but 9:15 passed, and the concert did not begin. 9:20 passed, and it did not begin. At a certain point, a man in a normal suit arrived and climbed onto the tiny stage, a type of very low mezzanine, it seems to me. Is it like that now, too?

SM: Not exactly. The Auditorium of Good Humor (Sala di Buonumore) (ironically, it is called exactly that) was restructured in recent years.

EM: He climbed onto the stage, took off his coat, hung it on a coat rack, took a ladder, put it against a little balcony, and climbed onto it. It was 9:30, and the people naturally talked, in expectation that the concert would begin, without paying attention to that man on the ladder, who in the meantime had begun to act in a very strange way, producing creaking noises . . . 9:40, 9:45 . . . Then the public began to ask itself whether that man up there represented something that perhaps it should pay attention to, and little by little silence fell. The man continued, undaunted, in absolute silence. 10:15 arrived. The man descended the ladder, took his coat, and left. End of the first half. The happening left the public very perplexed. Nobody understood the reason for that exhibition. However, they did not react like the public at Cage's concerts at Darmstadt,[89] where the audience turned the seats upside down, beating the feet of the chairs. The Italian public remained silent, well educated. I tried to figure out for myself why and arrived at certain conclusions. And they are conclusions that I think are useful for music, but for film music in a particular way. A sound, any sound from our life, taken out of the context that produces it, assumes with time, in silence, another value, another meaning. The buzz of a fly in front of a microphone, isolated from all the rest, listened to in silence, is no longer what we thought but something completely different.

I told Sergio Leone about the episode in Florence. He already had a particular interest in the expressive potential of noise. He made the first twenty minutes of *C'era una volta il West* (*Once upon a Time in the West*)[90] emphasizing isolated sounds, but it wasn't exactly the same thing. In the film, we see the mill that creaks. We see the drop that falls onto the hat of the killer. Thus emphasized, therefore, the sounds are part of a natural context. In any case, he treated himself to an important experiment, and everyone judged those two reels to be a genial solution.[91] Naturally, this also had consequences for my work.

I don't say that it was a lightning-swift reasoning, but rather a slow maturation, almost imperceptible. Little by little I found the key to solutions that traced back to that episode in Florence. For example, the choice of tone color and the reduction of thematic materials, perhaps all the resources that contribute to a musical aggregation, developed from that Florentine experience. Remaining on *C'era una volta il West*, I think of those three notes of the harmonica, above all the cue "L'uomo dell'armonica" ("The Harmonica Man"). They were so necessary precisely for their extreme autoreduction. They carried diverse implications: the coexistence of external and internal levels, the symbolic significance that those three sounds assumed in the story and, therefore, that their obsessive reiteration assumed.[92]

IMPORTANCE OF COUNTERPOINT

I think it is important to think clearly and to find the stimuli to reduce the material, as in the case of the duets about which I have already spoken. If we take two flutes and we make a counterpoint in two parts; and then eventually we double them with another two instruments, adding a bass that has a clear harmonic connotation; and then we double these two counterpoints with the whole orchestra—if the counterpoint is correct, we already have a piece of music, a composition that stands on its own feet. It would be useful to look at certain scores of Brahms in order to understand his duets with a bass. They are in three parts, often with the intervention of the brass that fixes the common sounds of the harmony. Anyway, the reduction of a theme to three sounds also guarantees its memorization, which in the cinema is very important.

Think about primitive music, that which is transmitted orally, with a provenance of Africa, South America, or Asia. Think of the sitar or the famous riffs of jazz. All these phenomena have in common the repetition of small, incisive melodies based on scales of four or five notes. It is repeatability that carries a certain monotony, but not in a negative sense—a monotony that is able to give force to the composition. From here the minimalists were born. They departed from primitive music, elaborating on it with a synthesizer. Today there are many connections between primitive and contemporary music.

Let's remain on the small, incisive melodies. We can put them in various tracks, and an example from *L'attentato*[93] in this sense has already been given, but now we can refer to another example that behaves in a different way from that principle. You could compose in advance a harmonically fixed sketch. I do not want to suggest which chords you should use, but it is possible to make it either in a traditionally tonal manner or with distant chords, with unusual harmonic transitions. You could create a first melodic part and a second that follows the first—I am not talking about duets. I am speaking of octets—and then arrange the octets on various tracks; and with this melodically identical base, made with a few sounds, try another manner of writing, perhaps more interesting and more entertaining, certainly more experimental, because in the mix you could entertain yourselves by pulling out infinite possibilities from those few sounds.

GESTURAL MUSIC IN *BUONE NOTIZIE* (*GOOD NEWS*)
(PETRI, 1979)

In the film *Buone notizie* (*Good News*),[94] I had an experience of this sort that in a certain sense was gestural music. I, the director of the orchestra/composer, called for the entrance of single instruments with a gesture, and these sounded as long as they did not receive the gesture to stop, while the other instruments continued. This type of writing (in various columns) came later than that which I have already described. That other—*Invention for John*[95] —was indirect, in the sense that the instruments played according to a common metronome and to a predetermined harmonic plan. Individually we recorded simple melodic structures, not atonal, not decaphonic, based on strophic plans, some longer, some shorter, repeatable into infinity. A simplification desired in order to permit a complicated movement of the parts was determined by the opening of the potentiometer for the track on which that certain instrument was recorded. Instead, here (*Good News*) the instrumentalists were all present and entered at my gesture. For this reason I spoke about gestural music.

SM: Excuse me, Ennio, but your explanation could be confusing. By "gestural" you mean music in which the visual element in an expressive sense is present and now and then decisive—a breed of "turn into something spectacular" gesture and of "staging" performance that imply allusions of various kinds.

For example, in *Novelletta*, by Bussotti, the pianist "plays" over the keyboard and finishes by caressing the legs of the instrument as if they were a woman's legs. (I remember Giancarlo Cardini's interpretation towards the end of the 1970s). The reference is to the "extreme" rite of nineteenth-century pianistic virtuosity. In your case, you speak instead of pseudo-aleatoric music, because there is the casual component (the entrances determined extemporaneously by the conductor's gesture), but there is also a well-defined musical notation. Therefore, a certain relationship with your experience in the Gruppo di Improvvisazione Nuova Consonanza seems evident to me.

EM: It could be. This is a piece that holds a little bit of everything that I talked about before, a strange mixture of types, of timbre. There is a jazz trumpet that deliberately plays badly, a bassoon, a mandolin, a viola, an accordion that does not play but "breathes." I had him do it by making the chords while opening and closing the bellows, and then I magnified the effect in the mix, because one hears this "folk" sound.[96] I told the musician that he had to breathe together with the instrument, too. This mixture of colors is very important. The strophic dimension and this timbral context that is so heterogeneous are the elements that I believe caused the results that I wanted, because I felt that one was dealing with a great film. But I have to tell you that initially I had composed a completely different kind of music. When I listened to it, the editor said in front of Petri, "From here on one does not laugh anymore." Then I started over from the beginning.

SM: Strange . . . it is a film that can inspire everything except hilarity.

EM: Yes, yes . . . but Petri hoped that one would laugh.

SM: But perhaps as a disguise for the tragic, as extreme irony.

EM: In any case, I rewrote everything. The references that here will suffice are the cues "Notturno un po' folle" ("A Night That Was a Little Crazy") and "Buone notizie" ("Good News").[97] Naturally, a strophic nature does not exclude certain particular solutions. For example, I played with stretching the intervals apart. In a discourse so almost folklike, I inserted something that has to do with a totally different thing, specifically the music of the second half of the twentieth century.[98]

And then about the work on its timbre: I played the jazz trumpet, because, I reiterate, I wanted it to be played badly, ruining the sound of the instrument. A certain irony was sufficient; it served as the destruction of the sound, equivalent to the destruction of a man, the protagonist of the film.

SM: Quite rightly the matter that Maestro Morricone is discussing pertains more strictly to composing than anything else, because the subject of the moment is elements of composition. . . . For certain traits of the film and score . . . I dedicated some pages in my book.[99]

In an extract from the aleatoric score one can see an extrapolation of some of the interventions. The only real and proper melody, the melody assigned to the viola, precedes the modules.[100]

But it could have been realized differently, for example, in a version of the aleatoric score that served Morricone for the composition "Titoli" ("Titles"). Imagine, then, a recording session with all the instruments present in which a common metronome starts to click, and at a sign, one or more instruments attack at the first measure. The others follow, count the measures, and enter at successive signals from the conductor. It is a modularity similar to that for *Invenzione per John* (*Invention for John*),[101] but in this case it is *live*.[102]

Buone notizie is Petri's last film, and I confess that I consider it almost a cult movie. Naturally, I do not pretend that this predilection is shared.[103] But for me it remains an important film, even though it is impossible to find.[104]

It is not an easy film. Petri carries to their extreme consequences all the elements—the auto-irony, the grotesque, the sarcastic pessimism—that distinguish it . . . and the intonation of the recitation is very close to Brechtian alienation.

To establish a relation between life and art is often misleading and leads inevitably to the rhetorical. In this film, death is the predominant subject (death and its *indifferent* and *unreasonable* actions).[105] As he died after working on the film, I have to ask whether Petri knew already that he was condemned. In any case, I find really extraordinary the stylistic range Morricone invented. The composition with which we are occupied is an emerging funeral music. It is, at least in appearance, in the New Orleans style, but then it is transformed by means of the entrances of the accordion and the mandolin. Their behavior is clownish, dense with symbolic references and absolutely tragic insight, but it is alienated, just like the recitation.

When I hear a result of this kind, I admire it profoundly. I find it much, much more meaningful—whether as music in itself, or for the function that it assumes in the film—than those "high" and complex results of which Maestro Morricone is, instead, prouder. I refer to the double fugue of *L'umanoide*,[106] for example, but also to *Finale di un concerto romantico* for inverted canon.[107] We have talked about them in part. I understand the exceptional procedure. It is really unique in the environment of specialists in film music.

However, I maintain the idea that the geniality of certain solutions reached with Leone, with Petri, with Joffé, in part with Pasolini, and with many others are more personal and inimitable stylistic characteristics. They are solutions that not even . . . a composer from an exclusively cultivated world would have known how to invent. But a double fugue can be within the reach of any number of good, newly graduated composition students. They are like that reconstruction *in the manner of* a concerto of the nineteenth century (contamination apart), without counting the danger of the implicit rhetoric in a musical event of this kind. On the other hand, there are films that break with tradition and inaugurate a tendency, of course risking the disapproval of the public, and films that prosper thanks to *clichés*.

MODULAR TECHNIQUES AND THE RELATION BETWEEN DETERMINISM AND ALEATORY

Let's turn to modular techniques, to superimpositions, and to the relations between determinism and aleatory.

EM: It is a type of writing that I inaugurated with the first film of Dario Argento, and then I used it in the second and third.[108] I continued for a few other films, and then that was enough. Otherwise, I would have had to leave my profession, because the results were sufficiently difficult for spectators to listen to. I wrote the structure for various sections, and then, recording, I indicated the entrances, exactly as I said before. But all this would not have made any sense had I neglected the tone-color factor and the mixture of musical and other sounds.

SM: For example, the electrical outlet, the milling cutter, and the welding machine for the cue "La classe operaia va in paradiso" ("The Working Class Goes to Heaven"). [109]

EM: It is a good example of what we have been saying. I obtained those sounds with Sinket, a synthesizer. I believe it was the first Italian one and perhaps one of the first in the world (even if then the Americans took all the credit). It was designed by the engineer Paolo Ketoff. [110]

SM: Apart from the "noisy" inserts, the score for the opening titles is sufficiently conventional in appearance. But after looking thoroughly at the piece, which is a march, one sees that it is constructed according to a structure that has many analogies with a chain of editing. And then there is a strange thing that seems to me typical of the Petri-Morricone fellowship, a decidedly kitschy passage made by the insertion of a violin that intones a species of little romantic cadenza.

EM: It is in contraposition to the trombone, to the vulgarity and the force that I wanted to express with the trombone.

SM: It is another example of how contrasts and stylistic "incoherences" can assume precise meanings. Those who have seen the film will remember the environment in which the worker Lulù Massa, her hairdresser companion, and her son live. There are souvenirs, little pictures, little embroidered things, soft toys, . . . all the bric-a-brac of a certain social condition in which little "aesthetic" ambitions are unfortunately all characterized by bad taste.

EM: This is a march tempo with strange tunings that are reminiscent of *Indagine*. [111] I revived that idea a little, because the success of *Indagine* was so extraordinary . . . Petri asked me explicitly to continue in that direction. It was justified, however, by the type of social condemnation that was found in his films.

TOTEM AND THE CONTRABASSOON

SM: Without counting the relationships with extracinematographic pieces, I think of *Totem secondo* (*Second Totem*) [112] and of the almost physiological emissions of the contrabassoon in the deep register that you had already tried out in *Totem*.

EM: *Totem* had its source in another Petri film but was thrown out because it was too difficult.

"L'ESTASI DELL'ORO" ("THE ECSTASY OF THE GOLD")

SM: This would confirm the relationship between the two productions. This is a typical process of accumulation analogous (though completely different as a stylistic framework) to "L'estasi dell'oro" ("The Ecstasy of the Gold").[113] The synthesized sounds are only some of the unusual occurrences. For example, there is that type of shout or lament.

EM: It is an electric guitar, distorted, with written notes: C-natural and B-natural. I annotated "electric guitar distorted," and the player was free to oscillate with quarter tones between those two notes.

THE HARMONICA IN *C'ERA UNA VOLTA IL WEST* (LEONE, 1968)

SM: A little like the harmonica of *C'era una volta il West*.[114]

EM: Yes, exactly. In that case I wrote only three notes. The orchestra previously was recorded live, and I left the attacks and above all the changes of notes, the crescendos and the diminuendos, to the player. Naturally, he was not one to do exactly what I said, but this served to make it stay above the instrumental base that he listened to over headphones.

SM: Before leaving *La classe operaia*,[115] I would like to add another observation. Many years ago I read of an association between this music and futurism, but the match is as facile as it is misleading. We know that the aesthetic of futurism is the exaltation of the machine, of the relation between man and machine. Of this vision there is not even a shadow in the film of Petri, where the machine signifies psychological and physical torture. It is alienation and mutilation. Think not only of Lulù, but also of the figures of the old worker, Salvo Randone, recovered in an insane asylum. Think of the tormenting tall tale that the workers shout and throw again from one position to another in the office. They are phrases without sense, reiterated, seasoned with sexual allusions, of arrogance and of challenges.

After the idealistic and fascistic heroism of *Acciaio*[116] and the little scenes sweetened with soft neorealism and Italian comedies, I do not believe that a director of our cinema is capable anymore of describing the climate that one really breathes in a mechanic's shop. But saying it this way, I do not want to conjure up an "objective" and documentary perspective. It seems paradoxical, but the "truth" of Petri's story resides exactly in the transfiguration to which the materials of the narration are subjected: the reiterated nonsense and exaggerated recitation that become something similar to metaphysical. The exorbitant facial expressions (also in the literal sense) of certain minor personages are not arbitrary caricatures or really allegorical. They are the essence itself of the processes of alienation. Therefore, I find that (having nothing to do with futurism) the music of Morricone has an interpretation that is more consonant with the ideological values and aesthetics of the film. It is not music of "good manners." It is heavy, dirty, sweaty, frustrated, and dissociated music. Thus, it is clear that the musical comment, as one usually intends it, doesn't mean anything here. This is a music that assumes in the first person all—I mean all—of the features of the film.

EM: We have talked about the reduction of the material, and in this sense there are still some examples to cite. But I want to turn also for a moment to the harmonica of *C'era una volta il West* that we have heard previously. How was this theme conceived? Why the choice of the harmonica? I was obligated to use it because the harmonica was in the script. I had to depart from a certain point in the film, halfway through, where there is a flashback to a youth who is constrained to hold his brother (who has a rope around his neck) on his shoulders. Naturally, the young man wants to prevent the hanging of his brother, but the torturer at a certain point puts a harmonica in his mouth. The young man is forced to breathe in, and so the theme was born (in fact, we, Leone and I, said to the harmonica player to breathe wheezily into the instrument, and Sergio almost strangled him in order to obtain the result). Therefore, the theme was born out of the necessity of the film and initially assumes a realistic character.

When for the first time we hear the principal actor (Bronson) play the harmonica, he does not have a name. He is "the man with the harmonica." We haven't yet seen the flashback, where the music is on an internal level. Little by little during the film, that realistic feature is transformed into a symbolic characteristic of dramatic force, of vendetta, especially after we have discovered the relationship that exists between this personage who is a little mysterious and the scene of the hanging. There we see him again, as he was many years before. At that point, it is clear that the sound of the harmonica that we hear offscreen belongs to a mediated level. As Professor Miceli has taught us, at that point, it is as if we were listening to his fixed idea of vendetta. Or is it an external level?

SM: In this case it depends on your instrumental treatment. We understand that we are dealing with episodes in which the character does not play. If the harmonica is alone or has a minimum of instrumental support, it belongs to the mediated level. If, on the other hand, it presents itself with the whole orchestra, perhaps by means of a gradual transition, at the highest point of the increase of orchestral instruments, it is an external level. The preceding implications make it an enriched, all-inclusive external level, because it contains within itself the other two levels. However, the more interesting aspect

(. . . earlier I touched on other examples of cases of transition between levels) remains in the fact that the mechanisms of flashback and of flash forward make the musical components assume a primary dramaturgical role in which the spectator can "reflect," even unconsciously, on how much he has seen and heard previously. It succeeds here, and it will succeed, in a masterly way, in *C'era una volta in America*.[117]

METTI, UNA SERA A CENA (LET'S SAY, ONE EVENING AT SUPPER) (GRIFFI, 1968)

EM: We move now to cues from *Metti, una sera a cena* (*Let's Say, One Evening at Supper*).[118] The first theme is based on reduced material—that is, on three sounds—but not from the point of view of timbre. It is constructed entirely with connected degrees of the scale, being an exercise of major and minor sevenths. By comparison to other cases of reduction, the scope is completely different. It is tonal, very simple, easy to listen to. In this film I wrote another piece, too, that I believed would be very successful, but, on the contrary, it did not happen as I had foreseen. It is a piece that I wrote to contrast with the first one. We hear immediately the second theme that is in contrast with the first one. . . . The characters are so far away from each other that it seemed right to me to construct it all with very disjointed degrees of the scale.[119]

One can create a musical logic in the interior of a film by departing from an idea that is only compositional but that is also able to find a symbolic reference in the story. In this case, it is the contrast between . . . absurd characters, love contrasted with rivalry. The theme demonstrates a very simple way of beginning. It is actually a modal theme, even if one might define it as being in B minor. In contrast, there is the first theme by connected degrees, about which I already spoke.[120]

We have a demonstration of how the contrapuntal artifices can be introduced in a piece like this one that is very easy, really "commercial," and (actually) danceable. There is the insertion of the augmented theme over the ostinato figuration of three notes.

Therefore, I invite you to reflect, always creatively, on such simple, normal things. I am not able to remember the genesis of all the ideas that are at the base of the pieces that I have written. However (if my way of working can be an example), certainly it is necessary to be curious even about a piece that is banal.

Naturally, there are also cases in which one can be less committed. The pieces at the internal level, for example, that come from a radio, those in a dance hall. . . . This music is of no importance to me, and I treat it like any old music. On the contrary, exactly because it should not be confused with commentary music, I make it a little worse. I don't know if it is good or bad, but I feel that I ought to be more attentive in order to distinguish between a realistic, casual music and a music that comments on the film, that represents the persons and ideas. This is true except in cases like the finale of *Io la conoscevo bene* (*I Knew Her Well*),[121] about which Professor Miceli spoke to you. There I acted differently because that piece assumes an extremely important significance.

SM: This confirms the fact that one ought to distinguish between various degrees of internal level. The classification tells us only that the music belongs to the scene, while to determine its importance and its function, of course, indirect and allusive, one has to analyze the narrative context and the director's intentions.

AUGMENTED THEMES

EM: In the last example, *Metti, una sera a cena* (*Let's Say, One Evening at Supper*),[122] I made a fleeting reference to an augmented theme. To augment a theme is a contrapuntal artifice, as all of you know, but in this case it is augmented so that one could call it a species of cantus firmus. Think of a cantus firmus contrasted with a profane piece like *Metti, una sera a cena*. These are the procedures that interest me and that give me a feeling of autonomy. *Metti, una sera a cena* is an example of exceptional augmentation, because over a passage written in half notes the theme becomes whole notes. Then the theme in connected notes has given way to the theme for pianoforte transposed into C minor, and over this one has superimposed a canon for brass at intervals of the fifth.[123]

AUGMENTATION WITH RESTS

Now I would like to talk about the expansion of a theme, . . . not only about the expansion of note values (because we are dealing with augmentation) but also about expansion by means of the addition of rests. To add silences to a theme is something that I discovered slowly in the cinema. (I also have written concert pieces in which I serialized all the values of the rests, but that is another discussion.) It is one solution, perhaps an expediency, that strengthened my ideas about the reduction of material and about the importance of tone colors. I applied this procedure pretty recently in a decisive manner to two films, *State of Grace*[124] and *Bugsy* by Barry Levinson.[125] It was necessary to notate the durational values of the three-note themes and the distance that passed from one repetition of the parenthesis to the total advantage of the tone color.

SM: We referred previously already to a cue from *State of Grace*, "Hell's Kitchen." Naturally, it is a welcome recurrence, because the same compositional process can be examined from different angles, to which one can then add its relation to moving images.

USE OF HARMONICS IN *STATE OF GRACE* (JOANOU, 1990)

EM: It is in *State of Grace*[126] that I applied this procedure for the first time, but I will tell you immediately that I could not get Joanou interested in it in the least. When I recorded this piece, he was very polite, but at the end of the editing he said to me, "Hmm . . . it isn't as though it works that well for me." He had not understood. After some months, however, a letter full of enthusiasm arrived. It was completely different from what I could possibly have imagined.

In sum, . . . this is a passage that is very important in my cinematographic writing. Apart from the theme, with those few sounds that every so often "run over" the other sounds, almost as if there had been an accident, there is one fixed dissonance that becomes like a theme. On the third major degree of the chord E-flat and D-natural occur together and, therefore, the dissonance that characterizes the piece. But it seems to me that I already have talked about these things. However, I have not finished, because I need to describe another feature.

In this piece there is a sequence of harmonics. In the saxophone part, which enters at a certain point, there are these "clicks" that I thought were sensual. I added the eleventh-degree harmonic, F-sharp, which is a dissonance in the normal context of C major but is not if one considers the sequence of natural harmonics. Then, in a certain case, the B-flat. Sometimes there is the B-natural, which is the harmonic still higher, the fifteenth degree, until the sixteenth degree, which is a repetition of the harmonic, four octaves above. In conclusion, all the harmonics are touched, a natural phenomenon that I tried to bring back to the cinema.

By using this example, I do not mean to advise repetition of the same procedure. Each one of us has to invent a way of working; these are only suggestions. I have been asked in what way I succeed in being free in the face of a director's request. One can be free in private, secretly. The director is not interested in the least in this particular aspect. Joanou did not know that there was an eleventh harmonic or the third minor. In fact, after the first hearing, he remained perplexed, unsatisfied, as I just explained.

AUGMENTATION AND *BUGSY* (LEVINSON, 1991) —
THE EXPRESSIVE USE OF THE PAUSE

Now we can move along to *Bugsy*.[127] Levinson heard *State of Grace*,[128] which didn't make a cent in America, and, as sometimes happens, he asked me to imitate it. The composer can mount a resistance, but in this case I did not have any reason to protest. Joanou was very angry. . . . He released a resentful interview against me, not exactly bad but resentful, because I had repeated the experience that I had with him. First he didn't like my music, then he liked it so much that he wanted an exclusive. . . . Poor dear!

SM: Entertaining. In any case, it is a constant in your career. Every time you have written music for a film that was not successful, you have reproposed it repeatedly, with opportune modifications, until you have found the winning combination.[129] But let's look at the example from *Bugsy*.[130]

EM: I will not repeat what I have already said about the "rotation" of the blues. The mechanism is the same. (We have been talking about) the pause. In this example, the music is even more augmented than in the cue from *State of Grace*, because after Levinson made his request, I thought about how to improve the procedure.

SM: But, apart from the pause, the impression that one gets is of a major transparency of the harmonic foundation. As Stravinsky would have said, there is less "marmalade." The dissonances appear more isolated, less fused with the tonal harmony. Really, for this reason it is more evident, more recognizable. Could it be that the occasion of a great production like *Bugsy* induced you to be prudent, reducing the complexity of the writing? Basically, it is one of your constants to be more experimental in films that are apt to be less remunerative and then to apply those solutions, but softened, to films that are economically more ambitious.

EM: It could be. However, I improved the same procedure even more in Oliver Stone's film *U-Turn*.[131] It is a piece[132] that actually does not have a melody. The melody, if there is one, consists of two notes and is played extremely sensually between a bass flute and a female voice. They repeat the same thing, but these two notes are not important. It is the framework that is important, because I used the true and proper *appoggiatura* of whole chords, not of just one note, but within an easy-to-hear tonal system. This is the challenge for the cinema: to be catchy but without sacrificing everything else in the writing.

SM: You have talked about how you extended the melody (or, to state it better, the microthematic segment) through augmentation and the insertion of rests, but you referred to recent examples while you yourself have said that they are discoveries that you arrived at by degrees.

It would be interesting for those following this discussion to think back to examples pertaining to a less complex phase from the melodic and harmonic point of view. Let's start with *Gott mit Uns (God with Us)*. Then let's go to *Marco Polo* and finally to *Il deserto dei tartari (The Desert of the Tartars)*. Notice that in this initial phase of the process that demonstrates the expressive use of the pause, you also establish, gradually, the presence of the pedal point. We have already discussed its function for the imperceptible entrance of music in a scene. Here, instead, we can understand it as compensation for a series of "lacks" and, in the development of this style, increasingly as harmonic anchorage until we arrive at *State of Grace* and others.

GOTT MIT UNS (GOD WITH US) (MONTALDO, 1969) [133]

The principal theme of *Gott mit uns* is constructed according to the classic structure A-B-A. With its progress from the passage of A to B, the chord bands in the strings gradually annihilate the sense of suspension and the expressive presence of the pause. The melody is typically Morriconian, solemn and enlarged, but still not at the extremity of its consequences, and the pauses between semiphrases fall within the logic of conventional phraseology. . . . [134] Consider next the semiphrases that constitute section B. They are much more linked together, until the extreme density of the bridge that brings us back to A. [135]

Also, the pedal is not an immobile pedal but follows the harmonic dynamics and therefore reduces in some way its own unambiguous impact. It is not by accident that this happens above all in the passage from A to B and affirms a basic characteristic of this writing. In the initial part, Morricone is much more "extreme" (it is relatively obvious within the context). Then it is as if he repents and, preoccupied with the reactions of the listeners, as one should be who writes music for the movies, he inserts, little by little, compensatory elements until the piece becomes much more conventional than it promised to be at the beginning. If one considers this procedure well, it is somewhat analogous to the tripartite structure of the music of the western. The ideology—so to speak—is totally different, but the result is similar. It commences in an unusual way and ends in a reassuring one. With *State of Grace*, [136] on the other hand, the unusual becomes ordinary, perhaps because of the ostinato, which, as noted, has this function for the listener. If one insists and insists, even the strangest concentration becomes acceptable.

MARCO POLO (MONTALDO, 1982) [137]

We move on now to the title music for *Marco Polo*. [138] In association with other sponsors, the movie represented a great production commitment for the RAI. (Not accidentally, the cast is international.) As far as I know, it was acquired by many foreign TV stations, representing an exception. . . . Italy is a great acquirer of foreign productions (even the worst ones), while it produces few and badly. The viola soloist is Dino Asciolla. [139]

EM: This piece is in D minor, but in the central part, where there is an explosion of intensity, I conducted an experiment. There are modulations to very distant keys and then the return to the initial D minor. But for these modulations to distant keys, I did not use the dominant, V. I always made them using the plagal cadence. It seemed opportune to work with the plagal cadence because it was much in use in the period in which Marco Polo lived. No one noticed this solution, but I was interested in applying it.

SM: The cadence of the subdominant to the tonic, called the plagal cadence, and, not by accident, the "Amen Cadence" by the English, is typical of ecclesiastical polyphony. Belonging to tonal harmony, I believe that it entered into use precisely in the epochs following that in which Marco Polo lived, astride the thirteenth and fourteenth centuries.

But philology here does not make any sense. The just or mistaken motivation aside, the important thing is something that you have demonstrated many times with great effectiveness. You search for completely musical solutions that stimulate you while you are composing. In connection with the previous discussion, you have noted the structural affinity with *Gott mit uns*. The thinning out in part A and the thickening of part B are analogous.

IL DESERTO DEI TARTARI (THE DESERT OF THE TARTARS) (ZURLINI, 1976) [140]

We arrive at the third example and will occupy ourselves with the opening titles, then with a related scene, and finally with the first sequence of *Il deserto dei tartari* of Zurlini, a film that was at times very intriguing. It had an exceptional cast, [141] but it did not have the reception that was expected of it. The music for the opening title music does not have anything to do with our discussion about extended melody.

However, since we are here, let us turn for a moment to the method of levels. The theme for piano that is present during these titles has all the characteristics of a typical external level. (I skip over the fact that, though consistent with the required closed and symmetrical structure for a piece of this kind, its scansion is perfectly aligned with the changes in the scene in the opening titles.)[142] However, it is a false external level.

Generally, the spectator receives the music for the opening titles with a certain critical neutrality because, more than the expected name of the director, presumed setting, and names of the cast, he or she still does not have many points of reference. The composition for the opening titles introduces a climate, an epoch, and exactly for this evocation it is considered a sort of curtain raiser or frame. It is connotative in the stylistic sense but without specific denotative, that is, dramaturgical, functions.

However, in this case, during the narrative development of the film, the protagonist returns to his ancestral home. He approaches a piano and plays the music from the opening titles. This is a solution that interests me very much. In agreement with the director and obviously with the screenwriter, who has given his consent, the composer writes music that can assume a retrospective value. It is useless to say that the model for this circularity comes from the musical theater (the overtures, symphonies, intermezzi, preludes) and from Wagner in particular.

In other words, here the composer throws out an apparently neutral seed from which he will much later collect the fruit. In terms of levels, what appears initially to be on an external level now proves to be an internal level. Consequently, in another context and in the absence of the piano, successive listenings can be interpreted as the thoughts and feelings of the protagonist, his musical memory, turned toward familiar objects of affection. Therefore, the music assumes a typical mediated level. In this way the circularity is complete.[143]

We turn to music with the melodic extension. Here there is a remarkable coincidence between the character of the narration and the compositional process. (As we have seen, independent of any single film, Morricone's writing is characterized by a compositional process that is in constant evolution. It is a stylistic feature of his work.)

To explain this better, it would be necessary to know the film and, before that, even the novel of Buzzati on which it is based. I remind you only that Lieutenant Drago[144] is assigned to a fortress at the edge of the empire and the desert. (This was already audible from the voice off-camera in the opening titles.) He will wait in vain for the arrival of the Tartars. He will get sick, and when the sentinels finally announce the Tartars' appearance, Drago will be conducted home almost dead. The climate is metaphysical, rarefied, and the apologue is clear. Maestro Morricone, if he wants, can explain other things. I can add only that after the passage of many years and repeated viewings, I remain amazed and fascinated by this theme.[145] The extension is responsible precisely for the same metaphorical values as the film. I am only sorry that the scene is too short and sacrifices the musical range. Really, I don't know how to explain it. A director receives a solution so extraordinary and does not have the courage that could be applied to the total advantage of the film. These are the cases in which one misses Sergio Leone. [146]

EM: The scene is not closed; it continues. Therefore, the music remains on a suspended chord. It should not be said that all pieces have to finish on the tonic. In fact, when the scene remains open, the piece can remain suspended as well. I often talked about this fact with the director, because I don't like to stop music in the middle of a scene. I have already explained the reason. The exit of the music is not as natural as its entrance. In this example, one is not aware of the cue's entrance. When one finally notices, it has already entered a while back.

For that reason it had to go away in the same manner, imperceptibly, within the sounds of the successive scene. When music remains suspended, as in this case, putting a chord in D major would not be very pleasant. On the other hand, there was not time to finish it. Therefore, it seemed to me more in keeping with the continuation of the scene to remain on the third facing the dominant, V.

CANONE INVERSO (INVERSE CANON) AGAIN

In the first part of this course I spoke about a case that had never happened in almost forty years of my being militant about cinema music, that of writing the finale for a concerto for violin and piano in a romantic style in which I had to insert a canon. It seemed to me in keeping with the fact that the film was entitled *Canone inverso* [147] and had two violinists and a pianist as protagonists. The two violinists were in part friends, in part rivals, and together played an inverse canon. Therefore, in any case, I had to write an inverse canon.

I wrote two types of inverse canon for the film. I wrote the second after the first had to be discarded because it was too difficult to play and was not catchy enough nor gypsy-like enough. (The film takes place in Prague; therefore, the director wanted it to reflect the influence of gypsy music.) But it is about the first canon that I would like to talk now. It is a very chromatic piece.

The inverse canon proceeds from four beats in four measures, and the motive is very simple. When I saw the playback list, I realized that the duration would be only sixteen seconds. Therefore, I would not be able to compose an inverse canon of the total duration of one minute and fifteen seconds (it seemed to me), because the inversion would be heard too late. For that reason I made sections that were in sixteen-second modules so that the inversion would be heard simultaneously with the development of the direct statement of the canon.

So where is the problem? To write an inverse canon with dodecaphonic technique presents no difficulties because the encounters, the clashes, the dissonances do not make an impression. Here, however, I found myself in a tonal context, and the situation was different.

I would like to note that this is an inverse double canon. When I wrote the bass, I did so only to justify the two parts harmonically and contrapuntally, because in the final version there would not have been a bass. I tried to invert it. It was perfect, miraculously perfect. Therefore, I do not merit this second result. Here is the *Canone inverso*, first version, for two violins and piano.[148]

It is not necessary to listen to the second version, for two violins.[149] This is an example of the kind of misadventure that can happen in the cinema. When I studied at the conservatory, I never composed a tonal inverse canon. I wrote it with twelve tones, but not the classic kind. We made canons at the octave, and therefore they were simple enough. . . . Professor Miceli has already indicated in a critical way the problems that arrive as a result of actors, who normally do not know how to imitate a musician. In this case, the actors who interpreted the two violinists studied in London with a maestro. They practiced for some time, not for five months, as with Tornatore's film,[150] but I believe for a couple of months. Naturally, one does not exclude the possibility that on playback—that is, at the internal level—situations of the external level may be added, perhaps even with the addition of a female voice.

SM: In any case, you are very content with this kind of test . . .

EM: Beh. It demonstrates that I can also be an academic composer when it serves. To make a fugue in six parts (as we have heard) is a service to the film that, it seems to me in all humility, succeeds.

SM: This also is an interesting problem and subject to multiple interpretations. . . . I would say that the concept itself of being "academic" after Webern, after Cage, after the neo avant-garde, does not have the significance that it would have had in the first quarter of the twentieth century. . . . The definition itself . . . ought to be contextualized. I want to say—for a moment outside of the writing for the cinema, to which we will return immediately— that an "academic" composer could be defined as a composer who continues today, unperturbed over the Shah of Schoenberg. He or she would be heedless of everything that has characterized the music of the second half of the twentieth century or is one who, struck by lightning (like Paul on the way to Damascus) by the *Symphony of Psalms* of Stravinsky, follows it more or less consciously in all his or her productions. It is academic in its rapport with classicism, and the classics of our time are, among others, the composers that I cited.

Instead, to write a concert in a romantic style or a double fugue on the model of Bach is not academic. It is a handcrafted product, *à la manière de*, in the manner of, totally outside of its own time. It can have some reason for being that is applicable only in the movies. And—having said this, I return to the point. There are reasons that most of the time I don't understand. As director of my own film, I would want original music, and if I had to be connotative in a stylistic sense, I would opt for preexisting music, . . . trusting in a musical consultant. Luchino Visconti did it; Ricky Tognazzi could do it. . . . So much more we are in a playback situation. I can understand the inverse canon (the piece for two violins, not the film, which, though not having yet seen it, I would be tempted to paraphrase as *Natale in casa Cupiello* [*Christmas at Cupiello's House*][151]), but to ask a composer today—and one of your caliber—to write the finale of a concerto in the romantic style seems to me an enormous waste of energy, a mannerism, a sort of cynicism or of ostentation of the nouveau riche.

EM: I do not know; perhaps this is a legitimate criticism from your point of view, as you are rightly very rigorous. I have an assignment. The inverse canon for two violins ought to be simple, catchy. I am talking about the second version. It has to be easy to execute and harmonically correct. Over so many obligatory roads I had to travel to be able to make a thing that was freer. On the other hand, the first version was more fanciful, but it did not achieve the effect that it should have. It pleased everyone, but it was not accepted because it lacked that catchiness. Now sometimes films have some-thing in common with publicity. The piece has to be easy to memorize, of course. It has to be in line with a middle public. (One could have a long discussion about this: What is the level of the cinema public? It is medium-low.) Therefore, this inverse canon is catchy, so catchy that even Claudio Villa[152] would have been able to sing it in his day.

NOTES

1. Here it was not possible to include all of Morricone's preanalysis for all the films with his music screened in their entirety during the seminar held at the Accademia Chigiana, nor all the analyses made by members of the seminar. For this reason it was decided to make a selection: *Indagine su un cittadino al di sopra di ogni sospetto* [DVD, Medusa Video, 2008; Eyescreen, 2003]; *L'attentato* [VHS, Lange, B004AH2DY0]; *Il prato* (*The Lawn*) [DVD, ArtHaus, B000PKHW3S, n.d.]; *Il deserto dei tartari* [DVD, *Il deserto dei tartari*, General Video, 2007; *The Desert of the Tartars*, Ryko Distribution, 2006]; and *The Mission* [DVD, Warner Bros., 2003]. The selection is valuable as an example and moreover has references to the text to preceding chapters or to that which follows.

2. Available on CD, Cinevox CD-CIA 5086.

3. See "Musical Example 25, Theme I from *Indagine su un cittadino ad di sopra di ogni sospetto*," in *Comporre per il Cinema*, 159–60.

4. Orchestrated differently, with the titles "Miraggio" [Mirage], "Miraggio second" [Second Mirage], and "Miraggio terzo" [Third Mirage] on the Cinevox CD.

5. The head of the homicide section (Gian Maria Volonté) and his lover, Augusta Terzi (Florinda Bolkan).

6. See "Musical Example 26, Theme II from *Indagine su un cittadino al di sopra di ogni sospetto*," in *Comporre per il Cinema*, 161.

7. See "Musical Example 27, *L'attentato*," in *Comporre per il Cinema*, 162.

8. On the CD CAM CSE 065 with the title *Il prato* (*The Lawn*).

9. The film unfolds in the Tuscan countryside near San Gimignano. The "fable," the result of Antonia's (Isabella Rosselini's) hallucination, takes place in an epoch vaguely like the Renaissance.

10. Here obtained from the reduction of A for flute and piano. See "Musical Example 28, Theme I of *Il prato*," in *Comporre per il Cinema*, 163.

11. On the CD, op. cit., with the title "Troppa luce, troppa ombra" ("Too Much Light, Too Much Shade").

12. The notes B-A-C-H from the German notation correspond to the succession B-flat—A-natural—C-natural—B-natural.

13. See "Musical Example 29, Theme II of *Il prato*," in *Comporre per il Cinema*, 153.

14. Directed by Valerio Zurlini, an Italian-French-German production, 1976. [DVD, General Video, 2007.]

15. On LP GM, GML 1005 it assumes diverse titles, among which is "La casa e la giovinezza" ["The House and Youth"]; the version referred to is, however, that of the piano solo, recorded on CD by Gilda Buttà (Frankfurt am Main: dfv, in press [2001]) as a piece belonging to the *4 Canzoni: Le due stagioni della vita, Gott mit uns, Il potere degli angeli* [*Four Songs: The Two Seasons of Life, God with Us, The Power of the Angels*]. The CD also contains the *4 Preludi* (*White Dog, Stark System, Indagine su un cittadino . . ., Metti, una sera a cena*), in addition to *Rag in frantumi, Nuovo cinema Paradiso*, and the *Quattro studi per il pianoforte*.

16. On the LP, op cit., it assumes various titles, of which *Proposta* can be considered the one referred to.

17. See "Musical Example 30. *Il deserto dei tartari*" in *Comporre per il Cinema*, 163.

18. [DVD, Warner Bros., 2003.]

19. The film, directed by Roland Joffé (GB, 1986), takes place in the first half of the eighteenth century.

20. See "Musical Example 31, *The Mission*—Gabriel's oboe," in *Comporre per il Cinema*, 164.

21. See "Musical Example 32, *The Mission*—'Finale,'" in *Comporre per il Cinema*, 164.

22. See "Musical Example 33, *The Mission*—'Fusione,'" in *Comporre per il Cinema*, 164.

23. See "Musical Example 35, 'On Heart as It Is in Heaven,' from *The Mission*," in *Comporre per il Cinema*, 175–76.

24. *Per un pugno di dollari* (*A Fistful of Dollars*) (Leone, 1964). [DVD, *Sergio Leone Anthology*, MGM/UA, 2007.]

25. The lapse—if that is what this is—is very interesting and symptomatic of a contradictory position. The constant hyperbole on which the cinema of Leone is based, even efficiently described a little above by Morricone, would make one think of a musical contribution revolving around incredibility more than credibility, around the obsolete more than the customary, as, by his own admission, his musical contributions are obsolete. The adjective betrays perhaps a constant preoccupation of Morricone, that of contributing to the consolidation of the film in terms of consensus. [SM]

26. *Il buono, il brutto, il cattivo* (*The Good, the Bad, and the Ugly*) (Leone, 1966). [DVD, *Sergio Leone Anthology*, MGM/UA, 2007; Mondo Home, 2007].

27. He is referring to *Giù la testa* [*Duck, You Sucker*] [DVD, *Sergio Leone Anthology*, MGM/UA, 2007]. For a detailed analysis of this music see Miceli, *Morricone*, op. cit., 93–169.

28. In an especially prominent way in the first three, *Per un pugno di dollari; Per qualche dollaro in più; Il buono, il brutto, il cattivo*; and in a softer way in *C'era una volta il West* [DVD, *Sergio Leone Anthology*, op. cit.] (but the discussion is valid also for *Il clan dei siciliani* [*Le clan des siciliens*] [France, Verneuil, 1969]; [DVD, *Il clan dei siciliani*, Twentieth Century Fox, 2006; *The Sicilian Clan*, Phantom, 2009], although with some adaptations).

29. He refers principally to the cue entitled "L'uomo dell'armonica" ["The Harmonica Man"].

30. He refers to the cue "La resa dei conti" ["The Rendering of the Accounts"] from *Per qualche dollaro in più*.

31. See especially the chapter "Dalla scuola di Petrassi a Darmstadt" in Miceli, *Morricone*, op cit., pp. 41–63.

32. The numerous discographic and republished editions of the musical tracks of Morricone, especially those with the most success, like *C'era una volta il West* [*Once upon a Time in the West*], render very relative the reference to one edition in particular. Therefore, we will limit ourselves, recollecting that the anthologies that are most easily available, attributed to productions of the sixties and seventies, are published principally by RCA/BMG, General Music, Intermezzo Media, CAM, and Virgin. (See "Musical Example 34, "'Jill's Theme,' from *C'era una volta il West*," in *Comporre per il Cinema*, 170.)

33. *C'era una volta in America* (*Once upon a Time in America)* (Leone, 1984). [DVD, *Once upon a Time in America*: Two-Disc Special Edition, Warner Bros., 2011.]

34. "L'uomo dell'armonica" ["The Harmonica Man"], cue from *C'era una volta il West* [DVD, *Sergio Leone Anthology*, op. cit.]

35. "Deborah's Theme," *C'era una volta in America* (1983).

36. *Nuovo cinema Paradiso* (Italy/France, Tornatore, 1988). [DVD, Arrow Video, 2001, 2003, 2007; Cecchi Gori, n.d.; Director's Cut, Cristaldi Film, n.d.]

37. Stefano Novelli.

38. *C'era una volta il West* [*Once Upon a Time in the West*] (Leone, 1968). [DVD, *The Sergio Leone Anthology*, MGM/UA, 2007; Paramount Pictures, 2010]

39. *The Mission* (GB, Roland Joffé, 1986). [DVD, Warner Bros., 2003.]

40. He alludes to the cue "On Heart as It Is in Heaven," track 1 of CD Virgin CDV 202, which represents what Morricone intended but which the director, Joffé, did not use. See "Musical Example 35, 'On Heart as It Is in Heaven,' from *The Mission*," in *Comporre per il Cinema*, 175–76.

41. More exactly, on the border between Argentina and Brazil.

42. Father Gabriel, interpreted by Jeremy Irons.

43. *Per un pugno di dollari* (*A Fistful of Dollars*) (Leone, 1964). [DVD, *Sergio Leone Anthology*, MGM/UA, 2007].

44. For a more detailed analysis, see Miceli, *Morricone*, op cit., 281–93.

45. Altamirano, played by Ray McAnally.

46. Don Cabeza, interpreted by Chuck Low.

47. Don Hontar, played by Ronald Pickup, already known to the Italian public by virtue of being the protagonist of a TV film about the life of Giuseppe Verdi.

48. Although in the film a laboratory of lute making prepared by the Jesuits is visible, here I am referring to the presence of music. [SM]

49. *Alexander Nevsky* [*Aleksandr Nevskij*] (USSR, Eisenstein, 1938). [DVD, Criterion Colletion, 2001; Eureka, 2003.]

50. Fernando Ghia.

51. Among the most recent occasions, we remember the concert directed by Morricone at the Academy of Saint Cecilia, the auditorium in Via della Conciliazione of Rome, on November 1998, of which precious testimony remains on CD Sony Classical SK 89054.

52. [DVD, *Sergio Leone Anthology*, MGM/UA, 2007; Mondo Home, 2007.]

53. See "Musical Example 36, 'The Ecstasy of the Gold' from *The Good, the Bad, and the Ugly*," in *Comporre per il Cinema*, p. 178.

54. [DVD, *Sergio Leone Anthology*, op. cit.]

55. Played, respectively, by Robert De Niro and Larry Rapp.

56. On the CD Mercury 822 334-2, it corresponds to the first part of the piece entitled "Poverty" (track 2).

57. On the CD, the version closest to this use carries the title "Friendship and Love" (track 13) and is connected to the song "Amapola" (here arranged by Morricone for solo instruments), corresponding to track 9.

58. On the CD, op. cit., also as "Childhood Poverty."

59. See "Musical Example 37, Theme 'Poverty/Childhood Poverty,' from *C'era una volta in America*," in *Comporre per il Cinema*, 180–83.

60. See "Musical Example 38, Theme 'Once Upon a Time in America/Friendship and Love,' from *C'era una volta in America*," in *Comporre per il Cinema*, 184–86.

61. See "Musical Example 39, 'Deborah's Theme,'" in *Comporre per il Cinema*, 187–88.

62. I make the case, for example, about the musical attacks in the film *Il prato*. [SM]

63. I don't like to be negative about authors that I esteem, but on the other hand . . . for those who have demonstrated that they can give a lot, it is legitimate to expect more.

64. *Il prato* (*The Lawn*) (Taviani, 1979).

65. *C'era una volta in America* (*Once upon a Time in America*) (Leone, 1984). [DVD, *Once upon a Time in America*: Two-Disc Special Edition, Warner Bros., 2011.]

66. Dino Rulli (1890–1930), Roman composer, was author of, among others, *Addio tabarin* and *Scettico Blues*.

67. [DVD, *State of Grace*, MGM/UA, 1990.]

68. See "Musical Example 40, 'Hell's Kitchen,' from *State of Grace*," in *Comporre per il Cinema*, 191–92.

69. "Hell's Kitchen" from *State of Grace*, directed by Phil Joanou, USA, 1990, MCA Records MCAD—10119.

70. "The Shootout" on the CD, op. cit.

71. The film was shot in our time in the Irish quarter of New York. The final episode was realized by cross-cutting. The images of the procession during St. Patrick's Day alternated with the shoot-out, in which Terry Noonan (Sean Penn), a policeman who has infiltrated an Irish gang, reveals his real identity and vindicates the assassination of his friend Jackie (Gary Oldman).

72. They correspond on the CD to the composition "St. Patrick's Day," a version of "Hell's Kitchen."

73. He is talking about Kathleen (Robin Wright), sister of Jackie and of Frankie (Ed Harris), killer of the brother.

74. See "Musical Example 41, 'The Shootout,' from *State of Grace*," in *Comporre per il Cinema*, 194–96.

75. At least 388 as of February 2013. [GBA]

76. By the way, then realized in Miceli, *La musica nel film e nel teatro di prosa*, op cit., 283.

77. The cue "Hell's Kitchen" from *State of Grace*, directed by Phil Joanou, USA, 1990, MCA Records MCAD-10119.

78. *Per un pugno di dollari* (*A Fistful of Dollars*) (Leone, 1964). [DVD, *Sergio Leone Anthology*, MGM/UA, 2007.]

79. *Rio Bravo*, directed by Howard Hawks, USA, 1959, music by Dimitri Tiomkin. [DVD, Warner Bros., 2003.]

80. He is referring in reality to a vocal composition.

81. Television broadcast, RAI, 1962, directed by Mario Landi.

82. *State of Grace* (*Stato di grazia*) (USA, Joanou, 1990). [DVD, *State of Grace*, MGM/UA,1990, 2002.]

83. *The Scarlet Letter*, USA, 1995. [DVD, Disney/Buena Vista, 2004.]

84. *Malèna*, being worked on in 1999 and released in the autumn of 2000. [DVD, Buena Vista Home Entertainment, 2001.]

85. Gillo Pontecorvo (1919–2006), Italian director.

86. *C'era una volta in America* (*Once upon a Time in America*) (Leone, 1984). [DVD, *Once upon a Time in America*: Two-Disc Special Edition, Warner Bros., 2011.]

87. He is referring to the jacket note from 1982 for the LP of *Gestazione e Totem Secondo* (*Gestation and Second Totem*), RCA RL 31650. The phrase referred to *Gestazione*.

88. He is talking about a concerto organized by the association Vita Musicale Contemporanea, founded by Pietro Grossi, who carried out his activities at the Conservatory of Florence from 1961 to 1967.

89. See Miceli, *Morricone*, op. cit., but, above all, see A. Trudu, "La distruzione del tempio, John Cage a Darmstadt nel 1958" (and before and after), in S. Miceli (ed.), *Norme con ironie: Scritti per i settant'anni di Ennio Morricone* (Milan: Suvini Zerbini, 1998), 313–46.

90. *C'era una volta il West* [*Once upon a Time in the West*] (Leone, 1968). [DVD, *The Sergio Leone Anthology*, MGM/UA, 2007; Paramount Pictures, 2010.]

91. In cinematographic editing, the unit of measure is a reel, corresponding to twenty minutes of projection (in the past, it was ten minutes).

92. See "Musical Example 42, 'L'uomo dell'armonica,' from *C'era una volta il West*," in *Comporre per il Cinema*, 202.

93. *L'attentat* [*The Attempted Assassination*] (Boisett, 1972). [VHS, Lange, B004AH2DY0.]

94. Directed by Elio Petri, 1979.

95. *Giù la testa* (*Duck, You Sucker*) (Leone, 1971). [DVD, *The Sergio Leone Anthology*, MGM/UA, 2007; *Sergio Leone—Cofanetto Grandi Classici*, Mondo Home, 2007.]

96. Morricone demonstrated with his voice.

97. They are found on LP Cometa CMT 1013/27. They have not been reissued on CD.

98. See "Musical Example 43, 'Buone notizie,' intonation of distant sounds," in *Comporre per il Cinema*, 204.

99. See Miceli, *Morricone, la musica, il cinema*, 274–77.

100. See "Musical Example 44, Modules from *Buone notizie*," in *Comporre per il Cinema*, 205.

101. *Giù la testa* (*Duck, You Sucker*) (Leone, 1971). [DVD, *The Sergio Leone Anthology*, MGM/UA, 2007; *Sergio Leone—Cofanetto Grandi Classici*, Mondo Home, 2007.]

102. See "Musical Example 45, Extract of the aleatoric score for *Buone notizie*," in *Comporre per il Cinema*, 206–8. This score is a tablature for diverse instruments. The composer decides who ought to play, what to play, and when. It is not written anywhere under the nine pentagrams that all the instruments will play contemporaneously.

103. From what I have been able to read of the film's critiques, it seems really not to be.

104. I do not know the reason for this, seeing as how everything is reprinted on videocassette.

105. Not the power of the media, as someone wrote: that is only the context-pretext.

106. *L'umanoide* (*The Humanoid*) (Lado, 1979). [DVD, American International Pictures; ILC, 2005.]

107. *Canone inverso* (*Inverse Canon*) (Tognazzi, 1999). [DVD, Cecchi Gori, 2000.]

108. *L'uccello dalle piume di cristallo* (*The Bird of the Crystal Feathers*), 1970 [DVD, Phantom, 2009]; *Il gatto a nove code* (*Cat O'Nine Tails*), 1971 [DVD, *Cat O'Nine Tails*, Videotape, 2004]; and *Quattro mosche di velluto grigio* (*Four Flies of Grey Velvet*), 1971 [DVD, 01 Distribution, 2009]. One finds an anthology of the compositions on CD Cinevox CD-CIA 5087.

109. Directed by Elio Petri, 1971. [DVD, *La classe operaia va in paradiso*, Minerva, 2009.] See "Musical Example 46, 'Opening titles of *La classe operaia va in paradise*,'" in *Comporre per il Cinema*, 210–14.

110. "The orientation of the industry in the direction of a technology based on the transistor made possible, at the beginning of 1960, the development of synthesizers controlled by voltage. Almost contemporaneously, Robert Moog in New York, Donald Buchla in California, and Paul Ketoff in Rome constructed equipment controlled by voltage for electronica music, and in 1964 the first synthesizers appeared." J. Chabade, "Il principio del 'voltage-control' e le sue implicazioni per il compositore," in H. Pousseur (ed.), *La musica elettronica* (Milan: Feltrinelli, 1976), 281.

111. *Indagine su un cittadino al di sopra di ogni sospetto* (*Investigation of a Citizen above Suspicion*) (Petri, 1970). [DVD, Eyescreen, 2003; Medusa Video, 2008.]

112. *Totem secondo*, for five bassoons and two contrabassoons, no. 24 in the *Catalogo delle opera*, dated 1981 but could be earlier, and anyway preceded by *Totem* (not in the catalogue) for the same ensemble with the addition of percussion instruments.

113. From *Il buono, il brutto, il cattivo* (*The Good, the Bad and the Ugly*). [DVD, Mondo Home, 2007.]

114. *C'era una volta il West* [*Once upon a Time in the West*] (Leone, 1968). [DVD, *The Sergio Leone Anthology*, MGM/UA, 2007; Paramount Pictures, 2010.]

115. *La classe operaia va in paradiso* (*The Working Class Goes to Heaven*) (Petri, 1971). [DVD, *La classe operaia va in paradiso*, Minerva, 2009.]

116. Directed by Walter Ruttmann, music by Gian Francesco Malipiero, 1933.

117. *C'era una volta in America* (*Once upon a Time in America*) (Leone, 1984). [DVD, *Once upon a Time in America*: Two-Disc Special Edition, Warner Bros., 2011.] Frank, played by Henry Fonda.

118. Directed by Giuseppe Patroni Griffi, 1968.

119. See "Musical Example 47, Theme from *Metti, una sera a cena*," in *Comporre per il Cinema*, 217.

120. See "Musical Example 48, [1st] Theme from *Metti, una sera a cena* (vocalized)," in *Comporre per il Cinema*, 218–21.

121. *Io la conoscevo bene* (*I Knew Her Well*) (Antonio Pietrangeli, 1965). [DVD, Medusa Home Entertainment, 2009.]

122. *Metti, una sera a cena* (*Let's Say, One Evening at Supper*; *Hurry to Me*) (Griffi, 1968).

123. See "Musical Example 49, Augmentation of the theme for *Metti, una sera a cena*," in *Comporre per il Cinema*, 222.

124. USA, 1990, directed by Phil Joanou. [DVD, MGM/UA, 2002.]

125. USA, 1991, starring Warren Beatty, Annette Bening, Harvey Keitel, and Ben Kingsley. [DVD, *Bugsy—Extended Cut*, Sony Pictures Home Entertainment, 2006.]

126. *Stato di grazia* (*State of Grace*) (USA, Joanou, 1990). [DVD, *State of Grace*, MGM/UA,1990, 2002.]

127. He is dealing with the composition "For Her, For Him" on track 2 of the CD Epic EPC 469371 2. Other versions of the same piece are found on tracks 18 and 21.

128. *State of Grace* (*Stato di grazia*) (USA, Joanou, 1990). [DVD, *State of Grace*, MGM/UA,1990, 2002.]

129. A few of the more striking examples are noted in Miceli, *Morricone*, op. cit., 295ff.

130. See "Musical Example 50, 'For Her, for Him' from *Bugsy*," in *Comporre per il Cinema*, 224–29.

131. *U -Turn*, (*Inversione di marcia*), USA, 1997, with Sean Penn, Nick Nolte, Jon Voight, and Jennifer Lopez. [DVD, Sony Pictures Entertainment, 1998.]

132. Corresponding to track 11 on the CD Epic EK 68778.

133. *Dio è con noi*. Directed by Giuliano Montaldo, 1969. [DVD, Stormovie, 2008.]

134. See "Musical Example 51, Semiphrases A1 and A2 from *Gott mit uns*," in *Comporre per il Cinema*, 230.

135. See "Musical Example 52, Semiphrases B1 and B2 from *Gott mit uns*," in *Comporre per il Cinema*, 231.

136. *State of Grace* (*Stato di grazia*) (USA, Joanou, 1990). [DVD, *State of Grace*, MGM/UA,1990, 2002.]

137. Directed by Giuliano Montaldo, 1982. LP Fonit Cetra LPX 108. [DVD, Elle U Multimedia, 2009.]

138. See "Musical Example 53, Principal Theme of *Marco Polo*," in *Comporre per il Cinema*, 232–35.

139. One of the most accomplished Italian violists of his time (Rome 1920–Siena 1994).

140. [DVD, Instituto Luce, 2008; General Video, 2009.]

141. Jacques Perrin, Vittorio Gassman, Philippe Noiret, Max von Sydow, Fernando Rey. The film is based on the novel of the same title by Dino Buzzati.

142. For a more complete discussion, see Miceli, *Morricone*, op. cit., 261ff.

143. See "Musical Example 54, Opening title music for *Il deserto dei tartari*," in *Comporre per il Cinema*, 236–37. On the LP, GM – GML 1005, (which was not reissued on CD) the piece was entitled *La casa e la giovinezza*. Subsequently it was inserted into *4 Canzoni* and recently recorded by Gilda Buttà.

144. Jacques Perrin.

145. On the LP cited, there exist versions that are different from this composition, but the one closest to the soundtrack of the film carries the title "Proposta."

146. See "Musical Example 55, 'Theme from the Desert' for *Il deserto dei tartari*," in *Comporre per il Cinema*, 238–40.

147. [DVD, Cecchi Gori, 2000.]

148. See "Musical Example 56, 'Canone inverso,' from the film of the same title (1st version)," in *Comporre per il Cinema*, 241–42. Dealing with a film being worked on at the moment of the seminar, the references to the CD (Virgin, op. cit.) ought to be taken with the benefit of an inventory. For example, track 1, entitled "Canone inverso primo," presents a version with orchestra and even first with the insertion of white voices, recalling solutions already heard in films of the sixties and seventies such as *Grazie zia* [DVD, Medusa Video, 2005] and *Il sorriso del grande tentatore*. (*The Smile of the Great Tempter*) (Damiani, 1974).

149. The less elaborate version corresponds to track 21 of the CD (Virgin, op. cit.).

150. *La leggenda del pianista sull'oceano* (*The Legend of the Pianist on the Ocean*). [Streaming video, Italia-Film TV, Guarda Online.]

151. A comedy by Eduardo Di Fillipo. [GBA]

152. Traditional Italian "light" pop singer of the 1950s and 1960s. [GBA]

Chapter Seven

Questions and Answers

Course Member [CM]: Maestro, in the presence of themes that are so beautiful, has it ever happened that you have arranged them . . . for other instruments, even if only for personal pleasure?

EM: I am not interested in arranging pieces that I have already written, because I want them to remain in their original environment. There are, however, exceptions tied to particular exigencies. The finale to *The Mission*, for example, I have done at the Santa Cecilia with ninety choristers and eighty instrumentalists. If I had left the oboe as it was in the original, who would have heard it? Therefore, instead of the oboe I put four horns in unison—in the octave below, naturally. I could not do otherwise. However, since we have now returned to *The Mission*,[1] I would like to add a little thing that I forgot to say before. The ethnic chorus was interpreted by English choruses, but if there had been a real ethnic chorus it would have been beautiful. Instead, I had to make a compromise, as in *Bambini del mondo*.

ETHNIC CHORUSES IN *THE MISSION*

SM: You said to me that to form the chorus of natives, you had to use people from different embassies in order to avoid having one sonority, a phonetic uniformity.

EM: Yes, in fact, that was exactly the case for this piece and the *Magnificat*. The idea was mine and also the director's. But it was not easy to obtain the hoped-for result, to fuse everything. We made five or six attempts, and we were not satisfied. Then the audio engineer proposed that he make a premix alone, without us disturbing him with our suggestions. Thus the oboe and the ethnic chorus were privileged to the disadvantage of the a cappella chorus.

CANONE INVERSO AND DIFFERENT THEMES

CM: I would like to know from Maestro Morricone if you immediately composed two versions for the *Canone inverso*.[2] Do you usually make two versions of each piece?

EM: Let me explain more fully. I wrote the first version and recorded it. The morning afterward, without talking to the director, I met the violinist Franco Tamponi, who had performed it, and he said to me, "Ennio, I had to consult with the actors for the film, and I believe that they want something very easy. What you have written is beautiful, but I do not think it will work well." For that reason I immediately wrote a second version, and I went to record it with him that afternoon. In this case I had prepared two versions, but in general I prepare six, seven from among which to choose. The director is thereby so bewildered that he cannot make a decision—seven themes of one type, then seven of another, four of still another. . . . In one morning he listens to twenty themes. It is not easy to find the right one.

However, I know some directors, too, who are musical, and therefore they resist aggression of this type. I ought to say that Tornatore was not among the bewildered. Zurlini, for *Il deserto dei tartari*,[3] had me play four measures, then he said, "Enough." (Perhaps he was afraid I would continue.) In that case, however, I had written only two themes. It was the first overture commission I received from Zurlini, who had told me for years that he wanted to work with me but then . . . always returned to Luciano Chailly.[4]

HENRY V[5] AND EXPLICIT AND IMPLICIT SYNCHRONIZATION

CM: You and Professor Miceli have talked about implicit and explicit synchronization. From the expressive point of view, I believe I have understood the difference, but I would like to know something more from the technical point of view. How are they realized in practice?

EM: We talked about the sequence that is so resonant, so extraordinary in Branagh's *Henry V*. It has an extremely rare long single shot. But one would not make an entire film from long single shots—it would be absurd and also boring. The cinema is segmented by its nature. A film is made by assembly, and within this fragmentation, within certain sequences of the montage, synchronization points for the music are decided. The synchronization points are where the changes, even slight ones, are programmed by the director and composer or by the composer alone. Therefore, near the timings I flag the frames where there are to be joins, the moments of synchronization, by marking them in order A, B, C . . . according to how many there are in that scene. Frequently, in order to avoid a misunderstanding with the director, I write next to my personal notes the actual words that he has used to comment on those potential sync points. Sometimes the director has second thoughts; therefore, one needs to protect oneself.

SM: The difference between an explicit and an implicit synchronization arises from the relationship between scene and music. We have already explained this point. It varies from one time to another. On the practical level, nothing changes. In any case, the composer will have to take into account the previously chosen sync point. Also . . . certain implicit sync points arrive casually, as Maestro Morricone has already explained. They are noticed afterward, when everything is done, but they are no less important for that.

TIMINGS

CM: In practice, how does one take the timings for a film?

EM: Once upon a time they took it from the Moviola. One stopped the film at the point where the part to be examined began. One put a zero in the counter of the machine and then one went ahead, stopping on the sync points or at the end of the piece, and one annotated the meters (with a calculation about which, it seems to me, I have already spoken). One does not do it that way anymore, and I am very content with that. Now the director comes to my house with the videocassette, upon which is imprinted a time code. With a beginning for the music established, I distinguish two columns for my notes. In the left-hand column I note the absolute time from the beginning of the film (that is, the time code)—let's put 00:07:00—while in the right-hand column I write the time relative to the duration of the music. I therefore begin writing at 00:00, while the final value I consequently deduct, making a calculation that is pretty infantile. I stop the videocassette at the point at which it was decided that the music ought to finish. I only have to read the time code. If it shows 00:08:40, it means that I have to make a cue that lasts one minute, forty seconds. I will write that in the right-hand column of my notes. This is a topic that I take for granted, but . . . it should not be, . . . as Sergio always tells me.

THEMES

Zeffirelli's *Hamlet*,[6] **Joffé's** *Fat Man and Little Boy* (*L'ombra di mille soli*),[7] **Bertolucci's** *La domenica specialmente* (*Especially Sunday*),[8] **Leone's** *C'era una volta il West* (*Once upon a Time in the West*),[9] **Tornatore's** *L'uomo delle stelle* (*The Man of the Stars*)[10]

CM: Maestro, is the theme that you write for a film above all the consequence of your inspiration, or is it the interpretation of a precise request from the director?

EM: It seems to me that I already talked about that in the initial part of the course. Unfortunately, in the cinema we get it into our heads always and only to speak of themes. This is really a very reductive condition for the music in a film. I have not told you about the episode with Zeffirelli, who for *Amleto* (*Hamlet*)[11] asked me to write music without any themes and then during the recording session became very angry, like a madman, because I had not written a single theme. Evidently he had forgotten about his initial request, so I wrote it for him immediately, for oboe, over the harmonic scheme of the cues that I already had prepared.

Because there is a cultural deficiency in the relationship between directors and composers, the director always and only asks for the theme (even if in certain films the theme does not matter at all and could be damaging). In my opinion, it works this way for two reasons. On the one hand, because of the theme, the director succeeds in understanding certain situations better. On the other hand, aside from the theme, he would not know what to suggest. Of course he might want something different, but he does not have the language to express it, to describe it. I have already told you that the theme is of little importance to me. If I had the time and an orchestra here, I would be able to write a few measures and demonstrate to you that a theme on the piano is really a silly thing; immersed within a certain sonority, however, it becomes another thing. It gallops in another dimension.

I did an experiment in a film by Roland Joffé about the travail of the inventors of the atomic bomb.[12] Joffé did not understand a thing about music—I would say even less than all the other directors I have worked with.[13] When he listened to an orchestra, he approved or rejected the cue, but if it was the latter case, it was a brutal business. . . . I made various versions of an orchestration, of a theme, but many times . . . they did not suffice. In the film about the history of the atomic bomb, he told me in a courteous and sorrowful tone that he did not like the theme that I had written. I took away the theme . . . and inserted in that same orchestration another theme that I invented on the spur of the moment. It went extremely well.

In the episode of *La domenica specialmente* (*Especially Sunday*),[14] directed by Giuseppe Bertolucci, I wrote a simple, extremely humble theme that was adapted to the slightly impoverished circumstances he wanted. I had immersed it in a very particular sonority. He had accepted it, but in the finale he wanted it only for accordion.

Then there are emergency situations. In the film *C'era una volta il West*,[15] Leone and I were aware only at the end that a theme was missing, Cheyenne's Theme,[16] the one with banjo. "What should we do?" We had not discussed anything; thus I put myself at the piano during the orchestra's break. I improvised something. I orchestrated it very quickly, and after two turns the copyist—always present—had copied and made the parts. It is the stupidest theme in the film, but I have to say that it works.

CM: When you have had to insert a new theme over an already-realized harmony and instrumentation, have you had to change the instrumental soloist in order to propose something to the directors that seemed different, or did you work on changing only the notes of the melody?

EM: In the case of Roland Joffé's film, I do not remember whether I changed the instrument or the instruments employed in the rejected version. In Zeffirelli's film I improvised a theme, but in that case there were no instrumentalists to confront because the cue that was already prepared did not have a theme; there was only a harmony. There is a way to make thematic and nonthematic music contemporaneously. Music that has many themes, precisely because it has so many, excludes the possibility of having a single identifiable theme. I am not talking about orchestration. I am talking about the thematic presence entrusted to five different instruments contemporaneously. I had an experience of this sort on a film by Tornatore, *L'uomo delle stelle* (*The Man of the Stars*).[17] A folk-style canon emerged that never ever finished, infinite. . . . It is a way to avoid being bored.

CM: Has it happened that the director criticizes—or rejects—the instrument to which you have entrusted the theme?

EM: Sometimes even this happens. The director confuses the theme with the instrument. This is a good example of the monstrosities that can happen in the cinema.

CM: From what you have said—and from what one hears in the cinema—is it difficult to make at least one theme from a traditional melody? Could one escape this slavery by writing an atonal theme?

EM: It depends on the context, on the requests. There are films for which it is necessary to make atonal themes—actually, athematic atonal—but apart from all the rest, this presupposes that you know how to utilize dodecaphonic technique.

USE OF DISSONANCE

SM: One could make it atonal without making it dodecaphonic, but I wonder how many directors are interested in or open to welcoming solutions of this type.

EM: Certainly. Then there is the problem of dissonance. I have used disso-nant music in the cinema for the most dramatic moments of a film, the most traumatic, the most threatening. I have done this, comforted by the fact that in the history of musical composition, dissonance has always had a signifi-cance of this sort. Verdi, for example, knew only one dissonant chord. That was the diminished seventh, and he used it always at the most opportune moments. . . . I also make use of dissonance, but they are dissonances that the public today can understand as traumatic, which means certainly not the diminished seventh. For this I have been criticized heavily by a certain illus-trious musicologist.

SM: Saying it in that way does not reflect the terms of our discussion. I am constrained to reply in order to demonstrate that it is not pertinent to our theme. First of all, one has to remember that dissonance is not an immutable phenomenon. The fourth, for example, sounded dissonant to the Middle Ages and consonant in the Renaissance. This is without reckoning with the fact that one moved contemporaneously from the conception of the interval to that of the chord. Therefore, the matter was very, very much more complicat-ed (it was the passage from an absolute feature to a relative feature).

If we go back to the question of music for film, there is nothing to wonder at. The use of dissonance simply reflects the models created in the musical language of Viennese classicism from the late romantic era to the beginning of the twentieth century. In the cinema, these are reduced to stereotypes. My criticism arises from a global appraisal of your figure as composer. When I studied your concert works (aside from some exceptions that use a complete-ly different musical language), I reflected on the likely disassociation. It raised a concrete question for me. Which of the two is the real Morricone? Obviously, it is a problem that for the cinema means nothing. My observa-tion was not addressed to the cinema composer but rather to the composer in general *tout court*. That is why at the beginning of this response I said that the argument did not belong in our course. And also, I repeat, for another time, that the example of Verdi, to whom you always refer, is not relevant, because in the homogeneity of the genre to which he was dedicated and to the homogeneity (relative but consistent) of the epoch to which he belonged, Verdi had an almost unambiguous, technical-expressive reference. It was a completely different climate with respect to that in which we live today.

As an aside—but this comment is not addressed to you in particular, because it pertains to a good number of the composers that work in the cinema—after all that has happened in the music of our century, I ask whether the association of dissonance with negative situations (neurosis, terror, madness, etc.) is not educationally harmful and deceptive for the spectator today. I would like to remind you that in the silent-film era, the people who were adept at compiling preexistent music had recourse to the music of Richard Strauss and Debussy to comment on dramatic situations (it is the case with *The Cabinet of Doctor Caligari*).[18] It is obvious that that sonority seemed strange, disquieting, and in the end sinister to the average spectator, but with time things changed. At least with the "emancipation of dissonance" from Schoenberg on, an evolution occurred in the tastes of the listeners, too. Is it possible that today only the cinema still remains, clinging to positions that are so backward and behind the times? It is possible, certainly, because I also know something about the productive mechanisms and the rules of the market. I understand why it happens, but it does not have to please me.

EM: The problem is always this: one has to consider the marketability of the film and make something musical that is perceptible to the average public.

THE VOICE

CM: In your music for film, above all from some years ago, you frequently used a voice, even in unconventional ways. Can you add something about this?

EM: It seems to me that I already have spoken about this, but I will return to it willingly if it can be helpful. Those who know my work know that I adore the human voice. I adore it because it is the best form of human expression and also the most ancient. Because it is a product of our bodies, we can modulate it, commanding ourselves without going through another instrument. In my opinion, it is the principal instrument. In fact, I have both used it and abused it, especially when I have had at my disposition a singer like Edda Dell'Orso, who is a very great artist. But what interests me very much goes beyond the melodic business. The voice that interests me does everything as if it were a reinvented instrument. I have prepared a list of some of the voice's possibilities with which it can intervene in the cinema:

- Simple phonemes
- Whispers
- Voices more or less reciting
- Exhale and inhale sounds: sighs, gasps. . . . The varieties are infinite.
- Catcalls, ugly sounds in general
- Sounds from the lyric [opera] tradition, from the folk tradition (those from the folk tradition can be sounds of war, sounds of love, sounds of protest)
- Sounds produced by the larynx and digestive sounds
- Animal sounds
- Choruses of various types: classic choirs, choirs from the liturgical and Gregorian traditions, choruses of different ethnic traditions
- Collective buzzing, crowds that emit phonemes and unorganized words, but organized within the score

Some time ago I was at dinner with a director, Stefano Reali, who—a very rare case—is also a composer. There were two singers, both sopranos, Fiammetta Izzo and Silvia Gavarotti, and in the course of the evening, Reali went to the piano and accompanied them in a sort of spirited contest. At a certain point, Silvia Gavarotti did something incredible. She put two fingers in her mouth while whistling like the shepherdess while she sang! A shouting voice came forth, gorgeous, extraordinary. I asked her if she was able to redo it softly, and she did it very well, in a lower range.[19] I wanted to use her as soon as the occasion warranted!

"VICTIMAE PASCHALI"[20] FROM *IL SORRISO DEL GRANDE TENTATORE (THE SMILE OF THE GREAT TEMPTER)*

All the examples that I have mentioned can be submitted to electroacoustic tricks, electronics of twenty-four to forty-eight tracks. I mean that you can try mixtures, slowdowns, accelerations, even inversions. Start with a sonorous object and transform it. We can give an example, "Victimae paschali," from *Il sorriso del grande tentatore (The Smile of the Great Tempter)*, tied of course to what we said about not using themes. I made five of these pieces. They are five *Sequenze* that I mixed, to the great disapproval of Professor Miceli, for whom it was in a certain sense a sacrilege. However, reflecting on the history of music, I concluded that music has always been the servant of the word. By comparison, in my work I have tried to invert this hierarchy. In setting to music the *Epitaffi sparsi*[21] and other components (I asked Miceli for them), I know that I neglected the texts. They were thus fundamental as he gave them to me. I do not say this in order to flatter him. I knew it, and for this reason I asked him for them, but I had to privilege the musical side. Also, in this example, listening to it, one does not understand one word of the text. In this composition there is modality, athematicity, and the use of a certain type of choir. Then there is a pretty shocking rock 'n' roll entrance. But there is a reason why I put it there. In the film, the Tempter is a devil who is made welcome in a convent, carrying all of his skepticism with him. He makes a nun fall in love with him and even goes to bed with her. This rock 'n' roll represents the profane with respect to the sacred, expressed through the other elements. Therefore, the composer can also serve a film morally, trying to transform the sounds into reflections and thoughts.

CM: Regarding the texts of this music, I have not understood whether there was a collaboration with Professor Miceli.

SM: No, none, no collaboration. I came into Maestro Morricone's mind by an association of ideas, because sometimes, always outside of the cinema, I wrote texts for him, or in the case of *Epitaffi sparsi*, I wrote them for my own entertainment, and he wanted to set them to music. Ennio is very generous in his judgment of my texts, but I have too much respect for those who write poetry for a living. Mine is an occasional, private activity, rendered public by involvement on the part of some composers,[22] but I have become increasingly embarrassed about it with the years. Therefore, I would prefer to glide over it. . . . Regarding my judgment about the use of the five *Sequenze*, I repeat, although without hope, that I am not raising a religious question but rather a musical one.

EM: After my having written it, it seemed a good result. Naturally, in the film we do not ever hear the piece for as long as it lasts on the CD. We hear only some tiny fragments. Damiani[23] listened to the music only after I had mixed it. There had been no anticipation at the piano. Then how, you may ask, had I been able to describe it to him? I tried to explain it somewhat, but in the end I said, "Trust me, I have a great idea." And he trusted it.

CM: What reactions did the director have to the mix?

EM: Naturally, he liked it a lot. But I would like to return to the discussion about the length. I said that there is a great difference between what we have listened to on the CD and what one can hear in the film. I would not have been able to realize my idea if I had had such a drastic time limitation. Therefore, I invite you to compose extensive pieces that you then reduce into shorter fragments according to the exigencies of the film. On the CD I put the whole version, because to the average person it does not mean anything to listen to a piece of eighteen seconds in length. My son wrote a very beautiful twenty-second piece, and I told him, "Triple it for the disc; what do you want to do with twenty seconds?" He had a moment of illumination, of beautiful intuition, but it finished immediately. One cannot make things that short in music, unless you are named Webern and you write the *Bagatelle*.

DIRECTOR'S TRUST

CM: How do you behave with a director when your intention is to compose something that is not immediately verifiable?

EM: It is a question of trust. I no longer work with directors whom I do not trust. I refuse because I do not want to suffer. I will suffer anyway, because it is not a foregone conclusion that everything will go well even with a director who trusts me, but at least I know that there is trust. At one point I accepted everything . . . in order to make a living, but at this point I have to live. Therefore, there has to be an exchange. Of course, one succeeds in becoming friends. One talks better. One discusses better.

Tornatore will begin to shoot his next film in September.[24] I am in an embarrassing position because he has told me, "I want music that is not ever heard," or "I want an instrument that is never heard." At the moment I do not know how I will resolve it. . . . I hear this request repeated by directors. According to them, you could always divide by zero, but this is not actually possible.

With Tornatore there is great reciprocal trust. But he knows very well that in his films, the things that he loves repeat. He has his tics, his stylistic features. . . . Beh, I also have mine. And why should I renounce them? In this moment I do not have any idea, but sometimes all the strange discussions that one has with the director carry one, incredibly, to a result. With Agosti, for example, it always goes like that. . . .[25]

TAKING UP THE PROFESSION OF COMPOSER IN FILM TODAY

CM: Maestro Morricone has talked to us about his experience, which is the result of a great career. I have read Professor Miceli's book in which he talks about the beginning of Morricone's career when he was an arranger, but perhaps those were different times. What advice can you give to a young person who wants to take up the profession of being a composer today?

EM: It is not easy to give advice. . . . You have to be an upstart, to make yourself known, to try. You live where?

CM: Bologna.

EM: First of all, you have to transfer to Rome.

SM: I want to respond as well.

EM: It is pathetic.

SM: In fact . . . it is clear that I am not in a position to give advice regarding the mechanisms for inserting oneself professionally into the cinema market. I think it would be useful to have experience (not well-paid, obviously) with some young directors who need a composer and do not know to whom to turn. Of course, they fall in with one of the many dilettantes armed with a synthesizer, when they may merit something better.

In 1997 and 1998 I was invited by Roberto Perpignani, who is among the most authoritative editors in Italian cinema, to hold two brief seminars at the National School of Cinema in Rome,[26] where Perpignani taught editing.[27] On that occasion I got to know some of the students who were studying directing. . . . It was a very stimulating experience, . . . a breeding ground to take into consideration. As you see, one needs to set oneself up, to have a spirit of enterprise, to wait for certain institutions to wake up from a lethargy now almost centuries old and look around. Many of you know to what I am alluding, seeing as how you study or have studied at a conservatory.

One would require very little. It would be sufficient, for example, if the Conservatory of Santa Cecilia would, at zero cost (thanks to the auspicious liberty derived from the imminent reform of the conservatories),[28] establish some kind of convention with the National School of Cinema. (Fortunately, the latter is presided over by Lino Miccichè, a historian of cinema who is particularly sensitive to the importance of the musical component in films.) He is ready to facilitate things.

I believe, in fact, that such a joint effort ought to begin in the formative phase of musical and cinematographic instruction, creating in that way the conditions for an unbroken passage between the world of school and work. But the didactic classification for film music is still to be invented, and the introductions are among the worst. Some sporadic initiatives have taken place in Italian conservatories and universities where, depending on the context, in terms of composition or history, the discipline has been entrusted to illustrious unknowns.

EM: How is it possible?!

SM: When one has to give an assignment for a teaching position, one makes a classification: didactic, artistic titles (I fly over old age, disability, et cetera, that can have their weight). I believe, however, that for this new discipline—where the judges are not generally able to judge—it is necessary to add a new, fundamental parameter: voices from the corridor.

CM: I would like to ask Professor Miceli two questions and Maestro Morricone one. Of Miceli I ask whether his theory of levels has found applications outside of his didactic activity—his or that of others. Then, in connection with the invitation that has been made for the next edition of this seminar, in which it is projected that there will be a composition test on a short film, will it be possible to use preexistent music? Of Morricone I ask this: If tomorrow, buying a newspaper, you were to read, "The best things Morricone has made are his arrangements," what would be your reaction?

MICELI'S METHOD OF LEVELS

SM: The method of levels has also been applied by others—for example, by Ennio Simeon, a musicologist who died prematurely a few years ago. He was the only Italian, besides me (he was much younger), who was occupied in a systematic way with music for film. I have also seen the method of levels in some articles, essays, and theses. As I think I have already said previously, above all I have found numerous references to it in France, although with substantial misrepresentations and omissions. However, I take into account that its diffusion was heavily conditioned by the scarce diffusion of the book in which it appeared for the first time.[29] I am certain that its reappearance in an essay in *Rivista Italiana di Musicologia* has not improved the situation, because the readers of that periodical generally do not lower themselves to such lectures. As for me, I have applied the levels also to cases other than Morricone, but, in order not to repeat myself, I prefer to pick up the discussion again when we pass on to the bibliographic information.

USE OF PREEXISTENT MUSIC

Now I come to the second question. Even if this (the next seminar is scheduled for Fiesole)[30] is a seminar directed above all at composers, I do not see why one should exclude a composition test with musical repertory chosen by directors, multimedia operators, or teachers of musical material. With some exceptions, they did not compose original music for silent films; rather, they used preexistent music, even if the compilation was in its way an act of "composition."

One can affirm it by virtue of two phenomena. The first pertains to the matching of the music to the images, where certain music assumes new, unpredictable functions and meanings (see Kubrick, just for a change). The second pertains to a well-documented psychological/perceptual process. As a result of that process, two compositions, the one very different from the other in classification, style, and so on, "sound" in a certain way if listened to in isolation and "sound" in a different way when juxtaposed the one with the other.

At a certain point in the seminar I emphasized the importance of the antecedent-consequent relationship in audiovisual analysis. Here the argument is analogous. In conclusion, in the future I will try to make room for exercises in recomposition for the use of directors and nonmusician professionals, because it can be a very educational experience.

EM: I am responding to your question. It would not be at all displeasing to me, but I would not be pleased if that journalist had not appreciated the film music, because in the cinema I recovered and developed experiences initiated in the arrangements, even if the best came afterwards in my opinion. However, it is in the arrangements that I made the greatest experimentation. For this reason I say that one has to be an upstart.

CONTENTMENT WITH THE MUSIC AND THE FILM?

CM: Maestro, one feels, with good reason, that you are very proud of your works—

EM: Excuse me for interrupting you for a moment. I am satisfied, but this contentment is always a reaction to depression. After all, I have to say, "If they continue to call me after forty years in the profession, I must not have done things that were always that bad." But I am also very critical of myself. Don't believe that I am so optimistic, because there are things that make me think a lot, that worry me. When I am about to record, I am always very nervous. Therefore, I am not so proud. Excuse the interruption, go ahead.

CM: Perhaps I should not have used the word "pride," but instead "love for what you have done." In part you have responded already. But I would ask you also, is there something that you have written that on the third or fourth hearing you did not like anymore, that even seemed really ugly?

EM: It is a very embarrassing question.

CM: You do not have to answer.

EM: It is true that here I am confessing. . . . You make me do a psychoanalytic session. . . . However, I can respond. . . . I have regretted that sometimes

I have put music in a film that was too important for that film. I was trying—
but this has already been said by Sergio—to save it with the music. Nothing
is more mistaken. One cannot put important music in a low-class film, because one obtains the opposite result from what one wanted. I realized this
when it happened, but it does not happen anymore. I can make other errors,
but not that one. On the other hand, I have never regretted experimenting
with something in the music. I made it pass under the nose of the director. He
accepted it, and this makes me proud.

SM: Finally, after all these seminars and innumerable public encounters, you
have made such an open, to me unexpected, declaration in which you admit
the poor quality of certain films. We can inaugurate a new analytic series,
you know?

EM: What series?

SM: The series "Pearls after Swine." You have spoken of psychoanalysis.
Then permit me to continue. Compositional talent apart, one thing that has
always struck me (and that is in my opinion one of the strong points in your
craft) has to do with . . . How to define it? . . . your critical threshold toward
the cinema. I have seen horrendous films—I mean not only just "ugly"—that
is, generic—but rather fake, unrealistic, ideologically confused, cynical, in
which you in some way have believed. Other composers who write music for
film—all belong to a later generation than yours; I do not know if this is
meaningful or not—have a very critical relationship with the film and with
the director.[31] For years, after going to the cinema to see a film about which
you have talked during the production, I have asked myself, "But what
makes Ennio speak well of this film?" Today I think that if you could not
have done that, you would not have been able to write the music.

EM: Pontecorvo says the same thing as you: "I should never ask your opinion of the film that you are making, because you like all of them so much." I
responded to Gillo, and I respond now to Sergio, that when I see a film for
the first time, I cannot assume a critical stance, not only because I have been
called out of courtesy and trust by the director, who expects rightly that I am
responsible for writing the music, but because the film, when I see it, is really
awful, always. Even a masterwork is like this. There are noises from the
scene and those of the camera, a stagehand that moves the scenery. The
recitation in some cases is provisional because it has to be dubbed. The sound
of the voices is not right. . . . One does not understand anything. I see the film
under terrible conditions. I should put myself in the position of a critic of that
film? I know the story—that interests me. I know how it will be for the trust
that I have in the director, and I say, "I'll take care of that." I will do my duty.

LA NOTTE E IL MOMENTO (THE NIGHT AND THE MOMENT) (TATÒ, 1994)

CM: Apropos of this point, I would like to ask your position regarding the film *La notte e il momento (The Night and the Moment).*[32]

EM: You have seen the film?

CM: Yes, actually, when it was presented for the first time in Venice. It seemed a pretty static film, not successful. I would like to know if the music that you wrote is among the errors that you talked about before.

EM: In this case also I was not critical of the film. I collaborated with Anna Maria Tatò only that one time, even though every so often I would encounter her, and she always would say she wanted to work with me. She talked to me about that film with such love, with such dedication. . . . She never threw herself on the ground as Agosti did,[33] but she communicated her enthusiasm to me. I believe I wrote pretty good music for her.

Then the film turned out to be of poor quality. I did not believe that . . . it would end up being of such poor quality. Therefore, Pontecorvo and Miceli are right, but one has to take into account that she had very little money at her disposition. And it is difficult for a production company to entrust a film to a woman. In these cases, what can the director do? She shoots the scene and has to say, "Okay, the first is good." She cannot make a second take, and the film is shot in two weeks. You understand? It is a dramatic thing. Therefore, the directors who are constrained to work in this way deserve respect.

In times past, when truly I did not have even a lira, films were proposed to me that were bad, the worst imitations of *Mondo cane (The Dog World).*[34] Notwithstanding my condition and . . . my being in a period when I accepted a lot, I refused them. But when I see the love of a director, the necessity that it expresses toward my behavior, I throw myself away.

GASPS, CATCALLS, BURPS, AND MORE IN L'ULTIMO UOMO DI SARA AND LA CORTA NOTTE DELLE BAMBOLE DI VETRO, GIÙ LA TESTA,[35] AND ESCALATION[36]

CM: Maestro, the catalogue of the possibilities for the use of the voice gave me great pleasure, and we have seen quite a lot, but, apart from *Giù la testa*, the examples were of the chorale type or based on a single voice. We have not heard gasps, catcalls, or other things of the type to understand how they can become an integral part of the music.

EM: Unfortunately, we have not carried with us the recordings of *L'ultimo uomo di Sara* (*Sara's Last Man*) and of *La corta notte delle bambole di vetro* (*The Short Night of the Glass Doll*),[37] in which there are examples of this type. Sergio has put so many inside his computer. . . . How is it that you did it?

SM: I transferred them from music cassettes, from the audio of VHS tapes, from old LPs, and from CDs, and I compressed them all in MP3 format.[38] Apart from the comfort of having a unique source always close at hand, of finding every title right away, and of being able to move instantly from one point to another in a piece, with a compression of 1:12, a minute of music generally occupies 1 MB of space on a disc. The extractable hard drive of my PowerBook has a capacity of 18 GB. Therefore the account is quickly made without mentioning that I can insert another hard drive and create an enormous new archive. In fact, I have one that contains all the musical examples I used during a course on the history of music. Moreover, the students certainly know what I am talking about because the use of the MP3 on the Internet is becoming a revolution, and not only a technical one. For that which pertains to me, the next step will be to make masters of all the video examples, scores, and score fragments from VHS tapes on a pair of DVDs.

EM: It is incredible. . . . I am still at the point of marveling at the use of the fax machine. But it was not possible to have everything, a full film archive. However, you have to imagine these sounds. If it is isolated from the rest and one puts in a little echo, a gasp can transmit a tragic sensation, but sometimes also the opposite is true. They are all entertainments that we treat ourselves to—you yourselves can do it—even if people do not realize it. I used the burp in *Giù la testa* in the rests in the *Marcia degli accattoni*.[39]

SM: In this piece, the citation from *Eine Kleine Nachtmusik*[40] always makes me laugh, exactly because it doesn't have anything to do with anything. The first time you make it "mistaken," flatting the B-natural, and look, this case coincides with the opening of the wrong door. The second time, when the prisoners turn up liberated and the research on the safe is about to be crowned with success, the phrase returns, but in the correct form.

EM: Then the chorus of children. . . . It is a collage of diverse things, compiled in a much less elegant manner than in the opening titles of *Uccellacci e uccellini*.[41]

SM: Now there, that is a small masterwork. We could listen to it as a synthesis of all the things said so far. . . .

AMOUNT OF TIME TAKEN TO WRITE A SCORE

CM: Maestro, from the moment when you agree with the director, how much time do you have to write?

EM: For the last few years I have asked for at least a month, but sometimes, in times past, they conceded much less: ten days, a week. I will tell you immediately what happens in the cinema. The date of release of the film is established, and they establish a program of the following type: the film is to be released on October 18. Therefore, we should begin the mix on the twelfth; therefore, we ought to record the music—that is the last thing to do—on the seventh. But saying it in this way, they do not think about the fact that it is already October 1! But they pay attention to. . . . Thus I have to write the music in seven or eight days. It has happened, but now I don't do it anymore.

CM: But really, in only a month you succeed in composing music for a film like *C'era una volta in America*?

EM: Yes, yes! Attention: a month includes the time necessary for the copyist, for reasons that I have already explained. He has to work without making errors, and the orchestra has to concentrate without accidents and interruptions. Therefore, I anticipate by a lot the delivery of the scores for the copying of the parts.

SM: I understand that it might cause astonishment. . . .

EM: Rossini wrote his operas in fifteen days. I ought to say that Warren Beatty, for the film *Bulworth*, slowed me down for months. In October 1997 I was supposed to see the film with him, in Rome, to take down the timings. Warren instead, after having telephoned me, presented himself on January 2, 1998, saying to me that he would be returning to Rome on the eighteenth of the same month for the recording session. Nevertheless, I made it on time.

CM: In that case, do you have to compose pieces for which a lot of very precise sync points are anticipated? How does one rely on the most correct possible execution, and how can one make successive corrections to the montage?

SCREENSOUND

EM: I ought to say that I put a lot of trust in ScreenSound; that is an extraordinary device. It can correct the smallest of my defects; I can make incredible cuts, dissolves already mixed.

CM: Can you explain better what ScreenSound is?

EM: It is a fantastic machine. I do not know how to use it. The sound technician controls it. I say what I want to obtain and he executes it. It is a computer in which one inserts all the recorded music. It looks for and finds it in an instant.

COMPUTER TECHNOLOGY FOR MUSICAL EDITING

SM: I can add something pertaining to this. As you know, at one point, in the analogical era, one operated physically on the magnetic tape, cutting and splicing. One defined "montage" as destructive and linear, and I don't think there is any need to explain why.

Today the recording and manipulation of the sound can be entirely digital and, as a consequence, neither destructive nor linear. Nothing remains of the analogical in the audio chain but the two extreme rings: the microphones and the diffusers. Maybe some of you have already used the hard drive recording directly or unloaded the recording from a DAT. That is the first step. The data is all available in digital. Access to whichever segment is almost immediate, and if you make a mistake, it is not too bad because one can work in the simulation modality and, moreover, on a copy identical to the original.

The machine to which Maestro Morricone refers is an example—the most expensive, I believe—of this system, but some alternatives exist that are based on the same principle. The advantages are many. No computer was created expressly for this work. A Power Macintosh G3 or G4 is more than sufficient and requires only one or more specific cards and a capacious hard drive that has a capacity of 20 GB or more. Consider that one minute of monophonic music recorded at 16 bits—44.1 kHz occupies 5 MB, while a 24-bit requires 7.5. If you want, if the internal slots are not sufficient, or if they are already occupied by other expansions (SCSI card, a sampler, etc.), you can connect the computer to an external box containing all the dedicated hardware.

Naturally, specific software exists that gives its name to the entire system. One of the most common is Pro Tools, which can be considered a de facto standard, just as Finale is for musical notation. In any case, the mode of working is fundamentally the same for all the systems of postproduction.

In 1987, when I finally abandoned Windows for Macintosh (because there is a limit even to masochism), there existed a program, SoundEdit, that permitted the first elaborations of sound. (With a much more advanced version I made the spectrographic analysis of *Dances with Wolves*.) Today there is, for example, Peak, which can be utilized with the TDM version of Pro Tools.

Already then it was possible to visualize the form of a wave, enlarging it to a detail of a fraction of a second, cutting a portion, working on it, and splicing it to another section. "Working on it" means operating on all the parameters of the sound as well as simulating infinite acoustic environments and, naturally, making dissolves of every kind.

I had "fiddled" with magnetic tapes for years under the influence of *musique concrete* and the Studio of Fonologia of Milan,[42] so I remember very well the emotion I felt when I saw and heard a sound of a few seconds in length extended in duration like an elastic band without modifying the pitch or tone color. Naturally, one was working on a frequency of sampling less than those actually used for a CD or DAT. So to obtain a modification in monaural of a not-very-complex sound of five to six seconds like the human voice, my Macintosh SE . . . worked for more than one minute to make the calculation. I have recounted this "prehistoric" experience without . . . entering into detail[43] in order to point out that those principles and methods are the same as those employed today for digital montage. They change the algorithms in the software and the possibilities of the graphic interfaces. The hardware is extremely powerful. The RAM is boundless. In sum, everything is in proportion—which means that, limited as I was back then to a single track (a little later to two), and above all by the total quantity of manageable sound data, today my prospects have been expanded in every sense.

You have at your disposition as many tracks as needed (eight, sixteen, thirty-two . . . with 192 MB of RAM you can arrange among sixty-four tracks), and the old bank of expensive, cumbersome mixers has been replaced by a virtual control panel that reproduces the same preset knob, the same linear sliders, the same level indicators. This is obviously in the premix phase. But coming to the point that interests us, . . . the final mix and the montage, the power of today's computers allows us to manage the entire soundtrack globally. On the monitor you have simply a list of folders and files relative to dialogue, effects, and music. Select the files that you intend to work on and display them on the virtual worktable, opening them. In this way you will have graphic images of the selected segments, and you will be able to manage them directly on the spectrogram, showing the portion of the track you wish to modify.

Do you want a dissolve of the effects at a specific point? You can establish the initial and final points of the intervention and the relative slope (that is, the progression of the intervention) with numeric data in a relevant dialogue window, or you can intervene in a graphic mode, literally designing the curve or the parallel line with the mouse. You can verify the result immediately (the wait times are minimal, on the order of tenths of a second) and decide to save it in a definitive manner. In every case you can always retrace your steps. I have taken for granted that on another monitor the film is running with the time code, obviously in sync with the virtual sound montage table (in addition, the images have been converted digitally with a compression system). The quality is inferior to the original, but it is of no importance, as one is dealing with a control copy. In conclusion, if for a certain sync point you realize that the music is behind the images by half a second, you can select the final portion of the sound and order the program to stretch the music by the amount necessary . . . and so forth. [44]

CM: Can this type of manipulation also be performed on the images?

SM: In the cinema, the treatment of sound is technologically more advanced than the treatment of the images, which are still tied to a chemical process. [45] But if there were no longer film, there would no longer be the cinema. Collaterally with our seminar, it seems important for me to make this clarification, which has apparently been taken for granted. I note often, in fact, that many of your generation, for reasons which I can easily intuit, ignore or flatten certain differences, but instead one needs to distinguish between them.

The movie camera is not a video camera, and, beyond the substantially different processes that each uses to acquire images, the difference in the result is perceivable by even a slightly trained eye. Personally, I study and utilize the technology tied to the audiovisual arts and to means of mass communication. Coming from a humanistic background, I am proud that . . . I have no difficulty in declaring that computer science and telecommunication have radically changed my ways of doing research, of producing, and finally of teaching (therefore, in a certain way, of my whole life). But blind, uncritical dedication leads to slavery and an inability to judge various contexts. One needs instead to historicize and contextualize the relationship between man and machine.

To do it in Italy is more difficult than elsewhere for certain philosophical and therefore pedagogical assumptions that I have already skimmed over in passing. But a history of science and technology in relation to the history of music and the figurative arts would still have a lot to teach us. For this reason, as much as to take a shortcut to a conclusion, I say use the digital photographic camera and elaborate the images with Photoshop. I do it with an excellent digital telecamera with three sensors [46] —"chapeau," as they say in French.

Every expressive form has had recourse to techniques that have conditioned and characterized the result. This statement is even more valid for the last one hundred years, to which belongs the geometric expansion of scientific and technological progress. Therefore, remember that the cinema is the cinema. The sentence is not new[47] but is always effective.

USE OF NOISE NOT DERIVED FROM THE EXPERIMENTS OF LIGETI; FRANCO FERRARA'S *CREATION*

CM: I would like to know whether the uses of the voice and of noises about which Maestro Morricone has spoken are derived from a cultivated sector such as, for example, Ligeti's *Aventures* or *Nouvelles Aventures*, or whether they are ideas that preceded the experiences at Darmstadt.

EM: Many years ago I was charged by the producer Dino de Laurentiis to write the music for *The Bible* (*La Bibbia*), but for reasons that I will not explain—editorial reasons[48] —that collaboration did not end well. I would have had to write some pieces, some tryouts, upon which I would have been judged. But the situation was not the best, because the commission had first been given to my teacher, Petrassi, and his music had been rejected by the director. I was asked to make a piece for *Creation*, which Franco Ferrara directed, but I also wrote another on my own initiative. I made a chorus for *Tower of Babel* (I had not seen even one frame of the film), and to make it, I went to a synagogue and asked for an appropriate Hebrew text. I had it translated into Italian in order to follow the meaning, and I wrote a score using all the single voices of the chorus of the RAI. Every voice sang and declaimed. The chorus grew, diminished, had some impulses . . . One could not understand anything. One was not supposed to understand anything, because it had to appear as a jumble of languages.

Ligeti had not yet written *Aventures*,[49] but I had not imitated anybody. I can swear to it. I did not, however, invent that manner of writing. It was in the air of the epoch. One could hypothesize an individual choral writing, not the classic unaccompanied choir. You can listen to that piece written for *Tower of Babel*—entitled, I think, "La porta d'oro"—in the film *Il segreto del Sahara.*[50]

COLLABORATORS

CM: In the end titles of Italian films, one usually reads that the musician does everything: orchestration, direction. In American films there is a directory of collaborators. How do they work in America?

EM: Also in Italian films there are those who do not write the music. Do you think that a singer-songwriter who takes the credit for the music of a film made the score? The singer-songwriters hardly know the chord symbols. They invent a melody (maybe they have not even written that much), and they pass it to an arranger, that poor soul who in times past was called the "negro." This practice has taken hold in Italy, because the arrangement exists in the songs. A song can be arranged in ten different ways by ten different arrangers, but music in the cinema is not an arrangement, so all the asses who do not know how to write music think they can entrust the music to an arranger as if it were a song. But it is not a song. In America, in France, in Italy they often operate like that, out of laziness or lack of ability, because they have too much work and they do not know how to carry it to a conclusion. Professor Miceli has already read one point to you wherein I expressed my opinion on this subject.

THE ORCHESTRATOR'S CREDIT

CM: In the cinema, is the orchestrator cited more than the arranger?

EM: In the end titles, in small letters. Years ago, together with Gianluigi Gelmetti, I organized a concert of film music in Parco dei Daini (Deer Park).[51] We asked for American scores, and they arrived from Herrmann, the composer who had written for *Psycho*. Very beautiful, written perfectly, a real composer. Then those of Max Steiner for *Gone with the Wind* arrived, but they were not scores; they were scribbling pads of four or five lines short scores, and with these the orchestrator had written the real, full score. Many composers do that.

HISTORIAN AND MUSICOLOGIST

CM: At a certain point Professor Miceli talked about critics and historians and made the distinction regarding the way they work, between the person who works on current events and the one who works on things of the past. You are a historian or musicologist, but you have written a book about Morricone, who, if I'm not mistaken, is a living author. How do you explain this choice?

SM: First, it seems to me that you have doubts about the definition of my role. "Musicologist" and "historian of music" are not synonymous terms. The function of the musicologist assumes a scientific approach to the material, whether in the method of research (think of the concept of *Musikwissenschaft* from which it was born) or in the technique adopted. In any event, it deals with a total discipline, or, if you prefer, with different sectors of specialization, including historic and systematic research. The analysis of a composition or of the entire body of a composer's work is, for example, among the specific tasks of the musicologist.

The historian of music, on the other hand, having been born from the same humanistic base and address, might not even be a musician and as such could deal with historical-aesthetic themes no less complex that disregard, however, the merely technical aspects of music. Naturally, there is not a hierarchy. I have already said this apropos the comparison between critic and historian. Also, here one can come up with extremely boring musicological research, historically speaking not influential, and above all myopic—or, on the other hand, with studies that have changed our way of reading the operations of a composer or a school of composition. And one can speak analogously of the work of a historian.

However, it is obvious that there is a vast terrain of common intervention for which the definitions have to be made on a case-by-case basis. Obviously, I will not take the time now to define myself. Consider the type of work on which you have assisted, perhaps read something from those works that are cited in the space dedicated to the bibliographic information. For what pertains to my choice, I don't know how to say it.

With time, history will put the Morricone "case" back into perspective. If one were to reread the past, one would be induced to conclude this, because those artists who during their lifetimes were very, very successful with the public have, more often than not, been reduced in importance after their deaths. It is not a written law, but a recurring phenomenon that in another place we could investigate. In my case, however, one would have to take cinematographic history into account that might move and modify, I suppose in a positive sense, the hypothesized process. In any case, with my interest in Morricone I do not have the pretext of hypothesizing the future, nor would I be interested in making a newspaper account, which is not a part of my profession.

THE CHOICE OF MORRICONE AS A SUBJECT FOR STUDY

Rather, I departed from a simple observation. In the panorama of contemporary music there is, I believe, no figure richer in experience and contradictions. No other composer has the capacity to communicate constantly with a public like his, one that is not only extremely vast but also includes different generations and social classes that are so diverse from one another. On the numerous occasions when I have conducted encounters between Morricone and the public (from university lecture halls to cultural associations in the provinces, in Italy as well as outside it), I have always been struck by the behavior of his admirers. . . . From over-fifty-year-olds to twenty-year-olds from extremely diverse social backgrounds comes, I summarize in one word, gratitude. Trying to understand the reasons for this phenomenon might mean understanding something that is not marginal and that pertains not just to Morricone but to the music, spectacle, custom, and culture of the entire twentieth century, however more or less popular it might be. Since by both vocation and formation I am a specialist in the twentieth century, I found and still find studying Morricone a task consistent with my role. . . .

At the beginning of the course Maestro Morricone told you not to delude yourselves into thinking that here you might become composers if you were not already composers, at least in a limited way. At the time, however, I thought and now wish to confirm the principle that is also valid for the aspiring director. Your interest in film music is legitimate. It is consistent with the times in which we live, but you need to follow this interest in such a way that it does not become exclusive and "sequestering." Contemporary music is made up of so many aspects. They call for a reflection that is both theoretical and historical. The reflection can ultimately project positively on our relationship with film music, even putting it into perspective (or not). If, of the music of the second half of the twentieth century, you have listened only to that by Morricone (or whomever else), I do not hide my diffidence. If, on the other hand, you have passed through the principal musical experiences of our time and continue to love above all the music of Morricone (or whom-ever else), then yours is a knowledgeable choice about which one can have a discussion.

CM: I remain, however, on the aspects that are tied to current events—for example, the interview of Maestro Morricone in your book on the Discant.[52]

INTERVIEW VERSUS CONVERSATION

SM: This is a common error that many fall into. In the old edition (and it will be the same in the new edition) it is defined as a colloquium, not an inter-view. The words are not synonyms, and the difference is not marginal. Inter-views are done by journalists, who today ask questions of a soccer player, tomorrow of a director, the day after tomorrow of a politician.[53] Naturally, they are very good, but this is not the point. Instead, while a colloquium or a conversation also contains questions, it involves an equal exchange between two specialists, each of whom operates on diverse titles in the same sector. Therefore, every other guarantee of knowledge implicit in this type of rela-tionship comes less from the character of "current events" to which you referred. The colloquium of Petrassi with Luca Lombardi,[54] or that of Stra-vinsky with Robert Craft[55] (one could cite many others) is a contribution to musical historiography, not current events.

SONGS IN FILM

CM: What role does one assign to a song in a film?

SM: The presence of a song in a film can have commercial or narrative motivations. The commercial motivation resolves in a very obvious associative process that carries little to the film and much to the recorded disc. Think of the songs present in the opening titles or end titles of the James Bond films. They are a frame, a logo. The narrative motivation, on the other hand, can be of various kinds. It can be, for example, a mechanism for the change between levels or a subtle game between connotative and denotative functions. More simply, a very well-known song can assume a temporal function from a system of signals. ("Yesterday" of the Beatles in *C'era una volta in America*).[56] It can also be a process of deformation and contrast. I think, for example, of the use of "Singin' in the Rain" in *Clockwork Orange*,[57] or of "Brazil" in the English film of the same title,[58] a cult movie that has not had a big circulation.

To return to Morricone and therefore to a song written on purpose, one needs to refer to the preceding ones to confirm a certain subtle sense of continuity that exists in the evolution of a composer. From his beginnings as an arranger he knew everything, and about that we have spoken. Morricone wrote very few songs, of which surely the most representative is "Se telefonando" ("If Telephoning"), which I maintained was indispensable to analyze briefly, even in the book about him. Now, however, I won't deal with it as a song per se, but rather for certain stylistic features that we find in the cinema. If you remember, you will have present in your mind the little scoffing chorus in the finale "Ta, ta, ta . . ." One finds it in *I pugni in tasca*,[59] or in other films of those years of challenge.

EM: *Grazie zia* [*Thanks, Aunt*].[60]

SM: Above all *Grazie zia*, in which the poison in the tribunes is assigned to white voices that by instinct we associate instead with the concept of purity and of candor. In sum, here also Morricone has created a model that is a part of that quality of even heavy sarcasm that characterizes much of his film music. Certainly at the base of a song there is adhesion to the needs of the market, an adhesion heavily creative but still always commercial. In certain parts of the music written for the cinema and, obviously, the musical soundtracks, there is a song. The problem, however, is not to eliminate the mechanism of consumption, which cannot be eliminated, but rather to render it dignified and thus to stimulate one's sensibility and intelligence.

Still, I have not decided whether to stay with the apocalyptic or with the integrated, to cite Umberto Eco.[61] Let's say that one day I wake up apocalyptic and one day I wake up integrated for the sake of consistency. But it is not an amoral question that the beat would make us imagine. More simply, if I meet up with the song "The Integration," by Paolo Conte, I feel good, also because it is not integration but lucid adhesion, conscious of a very specific model of craftsmanship and intellect. If, by comparison, I look at the spaces for publicity that the television reserves every day, selling them for information to the many musical nothings blown up and imposed by the record labels, then I feel more apocalyptic.

Precisely to demonstrate the difference between a passive and an active approach, I would like to refer to an example regarding Morricone as arranger. . . . In the sixties and seventies there was a privileged area, that of 33 1/3 LP discs. The print run was much reduced, and this allowed the greatest liberty of movement, creating almost an experimental area, because it involved a more refined public. It was actually a division of the market. The 45s were for everyone. The 33 1/3s were for the more affluent and demanding. RCA produced an LP by Miranda Martino entitled *Canzoni per sempre* (*Songs Forever*), all arranged by Morricone. Among these there was one from the end of the 1800s or the beginning of the 1900s that was called "Ciribiribin,"[62] a concentration of little sentiments both good and bad. Totò reprised it in the form of a parody in a variety show.[63] It is interesting to compare a recording from that period[64] with Morricone's arrangement.

For me, this is one of the obligatory passages needed in order to enter into Morricone's oeuvre. I dealt with it in the book but also recently during a roundtable organized in Cagliari by Antonio Trudu in preparation for the conferring of an honorary degree on Ennio Morricone by the University of Cagliari.[65] Franco Fabbri and Philip Tagg were present. Each one of us had prepared examples without the others' knowledge. Tagg started at the end— that is, with *The Mission*[66] —while Fabbri and I started at the beginning. Fabbri talked about "Se telefonando" and "Abbronzatissima." I used "Ciribiribin." Returning to the subject of song in film, a very important example goes back to 1966 and has to do with the first collaboration between Morricone and Pier Paolo Pasolini. But I want Morricone himself to talk about it.

PASOLINI

EM: Pasolini called me. He also had the director of production for Alfredo Bini, Enzo Ocone, call me. Pasolini asked for my help in making the music for *Uccellacci e uccillini* (*The hawks and the sparrows*),[67] and after saying this, he pulled out a list of compositions from the repertory that he had chosen (a little as the Taviani brothers do). But I responded, "I write music; I do not make adaptations of things by somebody else. In my opinion, you made a mistake by calling me." Pasolini thought for a moment and then said, "Then I will do what you want."

Except for Faenza, who on the first film said the same thing (that I have already told you), Pasolini was the only one to give me total liberty. It is useless to say that Pasolini was an extraordinary person, extremely polite, with a rare dignity. The only request he made for *Uccellacci e uccellini*[68] was to have a quote of an aria by Mozart from *Don Giovanni* or the *Magic Flute* (now I don't remember exactly) played on the ocarina. In the second film, *Teorema*,[69] he asked me for "dodecaphonic" music—by which he meant dissonant—in which to insert another quote from Mozart, this time from the *Requiem*. (He was really fixated on Mozart). I inserted that quote for mezzo in the clarinet, but naturally in a dodecaphonic context it was not recognizable.

Having him listen to the recording, I said to him, "Do you hear, Pasolini? . . . Mozart is the one that goes 'tiritiri' . . ." and he responded that it was good. Perhaps it was a spell, a weakness, one of his pleasures. However, little by little, working for him, I ought to say that by comparison with my initial demand, I made instead an unconditional surrender. I could have refused, certainly, but now I had entered into his work.

There was none of my original music in *Il Decameron*.[70] I recorded Neapolitan things that did not matter to me at all, but I did it. Afterward, in *I racconti di Canterbury* (*Canterbury Tales*),[71] it was almost the same thing. I remade a little in *Il fiore delle mille e una notte* (*The Flower of a Thousand and One Nights*),[72] but I surrendered completely in *Salò o le 120 giornate di Sodoma* (*Salò or the 120 Days of Sodom*).[73] In it there is only one of my original pieces, played by the pianoforte during the orgy. It precedes the suicide of the pianist.[74] The other pieces are my arrangements of terrible music from the time of the war, made for little orchestras of poor people dying of hunger for trumpet, sax, trombone, pianoforte, percussion, and contrabass and things of that sort. . . . He intones a nonexistent music; between the funeral and the idiot "Un giorno ti diro"[75] —played badly— would be an example of what I mean. They were pretty shameful things, but I did them.

SM: In any case, the idea of making opening and end-title music for *Uccellacci e uccellini*[76] was Pasolini's, wasn't it?[77]

EM: Certainly. The text is his.

SM: Those who know the film easily grasp the reason. The sense of a short narration with moral intent and of a fantastic narration, discovered, also has to invest the frame. Today it is easy to say it, but when the film was issued, a solution of that type made a great impression.

I am tempted to recount my experience as a young spectator. I was in a state of confusion, exiting from the Arlecchino Cinema of Florence (which then was an art cinema) immediately behind the Ponte Vecchio, where I saw for the first time *L'arpa birmana* (Burmese Harp)[78] and the films of Bergman. . . . Today it is a red-light hall. But maybe it would be better another time. Let's remain with the titles of *Uccellacci e uccellini*.[79] It is really a synthesis of languages, an anthology, almost a self-portrait. There is even a fragment of pointillistic writing.

EM: It pleases me that you realized it. It is in the last cues. It was like a prepared piano, but with organ. I was entertained. And I invite you to entertain yourselves when you write.

SM: In fact, I remember that the principal thread of our discussion was and is synthesis: how to adhere to the song without succumbing. How to redeem it and redeem them. Now we can make a great leap in time and arrive at *Sostiene pereira*.[80]

EM: The theme that Dulce Pontes sings is tertiary; over it there is a binary theme. It is another small example of how one can entertain oneself. Otherwise, if we did not have a flap of some interest, it would be an impossible profession. Here I certainly did not write a fado. It is the bravura of the singer that leads one to believe it.[81]

AUTHORS' RIGHTS

CM: I would like to understand better the mechanism of authors' rights in various countries.

EM: In Italy, Spain, Germany, and France, music receives a percentage of the cinematographic receipts. In America, the film is considered in its entirety. There is no percentage for music, but one makes money with the diffusion on the radio and with recordings. But if in Italy a composer obtains a copyright payment of "10," in America he obtains "200" and receives it immediately, independent of the proceeds of the film.

RELATIONSHIPS WITH PRODUCERS

CM: Maestro Morricone has spoken frequently about the rapport with the director. I would like to know whether there are also relationships with the producer.

EM: Only with Fernando Ghia, who, as I think I already said, followed *The Mission*[82] very closely, always giving his opinion. Once, a long time before, with Dario Sabatello—Sergio knows this little story already, but perhaps it is worthwhile to tell it to you also. Sabatello was not a real producer. He was an antiques collector who had a lot of money and had decided to produce the film *O.K. Connery*,[83] an imitation of a James Bond film. Imagine! In that case, I did not make the contract with the music editor—to whom the composer cedes the music—but with the producer. In the contract that Sabatello proposed to me, among the other clauses there was this one: "The music has to be beautiful, international, and a sure success."

NOTES

1. [DVD, Warner Home Video, 2003.]
2. *Canone inverso* (*Inverse Canon*) (Tognazzi, 1999). [DVD, Cecchi Gori, 2000.]
3. *Il deserto dei tartari* (Zurlini, 1976). [DVD, *Il deserto dei tartari*, General Video, 2007; Instituto Luce, 2008; General Video, 2009.]
4. [Luciano Chailly (1920–), Italian composer and author of theatrical works.]
5. *Henry V* (Branagh, 1989). [DVD, MGM, 2000.]
6. *Hamlet* (Zeffirelli, 1990), coproduction USA-Italy. [DVD, Warner Bros., 2004.]
7. *L'ombra di mille soli* (*Fat Man and Little Boy, Shadow Makers*) (USA, Joffé, 1990).
8. *La domenica specialmente* (*Especially Sunday*) (Bertolucci,Giordana, Tornatore, Barilli, 1991). [DVD, Cecchi Gori Home Video, 2008; Ripley's Home Video, 2008.]
9. *C'era una volta il West* [*Once upon a Time in the West*] (Leone, 1968). [DVD, *The Sergio Leone Anthology*, MGM/UA, 2007; Paramount Pictures, 2010.]
10. *L'uomo delle stelle* (*The Man of the Stars*) (Tornatore, 1995). [Streaming video at Italia-Film TV, Guarda Online.]
11. *Amleto* (Zeffirelli,1990). [DVD, Warner Bros., 2004; Cecchi Gori, 2007.]
12. *L'ombra di mille soli* (*Fat Man and Little Boy, Shadow Makers*), USA, 1990. [DVD, Paramount Pictures, 2004.]
13. The last film, *La lettera scarlatta*, I did not score for this reason. We did not understand each other, and I said to him, "I am sorry, Roland. We will remain friends, but let's call it quits."
14. Film in episodes from 1991 by Giuseppe Bertolucci, Marco Tullio Giordana, Giuseppe Tornatore, and Francesco Barilli. The episode directed by Bertolucci gave the title to the film. [DVD, Ripley's Home Video, 2008.]
15. [*Once Upon a Time in the West—Special Edition*. DVD, Mondo Home, 2007.]
16. See "Musical Example 57, 'Cheyenne's Theme' from *C'era una volta il West*," in *Comporre per il Cinema*, 248. The character is interpreted by Jason Robards.
17. The film, interpreted by Sergio Castellitto, is from 1995. [Streaming video at Italia-Film TV, Guarda Online.]
18. See Miceli, *Musica e cinema nella cultura*, 263 ff.
19. The range covered by the singer with this type of emission is of about three octaves, from F2 to E5, and produces a sound similar to a horn with mute (thanks to Stefano Reali for this precision).
20. Available on CD anthology NST, and on Beat CD CR 18.
21. *Epitaffi sparsi* for soprano, piano, and instruments, to preexistent texts by S. Miceli, composed between 1991 and 1993, n. 54 of the *Catalogo delle opera*.
22. Other than Morricone, with whom numerous collaborations are counted, Michele Dal'Ongaro, Fulvio Delli Pizzi, Egisto Macchi, Franco Piersanti, and Antonio Poce have composed to Miceli's texts.
23. Damiano Damiani (1922–), film director.

24. He is referring to *Malèna*. [DVD, Medusa Video, 2007.]

25. The collaboration with Silvano Agosti began in 1967 with *Il giardino delle delizie* [*The Garden of Pure Delights*].

26. First it was called the Experimental Center of Cinematography.

27. We have quoted him, for example, in connection with *Allonsafàn*.

28. The law was approved at the beginning of 2000.

29. Miceli, *La musica nel film*.

30. The seminar in 2000, run by Franco Piersanti and Sergio Miceli, took place at the CRSDM of Fiesole, April 14–16, and, other than a composition test, was effectively contemplated for the use of preexistent music.

31. See, for example, "Colloquio con Franco Piersanti," in Miceli, *Musica e cinema nella cultura*, 491–512.

32. Directed by Anna Maria Tatò, 1994. Soundtrack available on CD Epic EPC 4784752.

33. The collaboration with Silvano Agosti began in 1967 with *Il giardino delle delizie*.

34. A fake documentary by Gualtiero Jacopetti from 1961, filled with hypocrisy and racism, with music by Ritz Ortolani. It was so successful that it gave rise to a series of imitations. [SM]

35. *Giù la testa* (*Duck, You Sucker*) (Leone, 1971). [DVD, *The Sergio Leone Anthology*, MGM/UA, 2007; *Sergio Leone—Cofanetto Grandi Classici*, Mondo Home, 2007.]

36. *Escalation* (Faenza, 1968).

37. *L'ultimo uomo di Sara* (*The Last Man of Sara*) (Virginia Onorato, 1972). *La corta notte delle bambole di vetro* (*The Short Night of the Glass Doll*) (Aldo Lado, 1971). [DVD, Koch Media, 2006; Cecchi Gori, 2012]. A composition, *Emme Trentatré*, can be found on the boxed-set anthology of two CDs NST.

38. "MP3" is the contraction of MPEG 1 Audio Layer III and pertains to a group of algorithms of sound compression created by the Moving Picture Experts Group since 1988 [SM].

39. See "Musical Example 58, 'Marcia degli accattoni' from *Giù la testa*," in *Comporre per il Cinema*, 258.

40. He is alluding to the first movement of the *Serenata in Sol, K. 525* by W. A. Mozart.

41. Directed by Pier Paolo Pasolini, 1966. [DVD, Medusa Video, 2009.]

42. He is referring, respectively, to the Paris experimentations of Pierre Schaeffer in the forties and fifties and to those of Luciano Berio and Bruno Maderna in the sixties.

43. For an introduction to the themes of musical computer science, see S. Miceli, "Informatico per musicisti, serie organic" of four contributions (with numerous bibliographic indications) in *Musica domani* (1991), 78–81.

44. Part of the information reported here has benefited from an examination, in a definitive draft, based on the participation of Alessandra Perpignani anticipated in the already-cited seminar held by Franco Piersanti and Sergio Miceli for CRSDM in Fiesole in 2000. [SM]

45. It should be remembered that this statement was published in 2001. [GBA]

46. But with the memory of a Leica or a Contax of the fifties, of optically mythical names like Elmar or Summicron, and of many nights passed in the darkroom.

47. It refers to the Italian title (Milan: Garzanti, 1981) for a collection of writings by Godard, *Jean-Luc Godard par Jean-Luc Godard*, ed. P. Belfond (Paris, 1968). [SM]

48. One finds the major details of the episode in Miceli, *Morricone*, 77.

49. In reality (although a relation between the two events was improbable), *La Bibbia* of John Huston is from 1966; therefore, it followed by four years the *Aventures* of Ligeti.

50. *The Golden Door*, track 7 on the CD RCA BD 71559, for the made-for-RAI Television film *Il segreto del Sahara*, already cited.

51. Film in concert organized by the city government of Rome and the RAI, the Symphonic Orchestra of the RAI, in the Deer Park of the Villa Borghese, July 1–22, 1983, music by N. Rota (dir. C. Kellogg), M. Jarre (dir. Morricone), E. Morricone (dir. P. Urbini), M. Steiner, B. Herrmann, J. Goldsmith, L. Bernstein, and J. Williams (dir. D. Stahl).

52. The edition Discanto refers to *La musica nel film*; the new edition pertains to *Musica e cinema nella cultura*.

53. In English, the word "interview" does not have such a pejorative connotation, and serious interviews are conducted by scholars as well as extremely knowledgeable journalists. [GBA]

54. L. Lombardi, *Conversazioni con Petrassi* (Milan: Suvini Zerboni, 1980).

55. I. Stravinsky, R. Craft, *Colloqui con Stravinsky* (Torino: Einaudi, 1977) (including *Conversations with Stravinsky, Memories and Commentaries, Expositions and Developments*, New York, 1959, 1960, 1962).

56. *C'era una volta in America* (*Once upon a Time in America)* (Leone, 1984). [DVD, *Once upon a Time in America*: Two-Disc Special Edition, Warner Bros., 2011.]

57. Directed by Stanley Kubrick, GB, 1971. [DVD, Warner Bros., 2007.]

58. Directed by Terry Gilliam, USA, 1985. [DVD, *Brazil—3-Disc Special Edition*, Criterion Collection, 2006.]

59. *I pugni in tasca* (*Fists in Pocket*) (Bellocchio, 1965). [DVD, 01 Distribution, 2006.]

60. Directed by Salvatore Saperi, 1968. [DVD, Medusa Video, 2005.]

61. U. Eco, *Apocalittici e integrati* (Milan: Bompiani, 1965).

62. Written by the Milanese Tiochet and Pestalozza, 1898. See G. Baldazzi, *La canzone italiana del Novecento* (Milan: Newton Compton, 1989).

63. *Con un palmo di naso* of Michele Galdiere (1944), in which the ritornello was entrusted to the first actress, Anna Magnani. See Faldini, Fofi, *Totò: l'uomo e la maschera*, 207ff.

64. The version interpreted by Coppia Butterfly, *Fonografo italiano 1890–1940. Raccolta di vecchie incisioni scelte e presentate da Pasquito Del Bosco*. CD Fonit Cetra CDFO 3635. *Duettisti, comici, lirici, eccentrici*. The original version, LP RCA PML 10383, dated around 1964, is irreparable. For this reason it was rereleased as DC PD70324, but the voice of Miranda Martino was replaced by horrible mewing little voices.

65. The ceremony took place on March 31, 2000. The text of the inaugural lecture is reproduced in the appendices. The festivities concluded in the afternoon with a concert in the Chiesa di S. Chiara, organized by the Amici della Musica and by the University of Cagliari, in which Laura Gallenga (flute) and Elena Ciaffone (piano) played music by Rota, Crivelli, Barry, Piersanti, and Morricone. [SM]

66. *The Mission* (GB, Roland Joffé, 1986). [DVD, Warner Bros., 2003].

67. *Uccellacci e uccellini* (Pasolini, 1966). [DVD, Medusa Video, 2009.]

68. (Pasolini, 1966). [DVD, Medusa Video, 2009.]

69. (Pasolini, 1968). [DVD, Medusa Video, 2009.]

70. (Pasolini, 1971). [DVD, CDE, 2010.]

71. Italian-French production, 1974. [DVD, CDE, 2010.]

72. The last film of Pasolini, released in 1975 after his death. [DVD, CDE, 2010.]

73. *Salò o le 120 giornate di Sodoma* (*Salò or the 120 Days of Sodom*) (Pasolini, 1975). [DVD, BFI, 2001, 2008.]

74. Later entitled *Addio a Pier Paolo Pasolini*, it does not appear in the catalogue of the works but was played more times in public, above all by Gilda Buttà.

75. D. Bertini-Kramer. Written in 1935, it achieved success with the singer Meme Bianchi in 1943.

76. CD RCA 74321-36087-2(OST 130). There is the recent interpretation by Angelo Branduardi with the National Academy of Santa Cecilia Orchestra directed by Morricone, recorded in November 1998 on the occasion of the seventieth birthday of the author (CD Sony SK89054).

77. See "Musical Example 59, 'Opening Titles of *Uccellacci e uccellini*,'" in *Comporre per il Cinema*, 269–78.

78. Directed by Kon Ichikawa, Japan, 1956. [DVD, Medusa Home Entertainment, 2006.]

79. *Uccellacci e uccellini* (Pasolini, 1966). [DVD, Medusa Video, 2009.]

80. Directed by Roberto Faenza, 1995. [DVD, Cecchi Gori Home Video, 2005.]

81. CD Epic EPC 480383 2. See "Musical Example 60, 'A Brisa from *Sostiene Pereira*,'" in *Comporre per il Cinema*, 279–80. This excerpt does not contain the full score.

82. *The Mission* (GB, Roland Joffé, 1986). [DVD, Warner Bros., 2003.]

83. Directed by Alberto De Martino, 1967.

Appendix 1

Composing for the Cinema

A Manifesto¹

Cinema and music are joined by one element characteristic of their nature: temporality. The enjoyment of cinematographic works takes place through two sensory organs: the eyes and the ears. The eye has the better ability in the sense that the images, although composed, appear in all their integrity. The ear has a receptive limit when confronted by simultaneous signals of a more diverse nature, whether they are only musical (polyphonic—contrapuntal) or mixed (music, dialogue, noises, effects). In a film, the optimal enjoyment of the music depends on the generally neglected control of its temporal range, intensity, and clarity. One translates it into a reduced number of sound signals.

When I was young and frequented the School of Composition of Goffre-do Petrassi at the Conservatory of Santa Cecilia, I never imagined that I would be linked with the composition of music for the cinema. I had then (and I still have today) other aspirations. I wanted to write other music, not film music. Not that I look down on what I have done and what I do for the cinema, but certainly it does not give the spiritual satisfaction with which I think one should be rewarded at least in part. The other music I would have wanted to write is that which only rarely I succeed in writing for a film, because it is difficult to find someone who can accept it without complicating one's life with the public. Anyway, that life is already complicated by the ideas that motivate it. I allude to the so-called art film and *"film d'autore."*

For some of these films I have written music that I would not hesitate to present in front of a public that is more demanding than that of the cinema, in a concert hall, where the music is listened to for itself and is not just a complementary support for the image. But . . . in the cinema today (and not

249

just for me), to succeed in defending with dignity one's own personality and one's own natural creative requirements is increasingly rare. So, roughly speaking, barely 5 percent of the films that I have done are ones for which I succeeded in applying the music of my aspirations, and the reasons seem obvious to me.

Films are produced for a massive public that for the most part does not love complications, does not want obstacles that arise between the images and its understanding. The majority of the public wants—unconsciously, of course, but consciously on the part of the producers, who influence the product—a music that in slang is defined as "catchy," therefore, on a tonal foundation and concentrated almost always on a leading theme and on other collateral themes.

This desire reduces all, or almost all, film music to a "catchy" theme. Today, for obvious motives of the historical evolution of musical language, this situation cannot kindle any stimulus in the person who composes. It means the composer is led into a state of depression that after a long while can destroy him. So, many composers, also those who are not Italian, oscillate between rehashed music belonging to the so-called classical music repertory and music produced by discographic consumerism.

Since I took note of this situation unequivocally, I have reacted, perhaps even unconsciously, but I was always guided by a conviction that is in nature ethical, technical, and expressive. My reaction has carried me little by little to an out-and-out creative behavior, of which I became conscious over time, when the sum of my reactions had assumed precise connotations that were really mine and that I am now able to summarize . . . with four points.

1. I attempted to serialize tonal music (that which is vulgarly called "catchy").
2. Having to twist myself to write "catchy" themes, I wanted to limit them to a range of three or four sounds, imposing on them a serialization of intervals, dynamics, and timbre.
3. I wanted an instrumentation that took into account that which Webern and the post-Webern composers had added and consolidated in their experience, united to other contemporary experimentation in which I took part or did not take part.
4. I transposed aleatoric compositional techniques (even to the limit of a collective improvisation, organized in an elementary way) into music with a tonal or modal foundation.

All this, one can summarize further, was my attempt to find myself by way of my stylistic features or those that I unconsciously filtered (belonging to all the music that I would have wanted to write outside of the cinema) into the more commercial music that the cinema, with its exigencies of popularity and of cash receipts, forced me to make. This is why, even in such a compromising and conditioned context, I was able to find myself, redeeming myself in large part from the depression I described. But it was not only a moral redemption, because to the practical results I believe I added also a level of delightfulness and pleasure. All this became style, where the end was aimed at the not-otherwise-accessible individuation of a compositional syntax, like the sum of technical and expressive intentions.

Especially in the cases where I stressed the integration of experiences closer to my needs, to the needs of a composer of our time, I realized that a miracle happened, always unexpected, of approval—even if, many times, on the contrary, these same resolutions cost me some strong disapproval, for example, when I applied these ideas to films that could not assimilate them.

I ask, lastly, how would—or better, how ought—music for the cinema be? First of all, one needs to distance oneself from a dangerous assertion of Stravinsky, who about fifty years ago maintained that music for film should not disturb the spectator, just as the café orchestras did not disturb the customers of the locale.

The error of many illustrious composers (because one is dealing with errors) was to judge film music by the standards used for absolute music. Music for the cinema certainly will have a historical significance in the future, but it will have it with respect to its own time and relative to its own setting, without inadmissible and deceptive comparisons with classical music. With respect to its own time, film music, on the contrary, has a considerable value because it takes on the influences, fevers, distortions, and fashions that are the influences, fevers, distortions, and fashions with which the spectator identifies.

Here one would graft onto our theme a reflection about the social, political, and economic influence of the entertainment business market, with the consequence of analyzing the journey of a soundtrack from its financing to its commercialization in the form of reproduced music, but one is dealing with a long and complex analysis that lies outside my area of expertise in this venue. Concerning this I can add only that I have composed music for the cinema that I wanted to save on recordings. They are recordings that I had published but that no recording industry would have published, because they did not have that character of marketability to which I just referred. On these discs I collected those compositions, as I stated already at the outset, that could be executed in places and contexts in which music is the protagonist.

Turning back to the question, my response could be summarized with one formula: EST.

E—*Energy*, like tension, like the level in the transmission of the sounds.

S—*Space*, like the spatiality of the sounds, that ought to reach and envelop the spectator without equivocation and interference from other components on the soundtrack.

T—*Temporality*, like duration, like the staying power of the musical event.

Music written for the cinema is one component that is extraneous to the cinema itself, with the exception of music present at the internal level. To make one's own contribution, one has to be respectful of one's essential, constituent needs. That is possible if one takes into account *temporality*. That, as I just stated, is the element that music has in common with film. *Temporality* can justify and permit a happy coexistence between the two languages. Entering into the image—invading it—the musical sounds ought to be discrete, but contemporaneously, all, or almost all, of the other sound sources ought to give it *space*. The entrance of the music ought to be prepared by the composer and the director, arranging ahead of time a *space* of preparation for its entrance. This ought to be true, also and especially, for the conclusion and exit, even if gradual. But at the moment in which the psychological, expressive, and interpretive task is entrusted to the music, the sound's *energy* has to be able to liberate itself without delays.

NOTE

1. Document prepared by Morricone for the Fiesola edition and read at the conclusion of the lessons.

Appendix 2

Writing for the Cinema

Aspects and Problems of a Compositional Activity of Our Time[1]

Today one speaks of applied music with the intent of distinguishing it neatly from absolute music, and by saying such a thing one states at the same time both a half-truth and a half-lie. One describes a half-truth because the attitude of the composer before the commission of a piece of music destined for the concert hall is an attitude essentially free from at least conscious conditioning.

As one will note, it seems necessary for me to distinguish between conscious and unconscious conditioning. In fact, even the most unrestrained of composers relies unconsciously on a praxis more or less consolidated—genres, forms, personnel, technique of writing. It is so true that the radical breaks in the history of music, those that . . . in a single blow put into discussion genres, forms, personnel, and techniques of writing, can be counted on the fingers of one hand. (I think of John Cage, and I cannot think of many others other than him.) Instead, paradoxically, the great, the greatest authors of the past have been for the most part creators of synthesis and of concordances. They did not deny an epoch, but they summarized or recuperated all its aspects, carrying them to an extreme degree of perfection. Palestrina, Monteverdi, Mozart. . . . Finally, those that put in crisis a solidly preestablished system—Wagner, but also Stravinsky, also Schoenberg—they did it without denouncing the past. They did it with the means with which everyone already arranged; they did not invent again. When Schoenberg dedicated himself to dodecaphonic technique, he applied rules of composition practiced in the 1400s by the Franco-Flemish masters, and as a form he chose the suite, which as we know is one of the most diffuse forms from between 1600 and

253

1700, a form carried to its highest artistic degree by Johann Sebastian Bach. I believe that when Schoenberg composed the first entirely dodecaphonic piece—which, if I remember, is fixed as the Suite, op. 25 for pianoforte—he had in mind exactly this liaison with tradition, which by creating in this way he meant to confirm.

In other words, and to return to the basic concept, even in absolute music, total autonomy is a chimera, so much so that I feel the need to distinguish between an exterior independence and an interior independence. This last is the one that really counts. Therefore, I like to think—from the composer and not from the musicologist, and anticipating a concept to which I will return toward the conclusion—that Bach, when he had to compose a cantata every week for the liturgical office, was not very free exteriorly, as it is easy to imagine, but was free interiorly, because otherwise I cannot explain how he was able to renew the miracle of musical and spiritual poetry hundreds and hundreds of times within the same genre.

At this point, one probably will have noted that this dissertation is contradictory. I began by recognizing in composers of absolute music an elevated degree of freedom, but in fact, without saying so, I gave examples that demonstrated the opposite. Referring again to the last example that I called to mind, even assuming the absolute beauty of the cantatas of Bach, I cannot define them as an example of *absolute* music, but rather, in that case, as examples of *applied* music for the Lutheran liturgical office. I could resolve the contradiction by remembering that I spoke of a "half-truth," but to clarify now the intentionality of my process, I consider it necessary to take into consideration the other face of the coin—that is, the half-lie.

Above all, because of the effect of Crocean idealism, which in Italy has represented the more consistent part of the musical aesthetic of the first half of the twentieth century, musical criticism has looked down on every form of music that was not pure, not an end in itself, and as a result, musical historiography has passed in complete silence over the principal aspects of applied music, except for some individual studies conducted by an extremely restricted circle of musicologists who are without prejudice and who for this reason have not had an easy life, above all within the academy. I believe that you will find a first sign of the reversal of this tendency in the first volume of a new history of music of the twentieth century, curated by the Società Italiana di Musicologia, in which, finally, a chapter dedicated to the music for film and stage appears, signed by Sergio Miceli. This volume, entitled *Italia Millenovecentocinquanta* (*Italy 1950*),[2] was published last year (1999). Therefore, and I say it without irony, it demonstrates the tardiness with which music history has confronted the subject. If this fact conveys some idea of the marginalized state occupied by film music within official culture until now, it introduces but does not explain completely my argument about the half-lie. To deal with this I will redo still again the history of music, asking you to reflect with me briefly on the concept of applied music.

"Application," according to the vocabulary *Devoto-Oli*,[3] is defined as "functional arrangement, put into operation," and further as "concentration, constant and prolonged, of a determined activity, especially intellectual." In this sense, but not only this, all of Christian Gregorian chant (that is at the base of occidental music) is functional and applied music. One can affirm it without danger of being denied, without recounting that Saint Augustine had already said it when he reasserted that the *function* of music ought to be as support and as vehicle in relation to prayer without asking for anything for itself. The phenomenon continues in the first prototheatrical forms in the Middle Ages, in which the so-called ecclesiastical dramas served to tell the faithful in representative form the episodes in Christ's birth and death. Naturally, and to our good fortune, exactly there—where one declared that one did not compose for one's own or others' pleasure, but only to help with prayers and spiritual meditations, and therefore for the greater glory of God—the people in religious orders in the monastic centers scattered all over Europe began to elaborate the sacred monody, inserting interpolations into it, from recurring cells, dilating and contracting them, adding voices and finally instruments. Polyphony and counterpoint were born that way (the term "counterpoint" itself, as we know, derived precisely from the monastic practice of putting a note, called a point, in relation to another note: point against point). The outward appearance was a volley of sorts, but meanwhile, from the unambiguous *application* they formed a technique, a compositional conscience, a taste, and a praxis that went beyond official *function*. In a little while, I will try to return to this important lesson too.

I do not want, nor can I, now run over all the steps in the history of occidental music, but remember only that a lot of music was born as applied music. As a maximum example it will be enough to cite the baroque period and a good part of Viennese classicism. Haydn and Mozart, but still earlier Telemann, Handel, and Bach, wrote in a state of heavy submission and behind precise commissions, and it did not impede them—I already described it for Bach—from extraordinary success. But what to say about all the rest? It seems clear that all the great composers I have cited are divided between an absolute composing, also endowed with experimental characteristics, and an applied composing, tied to the times, to necessity, and to the desires for commissions.

At this point I would like to underline a paradoxical situation in our culture, product of that Crocean aesthetic that, to my mind, has harmed so much of the Italian music of the twentieth century. Let's make a hypothesis, completely ordinary, of a concert of baroque music in which two composers from the same period, Handel and Telemann, are on the program. In the first half we hear the *Musica per I reali fuochi d'artificio* (*Royal Fireworks Mu-*

sic), then a *Concerto per organo e orchestra*. In the second half we hear a *Concerto per flauto diritto e archi* and the *Tafelmusik per flauto diritto e basso continuo*. As you will have noted, both the composers are represented by pieces definable as "absolute" and pieces defined as "occasional," written for precise extramusical circumstances, applied music in name and fact. The paradox consists in this: today we don't normally accept a mixture of genre, putting it on the same level of respect and attention, but even so, we do not feel disappointed if the concert institution that has organized this evening has not scheduled contemporaneously with the performance of *Music per I reali fuochi d'artificio* a pyrotechnical spectacle. Similarly, we do not criticize if the concert institution is not preoccupied with setting the table on the stage to show us a group of women and men intent on eating an optimum supper while the *Tafelmusik* is performed. I do not think the metaphor requires other comments, but only a marginal addition: going to analyze the scores of Handel, one can easily ascertain that the same theme had been utilized in very diverse compositions, sonatas, concerti, suites—therefore absolute music—and occasional music, thus applied music.

I will not stop on the fact that in an evident state of necessity or for a proposition that they could not refuse, giants like Haydn, Mozart, and Beethoven wrote for carillons and musical clocks.

Nor will I insist on the much more relevant and significant fact that from Shakespeare on, therefore from Purcell until Mendelssohn and Schumann, but even to our Malipiero and Pizzetti, music for the stage reached an extremely high level. The *Sogno di una notte di mezza estate* (*A Midsummer Night's Dream*) by Mendelssohn, to cite only one case, is in the repertory of symphony orchestras all over the world, independently of its Shakespearean origin. I hope only to have demonstrated that the half-lie is made up, in reality, of many linked little lies, which perhaps would be more courteously defined as "forgetfulnesses," that are by this time commonplaces rooted in the taste and cultural conventions of our time.

At this point I wish to be clear, beside the semantic game implicit in the preceding, that the half-truth is, in reality, a half-lie, and vice versa, that the half-lie is a half-truth, trusting always the personal historical lecture that I gave, a prudent and respectful lecture of historical theses that are widely diffuse. In any case, musicians of whichever epoch are asked to interpret their own times, expressed now and then in terms of ideology, culture, and custom that are more or less ephemeral.

To come to the present and all the reasons for which I find myself at such a distinguished gathering, I will limit myself to another realization, which . . . I picked up from the writings of a scholar whom I already have cited here. Also, I have the certainty that if future generations want to try to understand our century, to understand it in all its implications—social, linguistic, cultural, customary—they will have in the cinema the most precious "evidence."

Without undervaluing literature, the figurative arts, and naturally music . . . absolutely, it is the cinema that better than any other language will speak of our time, perhaps precisely because it is a heterogeneous language, made up of so many languages, contaminated and therefore "impure" already from birth. It is not limiting to be like that; on the contrary, it was not so for the musical theatre, a primary example of contaminations, for a description of which I would have been constrained to have recourse to the same adjectives.

Today, the lyric opera does not express anymore those masterworks that, from Monteverdi to Alessandro Scarlatti, from Pergolesi to Gluck, from Mozart to Rossini, from Verdi to Puccini, from Weber to Wagner, from Debussy to Berg, have marked almost four centuries of our (not only musical) history. From many points of view it is the cinema that has collected this inheritance, precisely because among the thousands of routine works (exactly as in the musical theatre), it has consigned to humanity many great masterworks, but above all because it has demonstrated the capacity to speak to the hearts of the simple as well as to intellectuals. Paraphrasing once more the musical theatre, the cinema is capable of transforming itself from time to time into chamber opera and into opera buffa, into tragedy and into joyful drama, into comedy and farce, into popular spectacle and into the opera for a few elect.

My journey (which it does not seem to me to be the time here to go over in detail) has carried me to an identification with the cinema of the past forty years, not absolute but without doubt decisive, that I think I have confronted professionally in all its implications from the highest to the most common. An experience that I would not know exactly how to recapitulate, it was . . . rich in satisfaction but also delusions, in artistic fellowship and unforgettable people, but also (although rarely) in incomprehension and misunderstandings. If there were a Benedetto Marcello of our time, and if he were to write a satire—entitled, naturally, *Il Cinema alla moda* (*The Cinema alla Mode*), paraphrasing the celebrated *Teatro alla moda* of the Venetian composer of the 1700s—we would be able to have an idea of the complexity of the cinematographic environment. The analogies would be many: the producer in place of the impresario, the not-very-talented actress wanted by the producer instead of the not-very-talented singer wanted by the impresario, the screenwriter in place of the librettist, the whims of the celebrated actor protagonist in place of the whims of the celebrated tenor, and, naturally, the musician victim in both cases. I say "victim" without wanting, however, to victimize, even if the position of the composer of music for film is not among the more comfortable. The cinema has given me a lot, and even if during a certain initial period of my career I felt marginalized and hurt, in the suspicion that I had renounced my highest ideals of composition, I feel that I have recovered over time a certain serenity and that a confirmation of the changes came from within and outside of me. I believe it was also and above all on the occasion that sees us here reunited, including that rereading of musical history that I proposed to you a little while ago.

After the necessity of synthesizing my thoughts and deeds and trying to recover some ideas that I anticipated before, I would like to conclude by saying that, within the limits of my possibilities and frequently in the absence of determinants of exterior autonomy, I have always tried to pursue a sort of secret interior liberty. It was a liberty that, also with respect to clients, therefore from necessity often excluded the director and sometimes the production, and it gave me permission to maintain my own musical identity. Not by accident have I brought up the monks of the Middle Ages, because, in a perhaps analogous way, I have tried to work contemporaneously on more than one level: the first, evident to everyone and by everyone generally accepted, in which I have used my ability to write the music for a film characterized by certain specific necessities, from time to time receiving diverse and thick critiques for strictly musical implications; the second, secret and therefore ignored by a good number of the directors with whom I have collaborated, in which I have tried to put into action certain ideas, certain compositional experiments that I valued later on, in a more explicit way, I should say. And frankly, still today I do not see an alternative to this duplicitous choice, because one aspect without the other for me would not make any sense.

I like to think, finally—and perhaps this is the context in which it is more probable that my thought can appear legitimate—that the stylistic fusions, the mixtures among genres and forms, the attempt to synthesize areas and musical ideas that seem apparently irreconcilable, Orient and Occident, cultivated and popular, poetic and prosaic, are ascribable to a vocation but at the same time to the legitimate necessity of a composer of our time to express himself.

Perhaps, wanting to descend a little more into the details, I believe that the constant research and experimentation I have practiced in written film music, the utopian and antihistorical attempt to realize a compromise between writing based on a tonal foundation and that based on the Second Viennese school—I repeat: a private and silent attempt that evidently has reached the listener—was necessary to redeem the worn-out praxis of a craft. I tried to make the traditional harmonic simplification coexist with the serialization of intervals, durations, timbres, and dynamics with the result of bestowing on traditional harmony and melody an uncertain suspension appropriate to the music of our post–World War II era.

NOTES

1. Extract of the introductory speech of Ennio Morricone, read on the occasion of the conferring of the honorary degree in languages and foreign letters. Cagliari, Aula Magna of the Ateneo, March 31, 2000.

2. Guido Salvetti and Bianca Maria Antolini, eds. (Milan: Guerini & Associati, 1999).

3. Giacomo Devoto and Gian Carlo Oli, *Il Devoto-Oli: Vocabolario della lingua italiana* (Grassina: Le Monnier, 1971). According to *Webster's Encyclopedic Unabridged Dictionary of the English Language*, "the act of putting to a special use or purpose."

Filmography

For alternate titles see the index.

Accattone (Pasolini, 1961). [DVD: *Pasolini Collection: Vol. 2*, Waterbearer, 2003]. [DVD: *Accattone*, Medusa Video, 2006.] [YouTube: "Accattone di Pier Paolo Pasolini (prima parte)", posted by Bruno Esposito.]

Acciaio (Ruttmann, 1933). [YouTube: "audiodrop - Acciaio (shoogs New Cut)," posted by filmshoog; "Gian Francesco Malipiero: Quattro Invenzioni per orchestra (1933)," posted by TheWelleszCompany.]

Alexander Nevsky [*Aleksandr Nevskij*] (USSR, Eisenstein, 1938). [DVD: Criterion Colletion, 2001; Eureka, 2003.] [YouTube: "Battle on the ice," posted by rabbiattman; "Aleksandr Nevsky," posted by notbot.]

Alien (GB, Scott, 1979). [DVD: Twentieth Century Fox, 2000; 20th Century Fox Home Entertainment, 2003; Definitive Edition, 20th Century Fox Home Entertainment, 2007; Blu-ray, 20th Century Fox Home Entertainment, 2012.] [YouTube: "Alien Trailer (1979)," posted by Dav3ydav3.]

Allonsanfàn (Taviani, Taviani, 1974). [DVD: Delta Video, 2009.] [YouTube: "Allonsanfan finale Rabbia E Tarantella," posted by squilibriomentale89; "Allonsanfan - Filme Completo," posted by peteruivante; "Allonsanfan - ballata (video dal film)," posted by Stefano Fratini.]

Altri dopo di noi (Others after Us), from the film *Krăsnaja palata (La tenda rossa)* (Kalatozov, 1968). [DVD: Cecchi Gori, 2007.] [YouTube: "Tema d'amore (La tenda rossa) di Ennio Morricone," posted by cloudidogz.]

Amleto (Kozinčev, 1963).

Amleto (Zeffirelli,1990). [DVD: Warner Bros., 2004; Cecchi Gori, 2007.] [YouTube: "Amleto - Zeffirelli," posted by fandent; "Amleto di Zeffirelli," posted by kingartu83.]

L'arpa birmana (Japan, Ichikawa, 1956). [DVD: Medusa Home Entertainment, 2006.] [YouTube: "L'ARPA BIRMANA." posted by crissav08; "L'arpa birmana - Kon Ichikawa - 1956," posted by ilrepubblichino; "Biruma no tategoto.aka.The Burmese Harp.1956.KonIchikawa. Full movie.English subtitles" posted by DANA STARBUCK; "The Burmese Harp (1956) song scene english sub" posted by KatushiroOkamoto.]

L'attentat [*The Attempted Assassination*] (Boisett, 1972). [VHS: Lange, B004AH2DY0.] [YouTube: "L'attentat (Ben Barka)" posted by ChebRif; El atentado. Yves Boisset. Jorge Semprún," posted by fub401; "Extrait no. 3 du film l'attentat," posted by vFelix888.]

Ballet mécanique (France, Léger, 1924). [YouTube: "Le Ballet Mécanique (1924, Fernand Leger)," posted by Supercinema77; "Ballet Mecanique," posted by ATCFDrummer.]

Bambini del mondo (*Children of the World*), from *Ten to Survive* (UNICEF).

Bananas (*Il dittatore della Stato libero di Bananas*) (Allen, 1971). [DVD: *Woody Allen Collection, Set 1*, MGM, 2004.] Distributed in Italy with the title *Il dittatore della Stato libero di Bananas*. [YouTube: "Bananas (1971) - Trailer (english)," posted by MondAgave; "Bananas The harpist Woody Allen 1971 avi," posted by fede13fede13.]

The Band Wagon (variety show) (USA, Minnelli,1953). [DVD: Warner Bros., 2005, 2009.] [YouTube: "The Band Wagon - Vincente Minnelli 1953," posted by cawabobny; "'The Band Wagon' trailer," posted by Squawk82.]

Barry Lyndon (GB, Kubrick, 1975). [DVD: Warner Bros., 2001.] [YouTube: "Barry Lyndon - British Grenadiers," posted by Zappiss; "Barry Lyndon - Seduction Scene," posted by countvonfersen.]

The Bible (*La Bibbia*) (Huston, 1966). [DVD: Twentieth Century Fox Entertainment, 2005] [YouTube: "La Bible John Huston U.S.A. 1966" posted by Lynda Boccara; "The Bible: In the Beginning...(1966) – John Huston – Trailer" posted by The CineLady; "La torre di Babele" posted by colbymedia.]

Il bidone (Fellini, 1955). [DVD: Medusa Film SPA, 2003.] [YouTube: "IL BIDONE (The swindle) - Film di Federico Fellini del 1955," posted by 0peppone0.]

Blade Runner (Scott, 1982). [DVD: The Final Cut, Warner Home Video, 2007; 30th Anniversary Ultimate Collector's Edition, Warner Home Video, 2012.] [YouTube: "Blade Runner - Monologo finale," posted by Daniele Martinelli; BLADE RUNNER - ITA - le scene più belle," posted by daxrx7.]

The Blues Brothers (Landis, 1980). [DVD: *The Blues Brothers: 25th Anniversary Edition*, Universal Studios, 2005.] [YouTube: "The Blues Brothers (4/9) Movie CLIP - Shake a Tail Feather (1989) HD," posted by movieclips.]

Brazil (USA, Gilliam, 1985). [DVD, *Brazil—3-Disc Special Edition*, Criterion Collection, 2006.] [YouTube: "BRAZIL (1984) di Terry Gilliam - con Robert de Niro - Film completo.]

Bronenosec Potemkin (*Corazzata* Potemkin, *Battleship Potemkin*) (USSR, Eisenstein,1926). [DVD: Kino, 2007.] [YouTube: "Battleship Potemkin HQ," posted by James Huang; "Odessa Steps clip: Battleship Potemkin (1925)," posted by TheWesternReview; "Battleship Potemkin – the mutiny," posted by mrjoshuakearney].]

Bugsy (USA, Levinson, 1991). [DVD: *Bugsy—Extended Cut*, Sony Pictures Home Entertainment, 2006.] [YouTube: "'Bugsy' (1991) Main Title Sequence HQ," posted by Cinelation; "Bugsy (1991) - Trailer," posted by jonaspv.]

Bulworth (*Il senatore*) (USA, Beatty, 1998). [DVD: Twentieth Century Fox, 2003.][YouTube: "Bulworth - Movie Trailer," posted by zuguidemovietrailers; "Bulworth - Warren Beatty - View It!" posted by Richard Soria.]

Buone notizie (Good News) (Petri, 1979).

Il buono, il brutto, il cattivo (*The Good, the Bad and the Ugly*) (Leone, 1966). [DVD: *Sergio Leone Anthology*, MGM/UA, 2007; Mondo Home, 2007]. [YouTube: "The Good, The Bad, and the Ugly. Full Movie 1," posted by Dolsevita52; "The good, the bad and the ugly - Ecstasy of Gold," posted by RobertoGumpi; "The Good, the Bad & the Ugly Finale," posted by emas05.]

The Cabinet of Doctor Caligari (Wiene, 1919). [DVD: Eureka Entertainment, 2000; A2ZCDS.com, 2009.] [YouTube: "The Cabinet of Dr. Caligari (1920) - Full Movie," posted by LuckyStrike502.]

Canone inverso (*Inverse Canon, Making Love*) (Tognazzi, 1999). [DVD: Cecchi Gori, 2000.] [YouTube: "Canone inverso (Making Love - 2000) - 'Full Movie'" posted by Amy50290; "Canone inverso - Concerto Interrotto," posted by Alexis85bad; "Official Trailer Italiano - Canone Inverso: Making Love (2000)," posted by HMfansSpain.]

Caro diario (*Dear Diary*) (Moretti, 1994). [DVD: Warner Bros. Entertainment, Italia SPA, 2009.] [YouTube: "Caro diario Nanni Moretti in vespa 1993 parte 1," posted by serenaw3.]

Carosello napoletano (*Neapolitan Carousel*) (Giannini, 1953). [DVD: *Sophia Loren*, Lionsgate, 2008.] [YouTube: "Carosello Napoletano 1954 - Giacomo Rondinella - avi," posted by salvatore pirrone; "Sophia Loren Carosello Napoletano Part 1," posted by chicsoccer1.]

Il Casanova di Federico Fellini (Fellini, 1976). [DVD: Unilibro, 2010.] [YouTube: "El Casanova di Federico Fellini (1976) Trailer," posted by Danios12345]

Cassandra Crossing (Cosmatos, 1977). [DVD: Artisan, 2002.] [YouTube: "The Cassandra Crossing Part 1, 2 . . . 12," posted by Disasterflicks; "The Cassandra Crossing (1974) US trailer," posted by braniki1.]

The Cat Concerto (Hanna-Barbera, 1946). [DVD: Tom and Jerry Spotlight Collection, Warner Home Video, 2004.] [YouTube: "Tom and Jerry - The Cat Concerto," posted by AwesomeTVShows101312; "Tom and Jerry 029 The Cat Concerto HQ 480p," posted by Tomand-Jerry4011.]

C'era una volta il West (*Once upon a Time in the West*) (Leone, 1968). [DVD: *The Sergio Leone Anthology*, MGM/UA, 2007; Paramount Pictures, 2010.] [YouTube: "C'era Una Volta Il West," posted by adonterti; "C'era Una Volta Il West (Sergio Leone, 1968) - Jill arriva nel "selvaggio" West," posted by Betty Elms; "C'era una Volta il West (Trailer in inglese)," posted by trailersitaliani; "Once Upon a Time in the West (1968) - the Duel," posted by Bester B; "Once Upon A Time in The West---Ennio Morricone," posted by Amitoj Gautam; "C'era una volt il West - Duello iniziale-Harmonica (ita)," posted by maxarroja; "Harmonica History (Once Upon a Time in the West)," posted by Paolo Coelho; "Once Upon a Time in the West (1/8) Movie Clip (1968) HD," posted by movieclips (eight videos: 1/8–8/8).]

C'era una volta in America (*Once upon a Time in America*) (Leone, 1984). [DVD: *Once upon a Time in America*: Two-Disc Special Edition, Warner Bros., 2011.] [YouTube: "Once upon a time in America Trailer," posted by Buzzati; "Once Upon a Time in America (scene)," posted by youmontana55; "Once Upon A Time In America (1984) - Final Scene - The Smile," posted by cinemnemonic.]

C'eravamo tanto amati (*We Loved Each Other So Much*) (Scola, 1974). [DVD: Brigham Young University, 2001.] [YouTube: "C'eravamo Tanto amati - Ettor Scola," posted by Vale Stap; "C'eravamo tanto amati (1974)," posted by JohnLoffredo.]

Il clan dei siciliani (*Le clan des siciliens*) (France, Verneuil, 1969). [DVD: *Il clan dei siciliani*, Twentieth Century Fox, 2006; *The Sicilian Clan*, Phantom, 2009.] [YouTube: "Le clan des Siciliens (The Sicilian Clan) (1969) Trailer . . . Ventura)," posted by agelesstrailers.]

La classe operaia va in paradiso (*The Working Class Goes to Heaven*) (Petri, 1971). [DVD: *La classe operaia va in paradiso*, Minerva, 2009.] [YouTube: "The Working Class Goes to Heaven - 1971 - scene: 'Lulu Speech,'" and "The Working Class Goes to Heaven - 1971 - scene: 'Just think a pair of butts,'" posted by BISabbatH2; "La Classe Operaia va in Paradiso," posted by TomasRamalhete, by di redder73, and by 77zorro1.]

A Clockwork Orange (GB, Kubrick, 1971). [DVD: Warner Home Video, 2007, 2012.] [YouTube: "A Clockwork Orange - Trailer" and "A Clockwork Orange: Alex puts his Droogs in place," posted by megamushroom07.]

Un coeur en hiver (*Un cuore in inverno, A Heart in Winter*) (France, Sautet,1992). [DVD: Lorber Film, 2006.] [YouTube: "Scenes D'Art - 1992 - (Un Coeur En Hiver) (Real, Claude Sautet). Avi," posted by artescenes; "Un Coeur en Hiver/ A Heart in Winter - Trailer," posted by kochlorber; "A heart in winter clip 1," posted by highlightcinemage1.]

La corta notte delle bambole di vetro (*The Short Night of the Glass Doll*) (Lado, 1971). [DVD: Koch Media, 2006; Cecchi Gori, 2012.] [YouTube: "La Corta Notte delle Bambole," posted by Vetro di franzedge; "The Short Night of Glass Dolls - Trailer," posted by GialloTrailers.]

La cuccagna (*The Cockaigne*) (Salce, 1962). [DVD: Raro Video, 2012.] [YouTube: "La cuccagna (1962)," posted by JohnLoffredo; "La Cuccagna - La Ballata dell'Eroe," posted by Faustonet; "Luigi Tenco: La cuccagna (1962)," posted by JohnLoffredo.]

Dances with Wolves (*Balla coi lupi*) (Costner, 1990). [DVD: CVC, 2009; Warner Home Video, 2009; PolyGram & Guild Home Video—GLD51212; *Dances with Wolves—20th Anniversary Edition*, MGM/UA, 2011.] [YouTube: "Dances with wolves (1990)_Trailer," posted by inso99; "Dances with wolves - suicide ride," posted by bruce berger.]

Il Decameron (Pasolini, 1971). [DVD: CDE, 2010.] [YouTube: "Il Decameron di Pier Paolo Pasolini - prima parte, seconda parte," posted by Bruno Esposito.]

Il deserto dei tartari (*The Desert of the Tartars*) (Zurlini, 1976). [DVD: *Il deserto dei tartari*, General Video, 2007; Instituto Luce, 2008; General Video, 2009.]

Disclosure (Rivelazioni). (USA, Levinson, 1995). [DVD: Warner Home Video, 1994.] [You-Tube: "Disclosure - Trailer," posted by warnervoduk; "Disclosure - Taking Down Demi Moore," posted by NotoriousDillnger.]

Dr. No (GB, Young, 1962). [DVD: *James Bond Ultimate Collector's Set*, MGM/UA, 2007.] [YouTube: "Dr. No - Original Trailer," posted by ChocolateFrogPrince; "James Bond Dr. No opening," posted by plykshow.]

La dolce vita (Fellini, 1960). [DVD: Medusa Film SPA, 2003; Butterfly Music SRL, 2010.] [YouTube: "La Dolce Vita 'Fontana di trevi,'" posted by Matteo Paganella; "La Dolce Vita - Fellini - Finale," posted by AlTaMuRaPaNe.]

La domenica specialmente (Especially Sunday) (Bertolucci, Giordana, Tornatore, Barilli, 1991). [DVD: Cecchi Gori Home Video, 2008; Ripley's Home Video, 2008.] [YouTube: "La domenica specialmente III.wmv" and "La domenica specialmente VI," posted by Carlos Rangel.]

I drammi marini (Landi, RAI, 1962).

I due colonelli (The Two Colonels) (Vanzina, 1962). [DVD: Medusavideo, 2004.] [YouTube: "Totò 1962 I due colonnelli new," posted by MidasASD.]

The Duelists (GB, Scott, 1977). [DVD: Paramount Home Video, 2002.] [YouTube: "1977 - Los Duelistas," posted by trevorbuenhigo; "Sabre duel. The Duellists (1977)," posted by BrodatyOlo; "The Duelists," posted by Yarbols; "The Duelists (1977) - Epilogue," posted by Gabriele Martino.]

8½ (Fellini, 1963). [DVD: Criterion Films 2001.] [YouTube: "8½ Fellini," posted by David Davier; "8 ½," posted by tangodj.]

Elephant Man (GB, Lynch, 1980). [DVD: Music Video Distribution, 2007.] [YouTube: "1980 The Elephant Man - Trailer," posted by ennemme; "The Elephant Man (1/10) Movie CLIP - The Terrible Elephant Man (1980) HD," posted by movieclips; "Ending scene from David Lynch's The Elephant Man (1980)," posted by zarusama.]

The Endless Game (Forbes, 1989) (TVS Film/Reteitalia). [VHS, 1990.]

Entr'acte (France, Clair, 1924). [YouTube: "Erik Satie/René Clair: Entr'Acte (1924)," posted by TheWelleszCompany.]

Escalation (Faenza, 1968).

Fat Man and Little Boy, Shadow Makers (L'ombra di mille soli) (USA, Joffé, 1990). [DVD: Paramount Pictures, 2004.] [YouTube: "Fat man and little boy - tickling the dragon" and "Fat man and little boy - trinity test," posted by perryperks; "Fat Man and Little Boy Trailer (1989)," posted by gavinnorth72.]

Il fiore delle mille e una notte (The Flower of a Thousand and One Nights) (Pasolini, 1975). [DVD: CDE, 2010.] [YouTube: "Ending of Pasolini's arabian nights," posted by bancroft-dub; "Il fiore delle Mille e una notte introduction," posted by bancroftdub.]

Gamlet (Hamlet) (USSR, Kozintsev, 1964). [DVD: Hamlet, Mr. Bongo Films, 2011; Gamlet, Chicago, Facets Video, 2006; Gamlet, Moscow, RUSCICO, 2003.][Youtube: "Hamlet (1964) – Directed by Gigori Kozintsev – Clip 1" and "Hamlet (1964) – Directed by Gigori Kozintsev – Clip 2" posted by MrBongoWorldwide.]

Il gatto a nove code (Cat O'Nine Tails) (Argento, 1971). [DVD: *Cat O'Nine Tails*, Videotape, 2004.] [YouTube: "The Cat O'Nine Tails (US Trailer)," posted by thatscraptacular; "Cat O'Nine Tails - Rooftop Fight Scene," posted by friartuckk.]

Il giardino delle delizie [Le jardin des delices, The Garden of Pure Delights] (Agosti, 1967). [DVD: La vie est belle, B002UQ9UOO.] [YouTube: "Trailer Le Jardin des Delices un film réalisé par Silvano Agosti," posted by silvano agosti; "Le jardin des delices - Silvano Agosti 1967," posted by tarlait.]

Giù la testa (A Fistful of Dynamite/Duck, You Sucker) (Leone, 1971). [DVD: *The Sergio Leone Anthology*, MGM/UA, 2007; *Sergio Leone—Cofanetto Grandi Classici*, Mondo Home, 2007.] [YouTube: "Giù la Testa 1/2," posted by malefix82; "Giù la testa (1971) - German Intro," posted by Eurowestern; "Duck you sucker - Trailer," posted by Lindberg SWDB; "Duck, You Sucker Coburn & Steiger," posted by Aut0five; "Fistful of Dynamite/Duck You Sucker/ Giù la Testa," posted by patcalutube; "A Fistful of Dynamite (1972) - Rod Steiger, James Coburn - 'Sean Sean Sean,'" posted by Mr. Tarneyourself; "Giù la testa - Mesa Verde," posted by Ciro Campanile.]

Gott mit uns (*God with Us*, *Dio è con noi*) (Montaldo, 1969). [DVD: Stormovie, 2008.] [YouTube: "Vesztesek és Gyoztesek (1969) [Teljes film]," posted by XxxMr4rOnxxX.]

Grazie zia (*Thanks Aunt*) (Saperi, 1968). [DVD: Medusa Video, 2005.] [YouTube: "Grazie zia - Trailer italiano," posted by CGHomeVideo; "Grazie zia con Lisa Gaston (3/10) Sbirciare le gambe della zia . . .," posted by Eros Ottanta; "Grazie, zia - Salvatore Samperi (1968) English subtitles," posted by cinematomico.]

Hamlet (Zeffirelli, 1990), coproduction USA, Italy. [DVD: Warner Bros., 2004.] [YouTube: "Amleto - Zeffirelli," posted by fandent; "Bloody Deed - Hamlet (7/10) Movie CLIP (1990) HD," posted by movieclips.]

Hamlet (Olivier, 1948). [DVD: *Olivier's Shakespeare*, Criterion Collection, 2006.] [YouTube: "Hamlet - Sir Laurence Olivier - Parte 1 de 10," posted by luanurbec; "Comparing Productions of Hamlet, Act II, Scene ii (Part 2 of 4)," posted by John Kenneth Fisher.]

Hello Dolly! (Kelly, 1969). [DVD: *A Celebration of Song and Dance*, Twentieth Century Fox, 2007]. [YouTube: "'Hello, Dolly!' Barbra Streisand," posted by iLoveYouMeryl.]

Henry V (Olivier, 1944). [DVD: Criterion, 1999; *Olivier's Shakespeare*, Criterion Collection, 2006.] [YouTube: "St. Crispin's Day Speech - Henry V (1944)," posted by Robert Hicks; "Oliver (*sic*) Battle," posted by JBTulloch.]

Henry V (Branagh, 1989). [DVD: MGM, 2000.] [YouTube: "Henry V - Band of Brothers," posted by Martin Solomon.]

Indagine su un cittadino al di sopra di ogni sospetto (*Investigation of a Citizen above Suspicion*) (Petri, 1970). [DVD: Eyescreen, 2003; Medusa Video, 2008.] [YouTube: "Scene from 'Investigation of a Citizen Above Suspicion' (1970)," posted by Isinng; "Indagine Su Un Cittadino Al Di Sopra Di Ogni Sospetto - Interrogami" and "Indagine Su Un Cittadino Al Di Sopra Di Ogni Sospetto - Intro," posted by romalom1.]

Io la conoscevo bene (*I Knew Her Well*) (Pietrangeli, 1965). [DVD: Medusa Home Entertainment, 2009.] [YouTube: "Io la conoscevo bene - 1965," posted by pescespada; "Io la conoscevo bene (Pietrangeli) - il suicidio di Adriana (scena finale)" and "Stefania Sandrelli (Io la conoscevo bene) - Mina (E se domani)," posted by ataneila.]

Krăsnaja palata (*La tenda rossa*, *The Red Tent*) (Kalatozov, 1968). [DVD: Cecchi Gori, 2007.] [YouTube: "S.O.S. Nobile," posted by linusag.]

Il ladro di bambini (*The Stolen Children*) (Amelio, 1992). [Arrow Films, World DVD, FCD317. DVD: Medusa Film, 2007.] [YouTube: "Il Ladro Di Bambini," posted by LiberoCinemaUndergr; "Il Ladro Di Bambini - Al mare.flv," posted by Rolando Armillei.]

La leggenda del pianista sull'oceano (*The Legend of the Pianist on the Ocean*) (Tornatore, 1998). [DVD: Streaming video, Italia-Film TV, Guarda Online; Medusa Video, 2007.] [YouTube: "The legend of 1900 - piano scenes Duel part 1" and "The legend of 1900 - piano scenes Duel part 2," posted by kiritochii; "Legend of 1900 - Playing Love," posted by PervertedRogerEbert.]

The Life and Death of Richard III (Calmettes, Keane, 1912).

Lorenzo's Oil (Miller, 1992). [DVD: Universal, 2004.] [YouTube: "Lorenzo's Oil Trailer," posted by cheesebmahlvr.]

Love Affair (*Un grand amore*) (Beatty, Caron, 1994). [DVD: Warner Bros., 2002.] [YouTube: "Love Affair (1994) Katharine Hepburn playing piano)" and "Love Affair (1994) - 'It doesn't have to be a miracle,'" posted by mellow0w; "Love Affair - K. D. Lang," posted by docgina1.]

Malèna (Tornatore, 2000). [DVD: Buena Vista Home Entertainment, 2001; Medusa Video, 2007.] [YouTube: "Malèna (1/10) Movie CLIP - Watching Malena (2000) HD," posted by movieclips.]

The Man Who Knew Too Much (USA, Hitchcock, 1956). [DVD: Universal, 2006.] [YouTube: "The Man Who Knew Too Much Trailer," posted by Lydia Lane; "Symphony of Suspense," posted by PollardJGyroMeow.]

Marco Polo (Montaldo, 1982). [DVD: Elle U Multimedia, 2009.] [YouTube: "Marco Polo - prima puntata," posted by rai; "Marco Polo (1982) regia di Giuliano Montaldo," posted by kezzeta; "Primo incontro tra Marco Polo e Kublai Khan," posted by AntrocomOnlus; "Marco Polo - Morte della madre di Marco Polo.wmv," posted by The Taraka.]

Metropolis (Germany, Lang, 1926). [DVD: Masters of Cinema, 2010.] [YouTube: "Metropolis 1927," posted by Alessandro Drasso; "1927 Metropolis (restored) part 1/3," posted by Mitchell Baron; "Metropolis (1927) (2001 Restored Version) Original Soundtrack," posted by PlushiePokemon.]

Metti, una sera a cena (*Let's Say, One Evening at Supper; Hurry to Me*) (Griffi, 1968). [YouTube: "Metti una sera a cena (parte 1 di 2)," posted by Pridirector; "Metti, una Sera a Cena - Che cos'è l'amore?," "Metti, una Sera a Cena - Un amico con un amico o la fa molto grossa o non la fa," and "Ennio Morricone - Hurry to me," posted by Davide Leonardi.]

The Mission (GB, Joffé, 1986). [DVD: Warner Bros., 2003.] [YouTube: "The Mission - Gabriel's Oboe," posted by Julianapedreira; "The Mission - Trailer (1986)," posted by Worley-Clarence; "The Mission (De Niro legge la prima lettera di San Paolo ai Corinzi)," posted by Paolo di gennaro.]

Mondo cane (*The Dog World*) (Jacopetti, 1961). [DVD: Blue Underground, 2008.] [YouTube: "Mondo Cane 1962 (Eng Dub)," posted by languedamour.]

Morte a Venezia (*Death in Venice*) (Visconti, 1971). [DVD: Warner Bros., 2006.] [YouTube: "1971 Death in Venice - Trailer," posted by ennemme; "Last Scene in Death in Venice (Actual Scene)," posted by farah4.]

Mosé (*Nella voce di Dio, In the Voice of God*) (Del Bosio, 1975). [YouTube: "Mosé 1974 con Burt Lancaster Puntata 1 parte 2," posted by Antonino Governale.]

Napoléon (France, Gance, 1927). [YouTube: "'Napoleon' di Abel Gance," posted by Leo Pellegrini.]

Nella voce di Dio (*In the Voice of God*), from the TV film *Mosé* (Del Bosio, 1975).

Non c'è pace tra gli ulivi (*There Is No Peace among the Olive Trees*) (De Santis, 1950). [DVD: Lux Film, Cecchi Gori, 2008.] [YouTube: "Non c'è pace tra gli ulivi," posted by salvatorelp; "Lucia bose in: 'non c'e pace tra gli ulivi,'" posted by fondiudine; "canto di pastori dal film 'Non c'è pace tra gli ulivi,'" posted by zomaro74; "Non c'è pace tra gli ulivi 1950 (Sperlonga)," posted by Artiom Romashov.]

La notte e il momento (*The Night and the Moment*) (Tatò, 1994). [DVD: Cine Historico de Aventuras, B00279VCYK, 1995.]

Le notti di Cabiria (*The Nights of Cabiria*) (Fellini, 1957). [DVD: *Nights of Cabiria*, Criterion Collection, 1999.] [YouTube: "Le Notti di Cabiria - Federico Fellini 01.wmv," posted by ishimats; "Nights of Cabiria - Finale," posted by wellgard.]

Nuovo cinema Paradiso (Italy/France, Tornatore, 1988). [DVD: Arrow Video, 2001, 2003, 2007; Cecchi Gori, n.d.; Director's Cut, Cristaldi Film, n.d.] [YouTube: "Nuovo cinema Paradiso - La storia del soldato e della principessa (completa)," posted by giap01; "Nuovo Cinema Paradiso - Scena Finale," posted by albdurras.]

O.K. Connery (*Operation Kid Brother*) (De Martino, 1967). [YouTube: "Marinaie vs Marinai," posted by bellitalia1900; "Operation Kid Brother (1967) Trailer," posted by OurManInHavana.]

On the Town (Donen, Kelly, 1949). [DVD: Warner Bros., 2008.] [YouTube: "On the Town," posted by SLBxSami; "Prehistoric Man," posted by rm18607; "New York, New York - On the Town," posted by Jwingfield1588.]

Once upon a Time in America (Leone, 1984) See *C'era una volta in America*.

Once upon a Time in the West (Leone, 1968). See *C'era una volta il West*.

Otello (Zeffirelli, 1985). [DVD: MGM 2003.] [YouTube: "Trailer - Otello, de Franco Zeffirelli," posted by di versatilhv.]

Othello (Wells, 1952). [DVD: Second Sight, 2003.] [YouTube: "Othello (1952) - Part 1," posted by strangelovepsycho (seven videos: part 1–part 7).]

Pacific 231 (Mitry, 1949). [DVD: *Avant Garde: Experimental Cinema 2*, Kino, 2007.] [YouTube: "'Pacific 231' 1949 movie: Jean Mitry-music: Arthur Honegger original!" posted by Wouter Van Belle.]

Parsifal (Syberberg, 1982). [DVD: Image Entertainment 1999.] [YouTube: "Syberberg Parsifal," posted by plamen0.]

Per qualche dollaro in più (*For a Few Dollars More*) (Leone, 1965). [DVD: Clint Eastwood Collection, MGM/UA 2007.] [YouTube: "Per qualche dollar in più - Finale Completo.avi," posted by The FarGella; "For.A.Few.Dollars.More.1965 Full Movie, Clint Eastwood," posted by Kalyan Babu.]

Per un pugno di dollari (*A Fistful of Dollars*) (Leone, 1964). [DVD: *Sergio Leone Anthology*, MGM/UA, 2007.] [YouTube: "Per un pugno di dollari - 1964 - di Sergio Leone," posted by ziomichele45; "Per un pugno di dollari - scena finale," posted by Mickipower.]

The Piano (*Lezioni di piano*), coproduction France, Australia, New Zealand (Campion, 1993). [DVD: Ev, 1999; Ciby, 2000; Optimum Home Entertainment, 2006; Lions Gate, 2012.] [YouTube: "The Piano Trailer," posted by anotherrainbow2008.]

Platoon (USA, Stone, 1968). [DVD: MGM, 2008.] [YouTube: "Platoon - Trailer - (1986) - HQ," posted by ryy79; "Platoon - Welcome to the 'Nam!" posted by ucantstop43.]

Il postino (Radford, 1994). [DVD: Disney Buena Vista, 2004.] [YouTube: "Il postino, trailer," posted by Foarster.]

Il prato (*The Lawn*) (Taviani, 1979). [DVD: ArtHaus, B000PKHW3S, n.d.] [YouTube: "Taviano - Il prato (1979)," posted by Alexis Goussev; "Il prato; 1979," posted by jimshvante.]

I pugni in tasca (*Fists in Pocket*) (Bellocchio, 1965). [DVD: 01 Distribution, 2006.] [YouTube: "I pugni in tasca - Marco Bellocchio (1965)," posted by cinematomico.]

Una pura formalità (*A Pure Formality*) (Tornatore, 1993). [DVD: Cecchi Gori Home Video, 2011.] [YouTube: "Una pura formalità," posted by UPFishere; "Introduzione 'Una pura formalità,'" posted by Muad' Dib.]

Quattro mosche di velluto grigio (*Four Flies of Grey Velvet*) (Argento, 1971). [DVD: 01 Distribution, 2009.] [YouTube: "Four Flies Of Grey Velvet - opening," posted by kredencio; "Trailer - 4 mosche di velluto grigio," posted by John Trent; "4 mosche di velluto grigio: Finale," posted by lovecupboard.]

I racconti di Canterbury (*Canterbury Tales*) (Pasolini, 1974). [DVD, CDE, 2010.] [YouTube: "The Canterbury Tales 1972 Trailer," posted by Digho Vera; "I racconti di Canterbury (1972) [MultiSub] - (Paolo Pasolini)," posted by Art Cinema.]

Raging Bull (Scorsese, 1980). [DVD: Martin Scorsese Film Collection, MGM/UA 2005]. [YouTube: "Raging Bull Trailer," posted by mrmuga; "Raging Bull (1980) - Robert DeNiro," posted by RobertDeNiroClips.]

Rappresaglia (*Massacre in Rome*) (Italy, Cosmatos, 1973). [DVD: No Shame Films, 2006.] [YouTube: "Massacre in Rome (1973) War film," posted by trojanfan65.]

Rio Bravo (*Un dollaro d'honore*) (USA, Hawks, 1959). [DVD: Warner Bros., 2003.] [YouTube: "Rio Bravo starring John Wayne Walter Brennan Dean Martin and Ricky Nelson," posted by RiflemeRay1; "Rio Bravo Trailer HQ,"posted by Niravam0; "Music in jail, in Rio Bravo, by Howard Hawks," posted by Jérome Labbé; "Rio Bravo (1959) opening scene," posted by OuterBoroughs7.]

The Rocky Horror Picture Show (GB, Sherman, 1975). [DVD: Twentieth Century Fox, 2002.] [YouTube: "Rocky Horror Picture Show (Trailer)," posted by mattchbox.]

Romeo e Giulietta (Zeffirelli, 1968). [DVD: Paramount, 2007.] [YouTube: "Romeo e Giulietta - Zeffirelli - Scena del balcone," posted by dany200786; "Romeo e Giulietta. Franco Zeffirelli," posted by Myriam Immacolata Vitagliano.]

Rosa e il Mago (RAI, Nelli, 1975–1976).

La Roue (Gance, 1923). [DVD: Flicker Alley, 2009.] [YouTube: "La Roue," posted by lilacwine85.]

Salò o le 120 giornate di Sodoma (*Salò or the 120 Days of Sodom*) (Pasolini, 1975). [DVD: BFI, 2001, 2008.] [YouTube: "Salò o le 120 giornate di Sodoma (1975) (MultiSub) (Paolo Pasolini)," posted by Art Cinema.]

San Michele aveva un gallo (*Saint Michael Had a Rooster*) (Taviani, Taviani, 1976). [DVD: Fox Lorber, 2005; Butterfly Music SPA, 2010.] [YouTube: "San Michele aveva un gallo (final scene)," posted by the2661; "San Michele aveva un gallo - La canzone iniziale," posted by Stefano Fratini.]

The Scarlet Letter (*La lettera scarlatta*) (USA, Joffe, 1995). [DVD: Disney/Buena Vista,2004.] [YouTube: "The Scarlet Letter (1995) Official Trailer #1 - Demi Morre Movie HD,"posted by oldhollywoodtrailers; "The Scarlet Letter (1995) - Part 1," posted by Claudio Cavalcante Cunha.]

Il segreto del Sahara (*The Secret of the Sahara*) (RAI TV, Negrin, 1988). [DVD: Wide Vision, n.d.; RAI Trade, n.d.] [YouTube: "Sceneggiato rai (1988) Il Segreto del Sahara 5^ parte di 5 by Nino," posted by TelEmozioni; "Secret of the Sahara Il Segreto del Sahara Das Geheimnis der Sahara," posted by Haffschlappe.]

The Shining (USA, Kubrick, 1980). [DVD: Warner Bros, 2008, 2012.] [YouTube: "The Shining Code 2.0 (complete film)," posted by Michael Wysmierski.]

Singin' in the Rain (USA, Donen, Kelly, 1952). [DVD: Warner Home Video, 2010.] [YouTube: "Singing in the Rain - Singing in the Rain (Gene Kelly) [HD Widescreen]," posted by lbarnard86; "Singin' in the Rain - Moses Supposes.wmv," posted by david999mn; "Singin' in the Rain," posted by Flora Siami ("Make 'Em Laugh").]

Det sjunde inseglet (*Seventh Seal*) (Bergman, 1956). [DVD: Criterion, 2009.] [YouTube: "Ingmar Bergman The Seventh Seal," posted by quixotickitten.]

Solaris (USSR, Tarkovsky, 1972). [DVD: Criterion Collection, 2002.] [YouTube: "Solaris by Andrej Tarkovskij - Levitation (full scene)," posted by lurex; "Solaris," posted by flavianos75.]

Some Like It Hot (USA, Wilder, 1959). [DVD: MGM/UA 2007.] [YouTube: "Some Like It Hot 1959 part 1 Marilyn Monroe," posted by EUGEProductions.]

Il sorriso del grande tentatore (*The Smile of the Great Tempter*) (Damiani, 1974). [YouTube: "Il sorriso del grande tentatore (Film Completo)," posted by PrimoLoculoadestra; "Il sorriso dell sorriso del grande tentatore," posted by EXTRAVAGLIO0999.]

Sostiene Pereira (Faenza, 1995). [DVD: Cecchi Gori Home Video, 2005.] [YouTube: "Sostiene Pereira Trailer Ita," posted by JeanVigoFilm; "Sostiene Pereira Finale," posted by Oddlyshed.]

Star Wars (USA, Spielberg, 1977). [DVD: 20th Century Fox Home Entertainment, 2011.] [YouTube: "Star Wars Uncut: Director's Cut," posted by Casey Pugh.]

Stato di grazia (*State of Grace*) (USA, Joanou, 1990). [DVD: MGM/UA,1990, 2002.] [YouTube: "State of Grace (1990) full movie," posted by aaron stampler.]

La storia vera della signora dalle camelie (*The True Story of the Lady of the Camellias*) (Bolognini, 1981). [DVD: Ripley's Home Video, 2005.]

Teorema (Pasolini, 1968). [DVD: Medusa Video, 2009.] [YouTube: "Teoreme - Pier Paolo Pasolini (Film complete) Subtitles ENG SPA FRE," posted by di dinieghista.]

Thriller (USA, 1984). [DVD: *Michael Jackson: History*, vol. 2, Sony Music Video,1998.] [YouTube: "Michael Jackson - Thriller," posted by michaeljacksonVEVO.]

Top Hat (Sandrich, 1935). [DVD: Universal, 2007.] [YouTube: "Fred Astaire - Top Hat (Full Dance)," posted by gbcx777; "Top Hat (1935) Opening credits," posted by mickfoley.]

Tous les matins du monde (France, Corneau, 1991). [DVD: E4 Entertainment, 2006.] [YouTube: "Tous Les Matins du Monde," posted by mitekphoto; "Marche pour la cérémonie des Turcs (J. B. Lully)," posted by Peteronfire.]

Un tranquillo posto di campagna (*A Quiet Place in the Country*, *Un lugar tranquilo en el campo*) (Petri, 1968). [DVD: MGM; CD, 2007.] [YouTube: "A Quiet Place in the Country (1968) Giallo," posted by cultfilm66; "Un Tranquillo Posto Di Campagna," posted by StuntmanAustin.]

La Traviata (Zeffirelli, 1983). [DVD: Image Entertainment, 1999.] [YouTube: "La Traviata Zeffirelli parte 1," posted by lucyllebalth80.]

Trois couleurs—Bleu (Kieslowski, 1993), *Trois couleurs—Blanc* (1994), and *Trois couleurs—Rouge* (1994). *Tre colori: Blu Bianco Rosso* (Milan: Bompiani RCS, 1997) (original edition 1992). [DVD: Disney-Buena Vista, 2003.] [YouTube: "Trois Couleurs: Bleu (1993) Trailer," posted by Danios 12345; "Three Colours - Blue," posted by javatuan; "Trois Couleurs Bleu (1993)," posted by sungold22; "Three Colors: Blue (12/12) Movie CLIP - Can You Show Me What You've Composed? (1993) HD," posted by movieclips.]

2001: A Space Odyssey (Kubrick, 1968). [DVD: Warner Home Video, 2012.] [YouTube: "2001: A Space Odyssey - Original Extended Trailer #2," posted by the cultbox; "2001: A Space Odyssey #1 Movie Clip - Beyond the Infinite (1968) HD," posted by movieclips; "Kubrick's 2001: A Space Odyssey (widescreen)," posted by MikeszCZ; "Space Odyssey 2001 - Encounter with monolith (movie scene)," posted by tyhjyydesta.]

Uccellacci e uccellini (*The Hawks and the Sparrows*) (Pasolini, 1966). [DVD: Medusa Video, 2009.] [YouTube: "Hawks And Sparrows (Master of Cinema) Original Italian theatrical trailer," posted by Eurekaentertainment; "Uccellacci e uccellini (completo)," posted by Roninety; "Toto' 'Uccellacci Uccellini' parte 1," posted by Valentini Carlo; "Uccellacci e uccellini (1966) - opening credits," posted by rive5gauche.]

L'uccello dalle piume di cristallo (*The Bird of the Crystal Feathers*) (Argento, 1970). [DVD: Phantom, 2009.] [YouTube: "L'uccello dale piume di cristallo (Trailer Americano)," posted by neverlando74; "L'Uccello Dalle Piume Di Cristallo," posted by 66 Stincodisanto6; "The Bird with the Crystal Plumage intro (1969)," posted by discodelirio; "Shockcinema13 presents . . . The Bird with the Crystal Plumage," posted by ShockCinema13.]

L'ultimo treno della notte (*Night Train Murders*) (Italy, Lado, 1975). [DVD: Blue Underground, 2004.] [YouTube: "Aldo Lado - L'ultimo Treno Della Notte (1975) ('Scena finale')," posted by gilesnefandor; "Ultimo treno della notte," posted by horrorfictionmovies9.]

L'ultimo uomo di Sara (*The Last Man of Sara*) (Onorato, 1972).

L'umanoide (*The Humanoid*) (Lado, 1979). [DVD: American International Pictures; ILC, 2005.] [YouTube: "Scene from 'The Humanoid' (1979)," posted by CinemaDeBizarreDVDs; "The Humanoid (L'umanoide, 1979)," posted by ylivies.]

L'uomo delle stelle (*The Man of the Stars*) (Tornatore, 1995). [Streaming video at Italia-Film TV, Guarda Online.] [YouTube: L'uomo delle stele - Trailer," posted by guga85; "L'uomo delle stelle (piano sequenze) - Tornatore," posted by cosanostranapoli1.]

U-Turn (*Inversione di Marcia*) (USA, Stone, 1997). [DVD: Sony Pictures Entertainment, 1998.] [YouTube: "U Turn - Trailer - (1997)," posted by ryy79; "U Turn," posted by MrJowerty.]

Il Vangelo secondo Matteo (*The Passion according to Mathew*) (Pasolini, 1964). [DVD: Waterbearer, 2003; Legend Films, 2009.] [YouTube: "The Gospel According to St. Matthew (1964) - Pier Paolo Pasolini," posted by di crtv74MayGodLoveThee.]

La vita è bella (*Life is beautiful*) (Benigni, 1997). [DVD: Cecchi Gori, 2005; Miramax Lionsgate, 2011.] [YouTube: "La Vita é Bella_trailer," posted by dayishere.]

La voglia matta (Salce, 1962). [DVD: Medusa Video, 2008.] [YouTube: "Alfa Romeo 2000 Spider - La Voglia Matta ('62).mp4," posted by associnemalfa; "La voglia matta (di Luciano Salce, 1962) - Antonio e le donne (versione breve) (versione lunga)," posted by mafaldita224.]

West Side Story (Wise, Robbins, 1961). [DVD: MGM, 2003.] [YouTube: "West Side Story - Prologue - Official Full Number - 50th Anniversary," posted by DanceOn.]

Die Wunderbare Luege der Nina Petrovna (*The Wonderful Lies of Nina Petrovna, Sublime Menzogna*) (Schwartz, 1929). [YouTube: "Wunderbare Luege der Nine Petrowna (1929)," posted by Samotaaar (33 videos).]

Bibliography [to 1999]

Acreman, C., I. Ortosecco, and F. Razzi, eds. *Musica e tecnologia: industria e cultura per lo sviluppo del Mezzogiorno* (VI Colloquio di Informatica musicale, Atti, C. Acreman, I. Ortosecco, F. Razzi, ed.). *Quaderni di M/R 14*. Milan: Unicopli, 1987.

Adorno, T. W., and H. Eisler. *Composing for the Films*. New York: Oxford University Press, 1947. Reprint, London: Dennis Dobson, 1951. *La musica per film*, Rome: Newton Compton, 1975 based on German edition, München: Rogner and Bernhard, 1969.

Amyes, T. *The Technique of Audio Post-Production in Video and Film*. Oxford: Butterworth-Heinemann, 1999.

Anderson,G. B. *Music for Silent Films (1894–1929): A Guide*. Washington, DC: Library of Congress, 1988. Available online from the Music Division, Library of Congress.

Arcagni, S., and D. De Gaetano, eds. *Cinema e Rock. Cinquant'anni di contaminazioni tra musica e immagini*. Santhià, GS, 1999.

"L'avant-Scène." *Cinéma n. 360—Opéra n. 98*. Paris, 1987.

Bassetti, S. "Letteratura musicale tra passione e ideologia nel cinema di Pier Paolo Pasolini," in *Norme con ironie. Scritti per i settant'anni di Ennio Morricone*, edited by S. Miceli. Milan: Suvini Zerbini, 1998.

Bassetti, S., ed. *Sapore di sala. Cinema e cantautori*. Florence: GEF, 1990.

Bazelon, J. *Knowing the Score: Notes on Film Music*. New York: Van Nostrand Reinhold, 1975.

Un bel di vedemmo. Il melodramma dal palcoscenico allo schermo. Amministrazione Provinciale di Pavia, 1984.

Bell, D. A. *Getting the Best Score for Your Film: A Filmmaker's Guide to Music Scoring*. Los Angeles: Silman-James Press, 1994.

Beltrame, G., and F. Pavesi, eds. *Musica in cinema in 201 film*. Colognola ai Colli (VR): Demetra, 1999.

Bendazzi, G., M. Cecconello, and G. Michelone. *Coloriture. Voci, rumori, musiche nel cinema d'animazione*. Bologna: Pendragon, 1995.

Berg, Charles M. *An Investigation of the Motives for and Realizaion of Music to Accompany the American Silent Film 1896–1927*. New York: Arno Press, 1976.

Biamonte, S. G., ed. *Musica e film*. Rome: Edizioni dell'Ateneo, 1954.

Blanchard, G. *Images de la musique de cinéma*. Paris: Edilig, 1984.

Blaukopf, K., S. Goslich, and W. Scheib. *50 Jahre Musik im Hörfunk* (9. Internationalen IMZ-Kongresses). Vienna-Munich: Jugend und Volk, 1973.

Bolla, L., and F. Cardini. *Macchina Sonora. La musica nella televisione italiana*. VQPT 152. Rome: Rai-Eri, 1997.

Bordwell, D., and K. Thompson. *Film Art: An Introduction*. New York: McGraw-Hill, 1993.

Borin, F., ed. *La filmografia di Nino Rota. Fondazione Giorgio Cini—Archivi Nino Rota, I.* Florence: Olschki, 1999.

Bornoff, J. *La musique et les moyens techniques du XXe siècle* (Conseil International de laMusique 1). Florence: Olschki, 1972.

Boschi, A., and M. Dall'Asta, eds. "Audiofanie. Voci, rumori e musica del cinema." *Cinema & Cinema*, n.s., vol. 18, no. 60 (1991).

Brown, R. *Overtones and Undertones: Reading Film Music.* Berkeley: University of California Press, 1994.

Brusio, V. *Manuale del produttore di film.* Rome: Edizioni dell'Ateneo, 1956.

Burlingame, J. *Sound and Vision: Sixty Years of Motion Picture Soundtracks.* New York: Billboards Books, 2000.

Burt, G. *The Art of Film Music.* Boston: Northeastern University Press, 1996.

Calabretto, R. *Pasolini e la musica.* Pordenone: Cinemazero,1999.

Callegari, G., and N. Lodato, eds. *L'ultimo mélo. La vita cantata tra set e scena lirica.* Amministrazione Provinciale di Pavia, 1984.

Cano, C., and G. Cremonini. *Cinema e Musica. Il racconto per sovrapposizioni.* Bologna: Thema Editore, 1990; new and enlarged edition, Florence: Vallecchi, 1995.

Carrera, A. *Musica e pubblico giovanile. L'evoluzione del gusto musicale dagli anni Sessanta ad oggi.* Milan: Feltrinelli, 1980.

Casadio, G. *Opera e cinema. La musica lirica nel cinema italiano dall'avvento del sonoro a oggi.* Ravenna: Longo, 1995.

"C'era una volta il Musical." *Cinema e Cinema* 7, no. 22/23 (1980).

Chiarini, L. *Arte e tecnica del film.* Bari: Laterza, 1965.

Chion, M. *L'audio vision.* Paris: Éd. Nathan, 1990.

———. *La musique au cinéma.* Fayard, 1995.

———. *Le son au cinéma.* Paris: Éd. de l'Étoile, 1985.

Cineforum di Vicenza,ed. *Music in Film Fest.* Vicenza: 1987.

Cohen, A., ed. *Special Volume on the Psychology of Film Music, Psychomusicology* (Center for Music Research Florida University) 13 (Spring–Fall 1994) (published in 1996).

Coignard, M. La musique et l'image—Composition et orchestration. Réflexions, Conseils techniques et pratiques (Réalisation X. Escabasse). Paris: Éd. Max Eschig, 1994.

Colpi, H. *Défense et illustration de la musique dans le film.* Lyon: SERDOC, 1963.

Comuzio, E. *Colonna sonora. Dialoghi, musiche, rumori, dietro lo schermo.* Milan: Il Formichiere, 1980.

———. *Colonna sonora. Dizionario ragionato dei musicisti cinematografici.* Rome: Ente dello Spettacolo, 1992.

Comuzio, E., and G. Ghigi, eds. "L'immagine in me nascosta. Richard Wagner: un itinerario cinematografico." *Quaderni di musica e film*1. Venice : Comune di Venezia—Gran Teatro La Fenice, 1983.

Comuzio, E., and P. Vecchi, eds. *8 ½. I Film di Nino Rota.* Comune di Reggio Emilia, 1987.

Cueto, R. *Cien Bandas Sonoras en la Historia del Cine.* Madrd: Nuer, 1996.

Dalmonte, R., and M. Baroni, eds. *Atti del Secondo Convegno Europeo di Analisi musicale, Università degli Studi di Trento.* Trento: 1992. Contains "Relazioni strutturali fra musica e narrazione cinematografica," with contributions by Ph. Tagg, A. Björnberg, E. Simeon, H. Klempe, and R. D. Golianek.

Davis, R. *Complete Guide to Film Scoring: The Art and Business of Writing Music for Movies and TV.* Boston: Berklee Press, 2000.

De la Motte-Haber, H., and H. Emons. *Filmmusik. Eine systematische Beschreibung.* Munich: Carl Hanser Verlag, 1980.

De la Motte-Verlag, H., ed. *Film und Musik.* Mainz: Schott's Söhne, 1993.

De Santi, P. M. *La musica di Nino Rota.* Bari: Laterza, 1983.

Di Giammatteo, F., ed. *Viva Verdi, Quaderni del Cinestate.* Comune di San Gimignano, 1995.

Dizionario del cinema Italiano, I: Film, 6 vol.: 1930–2000. Rome: Gremes, 2000.

Erdmann, H., G. Becce (and L. Brav). *Allgemeines Handbuch der Film-musik.* 2 vols. Berlin-Lichterfeld: Schlesingersche Buch und Musikhandlung, 1927.

Evans, M. *Soundtrack: The Music of the Movies.* New York: Hopkinson and Blake, 1975.

Fabbri, F., ed. *Musiche/Realtà. Generi musicali/Media/Popular Music. Quaderni di M/R 23.* Milan: Unicopli, 1989.

Fabbri, F. *Il suono in cui viviamo. Inventare, produrre e diffondere musica.* Milan: Feltrinelli, 1996.

Fabbri, F., ed. *What Is Popular Music?* (Atti II Conferenza IASPM), *Quaderni di M/R 8.* Milan: Unicopli, 1985.

Farinotti, P. *Dizionario di tutti i film. L'unico completo.* Milan: Mondatori, 1999.

Farnè, L. *Vedere il Jazz.* Milan: Gammalibri, 1982.

Fayenz, F., ed. *Musica per vivere.* Bari: Laterza, 1980.

Ferraro, A., and G. Montavano, eds. *Estetiche del Walkman.* Naples: Flavio Pagano Ed., 1990.

Filmcritica 28, no. 279–80 (1977).

Filmlexicon degli autori e delle opere. 10 vols. (1958–1992). Edizione Bianco e Nero.

Film Music Society. http://filmmusicsociety.org/.

Fisher, J. P. *How to Make Money: Scoring Soundtracks and Jingles.* Emeryville, CA: Mix Books, 1997.

Fondazione Giorgio Cini—Studi di Musica Veneta n. 19. "Retroscena di 'Acciaio.' Indagine su un'esperienza cinematografica di G. Francesco Malipiero." Florence: Olschki, 1993.

Frater, C. B. *Sound Recording for Motion Pictures.* Cranbury, NJ: A. S. Barnes, 1979.

Geduld, H. M. *The Birth of the Talkies: From Edison to Jolson.* Bloomington: Indiana University Press, 1975.

Gorbman, C. *Unheard Melodies: Narrative Film Music.* Bloomington: Indiana University Press, 1987.

Hagen, E. *Advanced Techniques for Film Scoring* (book and CD). Los Angeles: Alfred, 1990.

———. *Scoring for Films.* New York: E.D.J. Music, 1971.

Helm, E. *Le compositeur, l'interprète, le public. Une étude d'intercommunication.* (Conseil International de la Musique 1). Florence: Olschki, 1972.

Hippenmeyer, J.-R. *Jazz sur Films ou 55 année de rapport jazz-cinema vus à travers plus de 800 films tournés entre 1917 et 1972.* Yverdon (CH): Éd. de la Thièle, 1971.

Hoffmann, C. *Sounds for Silents.* New York: DBS Publications, 1970.

Holman, T. *Sound for Film and Television.* Oxford: Butterworth-Heinemann, 1997.

Huntley, J *British Film Music.* London: Skelton Robinson, 1947. Reprint, New York: Arno Press, 1972.

Informatica: Musica/Industria. Pensiero compòsitivo, ricerca, didattica, sviluppo industriale (Atti del Convegno, N. Sani, ed.). Quaderni di M/R 1. Milan: Unicopli, 1983.

Jacquard, G. *La musique et le cinéma.* Paris: Presses Universitaires de France, 1959.

Julien, J. R. *Musica e pubblicità. Dai gridi medioevali ai jingle radiotelevisivi.* Milan: Ricordi Unicopli, 1992. First published 1989, Parsi.

Julien, J. R. ed. "Les musiques des films," *Vibrations,* 4. Paris: Privat, 1987.

Karlin, F. *Listening to Movies: The Film Lover's Guide to Film Music.* New York: Prentice Hall, 1994.

Karlin, F., and R. Wright. *On the Track: A Guide to Contemporary Film Scoring.* New York: Schirmer Books, 1990.

Keller, M. *Stars and Sounds: Filmmusik—Die dritte Kinodimension.* Kassel: Bärenreiter-Gustav Bosse, 1996.

Kermol, E., and M. Tessarolo, eds. *La musica del cinema.* Rome: Bulzoni, 1996.

Lack, R. *Twenty Four Frames Under: A Buried History of Film Music.* London: Quartet, 1997.

Lacombe, A., and C. Rocle. *La Musique du film.* Paris: Éd. Francio van de Velde, 1979.

Lang, E., and G. West. *Musical Accompaniment of Moving Pictures.* New York: Boston Music Company, 1920. Reprint, New York: Arno Press, 1970.

Limbacher, J. L. *Film Music: From Violins to Video.* Metuchen, NJ: Scarecrow Press, 1974.

Lissa, Z. *Aesthetik der Filmmusik.* Berlin: Henschelverlag, 1965. First published 1964, Krakau.

Lombardi, F., ed. *Fra cinema e musica del Novecento: Il caso Rota.* Dai documenti, Fondazione Giorgio Cini—Archivi Nino Rota, II. Florence: Olschki, 2000.

London, K. *Film Music.* London: Faber & Faber, 1936. Reprint, New York: Arno Press, 1970.

Lustig, M. *Music Editing for Motion Pictures.* New York: Hastings House, 1980.

Maas, G., and A. Schudack. *Musik und Film—Filmmusik. Informationen und Modelle für die Unterrichtspraxis.* Mainz: Schott's Söhne, 1996.

Maltin, L. *Leonard Maltin's Movie and Video Guide, 2000 Edition.* New York: Signet, 2000.

Mannino, F. *Visconti e la musica.* Lucca: LIM, 1997.

Manvell, R., and J. Huntley. *The Technique of Film Music* [1957]. Revised and enlarged by R. Arnell and P. Day. London: Focal Press, 1975. *Tecnica della musica nel film.* Rome: Ed. Bianco e Nero, 1959.

Masetti, E., ed. *La musica nel film.* Rome: Ed. Bianco e Nero, 1950.

May, R. *Le tecniche della realizzazione cinematografica. Dal soggetto allo schermo.* Milan: Ed. i 7, 1964.

McCarty, C. *Film Composers in America: A Checklist of Their Work.* New York: Da Capo, 1953. Reprinted with minor additions and corrections, 1972.

Mereghetti, P. *Il Mereghetti. Dizionario dei film 2000.* Milan: Baldini & Castoldi, 1999.

Miceli, S., ed. "Atti del Convegno Internazionale Musica & Cinema." *Chigiana*, vol. 42, n.s. 22. Florence: Olschki, 1992.

Miceli, S. "Cinema e danza. Dal "naturale" al coreutica," in L. Quaresima (ed.), *Il cinema e le altre arti*, La Biennale di Venezia – Marsilio, Venezia, 1996, p. 71-79.

———. "Forme visive e forme sonore. Le musiche di Ennio Morricone per *The Life and Death of Richard III* (1912)." *Musica/Realtà* 18, no. 54 (1997).

———. *Musica e cinema nella cultura del Novecento.* Milan: Sansoni RCS, 2000.

———. "La musica e il cinema. Il secondo quarto di secolo, Relazione per 1900–2000. Un secolo di musica in Italia," *Nuova Rivista Musicale Italiana* 34, no. 4, n.s. 3 (2000).

———. *La musica nel film: Arte e artigianato.* Florence: Discanto, 1982.

———. "La musica nel film e nel teatro di prosa. L'avvento dello specialismo," in *Italia Millenovecentocinquanta*, SIdM—CIDIM—CIM/UNESCO, *Musica nel 900 italiano*, edited by G. Solvetti and B. M. Antolini. Milan: Guerini, 1999.

———. *Morricone, la musica, il cinema.* Milan: Mucchi, 1994; Valencia: Fundació Municipal de Cine,1997; Essen: Filmwerkstatt, 2000.

———. "Le musiche del film: Una breve analisi." In *Il Gattopardo*, edited by L. Micciché, 28–39. Naples: CSC/Electa, 1996.

Miceli, S., ed. *Norme con ironie: Scritti per i settant'anni di Ennio Morricone.* Milan: Suvini Zerboni, 1998.

Miceli, S. "L'Opera in film: Seminario e tavola rotonda." *Quaderni dell'IRTEM*, vol. 5. Rome: IRTEM, 1987.

———. "Opera e Cinema: Seminario e tavola rotonda." *Quaderni dell'IRTEM*, vol. 6, 37–41. Rome: IRTEM, 1988.

Michelone, G. *Il Jazz-Film. Rapporti tra cinema e musica afroamericana.* Bologna: Pendragon, 1997.

Miller, L. A., and M. Northam. *Film and Television Composer's Resource Guide: The Complete Guide to Organizing and Building Your Business.* Emeryville, CA: Hal Leonard, 1998.

Morandini, L., L. Morandini, and M. Morandini. *Il Morandini. Dizionario dei film 2000.* Bologna: Zanichelli, 1999.

Morgan, D. *Knowing the Score: Film Composers Talk about the Art, Craft, Blood, Sweat and Tears of Writing for Cinema.* New York: HarperEntertainment, 2000.

La musica che si consuma. Quaderni di M/R 7. Milan: Unicopli, 1985.

La musica e il suo spazio (Seminario di studio, Atti, R. Pozzi, ed.). *Quaderni di M/R 15.* Milan: Unicopli, 1987.

Musica e sistema dell'informazione in Europa. Ricerca, produzione, consumo (Atti del Convegno, F. Rampi, ed.). *Quaderni di M/R 6.* Milan: Unicopli, 1985.

Musica e tecnologia: industria e cultura per lo sviluppo del Mezzogiorno (VI Colloquio di Informatica musicale, Atti, C. Acreman, I. Ortosecco, F. Razzi, eds.). *Quaderni di M/R 14.* Milan: Unicopli, 1987.

La musica in Italia. L'ideologia, la cultura, le vicende del jazz, del rock, del pop, della canzonetta, della musica popolare dal dopoguerra ad oggi. Milan: Savelli, 1978.

Musiche/Realtà. Generi musicali/Media/Popular Music (F. Fabbri, ed.). *Quaderni di M/R 23.* Milan: Unicopli, 1989.

Oppicelli E. G. (C. Bertieri's collaborator). *Musical! Il cinema musicale di Hollywood*. Rome: Gremese, 1989.

Pauli, H. *Filmmusik: Stummfilm*. Stuttgart: Klett-Cotta, 1981.

———. *Wagner e il cinema*. Torino, Regione Piemonte, Città di Torino, Goethe Institut, Teatro Reggio, Università di Torino e altri Enti, 1983.

Pellegrini, G., and M. Verdone, eds. *Colonna sonora*. Rome: Ed. Bianco e Nero, 1967.

Porcile, F. *Présence de la musique à l'écran*. Paris: Éd. du Cerf, 1969.

Pozzi, R., ed. *La musica e il suo spazio* (Seminario di studio, Atti, R. Pozzi). *Quaderni di M/R 15*. Milan: Unicopli, 1987.

Prendergast, R. M. *A Neglected Art: A Critical Study of Music in Films*. New York: New York University Press, 1977.

Provincia Autonoma di Trento, ed. *Trento Cinema 1987*. Trento: 1987.

———. *Trento Cinema. Incontri Internazionali con la Musica per il Cinema*. Trento: 1988.

———. *Trento Cinema 1990. Incontri Internazionali con la Musica per il Cinema*. Trento: 1990.

Prox, L., ed. *Film und Musik, Avantgarde Filme der zwanziger Jahre*. Oberhausen: 1983.

———. *Musik und Stummfilm*. Frankfurt: Alte Oper Frankfurt, 1988.

Pruzzo, P. *Musical Americano in cento film*. Recco- Genova: Le Mani-Microart's Ed., 1995.

Rampi, F., ed. *Musica e sistema dell'informazione in Europa. Ricerca, produzione, consumo* (Atti del Convegno). *Quaderni di M/R 6*. Milan: Unicopli, 1985.

Rapée, E. *Encyclopaedia of Music for Pictures*. New York: Berwin, 1925. Reprint, New York: Arno, 1970.

———. *Motion Picture Moods for Pianists and Organists*. New York: Schirmer, 1924. Reprint, New York: Arno, 1974.

Ratcliff, J. D. *Timecode: A User's Guide*. New York: Focal Press, 1999.

Reisz, K., and G. Millar. *Film Editing*. London: Focal Press, 1968.

Rona, J. *The Reel World: Scoring for Pictures*. San Francisco: Miller Freeman Books, 2000.

———. *Synchronization: From Reel to Reel: A Complete Guide for the Synchronization of Audio, Film & Video*. Emerysville, CA: Hal Leonard, 1990.

Rondolino, G. *Cinema e musica. Breve storia della musica cinematografica*. Turin: UTET, 1991.

———. *Dizionario del cinema italiano 1945–1969*. Turin: Einaudi, 1969.

———. "La musica nel cinema," in *Musica in scena. Storia dello spettacolo musicale*, vol. 6, *Dalla musica di scena allo spettacolo rock*, edited by A. Basso. Turin: UTET, 1997.

———. *Storia del cinema, Vol. IV, Dizionario dei film*. Turin: UTET, 1996.

Sabaneev, L. *Music for the Films*. Translated by S. W. Pring. London: Sir I. Pitman and Sons, 1935. Reprint, New York: Arno Press, 1978.

Sadoul, G. *Manuale del cinema*. Turin: Einaudi, 1971. First published 1960 in Paris.

Salizzato, C. *Ballare il film*. Milan: Savelli, 1982.

Sani, N., ed. *Informatica: Musica/Industria. Pensiero compòsitivo, ricerca, didattica, sviluppo industriale* (Atti del Convegno). *Quaderni di M/R 1*. Milan: Unicopli, 1983.

Schelle, M. *The Score: Interviews with Film Composers*. Los Angeles: Silman-James Press, 1999.

Schmidt, H. C. "Filmmusik," in *Musik aktuelle*, 4. Kassel: Bärenreiter, 1982.

Schmidt, H. C., ed. *Musik in den Massenmedien, Rundfunk und Fernsehen*. Mainz: B. Schott's Söhne, 1976.

Sibilla, G. *Musica da vedere. Il videoclip nella televisione italiana*. VQPT 165. Rome: Rai-Eri, 1999.

Simeon, E. *Per un pugno di note. Storia, teoria, estetica della musica per il cinema, la televisione e il video*. Milan: Rugginenti, 1995. Republished as *Manuale di Storia della musica del cinema*.

Skiles, M. *Music Scoring for TV & Motion Pictures*. Blue Ridge Summit, PA: Tab Books, 1976.

Solvetti, G., and B. M. Antolini, eds. *Italia Millenovecentocinquanta*, SIdM—CIDIM—CIM/ UNESCO, *Musica nel 900 italiano*. Milan: Guerini, 1999.

Stern, D., ed. "Angewandte Musik 20er Jahre," in *Argument-Sonderbände*. Berlin: Argument-Verlag, 1977.

Stiftung Deutsche Kinemathek, ed. *Stummfilmmusik gestern und heute. Beiträge und Interviews anläbich eines Symposiums im Kino Arsenal am 9. Juni 1979 in Berlin*. Berlin:Verlag Volker Spiess, 1979.

Sutak, K. *The Great Motion Picture Soundtrack Robbery: An Analysis of Copyright Protection*. Hamden, CT: Archon Books/Shoe String Press, 1976.

Tagg, P. *Fernando the Flute: Analysis of Musical Meaning in an Abba Mega-hit*. Liverpool: University of Liverpool, Institute of Popular Music, 1991.

Tagg, P. *Kojak: 50 Seconds of Television Music: Toward the Analysis of Affect in Popular Music*. Göteborg: Skriften från Musikvetenskapliga Institutionen, 1979.

————. *Popular Music. Da Kojak al Rave*. Edited by R. Agostani and L. Marconi. Bologna: CLUEB, 1994.

Philip Tagg website. http:/www.tagg.org.

Thiel, W. *Filmmusik in Geschichte und Gegenwart*. Berlin: Henschelverlag, 1981.

Thomas, T. *Film Score: The View from the Podium*. Cranbury, NJ: A. S. Barnes,1979.

————. *Music for the Movies*. Cranbury, NJ: A. S. Barnes, 1973.

Tone, K. *Digital Audio Post for Films on a Budget*. Van Nuys, CA: Sound Ranger, 1999.

Toulet, E., and C. Belaygue. *Musique d'écran. L'accompagnement musical du cinema muet en France, 1918–1995*. Paris: Éd. de la Réunion des Musées Nationaux, 1994.

Turco, M. Tedeschi. *Erich Wolfgang Korngold*. Verona: Cierre Ed., 1997.

Turroni, G. *L'arte e la tecnica del film*. Milan: Il Castello, 1965.

Uccello, P. *Il cinema: tecnica e linguaggio*. Rome: Ed. Paoline, 1966.

Vetro, G. N. *La musica come professione*. Parma: Spaggiari, 1970.

Vogelsang, K. *Filmmusik im Dritten Reich. Eine Dokumentation*. Laaber: Kronos, 1998.

Weis, E., and J. Belton, eds. *Film Sound, Theory and Practice*. New York: Columbia University Press, 1985.

What Is Popular Music? (Atti II Conferenza IASPM, F. Fabbri), *Quaderni di M/R 8*. Milan: Unicopli, 1985.

Wüsthoff, K. *Die Rolle der Musik in der Film-, Funk- und Fernsehwerbung: mit einer Instrumententabelle der Gebrauchsmusik, einer Einführung in die Studiopraxis und Kompositionsanleitungen für Werbespots*. Berlin: Merseburger, 1978.

Yewdall, D. L. *The Practical Art of Motion Picture Sound*. New York: Focal Press, 1999.

Index

Grossi, Pietro, 212n88
Gruppo di Improvvisazione Nuova Consonanza (New Consonance Improvisation Group), 191, 194
Guaccero, Domenico, 51n34
Guerritore, Monica, 52n48

Hamilton, Gay, 127n123
Hamlet (Olivier, 1948), 125n64, 265
Hamlet (Kozintsev, 1964) . *See Gamlet* (*Hamlet*) (USSR, Kozintsev,1964)
Hamlet (USA/Italy, Zeffirelli, 1990), 122n19, 220, 245n6, 265
Hamlisch, Marvin, 123n34
Handel, George Frideric, 255, 255–256
Hanna, William, 122n9
Harmonics, use of, 202
Harris, Ed, 212n73
Harris, Richard, 71n7
Hawks, Howard, 212n79
The Hawks and the Sparrows (Pasolini, 1966) . *See Uccellacci e uccellini*
Haydn, Franz Joseph, 255, 256
Hearing and sight, difference, 190
A Heart in Winter (France, Sautet, 1992) . *See Un coeur en hiver*
Hello Dolly! (Kelly, 1969), 106, 265
Hell's Kitchen (Morricone), 187, 202, 212n68, 212n69, 212n72, 212n77
Helm, Brigitte, 103
Henry V (Olivier, 1944), 75, 99, 100, 101, 125n64, 125n74, 265
Henry V (Branagh, 1989), 94–98, 101, 119–121, 124n56, 124n57, 124n59, 125n61, 127n137, 218, 245n5, 265
Henze, Hans Werner . *See Comporre per il Cinema*, 264
Herman, Jerry, 126n96
Herrmann, Bernard, 82, 146, 238, 246n51
Hitchcock, Alfred, 82–83, 123n23, 183
Honegger, Arthur, 74, 121n3
Hopkins, Anthony, 92, 124n48
The Humanoid (Lado, 1979) . *See L'umanoide*
Huntley, John, 122n10, 125n76
Hurry to Me (Griffi, 1968) . *See Metti, una sera a cena*
Hurt, John, 92, 124n48
Huston, John, 246n49

I Knew Her Well (Pietrangeli, 1965) . *See Io la conoscevo bene*
Ichikawa, Kon, 247n78, 261
Improvisation, 44
In the Voice of God (Del Bosio, 1975) . *See Mosé*
Incontro a sei(Encounter in Six) (Morricone), 144
Indagine su un cittadino al di sopra di ogni sospetto (*Investigation of a Citizen above Suspicion*) (Petri, 1970), 163–164, 197, 209n1, 209n3, 210n6, 213n111, 265
Indeterminacy, 136
L'Infinito (Leopardi), 124n44
Instrumentalists, choice of, 65–67
Instrumentation united to contemporary experimentation, 250
The Integration (Conte), 241–242
Internal level, 78–86
International Conference of Music and Cinema, Siena, 1990, 8, 122n16
International track, 141
Interview, 240
Invenzione per John (Invention for John) (Morricone), 136–137, 160n8, 161n9, 194, 195
Inverse Canon, Making Love (Tognazzi, 1999) . *See Canone inverso*
Inversione di Marcia (Stone, 1997) . *See U-Turn*
Investigation of a Citizen above Suspicion (Petri, 1970) . *See Indagine su un cittadino al di sopra di ogni sospetto*
Io la conoscevo bene (*I Knew Her Well*) (Pietrangeli, 1965), 81–82, 122n20, 201, 214n121, 265
Ionesco, Eugène, 50n14
Irons, Jeremy, 211n42
Iter inverso per 16 strumenti (Domino Guaccero), 51n34
Izzo, Fiametta, 224

Jackson, Michael, 17, 51n25
Jacopetti, Gualtiero, 246n34
Le jardin des delices (Agosti, 1967) . *See Il giardino delle delizie*
Jarre, Maurice, 246n51
Jarrett, Keith, 105–106

246n51, 247n65. *See also Comporre
per il cinema*, 259
Rotation of the blues, 184, 203
Roth, Tim, 72n26
La Roue (Gance, 1923), 74, 267
*Royal Fireworks Music (Musica per I reali
fuochi d'artificio)* (Handel), 255–256
Rozsa, Miklos, 146
Rulli, Dino, 212n66
Ruskaya, Jia, 93
Russell, Ken, 143–144
Ruttmann, Walter, 214n116, 261. *See also
Comporre per il cinema*, 259

Sabatello, Dario, 245
Saint Michael Had a Rooster (Taviani,
Taviani, 1976). *See San Michele aveva
un gallo*
Sala di Buonumore (The Auditorium of
Good Humor), 191
Salce, Luciano, 68, 71n24
Salerno, Enrico Maria, 71n10, 122n20
Salò o le 120 giornate di Sodoma (*Salò or
the 120 Days of Sodom*) (Pasolini,
1975), 243, 247n73, 267
Salò or the 120 Days of Sodom (Pasolini,
1975). *See Salò o le 120 giornate di
Sodoma*
Salone, Donato, 71n13
Salvetti, Guido, 121n2, 259n2. *See also
Comporre per il cinema*, 12 n5
Samperi, Salvatore, 247n60, 265
San Michele aveva un gallo (*Saint Michael
Had a Rooster*) (Taviani, Taviani,
1976), 109–111, 126n109, 267
Sandrelli, Stefania, 81, 122n20
Sandrich, Mark, 126n96
Saperi, Salvatore, 247n60
Sarandon, Susan, 124n50
Satie, Erik, 50n13
Satta Flores, Stefano, 45
Sautet, Claude, 72n29
Scarlatti, Alessandro, 257
The Scarlet Letter (*La lettera scarlatta*)
(USA, Joffe, 1995), 189, 212n83,
245n13, 267
Scarpelli, Furio, 52n53
Schaeffer, Pierre, 246n42
Schönberg, Arnold, 16, 208, 223, 253–254

Schumann, Robert, 256
Schwartz, Hanns, 79
Scion, Scion, Scion. *See Comporre per il
cinema*, 258
Scola, Ettore, 45, 52n53
Score organization, 60–61, 61–63
Score simplicity, 68
Scorsese, Martin, 16, 50n21
Scott, Ridley, vii, 114–115, 117, 145
Screensound, 234
Scriabin, Alexander, 16
Se telefonando (If telephoning)
(Morricone), 241
Second Viennese School, 258
The Secret of the Sahara (RAI TV, Negrin,
1988). *See Il segreto del Sahara*
Il segreto del Sahara (*The Secret of the
Sahara*) (RAI TV, Negrin, 1988), 237,
246n50, 267
Il senatore (Beatty, 1998). *See Bulworth*
Sequenze ufficiali, 143–144, 161n21, 224
Serena, Gustavo. *See Comporre per il
cinema*, 82 n21
Serenata in Sol, K. 525 (Mozart), 246n40
Serialization of tonal music, intervals,
dynamics, and timbre, 250
Seventh Seal (Bergman, 1956). *See Det
sjunde inseglet*
Shadow Makers (USA, Joffé, 1990). *See
Fat Man and Little Boy*
Shakespeare, William, 95, 99, 101, 256
Sheen, Charlie, 124n49
Sheen, Martin, 71n7
Sherman, Jim, 50n11
The Shining (USA, Kubrick, 1980), 102,
125n82, 268
The Shootout (Morricone), 187, 212n70,
212n74
The Short Night of the Glass Doll (Lado,
1971). *See La corta notte delle
bambole di vetro*
Shostakovich, Dmitri, 99, 101, 125n80
Sica, Salvatore, xi
La signora dalle camelie (Serena, 1915).
See Comporre per il cinema, 82 n21
Simeon, Ennio, 228
Sinatra, Frank, 126n96
Sinfonia Dell'attentato (Morricone), 132,
139

About the Authors and Translator

Ennio Morricone has written scores for nearly four hundred films. In 2007 he received an honorary Academy Award for his significant contribution to the art of film music, the only composer to be so recognized.

Sergio Miceli is an Italian musicologist whose many analyses, particularly of Morricone's scores, have established film music as a major artifact of the twentieth century.

Gillian B. Anderson is an orchestral conductor and musicologist who has reconstructed the scores for over 40 pre-1929 classic films and performed them with orchestras and at film festivals around the world. She has published numerous scholarly articles on movie music and the book, *Music for Silent Film (1892-1929): A Guide*. With Ronald Sadoff, she is a founding editor of *Music and the Moving Image*. See www.gilliananderson.it.